Community and Commerce in Late Medieval Japan

The Corporate Villages of Tokuchin-ho

HITOMI TONOMURA

Community and Commerce
in Late Medieval Japan

The Corporate Villages of Tokuchin-ho

STANFORD UNIVERSITY PRESS
STANFORD, CALIFORNIA 1992

Stanford University Press
Stanford, California
© 1992 by the Board of Trustees
of the Leland Stanford Junior University
Printed in the United States of America

Published with the assistance of a
special grant from the Stanford
University Faculty Publication Fund
to help support nonfaculty work
originating at Stanford

CIP data are at the end of the book

TO MY MOTHER AND SISTERS

Acknowledgments

MY SPECIAL GRATITUDE goes to the late Nakamura Ken for unreservedly sharing with me not only his collection of published and unpublished documents but also his sharp insights into the minds of medieval villagers. I greatly regret that I was unable to complete this book before he died. I also benefited from the wisdom of Wakita Haruko, whose stimulating work has influenced my thinking. Katō Mieko, Kurushima Noriko, and Umezawa Fumiko offered me friendship and intellectual guidance as they led me through the dense maze of village documents, and stood ready to discuss any historical questions I might happen to pose. Tsukamoto Yoshikazu, Nakajima Nobuo, Yamaoka Shizue, and Horii Yasue helped me to get closer to the realities of medieval village life and people. I am deeply grateful to Murata Sōkichi and Murata Sadahachi for allowing me—an outsider— a firsthand introduction to aspects of their impressive historical legacy. This book is an expression of gratitude for those who have shared with me the wealth of their ancestral past and for those scholars who, with persevering devotion to accurate historical knowledge, deciphered and interpreted thousands of extraordinarily difficult documentary passages.

In the early phase of writing, I benefited from the meticulous attention and criticism of Jeffrey P. Mass. The critical comments of Peter Duus, John Wirth, Anne Walthall, Suzanne Gay, and Carol Karlsen helped to reshape the manuscript at various stages of its development. I am particularly indebted to Kate Wildman Nakai for giving me unfailing support since the very beginning of my graduate-school years and for continuing to alert me to difficulties with her incisive analysis. I am also grateful to Margaret Van Bolt for applying her superb artistic skills to the illustrations in this book; to John Ziemer for his able supervision in bringing everything to order; to Mary Pasti for her warm, patient, and meticulous editorial guidance; and to Julia Routson and Patricia

Welch for freeing me of many hours of typing. The practical and moral contribution of Clay Ramsay to the creation of my first book cannot be measured in any tangible way. To Leo Abe Rainwater, I say thank you for being there and for forcing me to reevaluate the significance of joy, work, and time. Needless to say, I alone am responsible for any and all deficiencies this book may contain.

The completion of this project would have been impossible without the generous financial assistance of a number of organizations. I wish to express my appreciation to the Japan Foundation and the Social Science Research Council for grants in support of the initial research conducted in Japan. The write-up funds granted by the Mabelle McLeod Lewis Foundation and Social Science Research Council enabled me to turn the research results into a dissertation. I am indebted to the Northeast Asia Council of the Association for Asian Studies and to the Horace Rackham Graduate School and the Center for Japanese Studies at the University of Michigan for funding the later phases of research and writing as well as the production of illustrations and photographs.

Finally, I wish to thank the staff at Yōkaichi City Board of Education, who were generous in sharing its collection of local photographs for reproduction in my book; Bunka Geijutsu Kaikan (Culture and Art Hall) in Yōkaichi City for allowing me to photograph the plaques from the Imabori shrine; and the Historical Archive of the Department of Economics, Shiga University, who graciously accommodated my request to view and photograph the original documents from Imabori.

H.T.

Contents

10 pages of photographs follow page 36

Maps, Tables, and Figures

Preface

THE VAST MAJORITY of the population of medieval Japan were neither aristocrats nor warriors but ordinary people, to whom English-language works have paid scant attention. Even though our knowledge of elite institutions has advanced considerably in the recent past, we know little about how commoners organized their social space, how they made a living, or how they interacted with neighbors and authorities. It is these historiographical lacunae that have compelled me to write this village study. Because my immediate goal is to illuminate the social, economic, and religious order of medieval village life to the extent the records allow, I have adopted a consciously empirical approach in the formulation of questions and in the analysis of evidence.

For my sources, I have relied most heavily on the *Imabori Hiyoshi jinja monjo shūsei*, compiled by Nakamura Ken and published in 1981, which contains 982 documents from Imabori village, 946 of whose originals are now at Shiga University. Another 31 are held by Murata Sōkichi (an Imabori elder), and five still remain at the Imabori Hiyoshi Shrine, the original archive for the Imabori records. The Nakamura Ken edition also contains 35 records from Hebimizo, Shibawara, and Nakano villages. I have made use of those records, along with unpublished documents from Hebimizo and Nakano villages and documents appearing in local historical compendia, such as *Ōmi Gamō-gun shi* and *Yōkaichi-shi shi*.

I acquired additional knowledge about and insights into the history of the region through three on-site investigations—two in 1983 with Wakita Haruko and Katō Mieko and one in 1986 with Nakamura Ken. Under the guidance of these scholars and the direction of the archivists at Yōkaichi City Board of Education, I became familiar with the key features in the landscape, their original shapes and significance, and their correlation to the descriptions on old maps. Interviews with

Murata Sōkichi and Murata Sadahachi, *miyaza* members in Imabori, conducted with the help of Katō Mieko, also served to enrich my appreciation of the local tradition, especially the religious symbolism that governed the social and economic order of medieval village life.

Table of Weights, Measures, and Money in Medieval Japan

Weights, measures, and money were not standardized in medieval Japan. They varied greatly even within a small region. This list gives approximate equivalents.

Weights and Money

1 kan (= 1 kanmon = 1 kanme) = 1,000 mon (or, monme) = 3.75 kilograms

1 mon(me) = 1 sen = 3.75 grams

1 kin = 0.16 kan = 160 mon(me) = 16 ryō = 600 grams

1 hiki = 10 mon(me)

Area

1 chō = 10 tan = 9,917 square meters

1 tan = 360 bu = 991.7 square meters

1 bu = 2.75 square meters

1 semachi = unknown

Volume

1 koku = 10 to = 180 liters

1 to = 10 shō = 18 liters

1 shō = 10 gō = 1.8 liters

Distance

1 ri = 36 chō = 3.93 kilometers

1 ken = 1.82 meters

Community and Commerce
in Late Medieval Japan

The Corporate Villages of Tokuchin-ho

Introduction

IMABORI IS A TOWN about 1 kilometer square, situated 12 kilometers from Lake Biwa's eastern shore, in Shiga Prefecture. Today it falls within the administrative boundaries of Yōkaichi, a city of about 40,000 people and a major interchange on the nation's highway network. In the medieval period Imabori was a village in Tokuchin-ho, an estate (*shōen*) under the proprietorship of the great monastic complex of Enryakuji (see Map 1). Its geography retains much of its long historical tradition, locally documented since the thirteenth century.

The land in Imabori and the surrounding area is mostly flat, rising gradually in the east toward the Suzuka mountain range. To the south, west, and north, the flatness is brought to an abrupt end by the sudden appearance of mountains. Stretches of paddies and fields dominate most of the plain, interrupted here and there by grassy hills with wooded patches and by old and modern buildings. Footpaths and shallow ditches run alongside each other, dividing cultivated areas into the geometric configurations of individual plots. At its northern edge, Imabori is separated from the adjoining town of Nakano by a solidly built irrigation channel, flowing in from Yōkaichi's eastern edge and continuing west, a concrete reminder that these rural communities do not exist in isolation but are tied together by the flow of the water that nourishes their soil.

Four small stone steles, preventing incursions by evil spirits, signify the spiritual boundary of Imabori, while Hiyoshi Shrine marks its approximate geographical center. The shrine compound hosts three or four modest wooden structures. A well-used drum hangs from the eaves of the main building, suggestive of the village gatherings on festive and ceremonial occasions. A hollow tree stump of impressive girth in the corner of the compound serves as a marker of the centuries left behind.[1]

North of the shrine, a weather-beaten, half-meter-tall stone statue,

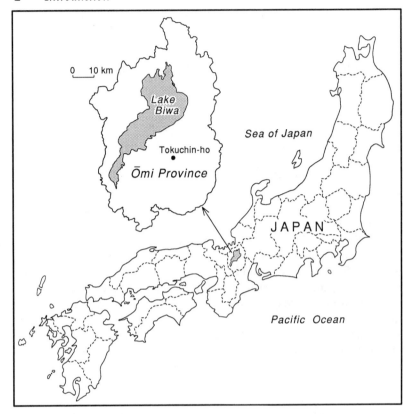

Map 1. Ōmi Province.

a *jizō* decorated with a hat and bib, marks a particular intersection of footpaths. The path extending directly northward is called Ichi-michi, or Market Road; in the past it integrated the residents into the market economy of the wider region. The cluster of spacious and solidly walled farmhouses to the south of the shrine is separated by a moat from the fields nearby. More compact frame houses line denser, narrower streets farther from the cultivated land.

The flat continuity of paddies and fields to the south of the moat accentuates a tree towering in isolation. No one seems to know its exact age; its real shape has been all but obliterated by luxuriant vines. Residents call the tree the Nogami, or Field Deity, and rely on its protective force for good harvests. Unlike the Nogami, the Yama-no-kami, or Mountain Deity, is not readily visible. Near the southern end of the town, behind what is now a grammar school, a winding dirt road leads to an unkempt hillside where one prominent evergreen tree stands high in a small clearing. The rope around the tree, like the upright sticks decorated with white and red paper (*gohei*), indicate the Yama-no-kami's sacred status and the worshipers' efforts to invoke its power.[2] Together, these deities figure prominently in the community's ceremonial calendar, since they can ensure favorable agricultural cycles.

There is nothing particularly unique about the irregular shapes of the paddies or the spiritual symbols that fill Imabori's landscape. Indeed, Imabori has the appearance of any semirural community with the usual long but indistinct historical tradition. But a closer look reveals its extraordinary feature: Imabori possesses a wealth of documents written locally and kept since the thirteenth century. The Imabori collection is the richest of its kind anywhere in Japan.

These village documents are doubly impressive viewed against general medieval record-keeping practices. Whereas the great bulk of medieval documents were the creation of the elites and their institutions—the imperial court and warrior governments, religious and aristocratic estate-holders, and warrior houses and their deputies—the Imabori collection was the product of commoners possessing neither formal political authority nor elegant handwriting. Whereas the elite documents view society from the top and cast the ordinary people in the simplistic general categories of taxpayers and tax evaders, the Imabori documents do precisely the reverse; they capture local activities and concerns, portraying the authorities in their capacity as tax collectors and dispute arbitrators. Here, villagers are the protagonists and village matters, the central issues. Local residents wrote and kept documents for their own and their descendants' sake, strictly to enhance the area's social and economic well-being.[3]

How did Imabori come to have substantial archives? The two forms of collective organizations, found at the territorial levels of village (Imabori) and estate (Tokuchin-ho), give a partial explanation. First, like its neighboring villages in Tokuchin-ho, Imabori was what historians have come to call a *sō* community, a village-based corporate group marked by various forms of collective ownership and administration. Keeping records was an important dimension in the institutionalization and perpetuation of this corporate structure. Second, merchants from a number of villages in Tokuchin-ho organized themselves into a collective widely known as the Honai ("inside the *ho*," i.e., inside Tokuchin-ho) Merchants Collective. Imabori villagers apparently played a dominant role among the Honai merchants and served as the group's archivists, keeping Honai records alongside those of the *sō*.

The internal structure of the sō also promoted the archival tradition and ensured its endurance. Although never formally defined, the sō's active constituents were members of the shrine association, or *miyaza,* the dominant local institution, which incorporated most of the village males over a certain age.[4] The miyaza's operational base was Jūzenji Shrine, which in turn was also the physical, spiritual, and administrative center of the sō. The shrine provided the common space in which the members discussed and planned the management of the sō. Despite ups and downs in the political and economic fortunes of the miyaza, its basic organization and ritual routines have persisted to this day at the very shrine that still stands in its original location.

Fortunately, Imabori and Tokuchin-ho were scarcely touched by the violence that supposedly affected a large portion of the population in the Sengoku, or Warring, period (late fifteenth through sixteenth centuries). From time to time since medieval days, the villagers have examined and reorganized their archival collection, which was, after all, a testimonial to their own past.[5] This persistence of the socioreligious tradition and the villagers' strong historical consciousness undoubtedly helped to preserve the Imabori collection.

The organizational structure of the sō and miyaza not only gave reason and means for the documents' creation and survival; it also determined the type and character of the document collection. Faithfully reflecting the organizational interests of the sō, the records were exclusively concerned with matters that influenced the corporate order or local economics. They therefore did not touch upon other aspects of community life, such as the family or the villagers' personal affairs, unless they interfered with the sō's goals or operations.

Documents in the Imabori collection can be grouped into three functional categories. First are the administrative records kept to ensure the maintenance of the sō organization in its political, economic, social, and religious dimensions. Under the second category fall the regulative documents, kept to impose the representative views of the sō organization upon the community at large. The third group consists of entrepreneurial records, kept to strengthen the area's commercial interests in the outside world, especially via market expansion.

In the main, the administrative records are strongly financial in character. Throughout its tenure, the sō was continually concerned with its finances, an element of fundamental importance to any corporate system. The sō accumulated its capital largely in the form of paddies and fields, mostly through purchase or commendation. The sō kept a systematic record of the status of its landholdings, with over 200 purchase and commendation records dating from the mid-fourteenth century to 1600. Besides these records of individual transactions, the sō occasionally compiled comprehensive catalogues of its landholdings. Thirty-five sets of these listings remain, dating from 1335 to 1566.

The sō also tracked more incidental transactions specific to certain occasions. Examples are the ledgers listing the names of participants in the *eboshi naoshi* (boys' coming-of-age ceremony) and the fees they paid, the cost of persimmons and fish placed at the altar, and donations toward the construction of the shrine bell tower.

Also included among the administrative records are letters and orders issued by the political authorities that had a direct impact on community management. A temporary exemption from taxes in a poor harvest year, the arbitration of a water dispute with the neighboring village, and an emergency request for wartime labor service are relevant examples here.

Most of the regulative records are formalistic, with penalty clauses intended for the long term. They were signed by a representative body (the sō or miyaza) with socially recognized enforcement authority and addressed a broad range of matters—membership status in the miyaza, and the use of common forest land or the shrine premises, for instance. Other rules addressed a specific act, such as the disagreeable behavior of a villager, usually in the form of a collective oath. In both cases these documents served as vehicles for transmitting the group's will to shape the community to its design.

The entrepreneurial records vary in form, content, and authorship, though all were kept for the single purpose of enhancing the competitiveness of local merchants in the region's trade network. Many record disputes with merchants of other areas over the use of markets and roads, and the arbitration efforts of the political authorities. These records were guarded with special care, because written proofs of precedents often paved the way for added future privileges. There are also fraudulent documents, forged to enhance authentic records and to give added prestige to the area's entrepreneurial past. (For translations of selected regulative and entrepreneurial records, see Appendix B.)

Though local people were interested in their own past and reviewed the village's documents from time to time, the academic community remained ignorant of this collection until the early 1900s and the compilation of the ten-volume history of Gamō County, *Ōmi Gamō-gun shi.* The chief compiler, Nakagawa Senzō, drew on many Imabori documents to describe the region's agriculture, markets, commerce, shrine activities, and political and military relationships.[6] Since then, these documents have attracted much scholarly attention, resulting in more than 50 articles and monographs.

At present the Imabori collection is available in several forms. In 1952, all but five of the original documents were transferred from Hiyoshi Shrine in Imabori to the Historical Archive of the Department of Economics at Shiga University, in Hikone. Incomplete sets of the documents also exist in *eishabon* form (precise manual reproduction—tracing—of the original handwriting) in the historical archives of Kyoto University and Tokyo University. These documents were published in 1975 under the direction of Nakamura Naokatsu.[7] Another printed version, edited by Nakamura Ken, followed in 1981—a volume with a more complete listing of documents as well as more accurate transcriptions of the originals.[8]

Other villages in Tokuchin-ho have also kept documents from the medieval period, though not nearly as many as Imabori has. The accessibility of these documents varies from one village to the next because discovering, cataloguing, and deciphering village records have proceeded in an uneven fashion. A limited number of these village records also appear in the *Ōmi Gamō-gun shi*. In the 1970s and 1980s, the cataloguing and compilation of these local records made great headway as the archivists at Yōkaichi City Board of Education arduously prepared the publication of *Yōkaichi-shi shi*.[9] But many are still inaccessible. For example, it is said that documents from Shibawara, Imabori's neighbor to the east, number as many as 4,000, most from the Tokugawa period and later. Though they too are "communal" records, they are placed at present under the protection of the town elders. Physically, the documents are kept in boxes, each of which is tied with hemp rope on whose knot a piece of rice paper is pasted; the paper is stamped with the personal seal of each elder. The opening of the boxes requires the presence of all the elders, who ceremoniously unseal and reseal them.[10]

In contradistinction to Shibawara's example, the records of Hebimizo, Imabori's western neighbor, were entirely overlooked by Nakagawa Senzō in the 1910s and were not discovered until 1973. Intrigued by the absence of Hebimizo records in the *Ōmi Gamō-gun shi*, Nakamura Ken asked the local people whether any old documents existed. Much to his joy, he was shown approximately 250 sets of village records resting in a building that had served as the communal meeting place in medieval days.[11]

Late medieval Japan was the period of the rising commoner. The sō village, manifesting the newly gained strength of the productive level of society, was a salient organizational feature of this era. Stimulating and reflecting the spread of the sō village was a particular set of economic and political circumstances: a notable advance in agricultural productivity, greater diffusion of political prerogatives, and a visible articulation of collective power at various levels of society.

Most fundamentally, the emergence of the sō village was related to the changes taking place in agriculture, the basic element in the great wave of economic expansion felt throughout Japan, starting in the mid-thirteenth century but gaining momentum in the subsequent two centuries. Intensification of cultivation, not expansion in cultivated area, caused the growth in yields. Double-cropping methods—planting wheat, say, or beans after harvesting the rice, or planting two successive crops of some grain besides rice—were introduced as early as the Heian period (ca. 794–1185) but spread throughout Japan in the fourteenth century. By at least the mid-fifteenth century triple-cropping was practiced in the capital region; barley or wheat, planted in the fall after harvesting the rice, was followed by early summer rice, then a crop of buckwheat that matured in early winter. Champa rice, a drought- and insect-resistant, high-yielding, early-maturing variety from the continent, was adopted throughout western Japan. The increased use of ash compost and animal manure as well as some use of human manure provided the fertilizers necessary for this intensified use of the soil. The greater access to draft animals and improved plows raised the level of efficiency in cultivation, and irrigation—fundamental to all farming efforts—was maintained or improved by the construction of reservoirs and the use of pumps. The resulting increase in surplus, coupled with a greater regional specialization in crops and handicraft products, promoted the development of rural and urban markets. Finally, an improved communication network facilitated the movement of goods and people, quickening the pace and expanding the scale of economic advance and bringing returns to the agricultural sector.[12]

The kind of collective social organization that developed in villages of this period was both a cause and a result of these economic advances, though collectives as such had existed much earlier. Rice-based farming had always required group efforts, and local initiatives in managing arable land, irrigation, and commons can be noted from about the eleventh century. A gradual distancing of the central proprietors from direct involvement in the productive processes tended to promote this pattern. By the fourteenth century, it was usual for most villagers to participate in these functions in order for the entire community to realize greater output and profit.[13] Intensified farming demanded togetherness more than ever, especially in certain seasons, such as the times of planting and harvesting, and for specific purposes, such as working to convert fields into paddies. Moreover, conflicts over rights and access to water sources shared with other communities often required villagers to confront the opponent with their concerted strength—a pattern distinctly different from that of earlier centuries, when the proprietors, not the commoners, disputed such rights. The increased importance of fertilizer and, in turn, of the commons in providing compost material also promoted the community's internal cohesion as the rights and access to the commons (whose borders were usually ill defined) spurred conflicts not only with other villages but also with local agents of the proprietor or the bakufu, the warrior government.[14]

The rise of the sō was also intimately connected with the late medieval political order, which hung in a shifting and precarious balance between two sets of divergent forces. At the center, the state authority was represented by a set of traditional proprietary establishments—the imperial family, aristocrats, religious institutions, and the Muromachi bakufu, all located in and around Kyoto. In the vocabulary of the time, they were the *kenmon* ("gates of power and authority"), which had, with the exception of the Muromachi bakufu (a fourteenth-century creation), occupied for centuries the pinnacle of the country's social and economic hierarchy: as the absentee proprietors of the vast network of shōen, or estates, spread across Japan and as the ultimate source from which prestige emanated.

But the tide of change steadily eroded their traditional prerogatives. In the provinces, local leaders of various ranks not only resisted the staying power of the kenmon but also challenged their very foundation by attacking the once well ordered alignment of power defined by the hierarchy of land rights basic to the shōen system. One benchmark of the transformation in this period was the increasing articulation of political authority at the local level, or, conversely, the downward diffusion to a wider spectrum of society of prerogatives inherent in the power of the kenmon.

The tenacity of the multiple actors making up the kenmon, ironically, contributed to the dispersal of central political authority. Although competition among the kenmon powers was acute, especially on the economic front, each knew that no one of them was strong enough to rule alone or survive the challenge of rising localism. Practically speaking, moreover, many kenmon members had personal ties with a number of kenmon institutions, as in the case of the third shogun, Ashikaga Yoshimitsu, who resigned the shogunal post to become the Great Minister of State (*dajō daijin*) in 1394, subsequently becoming a lay priest at two monasteries—Tōdaiji and Enryakuji. The kenmon, then, was a bloc of self-conscious elite institutions and their members that tended to play it safe and occasionally even upheld each other's interests, instead of eliminating one another in a struggle for sole paramountcy. Without a supreme ruler or institution, central authority itself remained diffuse, and its influence over the country eventually diminished.

The provincial challengers to the kenmon were mostly warriors. Their goal was not so much to displace the kenmon as to expand their own territorial grasp by eliminating obstacles, among them traditional influence from the top and threats from other local powers with similar ambitions. Unlike the warrior leaders of earlier times, these were often men of little hereditary prestige; their strength derived not from family status but from raw territorial connections. To realize maximum strength, they often organized themselves into collectives in which members were united by a nonhierarchical set of bonds. The circular style—commonly described as an "[open] umbrella form"—of signatures on written agreements for action symbolized equality among these warrior members.

From this collective base they sought to project political authority within their limited realms by drawing up internal regulations applicable to their members and to the local population. In this way they worked to transform the "private"—hence illegitimate—character of their "rule" into a "public rule" of regionwide validity. "Public" authority, which earlier had been the sole prerogative of the kenmon, was now shared by provincials.

The formation of politically conscious collectives was not restricted to warriors. At the basic level of production, villagers sought self-determination in local governance through the organizational strength of the sō. The sō villages,[15] a key structural manifestation of the decentralizing tendency, proliferated in the environs of the capital—the region with the most advanced economy and in geographical proximity to the kenmon. Sō villages administered their communities through a well-defined collective organization, which was marked by some or all of the following features: (1) the administrative role played by the miyaza, or shrine association, as the central organ of the corporate body; (2) collective jurisdiction over criminal matters; (3) issuance and enforcement of village ordinances; (4) communal ownership of property; (5) collective control of irrigation and the commons; and (6) communal responsibility for tax payment.

The kenmon responded to the rise of the sō villages in a manner that was more conciliatory than antagonistic. Already enfeebled, proprietary institutions greatly preferred the rise of villages to the rise of local warrior groups, who were sources of direct military and political competition, either as independent local figures or as nominal agents of the bakufu or the proprietors themselves. To villagers, the influence of proprietary institutions was typically more acceptable than that of local warriors who held the direct and effective means of squeezing local revenues. Disdained by the producers and the absentee proprietors alike, these warriors were often a common enemy of both. As in Okushima, a sō village in Ōmi Province, villagers might seek jurisdictional relief from the kenmon against the burdensome taxes imposed by local warrior managers.

While the sō found proprietary protection useful in increasing local autonomy, the governing strength of the sō village in practice helped conserve proprietary strength. Consequently, the capital elites and the direct producers often developed a supportive, reciprocal relationship while nonetheless preserving (or enhancing) the fundamentally extractive framework in which the status asymmetry went unquestioned.

The corporate structure of the sō villages was an institutional medium that facilitated the movement toward localism. By setting up provisions for local rule on its own initiative, the sō came to articulate some elements of political power previously embraced by the kenmon. The sō's appropriation of central prerogatives was, in a sense, an act of opposition to central rule. But in practice, empowering the village benefited the very source from which such authority originally derived. The sō village projected the power of the kenmon, at least in its structural self-representation.

Sō villages were strictly local institutions, shaped by the residents to meet their own communal needs in accordance with their own worldview. Although all villages organized into sō shared certain traits, they necessarily reflected local particularities, as did all villages in Japan. Different topography, history, relations with authorities, productivity, and other social and economic factors influenced their character.[16]

The sō considered in this investigation provides an exemplary case in which growing collective power and organization benefited both the proprietor and the village alike. It illustrates one variation among the relational forms giving advantages to those in authority and to the local population alike. Such patron-client relations are "a distinct mode of regulating crucial aspects of institutional order" characterized by, among other things, "simultaneous exchange of different types of resources."[17]

Political and economic resources, both actual and symbolic, flowed vertically between the client (the sō), with low ascriptive status, and the patron (the kenmon proprietor), with high political standing and countrywide prestige.[18] While the fundamentally exploitative dynamic between lord and peasant also marked this relationship, patronage by the kenmon directly and indirectly boosted local efforts to build up a village economy based on both land and commerce, and a socioreligious organization with political implications. Local accumulation of agricultural surplus, commercial profits, and political resources in turn benefited the patron by providing not only concrete material rewards but also the structural base for maintaining communal order. Local merchants also offered to the patron, based in the capital city, human resources that circulated over a broad geographical region. The patron institution lent its prestige and jurisdictional authority, crucial in the contests among the rival merchant groups.

Complex but interconnected factors shaped this particular form of lord-peasant relationship. The first was the unsuitability of Tokuchin-ho's terrain for rice cultivation, which led the community and the proprietor to deemphasize the area's agricultural potential and to promote supplementary commercial ventures. The ability of the residents to offer commercial profits, combined with the inability of the soil to produce much rice, promoted the proprietor's patronage of local enterprises alongside its expropriative requirements.

The kenmon's propensity to "encapsulate" nonagrarian commoners was not entirely new at this time but dated from as early as the eleventh century.[19] To diversify income sources, proprietors cultivated patron-client relationships with merchants and artisans by granting them tax-exempt sustenance land and by licensing them with exemptions from market dues and barrier tolls. In return for this greater security in their professional positions, the client entrepreneurs submitted labor and goods in a prescribed manner. Though only part-time traders, Tokuchin-ho residents' dealings with the proprietor closely resembled some traditional patron-client relationships that tied professionals to their lords.

A notable factor influencing this particular mode of patron-client relationship was the absence of direct control by an externally deployed warrior agent, such as the bakufu-appointed steward (*jitō*) or military governor (*shugo*), who frequently harassed the population and amassed local political power. Except on special occasions, political control over the village was simple and unitary, deriving from just one source—the proprietor. The absence of a shared enemy of warrior rank alleviated, for patron and client alike, the multilayered taxation structure that was common in many other Japanese villages. The absence of other authorities facilitated the direct and dependable mode of exchange between the two parties.

Through maximal investment of the resources available to them, residents nurtured a collective strength based on a highly organized and rationally administered corporate body, the sō. The sō members built up considerable local capital, which was then reinvested in projects enhancing the interests of the collective. The sō organization served as the institutional key to the growth of the local economy and the maintenance of the community's social equilibrium. The proprietor was conciliatory to the development of the sō, which served as an effective local governing organ, promoting a local economy whose profits inevitably "trickled up."

The mode of analysis based on the patron–client model differs fundamentally in emphasis from the mainstream postwar historiographical tradition in village studies. Though the latter has also focused on the relationship between estate (shōen) lords and subjects, it has stressed the elements of conflict, not those of cooperation or collaboration. This academic tradition was founded in 1946, in the postwar atmosphere of academic freedom, with the publication of Ishimoda Shō's influential work, *Chūseiteki sekai no keisei*. This book provided the conceptual model of *mura kyōdōtai* (*Dorfgemeinschaft*), a historian's term for the village collectives whose contemporary terms were *sō, gō, mura,* and even *shō*. In delineating the transformation of the ancient world into the medieval world, Ishimoda equated the dynamics of class conflict found in mura kyōdōtai with the moving force of history. The villages were an arena for conflict between the ruling class (the proprietors) and the ruled (the peasants). Mura kyōdōtai, the collective bodies of village-resident producers, struggled against the pressure imposed by the lord's efforts to appropriate surplus in the form of products and labor. Ishimoda used shōen sources in the Tōdaiji collection to trace the breakdown of primitive, kinship-based forms of *kyōdōtai* (*Gemeinschaft*) and the emergence of the private-property system—two processes that together generated the contradiction between producers and the lord that eventually transformed the ancient world. A characteristic of the newborn medieval world was the kyōdōtai now held together by territorial ties instead of kinship.[20]

Following this lead, scholarship in the 1950s and 1960s sought to clarify the process and stages of feudalism (*hōkensei*) as it developed in Japan by analyzing contemporary terms denoting personal status—*genin, tato, myōshu, ryōshu,* and *jitō,* for example—as they related to production and the control of land.[21] Efforts were made to interpret and define these terms according to Marxian class categories—slaves, serfs, and small peasants, for example—in order to explain the larger dynamics of social and economic evolution and, hence, the position of medieval (*chūsei*) Japan within this evolutionary process. Opinions were wide-ranging, from Araki Moriaki's theory that medieval Japan was a patriarchal slave society (in which not only genin but also myōshu were "slaves")[22] to Kuroda Toshio's characterization of genin as "serfs" and myōshu as "feudal small peasants."[23]

Within this larger trend, some authors focused exclusively on the sō and the kyōdōtai. Kikuchi Takeo, for example, proposed a three-part categorization scheme for the sō based on the degree of peasant autonomy vis-à-vis the shōen, the categories themselves reflecting differing economic conditions, such as the extent of local productivity or commercialization.[24] Kurokawa Masahiro's analysis, in contrast, focused on the process of fragmentation among the myōshu (upper-level peasants–cum–shōen agents) occurring alongside the growth of the sō village (sōson). The character or degree of autonomy of a given sō was determined by the intensity or mildness of antagonism between the new classes emerging out of the old myōshu.[25]

Addition of a temporal dimension helped Ishida Yoshihito to emphasize the transformatory character of the sō. To him, the sō was at first the lowest stratum in the vertical hierarchy of the shōen system of control (standing above the peasant class and its community) but later turned into a villagers' organization whose aim was to undermine the structure of control of which it had previously been a part. The contemporary terms sōshō (sō = shōen) and sōson (sō = mura, or village) signified the two stages. An organizational form associated with the Kamakura period (ca. 1185–1333), the former had a low degree of collectivism, with communal ownership limited to water resources or forest land, while arable land remained wholly subject to shōen control. Greater self-rule, including ownership and management of arable land, was accomplished by the sōson, arising against the background of the declining shōen system in the late fourteenth century.[26]

Further theoretical refinement and diversification of opinions occurred in the 1970s as historians attached greater weight to the problems of relations among various "systems"—for instance, the serf (nōdo) system and feudal state system.[27] But these works and those of the preceding three decades essentially belonged to one academic tradition; they shared basic analytical categories and affirmed the fundamentally conflictive nature of society, especially along the vertical axes of classes—between shōen proprietor and peasants, local tax manager and producers, or upper-level peasants and lower-level cultivators.[28] The patron-client model followed in this study provides an alternative view of late medieval rural society; it emphasizes a lord-peasant relationship predominantly marked by collaboration.

Postwar scholarship on the sō was built upon the analytical base developed in prewar times. Particularly noteworthy prewar works are those of Makino Shinnosuke and Shimizu Mitsuo, who, publishing in 1923 and 1942 respectively, advanced important propositions with a lasting impact on later scholarship.

Looking back from the Tokugawa period to the late medieval period, its immediate precursor, Makino inquired into the role of the sō structure in the creation of the centralized Tokugawa village system. With the unification of the country in the early seventeenth century, the newly empowered Tokugawa regime institutionalized the system of village self-governance, facilitating the functional split that it desired between the urban and rural sectors. The origins of this system, to Makino, lay in the late medieval sō structure. Its village-initiated collective order was exploited by the late-sixteenth-century unifiers, who integrated the organizational features useful to the ruling system, such as the power to enforce regulations, while neutralizing dangerous elements, such as the potential for violent protest against the authorities.[29] This interpretation has since become firmly established in the understanding of the sō.

Equally influential, though more inspirational than orthodoxy-forming, was Shimizu Mitsuo, who argued vociferously against the dominant view that estates constituted the essence of medieval society. The availability of extensive shōen documentation exhibiting ruling-class concerns[30] facilitated the prevalence of this view. In Maki Kenji's words of 1936, apart from the shōen, villages possessed no intrinsic character or substance of their own, at least until sō documents appeared in late medieval times.[31] Initially a student of the shōen system himself, Shimizu grew dissatisfied with the remoteness of this genre from the concrete particulars of village life. He vigorously advocated a methodological and conceptual separation of villages from the shōen and an independent examination of the villages on their own terms. Consequently, he argued that villages (mura) were not mere subunits of shōen, because the settlements of cultivators making up a mura's territory were often dispersed regardless of a shōen's borders. He further contended that the village as a whole, unlike villages in the manors of the West, was never an object of control by the shōen proprietor. To the latter, tax receipts and nothing else mattered. The mura was a "natural" community based on the mutual economic interests of its residents. Despite the artificial administrative dimension grafted onto the villages by the reforms of the eighth-century government, villages continued to carry the substance of a true community throughout the ancient and medieval periods. The communal characteristics associated with the sō were qualities that Shimizu supposed to be present in all villages. Although Shimizu's work was criticized in some postwar circles as an abandonment of the theoretical categories of Marxian analysis, his inspirational hypotheses left a lasting imprint on subsequent village studies.[32]

After many decades of village studies, a large number of questions remain. This is partly because of the limitations set by the sources themselves. At the same time, however, much previous scholarship has sacrificed detailed empirical analysis to a premature search for broad theoretical significance. The trend in the last decade has shifted toward taking the material for what it is, on the one hand, and following closely the geographical and topographical factors underlying the descriptions in the documents, on the other. This twin approach has helped to deepen and bring greater accuracy to our understanding of the setting and the social and economic structure of the village, as well as its relationship to authorities. Perhaps epitomizing this trend is the work of Nakamura Ken, the compiler of the Imabori document collection, who has walked the land on numerous occasions and whose documentary analysis extends to the minute details of handwriting and seemingly inconsequential scribbles.[33] Equipped with the documents of Imabori—the products of village life itself—and the wealth of previous scholarship on the subject, this study joins the new empirical current in order to analyze the village with whatever exactitude is possible.

The first of the six chapters that follow provides the geographical and political background against which Tokuchin-ho's sō communities and local merchant organizations developed. Fundamental to the particular forms that evolved locally were the region's geology and topography, access to transportation and communication routes, and the decentralized structure of political authorities.

Chapter 2 examines the structure and internal workings of the sō village by first clarifying the historical meaning of the "village" as it existed in the medieval period and then considering the local shrine, which coordinated the area's social, religious, and economic activities and resources. Broadening the scope of examination, Chapter 3 analyzes the reality and meaning of the sō's local prerogatives as they operated in relationship to the proprietor's sphere of influence. Here, land and water—the great points for convergence or conflict between proprietary and local interests—receive primary attention.

The significance of the patron-client relationship between the estate lord and village residents is thrown into relief by the commercial practices of the area's Honai merchants. Chapter 4 delineates the world of late medieval trade: its markets, its transport routes, its commodities, its toll barriers, and the merchant organizations that were its lively protagonists. Chapter 5 examines a series of disputes with other merchant groups that simmered over more than a century's time. The concrete ways in which village merchants sought to assert their commercial interests in the complicated web of social and political restrictions illuminate the crucial importance of collective strength and sound relations with the authorities in planning and executing winning commercial strategies.

At the end of the sixteenth century, radical political and economic changes were imposed on the land and people of Tokuchin-ho. New rulers eliminated the area's old patron, removed the merchants, and reassigned landholdings. Tokuchin-ho residents were legally transformed into a group of "peasants" whose primary duty was to meet rationalized tax requirements. How the population of the sō responded to these changes and influenced the new structure with their centuries-old collective strength is the topic of Chapter 6.

CHAPTER ONE

The Physical and Political Environment

THE WRITTEN HISTORY of Tokuchin-ho begins in the thirteenth century with the oldest authentic document in the Imabori collection.[1] The documented history did not rise out of a vacuum, however. Environmental conditions whose origins long preceded the appearance of the place name Tokuchin-ho gave shape and character to the subsequent course of the region's history. Topography and geography shaped the range of possibilities and limitations associated with the local social and economic structure. The locational factor also influenced local history by bringing the area into the orbit of a particular, but shifting, configuration of authorities.

The Physical Environment

The region that came to be called Tokuchin-ho occupies the greater part of the Gamō Plain, in an alluvial fan of the Ōmi Basin, situated on the narrow neck of Honshu where Wakasa and Tsuruga bays indent the Japan Sea coast and Ise and Osaka bays jut in from the Pacific Ocean. The Ōmi Basin nestles among a series of mountain ranges— the Kohoku range to the north, the Ibuki and Suzuka ranges to the east, the Shigaraki to the south, and the Hira and Hiei to the west—and hugs at its center Japan's biggest lake, Lake Biwa.[2]

The natural line of mountains around the basin marked the provincial boundary established in the seventh century by Japan's first centralized government. The province was named after the lake, then known as the Ōmi, meaning the "freshwater sea near (the capital)."[3] The lake's current name, Lake Biwa, which describes its lute shape, came into use in the Muromachi period (1338–ca. 1500).[4]

Lake Biwa was formed about 5 million years ago and at first covered a much larger area than it does now. Today, the southeastern region along the lake's curving shoreline is expansive and flat. "Mountains"

200 to 300 meters high, the former islands in the prehistoric lake, dot the plain here and there, accentuating the breadth of the landscape with abrupt vertical touches. Seven rivers flowing from the mountains to the lake almost parallel each other at irregular intervals.[5] Along their courses they deposit sediments carried from the mountains. The Echi River's accumulated sediment gradually created the alluvial fan in which Gamō Plain came to lie.

On the western side, only a narrow strip of land separates lake from mountains, and at the lake's jagged northern end the hills abruptly meet the water. The lake narrows to a sharp point at the southern end where it drains into the Seta River, which cuts through the terraces and hills to merge eventually with the Yodo River, flowing into Osaka Bay.

Historically, the Gamō Plain was a dry, unirrigated field not sown with rice. Japan's ancient literature gives a glimpse of the Gamō Plain's appearance. According to the *Nihon shoki,* Emperor Tenchi hunted[6] in the fields of Kamau (i.e., Gamō) in 668, accompanied by "the Crown Prince, the various Princes and Princesses, the Great Minister of the Center, and all the various ministers." Princess Nukada, the famous poet of the *Man'yōshū,* contributed a verse on this occasion by asking the Crown Prince, later Emperor Tenmu:

> Going this way on the crimson-
> gleaming fields of murasaki grass,
> going that way on the fields
> of imperial domain—
> won't the guardians of the fields
> see you wave your sleeves at me?[7]

Apparently, the ruling aristocrats viewed the Gamō Plain as being more suitable for hunting than for growing rice. This is borne out by the way the *jōri* system of land division and allotment, theoretically applied to all cultivated land in the nation, was carried out.

In Ōmi Province at large, the implementation of the jōri system was extensive. In the lake's southeastern region, the land was systematically divided into blocks, following the lake's shoreline, and the blocks were numbered, vertically for the *jō* from northeast to southwest and horizontally for the *ri* from southeast to northwest. Many of these numbers remain as place names. For the Gamō Plain, however, there is little evidence of land division and certainly none for the Tokuchin-ho area.[8]

A close examination of the geological setting helps to explain why the flatland of the Tokuchin-ho area was not converted to paddy land early in its history. The area in question is an elongated triangle lying south of the Echi River, with its tip pointing east toward the Suzuka mountain range. The southern leg of the triangle borders the foot of

Nunobiki Terrace, a tongue-shaped extension of the Suzukas. Several small "mountains" (Mitsukuri, Yukino) mark the western base line of this triangular plain.

This small plain wedged between the Echi River and Nunobiki Terrace was formed in two geological stages—before and after the shift in the course of the Echi River. The earlier course of the Echi ran south of its course today. In the latter part of the Pleistocene epoch (roughly 10,000 years ago) a seismic movement raised the fluvial basin and forced the river to move north, and eventually the new Echi formed a new alluvial fan. Within the triangle in question here, Tokuchin-ho lay in the old fan-shaped plain to the south of the river, which was about 5 meters higher than the river and the new northern plain. The use of Echi River water for irrigating the southern section of the triangle was thus a difficult proposition.[9]

Furthermore, the runoff from the surrounding mountains did not accumulate in this area and was not available for irrigation. Although the land sloped evenly and gradually away from the Suzuka range, dropping from a 220 meter elevation at the eastern end to a 100 meter elevation at the foot of Mt. Kamewari (over a stretch of approximately 23 kilometers), the runoff followed a line of cleavage—much lower than the surface of the plain—along the length of Nunobiki Terrace. This line caused by erosion was made ever deeper by the runoff from the Suzuka Mountains. Higher in elevation than either side of the triangle and unwatered, the old southern plain of the Echi River was thus unsuitable for rice cultivation (see Map 2).[10]

Although Tokuchin-ho was not favored by nature for producing rice, it nevertheless benefited from its location. Owing to its terrain and position, Ōmi Province played an important role for the nation's rulers from the beginning of the ancient period. The Asuka and Yamato region, Japan's earliest political center and the locale of the ever-shifting "capitals" of the seventh and eighth centuries, was situated directly south of Ōmi, over the Shigaraki Mountains.[11] Only a few kilometers west of the lake, beyond Mt. Hiei, lay the Kyoto Basin, which was the site of the imperial capital from 794 to 1869, most of Japan's premodern history. The mountain ranges surrounding Ōmi provided a natural fortification for the capital region. At the same time, because of its central location, Ōmi served as a gateway to the capital from the Tōkai, Tōzan, and Hokuriku regions beyond; it also adjoined seven provinces—Echizen Province to the north, Mino and Ise to the east, Iga to the south, and Yamashiro, Tanba, and Wakasa to the west.

In the aftermath of the Jinshin War (672) fought in Iga, Ise, Mino, and Ōmi provinces, Emperor Tenmu, who had emerged victorious, emphasized Ōmi's defensive capacities as part of his government's formal security plan. Barriers were set up at Suzuka, Fuha, and Arachi to check the movement of people from Ise, Mino, and Echizen provinces. By the late eighth century, the roads that these barriers guarded developed into major thoroughfares called the Tōkaidō, Tōsandō, and Hokuri-kudō. The Tōkaidō and Tōsandō ran together from Kyoto to Kusatsu, a point on the southeastern side of the lake, where the Tōkaidō bent eastward, following the course of the Yasu River into Ise Province. The Tōsandō extended farther north, perpendicular to the rivers' courses, and cut into Mino Province near the Amano River; the Hokurikudō ran close to the lake's western shore, eventually connecting the capital to Wakasa Province (see Map 5).[12]

The proximity of the Japan Sea to Lake Biwa's northern edge, as well as the closeness of the capital region to the lake's southern edge, made the lake an ideal water route connecting the Kinai with the Hokuriku region. Rice grown in Hokuriku, for instance, was shipped from Shiotsu (the lake's northern port) to Ōtsu (the southern port) and transported overland to Kyoto.[13] The Seta River, into which the lake drained, provided another water route for transporting items such as lumber to the Kinai, or capital, region.[14]

Its strategic importance and its role as a nexus of transport, then, placed Ōmi at Japan's economic and political hub from the beginning of the ancient period. This, as much as the dryness of its soil, proved to be a crucial factor in Tokuchin-ho's development.

The Authorities

Prior to the unification of the country in 1600, Tokuchin-ho residents lived under the pressure and protection of multiple overlords with overlapping spheres of authority, a situation attributable to the centuries of decentralized political structure. As was true of most peasants, they had little control over who would rule over them. Enryakuji and the Sasaki clan, the two major powers directly affecting village affairs, arose long before the Tokuchin-ho estate, each succeeding in carving a political niche by late Heian times. In the subsequent Kamakura period, Enryakuji stood as one of the country's most powerful religious institutions, enjoying a firm economic foundation and close connections with the court, while the Sasaki had won the favors of Japan's first shogunate, and the Rokkaku, one of its branches, was rapidly coming to dominate the Ōmi countryside through its locally based warrior power.[15]

Enryakuji, the monastic institution located near Kyoto, originally created the geographical and taxation unit called Tokuchin-ho. In securing its economic interests, Enryakuji utilized all of its resources, including doctrinal and ritual assets as well as the physical force of its low-ranking priest-warriors. The first political authority to appear in the Imabori documents, Enryakuji incorporated the Tokuchin-ho area into its network of landed estates sometime before 1279, the year for which a later directive reveals the nonpayment of tax (*nengu*) by the Tokuchin-ho peasants (*hyakushō*).[16] Documents illustrate that from this point on, at the latest, and throughout the medieval period, a complex of hierarchical relationships bound Enryakuji and Tokuchin-ho, as proprietor and tenant, patron and client, and tax recipient and tax-payer.

Enryakuji's proprietary significance began to weaken in about the mid-fifteenth century, the time that the landed prerogatives of many kenmon powers visibly slipped into the hands of the warriors. Subsequently the Rokkaku, a prominent warrior house in Ōmi, asserted greater economic and military influence under the politically legitimate title of *shugo* (military governor). The shugo's direct vassals were similarly ambitious, sometimes undermining their direct lord's authority by tapping into local resources. The formal warrior government, the bakufu, meanwhile had little relevance to the affairs of Tokuchin-ho; the Kamakura regime had no visible connection with Tokuchin-ho, and its Muromachi successor only occasionally sent orders concerning disputes.

The Estate Proprietor: Enryakuji

The origins of Enryakuji date to 788 when Saichō, a native of Ōmi, built Hieizanji on Mt. Hiei in order to promote the teachings of the Lotus Sutra. In 805, after returning from China, Saichō received permission from Emperor Kanmu to establish the Tendai sect on Mt. Hiei. The temple he built was renamed Enryakuji in 823, and eleven years later an abbot (*zasu*) was designated to replace a court official as the principal authority over the monastery. These developments set Enryakuji on its road to independence as a religious institution.[17]

In the tenth and eleventh centuries, the temple expanded greatly, and under the direction of the eighteenth abbot, Ryōgen, its internal structure underwent major reorganization. This was a development that would have important ramifications for the Tokuchin-ho residents. Partly to assist in the reconstruction of buildings ruined by fire, but also to steer ongoing factional disputes to his advantage, Ryōgen cultivated the patronage of the Fujiwara. Their financial contribution allowed Enryakuji to begin accumulating estates, a crucial step in further consolidating power.[18]

Architecturally, Ryōgen arranged the temple complex into three *tō* ("towers") and sixteen *tani* ("valleys"), the basic configuration that remains today. The three tō included Tōdō, Saitō, and Yokawa, administratively and architecturally separate entities that conformed to divisions in Mt. Hiei's topography. The tō were further divided into five or six tani,[19] each with its own financial arrangements, including the rights to its own estates. In addition, more than 3,000 buildings of various sizes, purposes, and levels of sophistication filled the valleys of Mt. Hiei, clearly displaying the power and prestige Enryakuji had achieved by that time.[20] Higashitani of Tōdō, the oldest and most prestigious of the three tō according to contemporary literature, held proprietary rights to Tokuchin-ho.[21] This political connection would prove to be a major asset to Tokuchin-ho residents, particularly in intervillage conflicts.

Meanwhile, the latent animosity between two groups of disciples— the Ennin faction and the Enchin faction—developed into a violent confrontation and ended in a permanent schism. The friction had its origin in Enchin's reconstruction of Onjōji (popularly called Miidera) as a detached section of Enryakuji in 858. In 993, the Ennin faction burned down the buildings on top of the mountain belonging to the Enchin faction. The Enchin faction responded by descending the mountain permanently and establishing a Tendai institution separate from and independent of Enryakuji. From this point on, Enryakuji came to be called the Sanmon ("mountain gate") in contradistinction to the Jimon ("temple gate"), applied to Onjōji.[22]

Even after the schism, further competition and factional splintering remained a feature of Enryakuji's organizational structure. One type of split followed the architectural divisions of the temple complex. The other major type included more informal and private divisions occurring through blood or master-disciple relationships, which became even more important with the entry of prestigious aristocrats into the order.[23] The Imabori documents illustrate that the architectural divisions in particular greatly influenced the way Tokuchin-ho history unfolded.

Enryakuji turned out to be one of the most successful estate proprietors in the country. By the twelfth century, the number of shōen units held by the temple and its subsidiary organizations numbered over 300, scattered in Yamashiro, Ōmi, Mino, Wakasa, Echizen, and Kaga provinces.[24] One scholar estimates that Enryakuji and its rival, Onjōji, held most of the land in Ōmi between them.[25]

In the course of accumulating estates, Enryakuji consolidated an administrative and financial structure in which its economic and spiritual interests interlocked. This structure was, in turn, built into a pyramidal hierarchy with two axes—that of the temple and that of the shrine, the two religious institutions that formed one inseparable bloc of power with many undifferentiated and interconnected features.[26] At its apex, there was Enryakuji itself, the locus of the original deity and the location of the central coffers, situated symbolically atop the mountain and looking down toward the lake and the capital. Hie Shrine (also called Hiyoshi Shrine today), located in Sakamoto, at the foot of Mt. Hiei, was Enryakuji's shrine counterpart. Below the apex, there was a network of daughter temples and shrines tied to Enryakuji and Hie Shrine. Some of these affiliates held estates in their own names and were commonly required to forward rents and services to the main institution.[27] Others were located in estates directly controlled by the patron institutions. They served as local centers of worship and as channels for the penetration of the temple's influence.[28]

A key theory that held together Enryakuji and Hie Shrine, and these two centers to their subsidiary institutions, was the symbolic and highly epistemological notion known as *honji suijaku:* manifestation of the Buddha's true nature in *kami,* or Shinto deities. By the late Heian period, this theory had evolved to promote direct identification between particular Shinto deities and particular buddhas and bodhisatvas.[29]

The mechanics of identifying one deity with another were complex, and tortured explanations were often required. One simplified contemporary account states that before the construction of Enryakuji, the deity of Mt. Hiei was called Ōyamagui-no-mikoto, according to the *Kojiki,* Japan's ancient chronicle. During Emperor Tenchi's time (r. 662–72), according to Enryakuji's own literature, Ōyamagui came to be called Obie ("small Hie") to differentiate it from another mountain deity, newly transferred from Yamato, which came to be called Ōbie ("large Hie").[30] This latter outside deity was Ōmononushi, the kami of Ōmiwa Shrine and of the prestigious Kamo family, worshiped as a protector of imperial residences. Hie Shrine was constructed in Sakamoto around this time to celebrate these and other local deities.[31]

In another explanation, each of the major sections of Enryakuji initially had its own symbolic buddha, which was associated with a kami of the three main shrines of Hie: Saitō, symbolized by Shaka-nyorai (Sākyamuni) and associated with the kami of the Western Shrine; Ōnamuchi (Ōmononushi); Tōdō, symbolized by Yakushi-nyorai (Bhaisajyaguru) and associated with the four kami of the Eastern Shrine (two different forms each of Ōyamagui-no-mikoto and Kamo-tamayori-hime-no-mikoto); Yokawa, symbolized by Amida-nyorai (Amitābha) and associated with the kami of Usa Shrine.[32] From the Heian through the medieval periods a rationale was introduced to treat all the associated kami and buddhas as a single entity called Sannō.[33]

Enryakuji's recent literature explains this last version in the following fashion: On Mt. T'ien-tai (Tendai in Japanese) in China, there resided a deity called Shanwang—Sannō in Japanese—who was said to be the Chinese counterpart of the Japanese deity Ōbie. When Enryakuji was built on Mt. Hiei to promote the Tendai doctrine, Sannō became joined with Ōbie in the form of Hie Sannō.

Linguistic and deific connection had its counterpart in the religious institutions themselves; Enryakuji and Hie Shrine became closely affiliated, with the latter serving as the protective shrine of the former, and their combined spiritual force won the visits and patronage of the imperial and court families.[34]

Deities associated with the central complex were in turn transplanted to the estates' local spiritual sites, mediating the proprietary influence through indigenous patterns of worship. Imabori's Hie Shrine housed many familiar deities, including Ōmiya (same as Ōbie) and Ninomiya (same as Obie); the shrine was formally called Hie Ninomiya Sannō Jūzenji-sha. Tangible deific connections and their symbolic ramifications both reinforced and ameliorated the primarily extractive economic relationship between the proprietor and the villagers. Ceremonies such as the Sannō-kō or Higan-kō, which integrated the celebrations of Sannō incarnations with celebrations of the local production cycle, probably called for the direct participation of Enryakuji priests.[35]

Across the country, the expansion of Enryakuji's economic power directly corresponded to the increase in both the number of these subsidiary institutions—absorbed voluntarily or under pressure[36]—and the number of affiliated deities. In the eleventh century, the names of such deities multiplied to more than 100.[37] On one level, then, Enryakuji extended its economic control through local administrators who managed tax-related problems. But on another, it maintained a spiritual and ideological continuum with its subjects through shared participation in the common ritual space. For the villagers, the presence of Mt. Hiei divinities on local soil was a tangible reminder of the prestigious connection between their community and the powerful central institution.

In addition to the land nexus, Enryakuji and Hie Shrine cultivated an interest in an ever-growing cash nexus. With the accumulation of shōen and the spread of their prestige in the late Heian period, the religious institutions began to influence the financial world, in particular through the lending of cash and seed rice by low-ranking priests and service people.[38] Called "sacred objects of Hie (Hie *shinmotsu*)," seed rice—the year's first seeds presented to the deities—was loaned before the spring planting. The borrowers used their paddies for collateral and repaid the loan after the fall harvest. Borrowing was made easy by a relatively low rate of interest, although severe pressure was applied to those negligent in repayment.[39] Consequently people of all classes, including courtiers, warriors, and commoners, made use of the loan services of Enryakuji and Hie Shrine. Their activities were not limited to the environs of Kyoto and Ōmi, nor to shōen with Enryakuji and Hie affiliations; the service people (*jinin*) of Hie Shrine could be found on estates held by other proprietors and as far away as Kyushu throughout the Kamakura and Muromachi periods.[40]

As the cash economy expanded in the late thirteenth century, money increasingly replaced seed rice as a loan medium, transforming this loan service into de facto moneylending.[41] The financial operations of Enryakuji and Hie Shrine were particularly noteworthy in the capital, where they served as patrons—operating what Suzanne Marie Gay calls a "protection racket"—for over 80 percent of the moneylending institutions (*dosō*) in Kyoto in the early fourteenth century. These institutions served as a type of banking system and even managed shogunal finances, in addition to promoting tax farming and storing clients' cash and valuables. They paid dues to Enryakuji and borrowed its moral authority and its muscle to facilitate debt collection.[42] The Muromachi bakufu sought to restrain the temple's influence, but with limited success. On several occasions (in 1370 and 1386), it prohibited Enryakuji and its affiliates from collecting overdue debts independently of the bakufu's arbitration. In addition, at the end of the fourteenth century the bakufu sought to absorb Enryakuji's customary prerogatives to impose fees on moneylenders. By the mid-fifteenth century the temple's effective resistance renewed its earlier position, and the moneylenders came to pay dues to both the bakufu and Enryakuji.[43] Needless to say, Enryakuji's solid financial status gave it powerful leverage in the economic and political power structure of the day, as well as attracted clients wishing to benefit from its protection. This financial power and the accompanying rational economic outlook were crucial characteristics of the institution that was the patron of Tokuchin-ho's residents.

Finally, alongside the economic and doctrinal bases of power, Enryakuji possessed a tremendous pool of coercive and military power, a necessity in resolving intertemple disputes or in competing against other estate holders, including warriors. Enryakuji, like other major temples, was equipped with its own fighting force, including priest-warriors (*sōhei*) and soldiers, although all priests of any rank would arm themselves on appropriate occasions.[44] Priest-warriors were low-ranking priests whose incognito attire (covered heads), clog-shod feet, and long halberds frequently arrayed the streets of Kyoto. They were instrumental in enforcing various measures to achieve institutional, or factional, aims—from protesting the symbolic gesture of a rival temple, punishing an estate agent guilty of encroachment, or threatening debtors with collection notices, all the way to weakening the contending faction by burning down its buildings. The size and strength of Enryakuji's military wing depended on the size of the temple's network of branch temples and shrines, which often provided these famous men of violence. For example, the priest-warriors of Gion Shrine, a branch institution, often led the disturbances staged in Kyoto wherein the holy palanquin was planted at a major intersection in an appeal to the deities to express their wrath.[45] Soldiers with a lay background filled the bottom rung in any large-scale mobilization effort. It is difficult to estimate the exact size of the total force, but several thousand were easily mustered.[46] Its military strength, coupled with its economic resources, made Enryakuji one of the most formidable institutions of the day.

The Shugo: The Rokkaku Family

The Rokkaku, a branch of the Sasaki clan, held Ōmi's military governorship, the shugo post, for nearly 400 years, from its initial grant in the late 1180s to its extinction in 1568 at the hands of Oda Nobunaga. Throughout a long (if occasionally interrupted) tenure, the Rokkaku and their vassals (*hikan*) left significant marks on Tokuchin-ho's history. As the dominant provincial power, the Rokkaku were in a position to arbitrate disputes and issue decisions, effect administrative measures, including tax and service levies, and wage war. For Tokuchin-ho residents, the most significant aspect of this vertical relationship was the authority of the shugo and his vassals to adjudicate disputes, especially intercommunity commercial conflicts. Matters related to expropriation had little significance, for throughout the medieval period, with the exception of one brief emergency, Tokuchin-ho was free of the shugo's imposts. More indirectly, however, the shugo's activities influenced the pattern of local production and commodity circulation owing to geographical considerations.

Before a Rokkaku was first appointed shugo, indeed from the ancient period on, the headquarters of the Sasaki and later the Rokkaku were all located within a few kilometers of Tokuchin-ho. Originally, the Sasaki lived in the area of Mt. Sasaki,[47] later called Mt. Kannonji, which was situated on the east side of the lake about 2.5 kilometers northwest of Tokuchin-ho, just on the other side of Mt. Mitsukuri. In about the tenth century they constructed a military headquarters in Owaki, almost on Tokuchin-ho's northwestern edge. This later became the shugo's headquarters. Sometime in the Kamakura period, the Sasaki built a loop road off the Tōsandō to reach Owaki, a passage much used by Tokuchin-ho merchants. In the latter part of the medieval period, they built a castle on Mt. Kannonji; at the mountain's southern foot the castle town of Ishidera developed (see Map 5).[48]

Tokuchin-ho residents and the shugo, therefore, had much in common; they shared the same transportation routes, and because they were both located in the Gamō Plain, they used the same water sources for irrigation. In the early 1300s, the Sasaki built a sluice to irrigate Owaki by drawing water from the Echi River. The irrigation channel cut through the northern half of the alluvial triangle and irrigated twelve villages located north of Tokuchin-ho before reaching Owaki. Water for Tokuchin-ho was drawn at a point upriver from the origin of this sluice.[49]

Apart from several houses on the fringes of the country, the Rokkaku family was the only shugo house to survive from the time of the first shogun, Yoritomo, to the end of the Warring period (ca. 1467–1568). This did not mean, however, that Rokkaku rule was marked by solid and continuous dominance in Ōmi. Rather, the family's resilience lay in its ability to withstand changes in the power structure above and below it. Of particular importance was the sort of federation formed by the Rokkaku vassals, which was solid enough to counter outside intrusions as well as to preempt the dominance of the Rokkaku themselves. Just as the shugo needed his vassals, likewise the vassals needed the power and authority embodied in the shugo.

Members of various Sasaki lines made up the core of the Rokkaku vassalage. (The origins of the Sasaki family and its branch lines are discussed in Appendix A.) The vassals' names remain in records describing famous incidents. At least seven Sasaki families can be numbered, for example, among the troops fighting under Rokkaku command, which, representing the bakufu side, clashed with an army of Enryakuji, representing Emperor Godaigo, during the Genkō Incident of 1331.[50] The vassalage structure continued to expand, and by the late fifteenth century, it had come to incorporate a large number of non-Sasaki families.[51] Many of these vassals also left their names in Imabori documents of later dates when their political significance increased in the region.

Structurally, the Rokkaku devised a governing system supported by a series of delegations of authority. As early as the 1270s, a three-tiered system composed of shugo, deputy shugo, and district-level deputy shugo was in operation. The direct descendant of the main Rokkaku line filled the post of shugo most of the time (with intervals for the Yamanouchi and Kyōgoku lines), and various Sasaki branches served in the deputy and district-level posts. This last was a position not widely found in other provinces at this time; it functioned as an enforcing authority for shugo orders in such areas as justice for commoners at the district (*kōri*) level. In the fourteenth century, when provincial administration was further rationalized, the title became "district commissioner" (*kōri-bugyō*). Holders of the position remained physically remote from the people they controlled, however. Much like their superiors (the shugo and deputy shugo), they spent most of their time in Kyoto and were absentee officials.[52] Despite this absenteeism and the absence of a shugo's regular imposts, these officials of various ranks made an impact on Tokuchin-ho by arbitrating commercial disputes and providing protection against incursions.

A Medieval Triangle: Competition and Cooperation Among Authorities

Changing relations of competition and cooperation among greater and lesser authorities characterized the fluid but resilient political conditions of late medieval Japan. As in any other region, at no time before unification was there ever a single political authority presiding over Tokuchin-ho. Instead of a single hegemonic power, the triangle of Enryakuji, shugo, and bakufu influenced local affairs in varying manners and degrees. The shape of this triangle was a mutable one; the nature of the relationships among them underwent continuous change, as did the internal structure of each of the elements. Thus, for centuries the distribution of power over Tokuchin-ho remained erratic. The villages' independent social and economic organizations benefited from this situation, for no authority had sufficiently concentrated political resources to restructure them. From their own collective base, the residents not only withstood all the political vicissitudes but sought actively to turn them to their advantage.

The efforts of the residents to promote the sō's activities were also facilitated by an absence of the violence and bloodshed that typically accompanied the struggles for a realignment of power in the Warring period. In the course of clashes between contending forces, villages could turn into battlegrounds, with houses destroyed and paddies and fields ruined.[53] Despite the frequency of armed confrontations among the powers in Ōmi, the Tokuchin-ho area escaped disruptions of this nature. The reasons for this are unclear. Perhaps the area was too flat to be suited for warfare, which was generally fought on hillsides or in the mountains. In addition, the Rokkaku never bothered to stake direct military or economic claims there, leaving the temple to enjoy unencumbered land rights. This freedom from destruction was no minor contribution to the success of local economic endeavors during a decentralized and tension-ridden era. The following pages will illustrate how the three authorities wove a fabric of political relations that served as the backdrop to the history of Tokuchin-ho.

Enryakuji had been the dominant power in Ōmi Province long before the establishment of the Kamakura bakufu. The appointment of the shugo to the province and the jitō to the estates was therefore an intrusion into the accustomed situation and a source of new friction. Collisions between the shōen proprietor and the shugo were commonplace throughout the medieval period. The temple and the Rokkaku clashed frequently over economic issues whose resolutions typically demanded intercession from the bakufu or the court.

Sasaki-no-shō, an estate with a history of Sasaki managers (*gesu*), was often the breeding ground for such conflicts. Enryakuji became its proprietor in 1184 upon commendation by the Taira, who, having attracted the Sasaki as their client, temporarily absorbed some of the latter's traditional prerogatives.[54] As early as 1191–93, for example, Enryakuji and Sasaki Sadatsuna opposed each other over the division of responsibility for this estate. Although the details are unclear, Sadatsuna apparently reneged on his obligation to forward the taxes, inviting the temple's retribution. A scramble followed that resulted in the injury and death of several low-ranking priests. The sacred mirror that they carried was also broken.

Symptomatic of the decentralized state was the involvement of both court and bakufu in the dispute's resolution, with the latter, at this early juncture, yielding to the former's decision. Responding to a petition by Enryakuji demanding punitive action against Sadatsuna and his sons (and to a subsequent march of priests on the imperial palace), the court exiled the guilty Sasaki and later executed one of them. Sadatsuna was eventually pardoned in 1193 as part of a general amnesty, then the bakufu awarded him three shugo posts.[55]

The temple and the shugo fought on many other occasions. Another clash in 1230 over the fees charged by the shugo to the carriers of portable Hie shrines led to the murder of a priest-official by a Rokkaku jitō.[56] The temple retaliated by demanding that the court issue a death sentence, and demonstrated its resolution by marching into Kyoto with the portable shrines of the seven Hie shrines. After some further violence, Enryakuji went on strike by closing the buildings of the three tō on Mt. Hiei, the Hie shrines, and all the daughter temples and shrines in the Gion and Kitano districts of Kyoto. Viewing this demonstration with utmost seriousness, the imperial court decided to exile the guilty jitō and relayed its sentence to the temple. But the bakufu, possessing newly gained confidence since the Jōkyū War (1221), took a different position.

While recognizing the sentence, the bakufu also ordered that a list of priests responsible for the coercive action be compiled. The temple provided a partial list—along with a plea for pardon. The bakufu refused the plea, however, and dispatched a mission to arrest the offending priests. Ultimately, the episode ended in stalemate, with the bakufu standing firm in its resolve but with no arrests actually made. After the culprits fled the temple, the court commanded the bakufu to track down Enryakuji troublemakers in all provinces.[57]

The bakufu's political posture toward Ōmi vacillated, however, depending on the shogun's particular outlook or needs of the moment. What remained constant throughout Kamakura and Muromachi times was the necessity to juggle the bakufu's relationship with the two major components of Ōmi's political structure: the Rokkaku and Enryakuji. For its own survival, it was often necessary for the bakufu to play up to one at the risk of displeasing the other.

During the height of Ashikaga rule, the third shogun, Yoshimitsu (r. 1368–94), sought to impinge on the Rokkaku's dominance while simultaneously ameliorating the tension between the bakufu and Enryakuji. In the 1380s, a series of measures was put into effect to check the growing power of the shugo. The first was the compulsory return to the original holders of the land rights acquired through *hanzei* from the 1350s on. (Hanzei was a legal measure by which a shugo, on the initial pretext of needing emergency provisions, might obtain long-term taxation privileges.) In the case of Ōmi, the new measure of the 1380s was calculated to promote dissatisfaction among the shugo's vassals, thereby weakening the shugo himself. Ōmi was one of the earliest provinces to put hanzei measures into effect, and the grant of hanzei land to the shugo's vassals or potential vassals was one of the surest means to consolidate their support. By the 1380s, the newly acquired land shares had already been distributed among the vassals. A reversal now would provoke discontent.[58]

An accompanying measure aimed at trimming shugo power was the appointment of the Enryakuji envoys (*shisetsu*) to the bakufu.[59] This step was also meant to reduce the tension between the bakufu and

Enryakuji. The envoys were chosen from among priests called *daimyō* whose duties included conferences with the shogun. The daimyō held low ranks in the temple's formal structure, though they possessed lucrative personal ties with priest families of prestige. For them, an appointment as envoy meant a new form of political leverage and a new bakufu-connected status.[60]

The authority given to these envoys duplicated some of the shugo's prerogatives. For example, they were authorized to adjudicate property-related disputes when ordered to do so by the bakufu, a responsibility hitherto held by the shugo for the entire province. Formerly, the bakufu gave an adjudication order to someone other than the shugo—a shugo of a neighboring province or a direct agent of the bakufu—only when one of the disputants was the shugo himself or his agent or when the shugo of Ōmi was unable to adjudicate for some reason. According to Shimosaka Mamoru, the bakufu's target here was the landholdings of the Rokkaku's direct and indirect vassals. In the 1380s alone, the temple's envoys terminated three known cases of "aggression" on the part of these vassals. The introduction of Enryakuji envoys, therefore, effectively cut into the economic base of the Rokkaku vassalage, a condition designed to weaken the shugo overall.[61]

The measures taken to weaken the authority and power of the shugo during the heyday of the Ashikaga shogunate apparently had results. To historians, the first indication of this is the disappearance of *kakikudashi,* a type of directive issued by the shugo himself or by his immediate agents. The important feature of these directives was their issuance independent of the bakufu. Some twenty written between 1350 and 1376 survive.[62]

The Ashikaga shogun who followed Yoshimitsu adopted a different attitude toward the Ōmi shugo. Yoshimochi (r. 1394–1423) also attempted to curtail the Rokkaku's hold, but he did so by promoting the Kyōgoku, another branch of the Sasaki and a competitive source of military authority in the province, instead of by catering to estate proprietors as Yoshimitsu had done.[63] In the last decade of the fourteenth century, the bakufu issued adjudication orders to the Kyōgoku to terminate any illegal acts committed by the vassals of the Rokkaku in northern Ōmi.[64]

By contrast, Shogun Yoshinori (r. 1429–41) campaigned vehemently against Enryakuji. In 1433 and 1434, Yoshinori named both a Rokkaku and a Kyōgoku to new posts called Sanmon *ryōō shi,* whose sole function seems to have been to confiscate Enryakuji property.[65] Records show that less than a week after the appointments, Enryakuji priests began a violent protest, indicating that anti-Enryakuji activities had quickly materialized.[66] The temple put up a stiff fight, but Rokkaku Mitsutsuna, with additional military aid from Ise and Mino provinces, succeeded in quelling the opposition; many priests died, and the temple's central building, the Konpon Chūdō, burned to the ground. "The Rokkaku did as they wished," commented Mansai, the abbot (zasu) of Daigoji.[67]

In the several decades preceding the Ōnin War (1467–77), the Rokkaku house was first shaken from within, then involved in a severe conflict with the Kyōgoku. These events presaged an era of countrywide instability marked by the fragmentation of warrior houses and the diminution of the central proprietors. It was symptomatic of this trend that by the end of the fifteenth century, Enryakuji ceased to adjudicate Tokuchin-ho's interregional disputes, while the residents busily sought vassal ties with the shugo's retainers for security.

A series of dramatic events highlights the general condition of disorder in which opportunism ran rampant. In 1444, the vassalage revolted against the current shugo (Rokkaku Michitsuna) for reasons that are unclear. He and his father were forced to take refuge, but finally met a violent end at the hands of his younger brother, Tokitsuna, who had the vassals' support.[68] It was an age in which internal divisions seldom remained private, and in the Rokkaku case there soon developed an intricate web of conspiring forces. To Tokitsuna's shock, the bakufu's deputy shogun (*kanrei;* Hosokawa Katsumoto) recommended another brother (Hisayori), a still younger brother of Tokitsuna's and a retired priest, to be the Rokkaku heir. Tokitsuna, however, retained the confidence of most Rokkaku vassals, and thus the bakufu was obliged to employ a Kyōgoku force to eliminate him. It is recorded that many retainers followed him in death in the ninth month of 1445.[69]

The main task left for the new shugo, after Tokitsuna's death, was to repair his relationship with the vassalage by allowing it more direct participation in Ōmi governance. One result was an increase in the number of directives issued by the administrative officials (*bugyōnin hōsho*)—usually to the deputy shugo, the post monopolized by one family, the Iba. Most of the shugo-related documents in the Imabori collection are of this type. The new shugo, in other words, did not promulgate direct orders under his own signature;[70] there were two levels of checks before the shugo's order could take effect in a given area. This pattern in the delegation of authority characterized Rokkaku rule for much of the late medieval period.[71]

A violent confrontation between the Rokkaku and Kyōgoku ensued in the 1450s. Though little information has survived regarding this conflict, we know that the shugo Hisayori ended his own life in 1456 "in order to save the situation."[72] The shugo post from this point went to a succession of holders, including the Kyōgoku for a two-year tenure, until the post became split between north and south in 1471. At this juncture the Kyōgoku held the three northern counties of Ōmi, and the Rokkaku were the shugo for the rest of the province.[73]

The Ōnin War, the historians' signpost for Japan's entry into the Warring period, split many warrior families, their members fighting in opposite camps. While the Rokkaku sided with the Yamana and the Kyōgoku fought for the Hosakawa, the rivalry here was complicated by internal friction within both families. Two Rokkaku men, for example, fought against each other; the one joined by a Kyōgoku man was largely successful.[74]

The war also marked the further decline of temples and shrines. In the confusion of the war, the Rokkaku and their vassals succeeded in appropriating a great deal of estate land in Ōmi, including that of Enryakuji. The temple attempted to block the takeover by announcing a mobilization in 1473. Though the bakufu approved the temple's action, peace was restored by a Rokkaku pledge not to seize temple land in the future.[75]

Nonetheless, the Rokkaku remained Enryakuji's enemy. In 1475, the Hosokawa faction of the bakufu came to an agreement with the anti-Rokkaku groups—Enryakuji, Kyōgoku (Masatsuna), and the shogunal vassals (*hōkōshū*)—to launch an all-out assault on their common foe. Against overwhelming odds, the current head of the Rokkaku house (Takayori) emerged victorious from the last major battle fought in Ōmi. By 1477, he and the bakufu had moved toward conciliation, and he once again became shugo.[76]

This in no way meant, however, that calm had returned to the province. Despite the bakufu's repeated order to return confiscated land,[77] the shugo and his men busily reaped the war's harvest. Ozuki Nagaoki, another courtier, for example, complained in 1481 that a suspected "vassal of the Sasaki shugo" who had "recently been invading land in western Ōmi" had seized his family's holding.[78] In the following year, a representative of the Kyōgoku reported to the bakufu that Takayori had forced his army into Takashima County "upon the pretext of pacifying the peasants."[79] Whether Takayori or his vassals had directed the land seizures was immaterial to the victims; as the shugo, Takayori was at fault.

This behavior on the part of the shugo apparently "angered" the shogun Ashikaga Yoshihisa.[80] He therefore announced plans for a punitive expedition to Ōmi, ostensibly to answer the grievances of temples and shrines but in fact to satisfy the demands of the shogun's own vassals (there were 46 hōkōshū in Ōmi).[81] The expedition was successful, but instead of returning the land to the original religious holders, he distributed it among his followers as wartime provisions.[82]

In 1491, the new shogun, Yoshiki, reconquered Ōmi and called the province his own "direct holding [*goryōkoku*]."[83] Once again it was his own vassals, the hōkōshū, who profited here, and only after a strong protest by the temples and shrines did the shogun begin to issue retrocession orders.[84] The estate proprietors, heads of the most powerful institutions of the early medieval period, were losing ground everywhere. To manage and protect their holdings, they were relying on warriors, many of whom, like the vassals of the Rokkaku, were their own natural enemies and took advantage of the situation.[85] Both the bakufu and the local vassals pressed against the established prerogatives of the proprietors at the very base of the latters' source of power—their landed interests.

The Imabori documents closely reflect this shift in the balance of power. In the first few years of the sixteenth century, there was a sudden increase in the number of directives issued by the Rokkaku vassals. But this also represented yet another series of ongoing power struggles—in this case involving the shugo and his vassals. The conflict between the shugo and the deputy shugo, a member of a former branch of the Sasaki family, was particularly severe. An accusation of inappropriate conduct brought in 1502 by the shugo (Rokkaku Takayori) against his deputy (Iba Sadataka) instigated a series of battles.[86] An accord was reached, but only temporarily; a second clash and the final defeat of the Iba came in 1514. The outcome of these events was the transfer of jurisdiction from the vassals to the shugo himself, but in the process, the fundamental weakness in the structure of Rokkaku power had been laid bare.[87]

Meanwhile, the Rokkaku's involvement in the affairs at the center—succession disputes in the Miyoshi, Hosokawa, and shogunal families—and in the affairs of other provincial houses, such as the Azai and the Saitō, further strained various strands of political relations. The 1563 murder of the Gotō, ranking vassals of the Rokkaku, by the shugo himself (Rokkaku Yoshisuke, later called Yoshiharu) shook the shugo's power base irremediably. The other retainers burned their own residences in Kannonji, retired in protest, and contacted the Azai house, the Rokkaku's archenemy. Although peace was reestablished, the Rokkaku's hold over their vassals was in fact broken forever.[88] Symbolizing the new condition was a compact, the Rokkaku codes, signed in 1567 after defeat in a battle against the Azai. Apart from the 67 articles covering a wide range of topics from land-related disputes to loans and liabilities, it contained a portentous oath signed by the last Rokkaku (Jōtei and Yoshisuke) and some twenty core families to mutually restrict their exercise of political prerogatives. In essence, it stood for a victory of the collectivist spirit and power of the key Rokkaku vassals—which had been growing since, at the latest, the murder of the Gotō—over the authority of the Rokkaku themselves.[89] The Rokkaku were unaware at this point, of course, that their final downfall was indeed imminent.

Before their collapse the Rokkaku waged aggressive wars both inside and outside the province, some of which came to involve the Tokuchin-ho residents. In 1536, for instance, the Rokkaku aided Enryakuji in resolving an armed dispute with priests of Honganji, a quarrel that had started with a theological debate.[90] In 1538 and repeatedly thereafter, the Rokkaku took the field against the Azai of northern Ōmi. And in 1556 and 1557, they pushed into Ise Province against the Chigusa.[91]

In the Chigusa campaign the shugo sought the services of the residents of Tokuchin-ho. Yet in doing so he again displayed the limits of his local influence relative to that of his vassals. Instead of commanding directly, he worked through Enryakuji, which conveyed his request to its own local agents in a voice of sweet reason: "Although there has never been a precedent [for this type of service, the shugo is making a special request] because this [war] is an important provincial matter. [Moreover, the shugo] considers the service to be an emergency employment [with payment to participants] that will not set a precedent for the future. . . . [Thus this request is delivered]."[92] The residents of Tokuchin-ho accepted the request because "there is not one peasant [hyakushō] here who is without a [warrior] master," that is, without ties to vassals of the Rokkaku, such as "Gotō, Fuse, Ikeda, Hirai, Kanzaki, Mii, Mikami, Shinmura, Misono, Kawai, and Yokoyama."[93]

In the eighth month of 1568, Oda Nobunaga dispatched a messenger to the Rokkaku asking for their cooperation when Nobunaga entered Kyoto. Because the Azai—the Rokkaku's longtime enemy—were allies of Nobunaga, the Rokkaku rejected this overture. When Nobunaga arrived, sixteen major vassals switched to the Oda side. The Rokkaku fled their headquarters in Kannonji, and the history of the family was effectively ended.[94]

Meanwhile, the Muromachi bakufu was approaching its own end, as its last shogun, Ashikaga Yoshiaki, became an object of Nobunaga's ideological control. After many exchanges of surface trust, suggested harmony, covert retaliation, and outright hostility, the last shogun was expelled from Kyoto, or, in Nobunaga's classic phrase, "abandon[ed] the realm," in 1573.[95] The fate of Enryakuji was more dramatic. In 1571, Nobunaga's troops simply burned it down, and although it was later reconstructed, its importance was over. The misfortune of historians was that all the documents of the temple, including those concerning Tokuchin-ho, also went up in smoke.[96]

These centuries of volatile political relations brought problems and possibilities to rural commoners. Most notably, the extreme insecurity of the authorities allowed the Tokuchin-ho residents much leverage in shaping and maintaining their own local system. The various authorities, all occupied by fights to hold or gain ground, did not trouble themselves with projects to restructure village life in any significant way. Capitalizing on the authorities' needs for resources that commoners could offer, the villagers asserted their local autonomy and won patronage where they could find it. Owing to their political acumen, and partly perhaps to luck, the residents of Tokuchin-ho garnered many benefits from their decentralized and shifting political environment.

But starting with Nobunaga, the process of unification transformed the entire economic base of the sō. The policies of Hideyoshi and the Tokugawa regime further reshaped the local institutions while simultaneously seeking to incorporate many of their time-tested features. Consequently, village collectives of the Tokugawa period would acquire a new meaning as they came to interact with the larger goals and interests of the new hegemonic state.

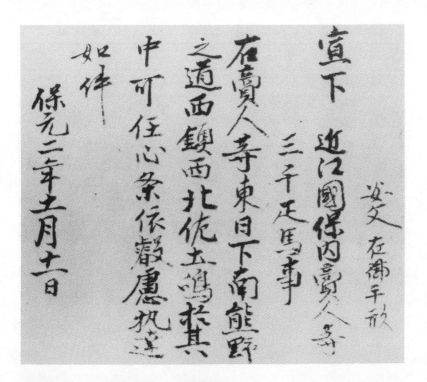

宣下

近江國保内賣人等

安文 在御平欸

三千疋馬事

右賣人寺東日下南熊野

之道西鏡西北佐立鳴其

中可任心免依敕慮执達

如件

保元二年十二月十一日

The *inzen,* a spurious decree of the retired emperor Goshirakawa. This is a medieval copy of the original, which is preserved at Imabori Hie (Hiyoski) Shrine and is said to bear a handprint of Goshirakawa. Courtesy of Yōkaichi City Board of Education.

Imabori Hie (Hiyoski) Jūzenji Shrine with the stump of the old tree that was cut down during the Pacific War. The girth of the tree suggests its age. Photographed by the author.

The Gamō Plain with the Suzuka Mountains in the far distance. Courtesy of Yōkaichi City Board of Education.

Nunobiki Terrace with Imabori in the foreground. Courtesy of Yōkaichi City Board of Education.

Stone *jizō* and the Ichi-michi (Market Road) leading north to Yōkaichi. Photographed by the author.

Nogami (Field Deity) in Imabori. Photographed by the author.

An irrigation ditch in Imabori. Photographed by the author.

Entrance to Imabori Hie (Hiyoski) Jūzenji Shrine. Photographed by the author.

Imabori Hie (Hiyoski) Jūzenji Shrine with a view of the drum hung from an eave.
Photographed by the author.

Two plaques from the *torii* gate of Imabori Hie (Hiyoski) Jūzenji Shrine,
now at Bunka Geijutsu Kaiban, Yōkaichi. The one on the right reads
"Sannō Jūzenji," a name showing the shrine's connection to the Tendai
school of Buddhism (Enryakuji). The plaque on the left, which reads
"Hiyoski [or, Hie] Shrine," was placed over the other, older one when the
Meiji government legally distinguished Shinto and Buddhism and
prescribed a strictly Shinto identification for all shrines in 1868.
Photographed by the author.

Yama-no-kami (Mountain Deity) with *gohei* sticks in the foreground. Photographed by the author in 1983.

Yama-no-kami (Mountain Deity) a few decades ago. From the photo collection of Murata Sōkichi.

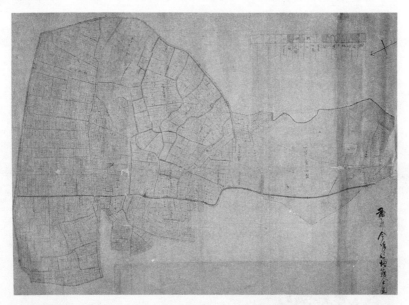

Map of Imabori drawn in 1873, Yōkaichi City Board of Education. Photographed by the author.

Map of the Lower-ho drawn in 1695. Photographed by the author, with permission of Historical Archive of the Department of Economics, Shiga Univeristy.

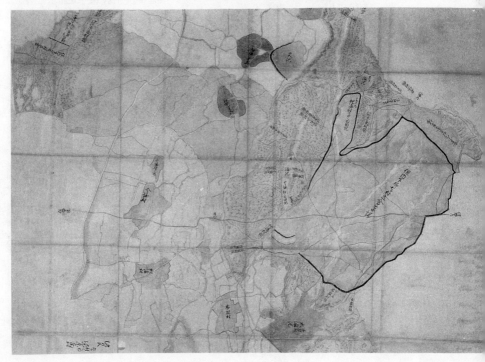

Buddhist statue preserved in Imabori
Hie (Hiyoski) Jūzenji Shrine.
Courtesy of Yōkaichi City Board of
Education.

Miko (popularly called an *oichi-san*
today) performing a purification
ritual. Courtesy of Yōkaichi City
Board of Education.

Hot water ritual in progress under the direction of a *miko*. Courtesy of Yōkaichi City Board of Education.

A ceremony dedicated to Nogami, showing the core members of the Imabori shrine association—*otona* (elders), *kannushi* (head priest), and *shōshi* (assistants). Courtesy of Yōkaichi City Board of Education.

The shrine of the Sasaki family. Members of a branch of the family, the Rokkaku, came to dominate Ōmi Province as its *shugo*. Photographed by the author.

Imabori Hie (Hiyoski) Jūzenji Shrine. Photographed by the author.

Remains of Kannonji Castle, the fortress built by the Rokkaku family and besieged by Oda Nobunaga in 1568. Photographed by the author.

CHAPTER TWO

The Sō Village

THE sō's own records show its organizational structure and function within the Imabori community at large. How were villages delineated geographically and socially? How did the life patterns of residents fit the structure of villages? What did the sō mean to the residents? While the documents reveal many facets of village life, they draw our attention most keenly to the sō's identification with the structure and operation of the local shrine. A focal point in communal life, the shrine was central not only geographically but also in the patterns of worship and local political authority. This chapter will seek to clarify the makeup and meaning of the sō within the larger context of the village community.

Villages: Geographical and Social Parameters

Medieval Japan lacked a standard designation for territorial units. Unlike in Tokugawa times, there was no single term defining the village, for example. What, then, do we mean when we speak of the sō village? If the sō was a corporate body built upon the common territorial affinity of its members, what was the shape of this territorial base? Put another way, what were the boundaries of a coherent social unit—a community—as perceived by its members? Did this perception of the residents match the understanding of the absentee proprietor with primarily economic interests? Our inquiry into these questions may begin with the examination of the various units making up the territorial hierarchy of Tokuchin-ho.

The Estate: Tokuchin-ho

Tokuchin-ho was an estate, or shōen, a unit of taxation, set up by Enryakuji for the purpose of drawing agricultural and commercial revenues, labor services, and other profits from the land and its inhabitants. It was a concrete geographical expression of the temple's design to colonize, so to speak, and to incorporate this region into its vast network of estates. The first documents in the Imabori collection testify that this proprietary relationship was operating by 1279.[1] Local legends concerning its origins suggest that some "natural villages" existed before the imposition of this artificial unit from above. According to the charter of Ōmori Shrine in Ōmori village, for example, an Enryakuji priest named Tokuchin came down to the area as early as 784. He renamed the shrine, which had its origin in 663, Tamaozan Chōfukuji.[2]

While exact dating is impossible, historians generally estimate the origin of Tokuchin-ho to be in the late eleventh century.[3] Nakamura Ken has hypothesized that, before that time, the area was a dry field used as a horse pasture.[4] Whatever the case, water and soil conditions strongly influenced the structure of proprietary control over the area. Geographical names, an innovation of the proprietor, identified the productive capabilities of each subregion and reflected Enryakuji's rational economic motivations. On the basis of the relative distance to the river, the area came to be divided into the Upper-ho (Kami-ho) located upriver, and the Lower-ho (Shimo-ho) located down and away from the Echi River. These two sectors also had descriptive names that reflected the irrigation capabilities of each: the Upper-ho was called the Tagata, or Paddy Side, and the Lower-ho was called the Nogata, or Field Side.[5] As we shall see, Enryakuji sought to maximize profits from both areas by encouraging agriculture in the Upper-ho and commerce in the Lower-ho.

Tokuchin-ho was the territorial framework that defined the vertical relationship between the proprietor and its subject population. In this sense, Tokuchin-ho functioned like any shōen, where the upward flow of goods was the primary purpose of its existence. In fact, people often spoke of Tokuchin-ho as a *shō* (short for *shōen*), as two agents of Oda Nobunaga did in 1589: "two plots of land . . . located in this shō."[6] The proprietor addressed the residents as *homin* ("people of the ho")— a word that implied circumscribed territorial affiliation—or as *hyakushō*—a term commonly used to denote (ideally) settled agriculturalists tied to plots of land encumbered with dues to their lords.[7]

Tokuchin-ho was an estate commonly identified by historians as an *ichien-ryō,* that is, a shōen under the exclusive control of one proprietor without the usual hierarchy of outside interests defined by various *shiki* (rights to profits and responsibilities to pay dues), including those of a warrior agent, such as the jitō.[8] This exclusive control tied Enryakuji and the residents together directly and simply. The temple's hegemonic exercise of economic and spiritual control encountered no interference from competitors; there was no local jitō to extract landed profits more efficiently than could the absentee proprietor, or to diffuse the residents' spiritual loyalty by establishing yet another center of worship honoring his ancestral deity.

The regional identity of Tokuchin-ho, or Honai, persisted as long as Enryakuji exercised political authority—however nominal—over the area. It was gradually and finally removed in the course of the territorial reorganization under Hideyoshi in the late sixteenth century, which also interred the remains of the medieval structure sustained by the shōen system.

Villages: Gō and Mura

In the Imabori documents the gō were subunits of the ho. Unlike the ho, which was clearly a creation of the proprietor, the origin and character of the gō are more complex. It is likely that at least some of the gō units originated as natural settlements and preceded the imposition of the artificial Tokuchin-ho framework, which served the interests of higher authorities.[9] In Tokuchin-ho's written history, at any rate, the gō was the basic administrative unit for facilitating proprietary control and a locally accepted formal unit for grouping the shōen residents.

As defined by Enryakuji, there were eight gō, four in the Upper-ho and four more in the Lower-ho.[10] The Upper-ho gō formed a line running from east to west, paralleling the sluice from the Echi River, while the Lower-ho gō stood in a cluster at the bottom of the triangle bounded by Mizukuri Mountain to the north and Fuse Mountain to the south (see Map 2). As stated earlier, Enryakuji differentiated its forms of control over the two areas, reflecting the agricultural potential of each, emphasizing rice-based taxation in the former and commerce in the latter.

The neighboring gō in Tokuchin-ho did not necessarily share common borders. As was typical in Japanese rural society, the gō adjoined plots of communal land, forestland, or grassland. This was a legacy of ancient times, when anyone could by law forage freely in the forest.[11] In Tokuchin-ho, the Gamō grassland was customarily shared by "the eight gō." When outsiders sought entry, Enryakuji issued a warning and threatened them with penalties.[12]

Though the ho was the sum total of the gō in an administrative sense, the gō together did not occupy the actual territorial expanse of the ho. The ho included water, fields, grassland, and mountains for communal use, suggesting that the residents' patterns of interactions

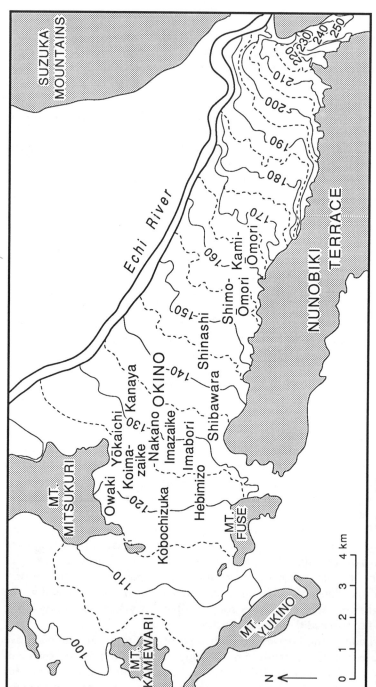

Map 2. The Tokuchin-ho area. Adapted from *YS*, II: 254, fig. 18.

based on productive needs stretched beyond the confines of each gō unit.

Individual gō were also a territorial medium through which the proprietor could extend its moral and spiritual authority. To promote this purpose, Enryakuji established a shrine in each of the gō, transforming the shōen into a collection of spiritually uniform subunits in which all the residents honored the incarnation of Jūzenji and other Hie-affiliated deities. In this mode of proprietary control, the gō became the defining feature of its specific shrine, and vice versa. In fact, the name of a gō often represented and identified its shrine, as in "a solicitation list for the bell of Imabori-gō."[13] The use of the gō name here distinguished this shrine from all the other Jūzenji shrines in the shōen. Instead of grouping the shōen population into units of spiritually disparate elements, the gō served to unify them via identical media of worship. By way of its shrine, each gō provided shōen-wide rhythms of rituals and ceremonies that gave the proprietor a sense of an organized structure of control.

Individual shrines were also differentiated from one another by the gō-specific local deities celebrated along with those universal deities associated with the proprietary institution. An oath dated 1337 that was signed (for purposes that went unrecorded) by 29 men of the gō (*gōmin*) pledged a collective action, involving retribution from various deities, including those "of the seven shrines of Sannō . . . and of the gō," as well as Amaterasu, Japan's founding goddess, for anyone who acted separately in his private interest.[14]

This did not mean, however, that the spiritual influence of one shrine was limited to the gō's residents or to its territorial limits. Far from restricting their religious affiliations in a territorial sense, the gō allowed residents to choose where to exercise their devotion. Just as people held land outside their home gō, they could worship at shrines in the other gō. People of other gō made contributions to Imabori's Jūzenji Shrine, and many of the parcels accumulated by it were scattered in the Lower-ho. In 1335, only one of the parcels enumerated in the list of shrine lands was actually located in Imabori, and all of the parcels were held by residents of other gō.[15] In the subsequent two centuries, Imabori's Jūzenji Shrine continued to receive contributions from outsiders but at a decreasing rate; the territorial boundary of the gō was gaining greater socio-religious significance.

The term for a village that was more closely associated with the people's own social sphere was *mura*. In medieval times *mura* signified a subunit of a gō, but it had no administrative dimension. For example, Higashi-mura was a natural aggregate of houses in the eastern sector of

Imabori, while Imabori's neighboring gō Shibawara had three internal divisions called Nishi-mura, Nose-mura, and Minami-mura.[16] Local residents used *mura* in the generic sense of the term *village*.[17] Most frequently, *mura* was used in a compound for "mura people"—*murando* or *muroto*. But the meaning of "mura people" was extremely complex, a topic to be dealt with later.

No political authority addressed Imabori as Imabori-mura until the era of unification in the late sixteenth century, when, under Toyotomi Hideyoshi, rural areas came to be organized into a series of units uniformly called mura. Standardization of villages into mura represented a revolutionary change, accompanied by a rationalized system of land taxation. Extensive cadastral surveys helped to demarcate the territorial limits of each taxation unit—usually a single nucleated village and its fields—and to determine the putative yield for each. This taxation unit was the new mura, a rural structure whose social significance has not vanished even to this day.[18]

Local particularities characterized the rural structure before Hideyoshi's surveys. As a result, the new mura represented a variety of previous territorial circumstances: some had been an entire shōen (e.g., Ikeda-no-shō in Yamato Province), others, at the other extreme, were villages already called by mura names (e.g., the seven mura in Nata-no-shō in Wakasa Province).[19] The medieval gō of Tokuchin-ho eventually became the mura of the Tokugawa period. But in this transition, more mura were created than there had been gō. An early Tokugawa record lists seven names of mura (where four might have been expected) in both the Lower- and Upper-ho.[20] Clearly, the number of viable villages had increased over the years. Perhaps an increasing population, and the concomitantly greater complexity in the actual patterns of habitation and in social and productive groupings, led villages to split. Imabori-gō, the focus of our study, however, simply transformed itself into Imabori-mura. At any rate, the proprietor perceived eight gō throughout medieval times—neat and fixed and thereby no doubt enhancing the proprietor's own sense of control.

The Sō

Compared to the territorial units we have so far been discussing, the sō was more clearly and inherently a people-oriented unit. This difference can be seen linguistically. In order to denote the "people of the village," the characters for *hito* (person) or *min* (people) were attached to the word *gō* (*gōmin*) or *mura* (*mura-hito*, pronounced "murando"). The term *sō* never formed a compound with *hito* or *min*. *Sō* already embodied their meaning. As a social organization, the sō often inscribed its own "personal" signature (*kaō*) on documents.[21]

The etymology of the word *sō* helps to clarify its meaning. Ishida Yoshihito has noted that the character *sō* that appears in Nara-period tax records and temple-related documents meant "the grand total."[22] Using the character *sō* to describe an organization, Maki Kenji has stressed, helped to emphasize the wholeness of its membership and representation.[23] Historically the character *sō* was used in a variety of contexts. Temples and shrines, for instance, referred to the *sōdera* ("the temple at large") and the *sōsha* ("the shrine at large"), both of which represented a united body of priests.[24] We are of course concerned primarily with the type of sō organization that began to emerge in about the thirteenth century and whose outstanding feature was a collective bond among members based on territorial affiliation.

This type of territorially based sō took a variety of forms. Some sō were organized by prominent local warriors (*kokujin*) and encompassed areas of varying sizes, from counties (*gun*) to entire provinces. Others, like Imabori, were village-based sō, whose members shared in local productive processes; of all the sō types this one most closely resembled the ideal "community"—*Dorfgemeinschaft,* or kyōdōtai.

The region under study embodied sō at the individual gō level and at the ho level, a structure that historians commonly call "double-layered." Available documents are explicit about the existence of sō in five gō: Hebimizo, Imabori, Imazaike, Nakano, and Shibawara. We can quite safely assume the presence of sō in other Tokuchin-ho villages as well.[25] This type of sō was what historians commonly call the sōson (sō village), the archetypal village of Japan's late medieval age. In the Tokuchin-ho area, the term *sōson* was never used, however, probably because the villages were called gō, not mura.[26]

The Imabori sō was, of course, the sō organization affiliated with Imabori-gō. In its broader sense, the Imabori sō signified a structure encompassing all residents of Imabori—both those with and without a voice in determining the sō's policies and programs. But the real significance of the affiliation between the sō and the gō lay not so much in the regional boundaries implied by the gō name as in the shrine particular to the gō. In its narrow sense, the Imabori sō was a corporate organization that operated out of the Imabori Jūzenji shrine and had intimate connections with its ceremonial activities. The sō's identification with the shrine was so intimate that a donor of shrine land addressed to the "Imabori sō" a statement of "commendation to Imabori Jūzenji."[27] Similarly, another donor commended land to the "Imabori sō sutra [*nyohokyō*]," in order to help finance the sō's sutra-copying activities.[28]

The sō organization that transcended the particularities of the gō was equated with Tokuchin-ho, the upper layer in the "double-layered" structure mentioned earlier. The local people called this sō of a wider scope the sōshō, but never the "sōho." Despite the implication of its name, the sōshō's membership was not ho-wide; it was an organization embodying only the lower four gō, whose residents shared agriculturally unfavorable but commercially favorable conditions.[29] "Honai ['inside the ho'] sōshō" frequently appeared in documents in connection with the activities of Honai merchants who were residents of the lower four gō.[30] The two types of sō—the gō-level sō and the ho-level sō— had dissimilar aims and functions, and many of the local residents were active participants in both.

There were yet other sō in Tokuchin-ho. Merchants who traveled over the mountain to Ise Province were organized into the "*yamagoe* ['over-the-pass'] sō."[31] Itinerant merchants of Shimo-Ōmori-gō were organized into their own merchants' sō (*shōbaishū sōbun*).[32] This was an area-specific and occupation-specific sō organization. In the late sixteenth century, yet another form of sō emerged; each gō of the Upper-ho and each gō of the Lower-ho was formed into a federation of sō identifiable by a "personal" signature.[33]

Collectives called sō, therefore, were a general historical phenomenon in late medieval Japan and a common form of organization in the area under study. But each sō had its particularities. Comparison of the Imabori sō and the Honai sō, the two most relevant to the remaining chapters, will illuminate their differences.

First, the two types of sō had dissimilar organizational goals. The objective of the Honai sō was commercial profit making, which in late medieval times required a group-based approach—as opposed to an individualistic approach—to trade safely and compete effectively with other merchant groups. The Honai sō made this goal explicit. In contrast, the objective of the Imabori sō was more complex. Although it was also profit-oriented, it did not articulate this orientation in economic terms. True, the Imabori sō did seek to consolidate its material base in land (and in cash on occasion) through donations or purchase, not unlike a modern corporate structure seeking investment capital. Purportedly, however, the final goal of all this was religious— to defray the costs of ceremonies and to increase the deities' protection of the community. The authorities recognized this religious component in the sō's raison d'être and exempted the land it accumulated from taxes. The Imabori sō and those who commended land to the shrine shared a deep religious affinity, which the Honai sō entirely lacked.

The Imabori sō and the Honai sō held contrasting outlooks on the outside world, and the difference between them was also reflected in their organizational structures. The Imabori sō was a tightly organized, inward-looking body. The membership of its executive body was meticulously defined in terms of number, seating arrangement, and function. The formal sō membership, in its narrow sense, required the payment of dues and adherence to the sō regulations. Ritual was one of the group's strongest adhesives, and in and of itself it was a main goal of the organization. In contrast, the Honai sō lacked a highly formal structure. Not ritual but commercial profit and a common enemy— other merchant groups—held the Honai sō together. The difference in formality between the two organizations can be seen by the Imabori sō's use of a "personal" signature on several occasions.[34] The Honai sō never employed this symbol of togetherness. Needless to say, how- ever, both organizations were concerned with the perpetuation of their structures.

What, then, was the relationship between the Imabori sō and the Honai sō? This seemingly straightforward question has no simple answer, but available evidence suggests that Imabori Jūzenji Shrine, and probably the Imabori sō itself, played a central role in the mer- chant collective that made up the Honai sō. To illustrate, the lower four gō (the Honai sō) wrote a regulation stipulating that "all those who go out to trade must pay 100 *mon* in cash to the monastic office [anshitsu] of [Imabori] Jūzenji Shrine and record it in the ledger." Failure to do so would cost the merchant a penalty of 300 *mon*, im- posed by Imabori-gō.[35] Imabori-gō, therefore, had the authority to impose fees and penalties on the merchants. According to Nakamura Ken, the Honai sō did not have its own administrative or secretarial offices but used the facilities of Imabori Jūzenji Shrine,[36] which would explain why the documents of the Honai merchants came to be assem- bled together with the Imabori sō records in the same wooden boxes at the shrine.

The sō organizations provided an important structural framework for the social and economic life of the villages, at both the gō and the ho levels. For the gō, the structure and activities of the sō closely over- lapped those of the local shrine. The sō acted as the collective manager of the shrine's material resources and ceremonial processes so that local people in many cases perceived the two as one undifferentiated whole. At the ho level, the sō was an occupation-specific organization lim- ited to merchants, but members came from a larger territorial space, namely the Lower-ho. These merchants of the Honai sō maintained a close connection with the Imabori shrine, which served as their institu- tional base. Many were involved in the activities of both sō.

Such was the structural side of this rural society. Within this struc- ture, how did people organize their lives? How did they interact, and how were they differentiated? What was the role of the sō in the internal workings of village society?

The Centrality of the Shrine

Patterns of human settlement and land use can tell us a great deal about the organization of a particular society. Scholars of the Annales school, such as Marc Bloch, and more recently those espousing regional-systems theory, such as Carol A. Smith and G. William Skinner, have demonstrated the importance of such categories of inquiry, despite their obvious methodological differences.[37] A good number of Japanese historians have also devoted themselves to analyzing the original setting in which historical processes unfolded.[38]

The task of reconstructing Imabori's medieval geography is complicated, however, by the absence of maps. We must compare and link information from different sources: the descriptions of land parcels for sale or commendation, and two maps from later periods, one from 1695 and the other from 1873.[39]

The seventeenth-century map, prepared as part of an effort to resolve intervillage disputes of medieval origin, shows areas of settlement in red ink, in addition to irrigation paths and the direction of water flow. The nineteenth-century administrative map marks residential plots with greater precision, along with roads, ditches, reservoirs, wells, paddies, fields, forestland, and grassland (see photo section and Map 3).

Juxtaposition of these maps shows that changes in the patterns of roads, ditches, and settlements over the approximately two centuries from 1695 to 1873 were minimal. The territory of Imabori resembled the shape of a filled-in question mark—an imperfect circle with a jagged northwestern edge and a handlelike rectangular extension to the south. The northern part was almost flat, but a slight tilt to the west was suggested by the flow of water toward Hebimizo, Imabori's western neighbor. Roads and irrigation ditches outlined the village and intersected within it, bringing into relief the plots of human settlement and agricultural production. A woodlot—an area free of houses—at the approximate center of the northern section surrounded Jūzenji Shrine. The southern rectangular section, which reached out to the Nunobiki Terrace, was a concentration of rice paddies irrigated from the reservoir of runoff from the terrace.[40]

Houses were found only in the northern section. They were grouped into three disjointed clusters in the belt south of what came to be called the Takayu River—a ditch running east to west about 100 meters north of the shrine. In the Meiji period, these clusters were called (from east

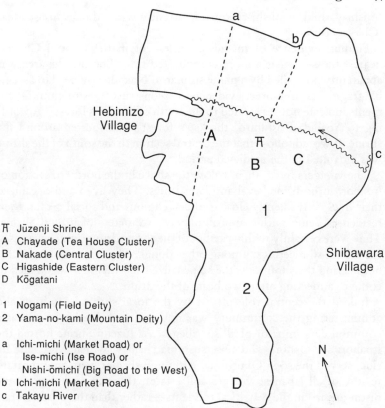

Hebimizo
Village

Shibawara
Village

Ŧ Jūzenji Shrine
A Chayade (Tea House Cluster)
B Nakade (Central Cluster)
C Higashide (Eastern Cluster)
D Kōgatani

1 Nogami (Field Deity)
2 Yama-no-kami (Mountain Deity)

a Ichi-michi (Market Road) or
   Ise-michi (Ise Road) or
   Nishi-ōmichi (Big Road to the West)
b Ichi-michi (Market Road)
c Takayu River

Map 3. Imabori village. Adapted from Nakamura Ken, comp., *Imabori Hiyoshi jinja monjo shūsei*, fig. on p. 731.

to west) Higashide, or the Eastern Cluster; Nakade, or the Central Cluster; and Chayade, or the Tea House Cluster. The Eastern Cluster stood about 150 meters east of the shrine. The Central Cluster was located almost immediately to the shrine's south and west and was separated into northern and southern sections by a road. The Tea House Cluster, farthest to the west, comprised houses that lined Ise-michi, a commercially strategic route running north and south.

The place names used in the medieval period suggest that these residential clusters had already taken shape. People spoke of "the eastern settlement" in the fifteenth and sixteenth centuries by using such descriptive terms as "Higashi-zaike,"[41] "Higashi-no-sato,"[42] and "Higashi-mura."[43] For the Tea House Cluster of the later period, medieval villagers used terms meaning "the western residential cluster"

(Nishi-yashiki or Nishi-zaike) concurrently with "the tea house area" (Chaya yashiki).[44]

Finding evidence of medieval settlement in the Central Cluster, nearest the shrine, is a more complicated task. Because the area was apparently not called by a name similar to Nakade, we need to assemble fragments of indirect evidence to reconstruct the situation. Documents indicate houses located to the south of the "sō's forest." According to Yoshida Toshihiro, the "sō's forest" was located around the shrine. It would follow that the central section to the south of the shrine was inhabited in the medieval period.[45]

The villagers lived, then, below the sluice in the northern section of Imabori in both medieval and later times. They lived and organized their lives conveniently close to their religious and social center, their residences being within approximately 250 meters of Jūzenji Shrine. They were certainly within earshot of the shrine drum, which was used for calling sō meetings, among other things. There was no excuse for not hearing the summons; the sō penalized any member who failed to come to a meeting after two beats of the drum.[46]

Indeed the central role played by the local shrine in uniting and administering the community was not unique to Imabori but was a common denominator of all sō villages. As Jūzenji Shrine hosted the Imabori sō, Ōshima and Okutsushima shrines, which were side by side, served the sō in Okushima. Although shrines were an important feature of all Japanese villages and estates, those in sō villages were distinguished in the way local residents—rather than the proprietor or warrior agents—took control of their operation.

The lives of Imabori villagers were intimately tied to the physical structure of Jūzenji Shrine and the formal and informal activities taking place there. Villagers visited the shrine throughout the year for a variety of reasons. The shrine combined the functions of a city hall, court house, notary, tax bureau, bank, fairgrounds, church, center for the performing arts, tavern, and playground, among others. The sō members met there to discuss current problems and plans for community management. Many of the commenders of land to the shrine probably drew up their documents using the shrine's inkstone or else dictated them to someone at the shrine. After harvesttime, commenders brought the produce from shrine lands and deposited it in a designated place. The shrine was the site of annual festivals that brought villagers together, not only in celebrations but in preparing for them and cleaning up afterward. For men, there were ceremonies and rituals that gave a social and religious significance to the recognized stages in their life cycles. Confraternities and sororities (*kō*) promoted social and religious activities, such as the arrow-shooting ceremony and sutra recitations. On occasion, villagers had the opportunity to enjoy forms of entertainment with religious roots, such as monkey dances (*sarugaku*), which were performed on shrine grounds. Dry spells also brought people together to make special prayers for rain. The shrine was the place to gather for gambling—we know this because gambling was formally banned on several occasions—and, most likely, for all sorts of other unrecorded activities. Of course, on any ordinary day people undoubtedly went there to ask for personal favors from the deities.[47]

The Miyaza, or Shrine Association

The sō administered, regulated, and oversaw shrine-related activities through Jūzenji Shrine's managerial body, a form of ritual organization historians call the miyaza.[48] According to Takamaki Minoru, among various types of shrine associations, those closely connected with local collectivism first evolved in the capital region in the latter part of the thirteenth century, in western Japan in late Muromachi times and thereafter, and in eastern Japan during the Warring or early Tokugawa period.[49] Hebimizo, Imabori's western neighbor, had a miyaza structure before the end of the thirteenth century, at least four decades earlier than Imabori did.[50] The structure of the medieval miyaza varied greatly from one location to another but always closely reflected the structure of the village itself. Where villages took on the sō form, the origins and maturation of the sō invariably paralleled the development of the miyaza.

The sō and the shrine association were the products of village life, not institutions imposed from above. They, therefore, took shape only gradually, keeping pace with the availability of required resources and the changing needs of the local residents for collective governance. The earliest evidence of a shrine association in Imabori dates from the 1330s, when 3 *tan* of tax-exempt land were set aside to support a "temporary shelter [*kariya*]," presumably to house miyaza functions. The local agents of the proprietor endorsed its tax-exempt status.[51] By the 1380s, the association had apparently achieved a higher degree of organizational coherence and, by extension, administrative quality; it ruled on the rotation system of headship in various ceremonies and on the disposition of new *za* members.[52]

Thereafter, the structure of the miyaza underwent some changes. At first, Imabori had one *za* ("seat," thus collection of seats, or "association"). By 1488, this had split into east and west za, perhaps signaling an increase in membership and greater organizational complexity.[53]

Eighty years later there were four za, a result of further divisions of the east and west za, again for reasons unclear to us.[54]

The primary religious purpose of the miyaza was to reinforce the sense of ritual community—encompassing both deities and human beings—by sharing in the circulation of food and drink: they were first offered to the deities and later consumed by the people.[55] Ceremonial gestures and objects provided the common code. In this process, the most exalted item was sacred rice, whose seedlings were passed down from one generation to another to be planted in a designated paddy by miyaza members in rotation.[56] Rice was also brewed into sake and reshaped into *mochi* (sweet rice-cakes). Other items included fruits and vegetables—burdock, beans, citrus fruits, tofu (bean curd), *daikon* (radishes), *kaya* (Japanese nutmeg), goby (fish), squid, and sushi made with sardines.[57]

The miyaza administered shrine affairs by regulating the processes and expenses of rituals, ceremonies, and festivals. Reinforcement of the miyaza's generational and seasonal routines was a crucial mechanism for maintaining the community's sense of peace and order, commonality among members, and a sense of distinctness from outsiders. The cycles of ceremonies promoted continuity and regularity in the rhythm of village life. The ceremonial calendar—"one of the most codified aspects of social existence," in the words of Pierre Bourdieu—had an important role in "orchestrating the group's activity" and "ensur[ing] the reproduction of the established order."[58] In the process, the miyaza—as the guardian of the calendar—obtained and projected moral authority deriving from the spiritual power inherent in the associated deities, including those linked to the proprietary institution.

Consolidation of the ceremonial routines began in the 1380s, when members discussed and decided what items were needed for the three major ceremonial events of the year: the Kechi, the Dō, and the Ninth Month Ninth Day ceremonies. The Kechi, taking place on the fourth day of the New Year by the lunar calendar, was an annual purification ceremony in which four arrows were shot (one to heaven, one to earth, and two to targets at human height) to eradicate lingering evil spirits and to ensure a good harvest.[59] For this ceremony, villagers figured that 2.8 *to* of rice was needed to cover the following expenses: the cost of setting up the arrow targets, the rice offering to the deities, sake for the regular (male) members, and sake for the women in the *nyōbō-za,* the "wives' seats."[60]

For the Dō ceremony, on the thirteenth day of the first month, the miyaza members stipulated 4 *to* of sake and 8 *shō* of rice—the latter for pounding into a large, round, sweet rice-cake to be offered to Yakushi-nyorai (Bhaisajyaguru Buddha). The ritual significance of this event is not fully clear to us, but Itō Yuishin has speculated that it was the initiation day for new za members as well as the commencement of service by the new *kannushi* (head priest) and the *shōshi* (his assistant). For the Ninth Month Ninth Day ceremony, 5 *shō* of sake was given to the deities, 3 *to* to the za members. This ceremony celebrated the beginning of the autumn harvest.[61]

Apart from the three great holidays, the miyaza oversaw a number of lesser ceremonial events throughout the year. These events were aimed at a motley assortment of ceremonial targets, including Buddhist images and folk beliefs, proprietary deities and local spirits. The New Year began with the Grand Gate Opening ceremony, which reconfirmed the presence of deities in the village.[62] On the third day, arrow targets were set up, and on the seventh, the Mountain Deity (Yama-no-kami) was given gifts of sake, mochi, and rice.[63] The Mountain Deity, a figure found across the country, commonly transformed itself into the Paddy Deity in the spring, protected the growth and harvest of rice, and returned to the mountain in the fall. Our records are imprecise on the transformatory character of the Mountain Deity, but in the absence of the Paddy Deity (reflecting the local agricultural conditions), the Field Deity may have represented the Mountain Deity in the spring.[64]

The ninth day of the first month was assigned as the day to read the Sutra of Great Wisdom (Daihannyakyō).[65] For the Jūzenji incarnation, the shrine held a festival on the third day of the second month. On the fifth day, the members recited prayers called "One Million Times *Nenbutsu.*" The equinoctial week in the second month was reserved for Buddhist services and sutra readings.[66] On specified days in the third, fourth, and fifth months, rice and sake were presented to the incarnations of the Jūzenji and Sannō deities. The Rice-Planting festival took place in the sixth month. On the twenty-third day of the sixth month, villagers celebrated a festival dedicated to the Daishōgun, a guardian deity with a martial personality who prevented evil spirits from entering the village.[67]

In honor of the Field Deity (Nogami), people presented millet wine and performed sumo (a sacred form of wrestling whose folkloric origins are intertwined with the creation myth) on the seventh day of the seventh month.[68] On the same day began the *bon* season, during which villagers paid homage to their ancestral spirits.[69] The fifteenth day of the eighth month was the festival day for Hachiman, an agricultural deity.[70] A ceremony for the annual change of *hijiri* (Buddhist monks from outside who served the shrine for a year—of whom more later) took place on the fourteenth day of the tenth month. Another dedication to Jūzenji was held on the third day of the eleventh month; and on the following day, the sō did its accounts for the shrine paddies and fields and calculated the payments to that year's kannushi and shōshi.[71] The eleventh month was the busiest time of the year for the sō members.

As a sideshow to the ceremonies, the miyaza sponsored performances of monkey dances by an organized troupe from a nearby village. These took place on the shrine grounds twice a year, in the second and sixth months, and were subsidized by the sō, which paid 1 *kan* out of its coffers on each occasion.[72]

Miyaza Members

The miyaza was the decision-making body of the community and its members constituted the dominant group within the village. Membership required certain qualifications, and there were gradations of rank among the members. One's sex, social status, length of residency, and age were some of the important criteria. Only men could be members. This gender imbalance, often explained in terms of the concept of female pollution,[73] was not a universal practice everywhere in Japan, however. There is evidence that in some regions women sat among men. In 1248, a za seat attached to the Usa shrine in Onoda, Kii Province, was even passed down from the father to the main daughter (*chakujo*).[74] Daughters entered the za and even acted as ceremonial heads (*tōyaku*) in fourteenth- and fifteenth-century Yamato. According to Takamaki Minoru, these women were qualified to enter the za when they were the actual or stipulated household heads.[75] In both cases, unlike in Imabori, a seat in the za seems to have been a heritable possession of certain families.

Apart from the main za, the socio-religious space set aside for men, Imabori had a "wives' za" (nyōbō-za), an auxiliary za that participated in the Kechi ceremony, described earlier.[76] We will review the women's role in the local structure of worship more fully in subsequent pages.

Among men, the status required for membership was that of murando (villager, sometimes called *jige*). Non-murando (*murando de naki mono*) had no right to join the za. In this, the miyaza structure reflected and reinforced the status distinctions that existed in the larger community. The sō prohibited non-murando from many of the social benefits that murando enjoyed, for example, "using a house rented from the sō."[77] For the crime of gathering leaves or cutting trees in the sō forest, non-murando offenders were evicted from the village, as were widows and orphans accused of the same crime.[78] For the same offense, murando lost their status and were, presumably, made non-murando.

What distinguished non-murando from murando? Our documents provide no direct clue. Most scholars consider the former to be drifters, who held no houses in the village, in contradistinction to the murando, who were permanently attached to the village through the houses they owned.[79] Non-murando may have been the people of *muen* (nonattachment) described by Amino Yoshihiko in the late 1970s. According to him, muen was a characteristically medieval spatial or relational state in which a clearly definable territorial or institutional affiliation was absent. By extension, *muen* often meant freedom from the social and political norms that dominated the medieval institutional order. People who held a muen relationship to society, for instance, were not bound by formal obligations, such as the annual levies due from agriculturalists tied to an overlord's income-producing land. Traveling entertainers and evangelists without ties to the land—land being the material foundation of the state—exemplified one group characterized by muen. These were itinerant people with primarily nonagricultural occupations, which were held in disesteem by the dominant society, built on the ideals of settled agriculturalists.[80] The muen population could also include *hinin* ("nonpeople"), a term attached to lepers and those engaged in various undesirable occupations, such as begging (*kojiki*), as well as *rōnin* ("wave people"), a label initially given to cultivators dissociated from the land of their original attachment but which, by the Heian period, came to mean simply "outsiders."[81] Hereditary servants (genin) of various types may have also been among the non-murando population, although they were in fact settled, permanent residents.

Between the two clearly differentiated groups, *mōto* ("in-between persons") represented a further refinement; although part of the miyaza, mōto were inferior to regular villagers. In 1403, the sō listed the names of eight mōto men and required them to take seats (za) lower than—presumably—the murando's, even if the mōto were three years senior.[82] Who were the mōto, and what accorded them the lower status? The scarcity of contemporary references makes this a challenging question. According to Nagahara Keiji, the mōto had two handicaps—the short duration of their residency and a low economic position. They were recent immigrants who had not attained full social recognition as local figures, and they were agriculturalists ranking below the myōshu (upper-level peasants holding considerable rights and obligations associated with a *myō,* or "name-field," recognized by their names).[83]

Evidence in the Imabori documents fails to support this clear-cut description of mōto. Myōami, the name of one of the eight mōto in the sō, is identical to the name of a myō located north of Imabori. Myōami was also named a holder of the *saku-shiki* (cultivation right) for the area bordering Myōami-myō itself.[84] Myōami, then, was possibly a myō- shu with additional rights to adjoining plots. But we must be cautious in reaching this conclusion. By the fifteenth century, the direct connec- tion between a myō and its holder (i.e., myōshu) had considerably broken down because of generations of land alienation and sales of myōshu rights; more often than not, the name of a myō merely desig- nated a conveniently demarcated unit of taxation with no implications as to the rights and status of the holder, which it had earlier conveyed.[85] Perhaps Myōami-myō was simply a place name with no significance as to the status of the man with the same name. But there is still the possibility that Myōami had been a myōshu. If so, we must conclude that the inferior status of mōto was purely social, not economic, in origin.

There is a further indication that differences in economic standing mattered less for membership than did status differences. To accom- modate people of different economic backgrounds, the za adopted a progressive fee system for the ceremony of becoming an *otona*, or elder; in 1504, those who owned horses or oxen paid 500 *mon,* and those who did not paid 300.[86] In this way, the miyaza articulated an important class division in Tokuchin-ho, in which the ownership of horses and oxen defined an economically superior group regardless of whether they were primarily peasants or merchants.[87] However, by demanding ceremonial dues commensurate with one's economic standing, the sō sought to integrate the have-nots as well. The community's economic structure depended on small cultivators and farmers of means, as well as on merchants with and without beasts of burden. The sō astutely included both groups in order to maintain access to all levels of produc- tion and all the threads of the trade network. Politically, the differenti- ated schedule of dues benefited the haves, for it reaffirmed their supe- rior position via an act of benevolence toward the less fortunate. At any rate, regardless of status, those unable to pay the dues were barred from participation in the miyaza.[88]

A gradation among members was also manifested in the seating order. The basis of this gradation is not altogether clear, but the crite- rion seems to have been some sort of seniority defined in terms of age, length of membership, or experience in ceremonial functions. This seniority system was also modified by factors related to one's status and the authority deriving from it. The seating arrangement discussed in the previously cited rule concerning mōto, which placed them in lower seats "even if they are three years senior" suggests the interplay of the age and status factors in determining the seating order. A system of gradation based on some sort of seniority seems to have evolved at least by 1403, the date of this regulation.[89]

At the core of the miyaza, the elders made up a group with more authority than the rest. At the start of the fifteenth century there were four otona, but the number increased to eight by the mid-fifteenth century, reflecting the multiplication of za from two to four, which in turn may have reflected the population increase.[90]

We do not know the specific qualifications for becoming an otona or how long persons served in that capacity. But attainment of a certain age, fulfillment of the headship for some of the important annual ceremonies, a record of undertaking various ceremonial expenses, and the passage of an otona ceremony must have been minimum requirements. Certain people, such as mōto, probably never qualified to become otona. The necessary financial obligations would also limit the selection to the economically secure. But the system was more open in Imabori than in some other villages. There was no monopoly of the za by certain families;[91] privileges were distributed among a large number of households ranked by seniority—actual or symbolic. Takamaki Minoru observes that miyaza arranged by seniority emerged in the late fourteenth to fifteenth centuries in villages free from the hold of strong lineages, such as those of local samurai.[92]

While otona exercised bureaucratic authority over the community, the kannushi or head priest, and, to a lesser extent, the shōshi, his assistant, occupied special positions of spiritual authority. But there was no clear professional division between otona and kannushi, for the latter was chosen from among the former, though the selection process remains unknown to us.[93] It is unlikely, therefore, that a kannushi possessed mysterious qualities attached to his person as a permanent condition. Nonetheless, as a kannushi, a man was closer to the deities, and from this position of elevated status he served as the intermediary between deities and people.[94] In origin, the kannushi was an emergency substitute for a formal priest and thus required no special training or ordination.[95] In Imabori, his primary function was to receive food and drink used as ceremonial offerings to the deities, an act of communion (called *naoshi*) with the deific order. The position of shōshi apparently rotated among miyaza members. A shōshi was exempted from paying dues associated with heading a ceremony, as explained below, and from paying fees for the monkey dances. He did miscellaneous shrine-related jobs.[96]

On various occasions, the za sought to reinforce inequality and hierarchy among its members. According to a record from 1556, new za members were less important than their seniors; the former were forbidden to express opinions as the latters' equals.[97] But by the 1580s, the *wakashū,* the young or junior members, began to assert themselves. A set of regulations, dated 1582, was written and signed by both the otona and the wakashū, emphasizing decision making through consultation and majority rule with a penalty of expulsion from the za for members who were too contentious.[98] We can only speculate on the background of this change. What tension caused this new rule to be drawn up? Did the regulation of 1556 backfire? Most likely this sharpened tightness and cohesion in the sō's organizational structure was a response to developments occurring at a larger political level—the dramatic transformation promoted at many sectors of society under the new hegemon Oda Nobunaga.

Miyaza members had the privilege and obligation of serving in rotation as ceremonial heads, as, for example, the *tō* (head) of the Ninth Month Ninth Day ceremony. While such a position accorded social importance, it was also a financial burden, for the head bore the ceremonial expenses, which ranged from 1 to 2 *kan* in cash.[99] Moreover, he was responsible for nonmonetary obligations, such as the cultivation of ceremonial land[100] and the pounding of sweet rice into mochi.[101] Negligence in these obligations could result in the lowering of one's seat,[102] probably a situation of considerable public shame. Rearrangement in the rotation of ceremonial obligations could also result, as in 1383. Although Sakonjirō was supposed to serve as head of the Kechi ceremony that year, the miyaza regarded him as inappropriate and ordered him to wait until his next turn.[103]

Thus, while membership in the miyaza accorded social recognition and local political power, it was also a costly and time-consuming job. A tension between privilege and obligation characterized the miyaza membership, as it would most public positions of high respect in a given society. How did Imabori villagers reconcile this tension? How did they view the miyaza? This, of course, is a question with a multitude of individual answers, varying with a respondent's social standing, economic condition, and age. The stability of the miyaza required approval and cooperation from the majority of villagers. Had disapproval taken on collective dimensions, the miyaza would have lost its institutional effectiveness and perhaps even collapsed.

In all likelihood, the social value of the miyaza (and the sō as well) underwent changes over the centuries, fluctuating between its image as an organization of privilege and its image as an organization of unwelcome obligations. For example, conflicts may have lain behind the sō's 1504 stipulation of progressively reduced fees for the ceremonial heads over the next four years.

The head of the Dō ceremony serving in the year of the ox shall pay 2 *kan;* [the head] serving in the year of the tiger, 1 *kan* 600 *mon;* [the head] serving in the year of the hare, 1 *kan* 200 *mon.* [For the head serving] in the year of the dragon and thereafter, do not reduce [the payment] below 1 *kan.*

Similar stipulations were made for the headship of the Ninth Month Ninth Day ceremony and for the Kechi ceremony as well.[104] In the same year fifteen men were barred from the za for owing various amounts of cash and rice.[105]

It is unclear whether these fifteen men were unable to pay or whether they deliberately neglected their obligations. Perhaps the social status of the local za was being reduced because of changes in the larger social structure. Commercial expansion and wider networks of communication might have diverted people's energies elsewhere in their search for opportunities and for security tied to prominent outside figures or institutions. At the same time, there might have been no deeper reason for the members' arrears than financial need. In either case, the loss of members handicapped the za, which could not operate its complex business or expect to wield local political power without a membership base. The continuation of its own structure depended upon continuous support by members. The za was strong only to the extent that its members were willing or able to uphold it. The za therefore set a relatively easy reentry requirement—payment of all arrears and the submission of "foot-cleansing" sake to the za.[106] In another example, a man who owed a great deal of money was placed at the bottom of the seating arrangement. Instead of expelling him and weakening the za's human base, the za shamed him with public rejection.[107]

Women in the Sō

In late medieval Japanese villages, the miyaza and the sō—the core record-keeping organizations—belonged primarily to the men. Women were not formally represented in these organizations and as a result occupied a social space that went largely unrecorded. Important documents that required collective signatures were, as a rule, sealed with men's names, although names of widows functioning in their husband's stead also might be included.[108] The perceived inferiority of women's spirituality and a social structure based on the male-centered household tended to debase the communal position of women. Women were excluded from miyaza membership and remained subordinate members of the sō, represented by the heads of households, who were almost always men.

The women's life cycle, unlike men's, was not segmented into publicly documented ceremonial stages. Women celebrated no ceremony equivalent to the eboshi naoshi, for example, which accorded boys a full public and spiritual status within the community. Women did have functions in the village's religious life, however. Imabori had a nyōbō-za (wives' za) apart from the men's za. And, as mentioned earlier, the Kechi ceremony, which launched the annual agricultural cycle, called for the participation of women. In Namazue, located about 3 kilometers north of Tokuchin-ho, women also took part in the Kechi ceremony, and their names were listed alongside their husband's in the Kechi records.[109] The role of women in these instances were, at any rate, dependent on their relationship to a man (their husband), and their status was subordinate to that of men; they remained outside the formal miyaza membership and thus outside its central structure and functions.[110]

Some women and girls generated a greater influence by serving as a *miko*, "the shamanic medium who acts as mouthpiece for the *kami* or ancestor," according to Carmen Blacker's definition.[111] A shaman, endowed with charisma—supernatural power from the otherworld—could pass between the worlds and communicate with the spiritual beings on whose disposition the community's well-being greatly depended. In Ōyamazaki, Yamashiro Province, there was a special za for miko, and the shrine's ceremonial records show that the daughter of a regular miyaza member entered the za in 1522.[112]

Evidence of miko in Imabori records is sketchy, but a miko is named as a commender of shrine land in lists dated 1384, 1481, and 1482.[113] Miko were also donors in solicitation campaigns in 1474 and 1497; the former campaign was for a bell and the latter, for a statue of Jūrasetsu, toward which a miko contributed 100 *mon*.[114] What was the specific function of miko? An undated document from the Tokugawa period shows that miko (also called *ichi*) were in charge of the hot water ritual, an act of purification that preceded formal rituals and ceremonies.[115] Although the Imabori records do not indicate whether the miko was male or female in any given instance, it would be safe to assume that most were female, given the nature of the ceremony, the above example from Yamashiro, and the long-standing tradition of female miko in Japanese history.[116]

Women's participation in ceremonies, however, did not alter the fact of exclusion from the formal system of za. Women's names went unrecorded among members occupying the formal za even in Oku-shima, for instance, where women participated as heads of ceremonies.[117] Since women carried both sacred and profane spiritual forces at once, they could be both recruited into and excluded from ritual occasions. But the institutional structure of the miyaza, with its public and political implications, remained outside the women's sphere.

At the same time, the miyaza was capable of drawing women's material resources into its support system. Women supported the miyaza by commending land to the shrine, as did Torame in 1465 "in order to have prayers recited for the repose of her departed soul."[118] They could do so because they were property holders in their own right with the independent power to alienate land (shares). They could sell their holdings, as Fukumatsume and Kokurime did in 1366 and 1434 respectively.[119] Torame's parcel was one she had purchased five years earlier.[120]

Despite financial contributions, then, women received no recognition as publicly sanctioned members of the miyaza. In this context, how were women viewed by the estate proprietor? It is generally believed that peasant women's property rights existed outside what came to be recorded in the tax registers (*tochi daichō*) submitted to the proprietor.[121] There was a separation between the private right to hold land and the public right to hold the responsibility for paying taxes as expressed in a shiki title. In other words, proprietors discounted women as legitimate bearers of tax burdens and thus only men's names appeared as the legitimate holders of taxed land.

Our records reveal a somewhat different pattern. Women's names appear occasionally as holders of saku-shiki, which combined the rights to income from the land with the responsibility for tax payments. A 1 *tan* parcel located in Hebimizo, for instance, was identified as "Chiyome *saku*" in 1510 and in 1566.[122] The name Chiyome describes a woman without connecting her to her husband—a female who probably purchased the cultivation rights or inherited them as a daughter.

Our other examples suggest the transfer of titled rights from deceased husbands to their widows. A parcel in Imabori bore the description "cultivated by Umagorō's widow [Umagorō *goke saku*]" on a sales record of 1442. "Matsuisho goke saku" described still another plot in a document of 1528.[123] Admittedly most saku-shiki were held by men. But women were sometimes recognized as the holders of such a title, whether independently (acquired through purchase or inheritance) or in place of their late husbands. In Okushima and Sugaura as well, women were publicly recognized holders of titled lands encumbered with tax responsibilities.[124]

In addition, women had the authority to provide cosignatures on records of land transfer; Torawakame cosigned with two males (her

brothers?) when a parcel was sold to Jūzenji Shrine in 1381.[125] A
mother cosigned her son's deed of sale in 1407.[126] Akurime and her
main son (*chakushi*) cosigned when selling land in 1395.[127] These cosignatures served to safeguard the transaction by preempting the possibility of future interference by close relatives, including women.

The social structure centering on the shrine recruited women's financial resources in yet another way. Though less frequently and to a lesser
degree than most men, women had the means and motives to contribute to solicitations for money. Perhaps their enthusiasm for a solicitation depended on the object of donation. In 1497, close to 90 women
responded to a solicitation for money to set up Jūrasetsu images, that is,
images of the ten female deities who protect the worshipers of the
Lotus Sutra. Five of the women donated 200 *mon* each, a large sum
exceeded by the donations of only five men.[128] In comparison, the
solicitation for the shrine's bell interested only four women, one ninth
the number of men who responded.[129]

The near exclusion of women from the miyaza had its corollary in
the structure of the sō in the broad, villagewide sense of the term. As a
rule, women's names did not appear on the sō's collective roster because households, almost always headed by men, made up the list.
Women's names could appear only if the signature of every household
was needed, including those lacking adult men. Among the 89 signatures representing the sō in 1583 (during the sō-wide opposition to
Hideyoshi's new surveys), for example, we find one female name.[130]

The unusual situation brought about by the nationwide wartime mobilization of the 1590s temporarily brought women to documentary
significance, however. A list of households in 1592 shows women—all
widows and nuns—heading 21 of the 75 households in Imabori.[131] This
was the year of Hideyoshi's first campaign to Korea, and it seems
possible that large numbers of able men had been conscripted to fight or
had died in the wars of unification. As in other wartime contexts, this
society could accord women greater public recognition on a temporary
basis.

Female status in the long term is perhaps better indicated by regulations drawn up by the sō, which imposed far harsher punishments on
widows than on murando men. An article in the regulation of 1502
concerning the harvesting of foliage called for eviction from the village
for offenders who were widows or orphans. For the same offense,
murando merely lost their places in the za.[132] Women without husbands—who would have provided the connection to the miyaza—
were thus particularly vulnerable to the severe measures imposed by
the sō. Viewed in a larger context, this regulation in fact spelled out and

reinforced the kind of circumstantial hardship visited upon peasant widows (and other husbandless women) in late medieval Japan. In Hine estate, during the famine of 1504, some villagers were caught stealing others' bracken (gathered in the hills to substitute for grain) as it was soaking in the river to be bleached. All but one turned out to be widows and young children. A month earlier, a miko and her children had instantly been cut down by the villagers when her son was indicted as a thief.[133] The inhospitable atmosphere generated by economic hardship harmed women and children before it harmed men.

Outside Participants in Village Life

Outside religious professionals played an integral role not only in the shrine's operation but also in the villagers' daily lives. Called hijiri, they provided an important ideological link between the proprietary institution and the village. Through hijiri, Enryakuji ensured the appropriate dissemination of the religious influence that formed an element of its proprietary control. These men were, according to Nakamura Ken, ordained Tendai-school priests with a close affiliation to Enryakuji, and were based in temples near Tokuchin-ho, such as Jōganji in Owaki and Ishidōji in Ishidōji.[134]

Generally speaking, hijiri of the Muromachi and Tokugawa periods filled many miscellaneous functions at large temples and shrines, serving as bell ringers, for example. They also traveled in the provinces soliciting contributions for pious projects, as well as for their own Buddhist magic or prayers.[135] They undoubtedly contributed to the spread of culture and literacy in the countryside.[136] At Imabori's Jūzenji Shrine, these priests resided in the "monastic office" (anshitsu) one at a time on a temporary basis[137] and conducted specifically Buddhist rituals, such as sutra recitation and the annual meditation rite of ge, which lasted three months. Murando worked closely with the hijiri by, for example, supplying necessary items, such as miso (bean paste) and rice during the ge season.[138]

Hijiri were local promoters of Tendai Buddhism within the shrine complex. Aside from spiritual activities, they organized solicitations to pay for new Buddhist images. The collection, mentioned earlier, to acquire statues of the Jūrasetsu serves as an illustration.[139] Its main sponsor was the incumbent hijiri, Gyōin. He successfully collected 17 kan 200 mon in cash over approximately two months' time from 123 men and 86 women, mostly residents of Imabori but also of other villages, such as Shinashi, Imazaike, Takebe, and Ishidōji. Gyōin himself contributed 1 kan;[140] the sō of Imazaike, Nakano, and Hebimizo donated 200 mon, 300 mon, and 5 to of rice respectively, while women typically offered small sums ranging from 1 *mon* to 20 *mon*, with the exception of three contributions of 30 *mon*, one of 50 *mon*, and nine ranging above 100 *mon*.

Solicitation campaigns by itinerant priests (*kanjin hijiri*) were important means of building up grass-roots support for monastic doctrines and institutions. During the Kamakura period such campaigns came to be controlled and well organized by the central temples, such as Enryakuji. They collected donations for various projects—repairing temple buildings, making images, copying sutras, and launching secular public-works projects, for example. Janet R. Goodwin attributes deep penetration of Buddhism into the countryside in the fourteenth and fifteenth centuries to this network of solicitation agents as well as to the new popular doctrines.[141]

Some hijiri associated with Imabori were closely integrated into the local economy. They held land in Imabori and contributed to the sō's coffers by making land commendations.[142] Their involvement in economic affairs could be even greater. The hijiri Shukuei of Ishidōji served as leader of the *tanomoshi*, a form of local credit association found in many medieval villages.[143] One case will illustrate the hijiri's activity: through Shukuei's mediation, an Imabori villager named Sakon took out a loan for 2 *kan* with 1 *tan* of land as collateral. After an unknown number of years, Sakon was forced to forfeit this land for 4 *kan*, representing the original loan and accumulated interest. This land was then transferred to the sō.[144]

The nature of a tanomoshi in medieval Japan depended greatly on the organizer's intent.[145] Some tanomoshi benefited the participants by helping out the needy, and others exploited them by forcing participation or requiring unreasonable collateral. In Imabori, the tanomoshi strengthened the economic foundation of the sō while benefiting the members. Debtors' collateral land served as another means of adding to the sō's holdings.[146] A similar structure, run by another hijiri, also operated in Hebimizo. One Hebimizo man, Magosaburō, put up a 200 *bu* paddy as collateral for the tanomoshi. Failing to keep up the payments, he was forced to borrow money from the tanomoshi. When his debt amounted to 2 *koku*, he sold the land to Gyōbu of Imabori for 2.25 *koku*. With this money, Magosaburō was able to pay the organization back and was left with 0.25 *koku*.[147] In both instances, the hijiri held the leading role in promoting this economic organization, which was closely linked to the corporate structure of the sō.[148]

Shrine Land

The perpetuation of ceremonies, the upkeep of the shrine premises, and the overall maintenance of the shrine's religious and symbolic image required a solid and reliable financial base. To this end the shrine held land that yielded material profits in the form of agricultural produce or cash. Broadly called *shinden* ("gods' paddy" or "sacred paddy") or *shinbata* ("gods' field" or "sacred field"), such land was held by the sō. Shinden were neither new in the medieval period nor specific to the sō-type villages. They had existed in different forms since ancient times, providing economic resources for the upkeep of religious institutions. The *ritsuryō* government of the seventh and eighth centuries granted tax-exempt shinden to shrines and temples in nationalizing the country's arable land. This form of shinden deteriorated along with the government's land-allotment program. The spread of shōen in subsequent centuries gave reasons and opportunities for temples and shrines to create their own shinden on their own estates—cultivated land marked off for the sole profit of the proprietary institution.[149]

The type of shinden that Imabori and other sō villages developed on a broad geographical scale[150] was different again from the types above: it was not a creation of the proprietor but an institution built by the residents in support of what they perceived to be their own patterns of worship. It was, indeed, a crystallization of the collective effort to extend control over local productive resources and surpluses. But it did not evolve in defiance of the proprietary institution; instead, it gained stature with the proprietor's explicit and implicit recognition. It accommodated the mutually contradictory interests of the proprietor and the local collective and helped to preempt potential conflicts.

On the one hand, shrine land was the concrete manifestation of the residents' wishes for personal and spiritual benefits and for the well-being of the shrine-centered social structure. Instead of the yield being forwarded to Enryakuji, an absentee proprietor, the shinden profits were kept locally and invested in activities that had direct spiritual or economic benefits for the villagers. On the other hand, Enryakuji recognized the importance of shrine land in supporting various ritual and ceremonial functions, for an active shrine organization with a solid economic base provided an acceptable element of autonomy at the village level, obviating the need for a more coercive form of estate control. The shrine land represented a form of investment and long-term symbolic capital for the proprietor; it provided security for the structure of proprietary patronage and dominance and in return ensured the continued dependence of its subjects. During the medieval period, when shrine and temple (Shinto and Buddhist) affairs formed a mostly undifferentiated whole, the local shrine benefited Enryakuji by serving as its religious outpost.

During the two and a third centuries from 1335 to 1566, shinden and shinbata multiplied. Six registers, dated 1335, 1384, 1416, 1463,

1510, and 1566, chart the progress the sō made in accumulating shrine land.[151] Starting with 4 *tan* in 1335,[152] by 1384 it held almost 4 *chō* 10 *tan*, and by 1463, this figure had increased to 8 *chō* 5 *tan,* and vegetable plots had been acquired as well. The growth in the following century took a somewhat different course; while the total area of the paddies and fields only reached slightly above 9 *chō* by 1566, the total rows of planted vegetables more than tripled.[153] Although the comparison is somewhat artificial—inasmuch as what mattered to the sō was not the size of the land but the amount of share (*tokubun*) derived from each parcel (which varied)—the pattern of upward accretion is unmistakable (see Table 1).

Differentiated according to the nature of the tax obligations, shrine lands can be grouped into three types. The first type was normally taxable land whose entire yield was forwarded to the shrine instead of being channeled to Enryakuji. To acquire tax-exempt parcels of this type, the sō negotiated with the proprietor when land was being newly developed. In 1448, for example, Imabori villagers complained that 1 *tan* 200 *bu* of newly developed land should have been classified as Jūzenji Shrine shinden and they therefore asked for tax exemption, which was granted.[154]

The second and more common type of shrine land provided a percentage of the yield for the shrine beyond the obligation already due to the proprietor. From the 1380s on, the amount of shrine land based on this "added share or supplemental rent [*kajishi*]" gradually grew until the 1440s and 1450s, when a dramatic jump occurred, then tapered off in the famine of the 1460s.[155] This share, kajishi, represented the surplus yield from a given parcel of land. The shrine accumulated shares through both purchase and commendation. This was an important means of keeping the village surplus in the hands of the villagers.[156]

The third type of shrine land involved accruing interests in non-paddy areas not highly desired by the proprietor. Starting in the latter part of the fifteenth century, parcels described as "newly sown vegetable land" were sold or commended to the shrine. Many of these parcels were located in the immediate vicinity of people's homes or in previously wooded areas with such names as "pine forest [*matsubayashi*]" or "road forest [*dōrin*]." Although inferior in quality, these parcels remained outside the proprietor's taxable land category and thus added greatly to the shrine's coffers. Apparently the development of this type of untaxed parcel was a common pattern in late-fifteenth- and sixteenth-century Japan. Fujiki Hisashi found such parcels in Izumi, Yamashiro, and Tanba provinces, as well as in Ōmi.[157]

Apart from proprietary recognition, accumulation of shrine land and in turn the very success of the communal organization depended

TABLE I
Land Held by Imabori Hiyoshi Jūzenji Shrine, 1335–1566

Date	Total holders	Outside holders[a]	Paddy and field land	Vegetable plots (in *semachi*)[b]	Residential plots
			Amount of land		
1335	6	5 or 6	4 *tan* 0 *bu*		
1384	40	5	4 *chō* 9 *tan* 270 *bu*	7.0	2
1416	41	9	5 *chō* 2 *tan* 294 *bu*	9.0	2
1463	48	5	8 *chō* 4 *tan* 226 *bu*	22.5	4
1510	98	6	8 *chō* 1 *tan* 19 *bu*	72.5	18
1566	78	6	9 *chō* 0 *tan* 79 *bu*	72.5	23

SOURCE: Adapted from Maruyama Yoshihiko, "Shōen sonraku," p. 305, table 3. The extant version of the 1335 list is lacking the first portion (probably one entry), and the one from 1566 is missing the last portion.
[a]Holders who were clearly not Imabori residents.
[b]The *semachi* is a unit for counting vegetable plots, not in area, but in rows of planted vegetables.

greatly on the initiative of local landholders in releasing income from land to the shrine. The over 200 sales and commendation documents surviving from between 1314 and 1589 testify that the residents of the area actively participated in this endeavor.[158]

Landed interests were passed to the shrine in various ways. In 1426, for example, one Genpō commended 6 *to*'s worth of shares derived from 1 *tan* of paddy located in Kuromaru, a newly opened area to the south of the residential areas. He dedicated this gift to the lighting of Jūzenji Shrine and stipulated that the transfer take place upon his death. He had purchased this parcel for 3 *koku* of rice from an Imabori man a year before. Judging from the notation that the cultivation right (saku-shiki) to the land belonged to a man from Hebimizo, Genpō himself held some other rights to it, perhaps the myōshu-shiki.[159] In another case, Kokurime, a woman from Mabuchi (a village outside Tokuchin-ho; see Map 4), sold a vegetable plot to the Imabori sō for 1 *kan* 700 *mon* in 1434. It was 1 *tan* in size and was located behind the shrine. Kajishi shares in this parcel were worth 250 *mon* each year. Kokurime's reason for the sale was "financial need [*atai yōyō*]."[160]

Through commendation, the shrine in essence inherited landed interests from the donor, though the release of interest usually occurred at the time of commendation, not after the donor's death as in the Genpō example. Commenders were often specific in assigning the use of their contribution. Included in their consideration were certain statues, such as the statues of Yakushi[161] and Hachiman,[162] certain activities, such as sutra reading[163] and arrow shooting,[164] and architectural elements of the shrine, such as its bell[165] and its roof.[166] People also made commendations for lighting shrine lanterns and lamps, subsidizing the cost of oil, as did Genpō.[167] Some commendations were made specifically to defray food expenses, such as sake for the Mountain Deity on the seventh day of the New Year[168] or for the banquet held on the ninth day of the New Year.[169]

Commendation in no way meant a one-way transfer of value, however. The expectation of a reward in the form of long-term spiritual peace accompanied the giving of material gifts. This expectation was often explicitly stated and varied in comprehensiveness. The "repose of my soul" was the most frequent wish.[170] Other donors were more inclusive and sought the salvation of their mother, father, and brothers[171] or of the generation to come. The most ambitious wish was that of Gyōbu, who, in commending two fields in Higashi-zaike to "Jūzenji Imabori sō," expressed hope for the "repose of [his] soul after death, the prosperity of the shrine, peace within the gō, happiness to everyone, good fortune to the family, attainment of Buddhahood, easy passage into paradise, extension of the law of Buddha to all sentient beings, and the universal distribution of divine favor."[172] In contrast, Sakon was more specific, commending a field to the sutra "in order to pacify the spirit of Hikojirō, whose ghost has appeared in the past."[173]

Selling land to the shrine held a meaning somewhat different from that of commendation. Through purchase, constituting about 16 percent of the total extant transactions, the shrine invested in a piece of income-producing property. As in commendation, the sale could be directed to a specific component of the shrine's structure and operation, but the great majority (80 percent) of the sales were made to Jūzenji Shrine, the Imabori murando, the Imabori sō or simply "shinden." Moreover, a sale carried with it no built-in expectations of spiritual returns. It was strictly an economic transaction meant to suit the material interests of the seller. As with Kokurime, "financial need" was the usual reason given for the sale.

Commendation was a process that satisfied both the personal and collective aims of the original property holders. The value of property, assessable in concrete economic terms, contributed to the maintenance of communal activities and objects. Simultaneously, transactions represented a form of calculated investment whose returns were to satisfy the commenders' inner desires. The visible items to which donation was directed symbolized and objectified the two-way exchange occurring between the economic and spiritual realms.

While the miyaza held no final responsibility to make all these wishes come true, it was nonetheless required to abide by a commender's terms. Gensai, who commended 100 *bu* of new paddy in Kōgatani to the Kechi ceremony, required that this paddy be cultivated by the ceremonial head of the Kechi.[174] He explained that the paddy was to commemorate his deceased grandparents, but its previous holder had failed to perform the appropriate rites. Gensai commended the paddy to Jūzenji Shrine so that the rites due to his grandparents would be performed. It was the shrine's responsibility to annually assign the paddy to the head of the Kechi ceremony according to Gensai's wishes.

The management of shinden and shinbata required organization and vigilant attention to detail. For example, the sō had to arrange for prayers on the seventh day of the third month for one Shōshū, who "died a mysterious death," in accordance with the commendation statement of his successor, Seishū.[175] In another instance, the sō needed to assign a cultivator to a parcel of commended land because in this case the cultivation right, not just the yield, was commended. Moreover, the yield from this land was to be used specifically for the ceremonial breakfast for the eight otona.[176] Keeping track of individual commendations that specified different objects of commendation and varied by size and type of land, percentage of yield, and terms of maintenance was an important task of the sō.

The commenders and sellers of land were not just men and women of Imabori. The shrine was sustained by those who felt the spiritual influence of Imabori Jūzenji Shrine and those who wished to extend its influence on the corporate structure of the sō. The commendation or sale of land to Jūzenji Shrine by outsiders was quite common.[177] Residents of Shibawara, Hebimizo, Kobochizuka, and Imazaike—Imabori's neighboring gō, which shared access to the commons—were frequent contributors. But so were people from an even wider area, including such places as Fuse, Futamata, and Ishidōji, as well as Mabuchi, the home of Kokurime in the earlier example.

Over the centuries, however, the rate of participation by outsiders decreased. Of the five original donors in 1335 none lived in Imabori.[178] The register of shinden from 1384 shows that about 38 percent of the holders were from outside.[179] The Imabori villagers apparently made efforts to absorb the interests of outsiders in their shrine land. "Because Imabori murando desired it," the Shibawara murando sold, in 1384, 1 *tan* of vegetable land located in Imabori for 1 *kan* 300 *mon*.[180] By 1416, only nine holders were outsiders. The register of that year conveniently illustrates the transfer of land from the hands of outsiders to Imabori residents by noting, in each instance, the names and residency of both the former and current holders. One *tan* of land located in the eastern section of Imabori, yielding 6 *shō* of rice income, for example, was "held previously by Jirōsaburō of Shibawara but is now in the name of Gorōsaburō of the Eastern Cluster."[181] Six outsiders were noted on the 1510 and 1566 lists constituting 6 percent and 8 percent, respectively, of the total donors.[182] The percentage of outside holders decreased from 100 percent in 1335 to below 10 percent in the 1500s, suggesting a growing sense of localism among Imabori residents. The boundaries that defined the social group upholding Imabori's miyaza became increasingly articulated in terms of the geographical space associated with the gō name. Imabori residents purchased the outsiders' interests and kept them among themselves.

The locations of shrine land also varied, extending to nearby villages—Shibawara, Hebimizo, and Imazaike, as well as Yōkaichi. There was no predictable relationship between the location of the land and its holder. Unlike the increase in the number of Imabori residents among shinden holders, however, shinden plots did not become concentrated in Imabori over the centuries. In fact, the reverse was true. Initially, in 1335, four of five parcels, amounting to 3 *tan* 120 *bu,* were located in Imabori.[183] The record from 1416 shows a similar figure, about 3 *tan* 110 *bu.*[184] But between 1416 and 1463, the figure almost doubled as the sō received or purchased outside land totaling at least 3 *tan* 120 *bu.*[185] This increase is also reflected in the register of 1463, which mentions about 6 *tan* of outside land. In the subsequent half-century or so, the sō gained approximately 2 *tan* more of non-Imabori land.[186] While seeking to limit outsiders' interests in Imabori land, the sō expanded its own geographical scope of investment.

The Cosmological Spatial Order

Medieval village life was imbued with a perpetual sense of otherworldliness nurtured by concrete and abstract symbols derived from a mixture of belief systems—kami worship, Buddhism, and folk beliefs. These symbols formed a normal part of the landscape, just as any tree in a field did. Living with these symbols on a daily basis, people internalized the associated values into their own subjective construct. The villagers' eagerness to contribute to shrine land and their responsiveness to solicitation expressed their personalized and intimate relationship with the otherworldly powers and their hope for reassurances from them.

Spirits, deities, and bodhisattvas were abundant, and people needed to bring order to these multitudes of cosmic influences. They did so by arranging them along the twin axes of time and space. The calendar of ceremonies and rituals expressed the villagers' attempt to bring the spirit world into tune with temporal human needs. They also organized the spirits on the horizontal plane of the village landscape, in spatial harmony with the people's living and working patterns.

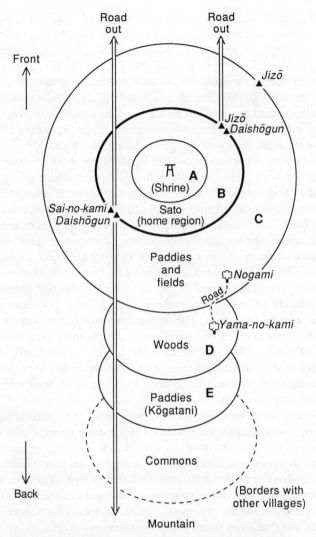

Fig. 1. The cosmological spatial order in medieval Imabori.

Records of ceremonies and rituals can be combined with the information on contemporary maps to construct a view of the local cosmological spatial order. By modifying a concentric-circle model proposed by Miyake Hitoshi for all Japanese villages,[187] we can sketch an
iconographical representation of the Imabori community.

The focal point of our community was the shrine and the area
immediately surrounding it, including the sō forest. Represented in

Figure 1 by circle A, this was an area where there was close communication between deities and people, the spiritual world and the secular world, and forces of extreme sacrality and profanity. The miyaza met there to ensure the perpetuation of this interaction between two dichotomous forces through the symbolic gestures of ceremonies and rituals, most vividly illustrated in *naorai,* the circulation of food between deities and humans. The area hosted the proprietary penetration of moral influences, and the village's dominant groups tended to monopolize the institutional privileges associated with circle A.

The intensity of the sacred and the formality of its expression found in circle A dissipated in circle B, which represented something in the order of a "home region" (*sato*) for the community. It was the habitation for villagers of all ages, sexes, and economic status and was marked by a clearly defined border. Waterways encircled it, servicing vegetable fields within it and demarcating in from out. The "in" area was insulated from the entry of harmful spirits, ghosts, and insects (which tended to roam around borders) by protective deities—jizō, Daishōgun, and Sai-no-kami. It also served as a buffer belt for circle A.

Immediately adjoining the residential area lay the space for cultivation and, ideally, irrigation. This region had little in the way of architecture but was covered with fields and paddies and interwoven with paths and ditches. The outline of circle C was a road, marked by a single jizō at its northeastern edge. Nogami, the Field Deity, presided over agricultural production. People spent most of their time here during the day.

Extending southward and farther away from the community's sacred core, woodland formed another delimited region, circle D. Its main occupant was Yama-no-kami, the Mountain Deity, whose benevolent and destructive forces called for an annual ceremonial dedication right at the foot of its symbolic manifestation (a tree). The area was an important source of building materials, fuel, and nourishment; it provided lumber, compost, firewood, herbs, and nuts for the villagers. The area was free from proprietary intervention.

In contrast to the woodland, the adjoining circle E (Kōgatani), provided little autonomy for the villagers and housed no significant deities. It was, instead, the product of the proprietor's development— paddies created by drawing water from the reservoir located still farther south. Thin in its spiritual dimension, the area was characterized primarily by straightforward economic considerations. The proprietor's moral and religious influence, densest in circle A, had its counterpoise here, where the function was clearly extractive.

Despite the outlines of these five circles and their implied borders,

Imabori was never a closed entity. It connected with the outside world, at its own chosen points, through the roads and paths that pierced the circles. One road (Ichi-michi, or Market Road) originated at the point guarded by the jizō and Daishōgun; it intersected circle B and extended north. Another road ran the entire length of Imabori from north to south. As with the first road, protective deities, Daishōgun and Sai-no-kami, stood at the junction of the road and circle B, guarding against unwanted trespassers. Linking with national roads and market towns, these roads represented avenues to the world of the unfamiliar—and to the world of opportunities.

CHAPTER THREE

The Sō Village in Its Estate Setting

The sō's extension of its economic base and its independent political authority did not occur in a vacuum, but in relation to the proprietor's assertion of its own vested interests. In terms of human geography, Imabori was a village existing within a shōen. The shrine land producing income for the sō occupied ground within the territorial borders defined and claimed by the proprietor. Even at the height of shrine land accumulation, the sō drew income from only about 15 percent of the total land cultivated.[1] The sō was an organization composed of a population living on soil overseen by an absentee lord with enormous political and economic power.

Given this context, how extensive were the sō's localist prerogatives? How did the sō build them? An inquiry into the patterns of rights and obligations pertaining to land and water, the clearest point of convergence for proprietary interests and sō initiatives, serves as the base from which to answer these questions. We will then turn to the question of authority and control that shaped the lives of Imabori residents.

Land and Water

The proprietor and the sō shared and competed over Imabori's agricultural potential. It was the proprietor's prerogative and obligation to develop land and water resources and to maintain the productivity of those resources in order to extract taxes. The sō's interest lay in the accretion of untaxed shrine land. The two forces shared a larger agricultural goal but differed in their underlying motivations.

Irrigation Development

Because rice culture—unlike the dry farming of the West—dominated Japanese agricultural life, irrigation was of fundamental importance in determining the level of local productivity.[2] Even in dry areas such as Imabori, the ideal mode of production for the lord and, to a lesser extent, for the producers was based on the primacy of rice.

From ancient times on, the high caloric content and dependable exchange value of rice secured its political and social status. The tax collector (initially the state, gradually displaced by estate holders) valued it for settling the population, for stabilizing the tax base, and for being a source of gastronomic pleasure[3] in ancient Japan. Despite initial resistance to pressure from above, taxpayers eventually came to internalize the high social and economic status of rice.[4] Both the elites and the commoners reinforced this value system in the seasonal ceremonial cycle. Whether at the proprietors' shrines in the capital or at shrines in hamlets, products made from rice, such as mochi and sake, were regular fare for the beneficent spirits and deities associated with rice production.

Irrigation developed in Imabori along the axes suggested by E. Walter Coward, Jr.: development in "agency-operated systems" and development in "community irrigation systems."[5] The agency in Imabori was Enryakuji, which sponsored large-scale land improvement projects. The sō, as the representative body of the community, maintained the local network of smaller waterways.

Overcoming some of the topographical disadvantages of the region, Enryakuji had tapped into two major sources of water for irrigation by the late medieval period: the Echi River and the runoff from Nunobiki Terrace. Originating at the Echi River was the Takayu River, a sluice said to have been developed through the efforts of the priest Tokuchin in the early medieval period.[6] The sluice originated about 7 kilometers east of Imabori in the village of Ikeda, in Kanzaki County. The water was channeled westward, entering Tokuchin-ho from its eastern end, through Ōmori and other villages, eventually reaching Imabori via Shibawara.[7] In Imabori it outlined the northern edge of the residential section, and its water was drawn off in various directions via smaller irrigation channels.

The Takayu successfully irrigated the eastern half of Tokuchin-ho, the Upper-ho, or the Paddy Side. It failed, however, to provide a stable water supply to the western side of the shōen, the Lower-ho or the Field Side.[8] Even in the nineteenth century, the Takayu was dry in Imabori "from mid-May to mid-September [Gregorian calendar] because of the long distance from its water source."[9] This meant that Imabori was affected during what would have been the months of heaviest irrigation. Despite the efforts of the temple, therefore, fields far outnumbered paddies in Imabori until the late sixteenth century, when about half the arable land was planted in rice.[10] Imazaike, another gō in the Lower-ho, located to the north of Imabori, had no paddy land whatever.[11]

In addition to the irrigation development that depended on the Echi River, efforts were made in the mid to late fourteenth century to utilize runoff from Nunobiki Terrace. This water was collected in a reservoir with the capacity to irrigate at least 5 *tan* 80 *bu* of "new" paddy located in Kōgatani, occupying the lower tip of Imabori's southern rectangle and extending into Shibawara. Kōgatani remained important as a stable rice-growing area.[12]

Apart from water improvements made by the temple, the sō developed irrigation on its own initiative. This type of localist effort to improve irrigation was found in other sō villages as well. It is recorded that villagers in Kii Province, for instance, purchased a piece of land at the end of the thirteenth century in order to construct a pond.[13] Frequently documents suggest local rights to and management of irrigation facilities through cases of intervillage conflicts. Villages in Mabuchi-no-shō, another estate in Gamō County, illustrate this pattern in their peace agreement dated 1487.[14]

In Imabori many a ditch was called a "sō ditch" because the sō managed it. For example, a plot sold in 1460 had the following borders noted: to the east, a sō ditch; to the west, a sō ditch; to the south, the sō land; and to the north, land cultivated by Sakon.[15] The sō managed its ditches with considerable sophistication. For the most part, they were probably intended to irrigate the land designated as sō land in documents. But they also represented a capital investment that brought financial profit to the sō. In 1555, for example, the sō rented out a 12 *ken* segment of one of its ditches to five people at the monthly rate of 20 *mon* per *ken*, except in the seventh month, when it was 10 *mon*, a discount rate due probably to the predicted low water level.[16]

The sō's construction projects potentially threatened the traditional proprietary prerogatives to draw income from the land. The threat became reality in 1460, when the villagers dug a new ditch, "because new water supplies are urgently needed," to irrigate several *tan* of land, at the apparent sacrifice of arable land on which tax and service obligations were owed to the proprietor. How was this problem of overlapping interests resolved? The villagers avoided conflict; they sent a request to Enryakuji for permission to go ahead with the construction and promised to discharge taxes and services as before.[17]

A case from the mid-sixteenth century demonstrates more precisely how this type of problem might have been handled. A parcel of land, apparently encumbered with service obligations to the temple, was going to be transformed into a sō ditch. In order to relieve the holder, Emontarō, of responsibility to the proprietor, the sō promised to dispatch a person to fulfill these obligations instead. The sō also established a compensatory relationship with Emontarō by guaranteeing payments of 100 *mon* in cash to him and to his descendants for each use of the ditchwater. Moreover, Emontarō and the sō agreed that if the sō found other usable water sources (i.e., hand-dug wells), the payments would cease, presumably because the owner could then convert the ditch back to arable land and harvest the yield to pay the required taxes and services.[18]

The sō exhibited innovativeness and good rational economic sense in their ditch enterprises. But in their attitude of compliance, they unquestioningly upheld the established structure of authority and interest distribution.

Residential Blocks: A Kaito Settlement

The available maps do not show us all the small ditches running through Imabori. But the major ones are marked in the seventeenth-century map, revealing a clear relationship between the lines of ditches and residential sections: ditches surrounded the Eastern and Central clusters completely and waterways wedged in the Tea House Cluster on two sides. Despite the scarcity of water, then, a network of ditches, in addition to roads, bounded Imabori's residential blocks. This pattern began in the mid-fifteenth century, suggested by the sudden increase in the notation of "ditch [*hori* or *mizo*]" in describing land parcels in the documents.[19]

What was the significance of this ditch building and encirclement of residential areas? Late medieval Imabori fits a type of settlement pattern historians commonly call a *kaito* ("enclosed") or *kangai* ("irrigated") village, that is a village outlined by moats or ditches. Kaito villages were most typically located in the outskirts of the capital. Exemplified by those in Ikeda-no-shō, Yamato Province, many of the kaito settlements were found within rectangular plots of land remaining from the ancient equal allotment system.[20] Imabori's kaito settlement was different in this respect; the settlement was not rectangular because Tokuchin-ho fell outside the ancient plan of equal allotment and was most probably created by the efforts of the residents. Perhaps to celebrate their own local initiatives, people of medieval Imabori incorporated the term *kaito* in place names, for example, Great Kaito, Central Kaito, and North Kaito.[21]

What factors gave impetus to the organization of the kaito in Imabori? Our documents provide no direct clue to the answer. In other areas as well, the origins of, and the purposes behind, the kaito settlements are obscure. Makino Shinnosuke posits that they emerged out of the villagers' perceived need for self-defense, most likely during the tumultuous years of the Ōnin War (1467–77).[22] This theory is unconvincing when applied to the situation in Imabori. Unlike many other villages,[23] Imabori has no recorded instance of a potential or actual armed conflict involving its villagers, with the possible exception of an act of arson committed by an agent of the neighboring shōen in the thirteenth century.[24]

Instead of strategic necessities, which Makino suggests, a more indirect socio-spiritual response to the wartime atmosphere might have given rise to Imabori's kaito settlements. The process might have involved self-articulation—rather than self-defense—and a strengthened notion of in and out as it came to be applied to both humans and spirits. The outer parameter of the ditches coincided with the spiritual border marked by local protective deities, such as Daishōgun and Sai-no-kami. The ditches that encircled settlements symbolized the villagers' desire to bar harmful spirits and to welcome beneficial ones.[25] A similar exclusiveness found its way into the writing of village codes, which applied to mortals. For the first time, in 1460, codes forbade villagers to accommodate travelers and prohibited outsiders from wearing an *eboshi* outfit like a villager.[26] Similar regulations barring outsiders appeared throughout the fifteenth and sixteenth centuries.[27] The sō probably constructed these ditches and certainly maintained the effectiveness of the enclosure by instituting regulations such as "Do not build a house to the east of the moat."[28]

Equally significant in strengthening the sense of exclusiveness was a practical economic consideration related to production. Kaito arrangements probably emerged in conjunction with the late-fifteenth- and sixteenth-century expansion of cultivated areas in the form of vegetable plots occupying the traditionally tax-free residential section. With the gradual weakening of the old proprietary structure, villagers found opportunities to assert greater autonomy in consolidating their economic base. As Nakamura Ken notes, the *semachi,* the measurement unit used for these vegetable plots, had no consistent relationship to the traditional units of land measurement, such as *tan* or *bu,* used for assessing taxes. Instead of area, *semachi* expressed loosely the shape or length of furrows and manifested a productive mode that was entirely independent of proprietary concern.[29]

A particularly noteworthy venture was the "newly sown [*shinmai*] kaito" which began to make an appearance in the 1510s.[30] This kaito area was organized in systematic rows, as suggested by such phrases as "the twentieth on the north side of the newly sown vegetable plot."[31] Villagers probably planted crops there for their own consumption as well as for sale at nearby markets. Japan's expanding economy and commercialization in these centuries most likely stimulated the growth in tax-free profit-oriented farming. Holders of these plots also sold or commended portions of the profits to the sō. As noted earlier, the sō's assets in vegetable plots more than tripled between 1463 and 1510 (see Table 1). Imabori's kaito arrangements, then, were yet another expression of the community's enterprise exercised in an area free of proprietary control.

Paddy, Field, and Field-Paddy

In records of land transactions, it was customary to describe the type of land, its dimensions, and its four boundaries. These notations inform us that Imabori's land fell into the following categories: dry field (*hatake*), paddy (*ta*), field-paddy (*hatada*), vegetable plot (*sounachi* or *nahata*), residential ground (*yashiki*), and woodlot (*hayashi*). These categories did not suggest rigidly fixed conditions, however; while some parcels remained in the same state, others underwent changes depending on the water supply. A comparison of transaction records for a given parcel that changed hands more than once can reveal its long-term usage. The 1 *tan* located to the north of the shrine's woods was a dry field in 1366 and, again, in 1373.[32] Land in Kōgatani, at Imabori's southern end, tended to remain paddy land, as did the 210 *bu* surrounded by water on three sides and sold twice (in 1378 and 1410) before being commended to the shrine in 1499.[33]

In contrast to the examples above, a parcel 260 *bu* in size, located to the south of the shrine and sold at least five times over a period of 40-odd years, began as paddy but had turned into field-paddy by the time it was commended to the sō in 1447 (see Table 2). Apparently, the two waterways bordering the parcel to the north and south failed to provide water adequate for continuous flooding. The designation "field-paddy" articulated the precarious state of this paddy, which reverted to a dry field during a water shortage.

Some parcels with the "paddy" designation were as likely to change status as those called "field-paddy." One *tan* located to the south of Higashi-zaike was a paddy on a sales slip of 1473, but with a notation suggesting its alterability: "as for levies, 300 *bu* when it is a paddy ["paddy time," *ta-doki*] and 1 *tan* 30 *bu* when it is a dry field ["dry-field time," *hata-doki*]."[34]

The proprietor and the sō handled the changeable condition of land each in its own way. Enryakuji's aim was to maximize its income in the

TABLE 2

Records of Transfer for a Parcel of Land South of Imabori Hiyoshi Jūzenji Shrine,
1403–1447

1. 1403.12.11. 260 *bu*, paddy, in front of Yakushi-dō (hall)
Boundaries: east, Emonjirō, cultivator; west, Myōdō, cultivator; south, ditch; north,
river
Sold by Myōdō to Emonsaburō
Price: 4 *kanmon*
2. 1407.11.10. 260 *bu*, paddy, in front of the Imabori shrine
Boundaries: east, Zaimonbō, cultivator; west, Hikojorō, cultivator; south, ditch;
north, the Imabori river
Sold by Emonsaburō and his mother to Jōjū of Kōfukuan (monastery)
Price: 3 *kan* 800 *mon*. Annual income 8 *to*
Dues: 2 to 3 *shō*; 25 *mon* for services. *Hamakudashi* obligation: once every three years
3. 1439.11.26. 260 *bu*, paddy, no location given
Boundaries: not described
Sold by Sochin of Kōfukuan to Imasato Eikyū
Price: 4 *kan* 200 *mon*. Annual income: 8 *to*
4. 1440.2.2. 260 *bu*, field-paddy, no location given
Boundaries: not described
Sold by Imasato Eikyū of Owaki to Suketarō of Imabori
Price: 4 *kanmon*
5. 1443.12.23. 240 *bu*, field-paddy, to the south of Nishi-zaike
Boundaries: east, Chikurinbō; west, Saemon; south, ditch; north, river
Sold by Suketarō of Imabori to Priest Shōshū of the temple Ishitōji
Price: 4 *kanmon*
6. 1447.11.14. 260 *bu*, field-paddy, in front of shrine, Daikaito
Boundaries: not described
Commended by Shōshū to the Imabori sōbun
Annual income: 8 *to*. Proprietary obligations levied.

SOURCE: (1) Doc. no. 477, Ōei 10 (1403).12.11: Myōdō denchi baiken; (2) Doc. no. 511, Ōei 14 (1407).11.10: Emonsaburō tō rensho denchi baiken; (3) Doc. no. 617, Eikyō 11 (1439).11.26: Kōfukuan Sochin denchi baiken; (4) Doc. no. 489, Eikyō 12 (1440).2.2: Owaki Eikyū hatake baiken an; (5) Doc. no. 561, Kakitsu 3 (1443).12.23: Minami Suketarō hatada baiken; (6) Doc. no. 224, Bun'an 4 (1447).11.14: Shōshū hatada kishinjō.

NOTE: The 240 *bu* listed in the fifth record is probably a transcription error.

form of rice. Therefore it sought to execute reclamation projects, as it did successfully in Kōgatani, and to convert dry fields into paddies. In 1378, for instance, Enryakuji transformed a field into a "newly opened" paddy, which, however, apparently could not be relied on for rice production. The cultivators responsible for paying taxes pleaded with the proprietor for a conversion of the rate based on rice to a rate based on legumes. Enryakuji's agent relayed the response from the proprietor: "Concerning the paddy newly converted from a field: tax shall be levied at the rate of 1 *to* 5 *shō* per *tan* [normally]" but "in a poor year, 3 *shō* of cowpeas [*sasage*] shall be forwarded [instead of rice]."[35] Enryakuji recognized that this new paddy was still not fully established, and it set differentiated tax terms to match annual crop conditions.

The proprietor maintained a basically flexible attitude toward taxation by allowing payment in crops other than rice. In so doing, it guaranteed itself a fixed amount of income, except in cases of newly opened paddy land. The example from 1473 illustrates how it adjusted taxes to the cash value of crops. The tax during the "paddy time" was equivalent to that assessed on 300 bu of paddy, but during the "dry-field time," the tax rate matched that for 1 tan 30 bu (i.e., 390 bu) of field. Because the dry crop ranked below rice in monetary value, the percentage of payment per field harvest was larger. The taxpayer had to make up the difference in value between rice and other crops.

Shinden and shinbata, from which the sō drew its income, were no less subject to the scarce water supplies. But in contradistinction to the proprietor, the shrine did not attempt to stabilize its income by pressuring cultivators. The shrine received sake in the amount of 7 shō during the "paddy time" and 5 shō during the "field time" from the 120 bu of land held by Shōenbō.[36] Another parcel of Shōenbō's described as "river-paddy [kawada]" offered 5 to of rice normally but 2 to 5 shō during the "field time."[37] "During the 'field time,' [the amount and type of share] will depend on what is being planted," stated Eichin as he commended a land share of 5 to from his 1 tan of field-paddy in 1442.[38]

While the proprietor focused on taxing rice land, the type of land from which the sō accrued profit (tokubun) consisted mostly of non-paddy land. The villagers—through the collective efforts of the sō—maximized the productive potential of the land by developing irrigation works and by planting various other crops in whatever area was cultivable, including the tax-free areas around homesteads.

The area's irrigation pattern, the material base of production, influenced the type of relationship that developed between the proprietor and the local people. The proprietor maintained full taxation privileges over most paddy land but cared less about taxing legumes—except on "convertible land," where rice would have been grown under normal (or even ideal) circumstances. This policy left the villagers ample opportunity to consolidate their own economic base. Consequently, certain separate spheres of interest emerged, decreasing the chances of the two parties having a head-on collision over the fruits of the soil.

Non-rice Crops and the Commons

Particularly important to the economic and nutritional well-being of the villagers were the non-rice crops, which were probably grown both for consumption and for sale, as well as for payment as tax. The variety of products have left documentary traces, typically as taxes owed to the proprietor, parts of land parcel descriptions, or elements in the sō regulations. Wheat and millet were commonly grown and were probably a staple of the population.[39] Tax obligations attached to a vegetable plot of more than 18 rows, located close to the market town of Yōkaichi and commended to the sō by an Imabori man in 1474, included 4 *shō* 2 *gō* of cowpeas, cloth (*gofuku*) equivalent to 130 *mon* in cash, bamboo worth 6 *mon,* and eggplants worth 7 *mon,* among other things.[40] Of course, cloth was not an agricultural product, but this obligation suggests that either cotton or mulberry for feeding silkworms was grown there. Land descriptions from 1479 on frequently mention the tea fields located around the Tea House Cluster, on the west side of Imabori village.[41] Tea continued to be an important cash crop for Imabori until the nineteenth century.[42]

Practical details about crop production—ground preparation, fertilizer application, and weeding, for example—are not available. But products of the commons must have been essential to the nourishment of the soil in addition to the fulfillment of the villagers' eating, heating, and housing needs. The spread of double-cropping, which required heavy composting,[43] increased the importance of the commons in the late medieval period. Imabori residents had access to three categories of communal land: the woodlot, traditionally free of proprietary interference; grassland under the supervision of the proprietor; and the land claimed by the sō.

Documents are silent about the use of the woodlot (circle D in Figure 1), which housed the Mountain Deity and was located to the south of the cultivated area. We must rely on this negative evidence to assume that residents held unencumbered access to mulch and herbs. This seems a reasonable assumption, considering that a firmly established local practice—such as the use of the commons—involving no supervision by the authorities or financial transactions among users would hardly come to be recorded, unless innovation or conflict disturbed the accepted order. Enryakuji apparently never challenged the traditional arrangement, and, perhaps because the woodlot was located clearly within the village boundaries, no outsiders intruded. Just as the patterns of family and kinship went entirely unrecorded, so did the activities in the woodlot.

In contrast, we know more about the "grass-cutting area [*kusakari ba*]" in Gamō Field, which fell under the protection and supervision of the proprietor. The field was apparently located in an area within Tokuchin-ho that was easily accessible to outsiders (non–Tokuchin-ho residents). Inter-shōen conflicts arose, and Enryakuji was obliged to intervene in 1468, guarding the Honai residents' exclusive rights of access. The wording in the statement suggests that some crops were grown there in addition to native grass; the harvesting of cultivated plants (*sakumō*) was forbidden to outsiders, as was the grass.[44]

Another instance of trouble about a half-century later reveals the level of complexity inter-shōen conflicts could attain. In 1525, the Honai residents appealed to Enryakuji to resolve a conflict: men from Misono, located northeast of Tokuchin-ho, had entered the Honai's grass-cutting area and brought in people from Nomura, another village, to harvest the grass. Meanwhile, the residents of Takebe, located to the north of Yōkaichi, claimed to have purchased this land from Misono and also cut grass there.[45] We are unclear as to the precise location or size of this grassy field. It was a preserve for the Honai residents at large, but outsiders obviously had easy access. Before the time of unification, at any rate, conflicts over the commons were limited to those involving outsiders.

The third category of communal land was the sō land. The sō's forests make frequent documentary appearances as one of the borders of a land parcel being sold or commended. They were located close to the shrine and were also called the "shrine's woods [*miya no mori*]."[46] We learn more about them from the sō's regulations, however, which set clearly defined strictures against their misuse. Starting in 1448, the sō began imposing cash penalties for such offenses as cutting down trees, damaging branches, and collecting soil, firewood, and mulberry leaves.[47] As in the grass-cutting area, the sō apparently prepared the ground for crops, as is evident from the regulations against damaging wheat or taking millet husks or cowpea vines.

How was the sō land utilized? It was earmarked for "public" use in support of the shrine and its functions. Firewood and charcoal belonging to the sō, for instance, were to be used for an unnamed shrine activity, according to a 1489 regulation.[48] Lumber and grass were used, it is certain, in building and repairing shrine structures as well as houses owned by the sō.[49] The cultivated crops most probably reached the altar as food for the gods or filled dishes during meetings and ceremonies.

The sō's land was communal insofar as the sō's property was communally held. More precisely, however, it was institutional and corporate property, not open commons. Thus an elaborate set of prohibitions accompanied its use. Penalties against misuse were graded according to the method or tools employed to commit the offense and according to the social status of the offender. In 1502, the offense was considered least criminal if no tool was used, calling for a fine of 100 *mon*. The use of a sickle ranked next (200 *mon* fine), followed by the use of a hatchet (300 *mon* fine). An act committed with a broadax ranked as the most heinous, and the perpetrator was fined 500 *mon*.[50] According to the 1489 regulation, for the same offense of gathering leaves or cutting trees in the sō forest, murando would lose murando status, while non-murando were to be evicted from the village.[51] In a 1502 regulation, the offender, if a village man, would lose his seat in the shrine association, though a widow or orphan guilty of the same crime would be evicted from the village.[52] Despite, or because of, the elaborate repetition of similar regulations, there remains no recorded instance of an actual offense.

All in all, the extent to which residents could tap the resources of the sō land for personal use without committing offenses was extremely limited.

Proprietary Intervention

How did Tokuchin-ho operate as an estate, which, after all, was a unit of taxation created for the benefit of the proprietary institution? What were the modes of intervention adopted by the absentee proprietor? For the purpose of rationally calculable extraction of local resources, Enryakuji initially organized Tokuchin-ho's arable land into blocks called myō ("name-fields"). Each myō unit was named after an upper-level peasant who held the status of myōshu ("name-field holder"); the myōshu was responsible for collecting the tax attached to the unit and was accorded the right to keep a percentage of the yield. This was no innovation but was a pattern commonly followed by estate holders as early as the tenth century.[53] The organization of myō in some estates clearly demonstrated the proprietary interest in efficient assessment and collection of taxes. In Okushima, another Enryakuji estate on the eastern shore of Lake Biwa, for example, the arable land (about 21 *chō*) was organized into 31 myō units of approximately equal size (7 *tan*), each named after a myōshu.[54] This list, dating from the mid-fifteenth century, probably did not reflect the reality, however. By that time, most myō arrangements were far more complex than met the eye. Because the right and responsibility to the myō, defined in the myōshu-shiki, functioned as private property that could be bought or sold, commended or pawned,[55] it could easily be dispersed, the unit dismembered. Over time, the myō units were transformed into purely artificial units of taxation, separate from the land that originally bore a myōshu's name. A myō unit could embody, for instance, several parcels of land scattered over the estate, and the myō's name might have no actual human counterpart.

We know little about the particular myō setup in Tokuchin-ho because the proprietary records are lost, but scattered evidence reveals that Tokuchin-ho was never organized into equal myō units, such as those in Okushima. The myō's first documentary appearance for Tokuchin-ho comes in a sales slip dated 1351, in which a large portion of the land being sold had its tax calculated as part of Suketarō-myō.[56] A commendation slip from 1362 describes a plot in Toratarō-myō, on the Field Side of the estate, as bordering Seijirō-myō to the east and Jirōsaburō-myō to the west.[57] Such names as Toratarō, Seijirō, and Jirōsaburō might very well have been the names of the original myōshu associated with these myō.

Because of the freely alienable rights associated with the myō, the myō underwent change over the generations. A sales slip of 1371 locates one Yorimune's dry field in "Tokuchin-ho Yōkaichiba, formerly Genjirō-myō."[58] An area that had been a myō apparently became subsumed under a new name, Yōkaichiba, "field of the day 8 market." Some myō, on the other hand, became mere place names. A dry field sold in 1386 was located in Tatsutarō-myō, which was merely a place name (*azana*), according to the notation on the sales slip.[59]

However the land itself was subdivided or renamed, the proprietor still taxed it on the basis of myō divisions. In 1378, "a peasant [hyakushō] who managed various myō" forwarded complaints regarding his tax burden during a period of bad harvests. Enryakuji responded by granting permission to substitute cowpeas for rice in payment.[60] As late as 1438, a myō located to the south of Yōkaichi clearly held tax obligations in the form of "cowpeas, eggplants, services, cloth, and bamboo."[61]

A major change in the mode of assessment came in the mid-fifteenth century. Enryakuji restructured its taxation system, moving to levies mainly based on the gō without abolishing the myō entirely. To facilitate this transition, the temple conducted a survey of paddy land in the Lower-ho, the Field Side of Tokuchin-ho, from the sixteenth day to the twentieth day in the ninth month of 1442. The records that remain are for Imabori-gō; they list the amount of paddy followed by the names of cultivators, with no mention of myō. From notations at the beginning and end of the list, we can see that the survey was conducted systematically from the northeastern section to the southern section of Imabori.[62]

Despite this new effort, some myō apparently continued to serve as units of taxation. An Enryakuji order issued half a month later, for example, indicates that a preexisting myō, Dankōbō-myō, came to incorporate new taxable paddies as they were opened up in Kōgatani. This document is useful in illustrating the myō's artificial quality, as it shows that Dankōbō-myō was composed of land parcels dispersed over different areas in the estate: a newly developed parcel in Kōgatani as well as another located elsewhere in the Lower-ho.[63] Half a dozen other notations of myō have survived in the post-survey years and suggest that some were simply place names, while others functioned as units for tax collection.[64]

Why did Enryakuji implement a new mode of tax assessment at this time? Perhaps the outmoded myō system was becoming increasingly inoperative in the rapidly expanding economy. The visible spread of the new vegetable plots and the accompanying rise in the sō's accumulation of shrine land may have prompted the temple to demonstrate its proprietary status to the residents. A proprietary sense of insecurity may have been caused by the turbulent events of the 1440s, occurring both in the capital and in Ōmi Province: the murder of the shogun Yoshinori in 1441 brought chaos to the bakufu and warrior bureaucrats; and peasant uprisings shook Ōmi, although Tokuchin-ho remained quiet. Meanwhile, the Rokkaku issued a series of *tokusei* (debt-cancellation) edicts, seeking to ameliorate peasant discontent but threatening the economic basis of Enryakuji, a major creditor. As Maruyama Yoshihiko suggests, the survey had both symbolic and practical aims for Enryakuji: to reemphasize proprietary authority and to renovate the tax-collection mechanisms.[65]

Enryakuji was not alone in seeking to upgrade the system. At this time, other large absentee estate holders, including Tōdaiji and Kōya-san, also conducted what would be their final large-scale survey in order to offset the steady erosion of their authority over the land.[66] The timing and the content of the new arrangement also found convergence with the kind of social transformation occurring at the village level. The gō was gaining importance as a geographical unit that defined the settlement pattern and social organization in Tokuchin-ho. In less than two decades the first sō prohibition against outsiders would be issued.[67] More and more of Imabori's shrine land was being held by the residents of Imabori gō. Enryakuji's new system more closely reflected the changing social reality.

Because Enryakuji was an absentee proprietor, it required the work of subordinates to collect and transport the tax profits. The temple dispatched agents, but it also depended on the myōshu. Agents called the *zushi* (mapmaker) and the *kumon* (scribe) served as intermediaries between the proprietor and the villagers. They relayed orders from above—for instance, the authorization for converting the rice tax to a payment in cowpeas during the bad harvest in 1378.[68] They also recognized the tax-exempt status of shrine lands, endorsing the location, ownership, and size of each plot.[69]

The signatures of the zushi and the kumon suggest that the two agents held unequal authority. While the zushi signed independently, the kumon always signed with the zushi. But they shared the responsibility for land registration in Tokuchin-ho, which was recorded in two books: the "zushi register" and the "Nakamura register." Nakamura was the name of the kumon's family.[70]

The zushi and the kumon were agents of the proprietor, but they also had a personal interest in the local economy. Their names (Tani and Nakamura) appear in land documents, where they are cited as cultivators of taxable paddies and holders of shrine land. They, therefore, worked for both proprietary and local interests. Their status carried local prestige, judging from the honorific *dono* villagers used to identify them.[71]

For reclamation purposes, there were special agents called reclamation commissioners (*shinkai bugyō*). Their responsibility was similar to that of the "mapmaker" but pertained only to newly reclaimed land. When villagers pleaded to have a newly developed Kōgatani parcel recognized as shrine land in 1448, for instance, the commissioners were the first to receive Enryakuji's reply, which was then relayed to the villagers.[72] Sometimes the commissioners cooperated with the villagers in obtaining tax reductions. They supported the peasants of Imabori and Hebimizo in requesting a 50 percent reduction in the tax charged on a recently reclaimed area because of a bad harvest. The commissioners added their own appeal to the temple.[73] They seem to have held no vested interest in the local soil, however. They were a temporary presence, perhaps appointed only for the duration of new development projects.

Perhaps the most crucial human components of the tax-collection processes were the local myōshu. The specific activities of the myōshu within the village are not well known, although scholars have exercised their pens writing about their general political and social significance to the broad process of historical transformation. The classic article by Matsumoto Shinpachirō, written in 1942, established the basic premise regarding the role of myōshu in late medieval communities (kyōdōtai). On the one hand, they were tax collectors for the proprietor as well as extractors in their own right, not only of the profits defined by the myōshu-shiki but also of any supplementary rent (kajishi) that could be squeezed out of the cultivators. On the other hand, as the "middle stratum"—between the local warrior agent, the jitō, and the cultivators—myōshu led the small peasants (shōnōmin, the historians' term for the majority of peasants) in collectivizing in order to secure the equitable use of the commons and the irrigation works. The myōshu protected the interests of these small peasants; the ability of the latter to maintain production affected the ability of the myōshu to secure their own profits.[74]

Others have elaborated on this theme. Kurokawa Masahiro argues, for example, that the role of the myōshu did not remain static, nor did that of the small peasant. Starting in the mid-fourteenth century and continuing through the fifteenth, increased productivity, the development of a cash economy, and the availability of a growing surplus allowed the growth of small peasants; they came to hold land in their own name, although their holdings were small (5 tan or under). They became a new type of small myōshu. Simultaneously, the original myōshu class decreased in size (because of the demise of some myōshu who had failed to exploit the economic opportunities) but increased in stature; its members held greater amounts of land than before and were often identified by surnames followed by an honorific dono.[75] This "fission within the peasant class [nōminsō bunkai]" had a direct impact on the formation of the sō. It was these upper-level peasants, still called myōshu (or dogō), and the newly risen small myōshu who organized the local productive resources—both natural and human—by instituting the sō political organization in alliance with the proprietor.[76] The sō, therefore, was an establishment devised for the security and convenience of the broad myōshu class, which had close ties with the proprietor.

Given the basic dearth of sources, it is difficult to prove how closely this representative model, described by Matsumoto and Kurokawa, fits the Imabori case. The nearest possible available source consists of the survey records of 1442, which list only paddies. Fields, vegetable plots, and residential land, which covered the greater part of the landscape, are omitted. With this shortcoming in mind, we can calculate the distribution of rights to land measured in tan. Of the 65 people listed, 17 are outsiders; the status of one is unclear. The remaining 47 people, who can be considered Imabori residents, are grouped in Table 3.[77]

Clearly, the two names in the 10 tan category stand far above the others. They contrast with the nineteen occupying the bottom rung, with holdings of less than 1 tan. Combined with the eleven names in the 1 tan category, these thirty names make up 64 percent of the total

TABLE 3

Distribution of Land in Imabori, 1442

Size of paddy	Number of people
10 *tan* or more	2
9 *tan* or more	0
8 *tan* or more	0
7 *tan* or more	0
6 *tan* or more	1
5 *tan* or more	5
4 *tan* or more	1
3 *tan* or more	3
2 *tan* or more	5
1 *tan* or more	11
Less than 1 *tan*	19
TOTAL	47

SOURCE: Based on Nakamura Ken, *Chūsei sōson shi no ken-kyū*, p. 303, table 5.

number of landholders in Imabori. Between the two extremes, there are fifteen men who hold between 2 and 7 *tan*. "Fission within the peasant class" is clearly evident in mid-fifteenth century Imabori if measured strictly in terms of paddy holdings.

To what extent does this conclusion stand up when examined in a broader context? Would the inclusion of non-paddy land yield a similar vertical spread? Scholars have repeatedly analyzed the shrine land registers in order to answer such questions.[78] A consequence of their labors is an outline of the local class structure. Miyagawa Mitsuru, for example, has observed the coexistence of two types of myōshu in fourteenth- and fifteenth-century Tokuchin-ho: the locally rooted myōshu of the warrior (*jizamurai*) type, who were few in number, and the small-myōshu-cum-independent-small-peasants, who increasingly dominated the rural scene.[79] Miyagawa also found a similar structure in Kuze-no-shō in Yamashiro and Ōyama-no-shō in Tanba.[80]

This methodological trend—analyzing the class structure based on shrine land registers—reached an important watershed in 1960 with the publication of an article by Wakita Haruko pointing out the fundamental shortcomings of the method.[81] No one before Wakita had given sufficient attention to the crucial fact that shrine land constituted only about 15 percent of the total land in Imabori. Given that fact, we must exercise caution in attaching validity to the conclusions reached by such scholars as Miyagawa. Even so, there is a basic congruence in the class structure construed from the 1442 survey and the records of shrine land: a large number of small holders and a small number of large holders with a gap in between. Perhaps, then, it might be safe to assume that a healthy nucleus of "small myōshu" had recently emerged below men of greater wealth. Perhaps the core body of the sō was composed of the small myōshu class.

Whatever the nature and historical significance of the myōshu, they were, at any rate, responsible for forwarding taxes to the proprietor. In documents, the myōshu appear most frequently in communication with the proprietor regarding obligations. An Enryakuji order of the fifteenth century, addressed to Honai peasants (*hyakushō-chū*), demanded all the myōshu of both "the Field Side" and "the Paddy Side" to forward the taxes calculated for the newly developed land.[82] In 1463, myōshu petitioned the proprietor, claiming that the zushi's demands for compensation for tax arrears were erroneously applied to parcels of shrine land.[83]

Apparently, the status and function of the myōshu provided them access to sufficient surplus to acquire means of transportation (horses or oxen) and the capital for other forms of investment. Judging from the signatories in the records of trade disputes occurring in the fifteenth century, some myōshu emerged as prominent merchants.[84]

The rate of taxation is an important index for assessing the intensity of proprietary imposition on the local population. Some land sale documents suggest that the rate of taxation was different for Kōgatani and other non-paddy areas. A new paddy in Kōgatani, 150 *bu* in size, for example, owed 2 *to* in rice to Enryakuji and 4 *shō* to the Imabori sō. An additional 5 *gō* was paid for water use (*iryō*), presumably to Enryakuji.[85] If we assume that 1 *tan* of paddy yielded 1 *koku* of rice, we can estimate a 4 *to* yield from 150 *bu* of land. Tax in the amount of 2 *to* would have been 50 percent of the yield, an average rate of taxation for the medieval period.

On the other hand, a strikingly small tax was levied on a field outside Kōgatani. From a field sold by one Hebimizo man in 1426, only 5 percent of the total yield went to the temple. This plot (2.5 *semachi*) yielded vegetables assessed to be worth 3 *to* in rice. Only 1 *shō* 5 *gō* (i.e., 0.15 *to*) was paid to the proprietor.[86] As stated earlier, the vegetable plots typically owed no tax. "No obligations," stated one Sanehisa as he commended his plot in front of Higashi-zaike in 1499.[87] Enryakuji's rice-centered outlook influenced the differentiated mode of taxation, a convenient formula for the residents with a greater stake in non-paddy land.

Some paddies and fields were additionally encumbered by what Nakamura Ken speculates to have been labor service. Denoted by an altogether ambiguous term, *hamakudashi* ("down to the shore"), this duty entailed overland transportation of annual dues to Lake Biwa's eastern shore for their shipment across the lake to the western shore. The levy apparently came around once every three years.[88] Another notation (*chōfu*, "labor imposition") on another document also suggests an additional form of labor service.[89] But the documents are silent on further details.

Unlike other sō villages, Imabori did not institutionalize collective payment of taxes; tax matters fell outside the sō's purview, and each cultivator was individually responsible for his or her obligation to the proprietor.

The efficient exercise of proprietary privileges to secure tax and labor levies required freedom from internal disorder and from incursions by outsiders. As the following section will discuss, the sō played an important part in maintaining internal order. Eliminating incursions involved, first of all, protection of the shōen's resources against transgressors who might violate the established territorial boundaries. But boundaries were frequently disputed, for they were sometimes unclearly drawn or were otherwise unrecognized by competitors. In the late thirteenth century, when Tokuchin-ho's borders were still nebulous, the shōen's local foes—officials of Haneda-no-shō (a neighboring shōen under Muromachiin proprietorship)—destroyed Honai property and burned down three peasant homes.[90] This attack explicitly undermined Enryakuji's proprietary interest. The priest-officials in Higashitani denounced the act strongly and demanded permanent exile for the responsible officials. The outcome of this incident is unknown, but no further violation was recorded, suggesting a conclusion with agreed-upon boundaries.

Conflicts involving shōen officials who challenged each other's territorial interests at the highest level were common in the early medieval period. Hōgetsu Keigo has demonstrated that, in the Kamakura period, shōen proprietors initiated aggressive irrigation disputes by arming themselves and by mobilizing their residents. But the actors in later conflicts were those on land directly concerned with productive processes, and in the words of Hōgetsu, "self-governing units formed within villages and shōen."[91]

In Tokuchin-ho in 1468, outsiders interfered with the residents' rights to communal grassland, whose value was increasing with the spread of double-cropping, as mentioned earlier. Enryakuji, according to a statement it made, found that outsiders pretending to be Honai residents made use of a commons located in Gamō Field, which was reserved for grass cutting and crop cultivation by residents of the eight gō. Enryakuji therefore issued a strict order prohibiting this trespass.[92]

The mode of resolution here illustrates that Enryakuji's proprietary umbrella was a useful protection for the villagers' collective interests. The weight of the public authority displayed by the proprietor helped to prevent the actual use of force in keeping outsiders away. Whatever its ultimate motive had been, the temple acted as a patron and guardian of local interests.

Disputes also occurred between villages inside Tokuchin-ho. In the 1550s, Imabori and Hebimizo fought over a road and ditch called Nishi-ōmichi that divided the two gō. Villagers of Imabori and Hebimizo held differing opinions as to the nature of Nishi-ōmichi. Imabori villagers wanted it to be a ditch, while Hebimizo villagers considered it a road, so time and again the former emptied it, and the latter filled it with dirt. Finally Enryakuji sent agents to arbitrate the conflict, and they determined that Imabori was in the right. The ditch was needed to irrigate paddies owing proprietary dues.[93]

While Enryakuji continued to hold jurisdiction within Tokuchin-ho, its abilities to arbitrate inter-shōen conflicts sharply deteriorated by the sixteenth century, for the configuration of political power in the country had undergone a major transformation. The traditional kenmon (the powers in the capital) were losing ground to provincial forces, which in Ōmi meant the shugo. When Honai residents complained to Enryakuji in 1525 about the infringement of their rights to the grass-cutting area,[94] the temple responded by indicating that the case was in the hands of the shugo and that there would be some time before a resolution. To assure a favorable outcome, Enryakuji advised Honai residents to prepare all necessary expenses in advance—an implicit reference to generous gifts for the shugo.[95] By the early sixteenth century, then, the temple had ceased to exercise jurisdiction over conflicts involving outsiders. The shugo took charge instead. Similar acts of deferral by shōen proprietors were common as early as the fifteenth century in other inter-shōen conflicts as well. In a border dispute between Fushimi and Sumiyama, dated 1433, for example, the proprietors likewise recommended settlement by the shugo or the bakufu.[96] But the pattern of resolution of intra-shōen disputes changed little throughout the medieval period; Enryakuji continued to hold jurisdiction within Tokuchin-ho well into the sixteenth century.

Local Governance

One of the sō's outstanding historical features is its local self-governance. But the nature and extent of local rule varied from case to case. Tabata Yasuko has proposed a three-part categorization of villages around the capital according to their local authority structure.[97] This can serve as the basis from which to evaluate Imabori's level of local governance.

The first type, represented by Kawashima Minami-no-shō in Yamashiro Province, had a strong local agent who held delegated authority from both the shōen proprietor and the Muromachi bakufu (*gesu-shiki* and *jitō-shiki*). He had jurisdiction over criminal matters and other local disputes concerning production and irrigation. He held authority not only to collect taxes from the local population but also to forward it to the proprietor in a lump payment. This allowed him to cut easily into the local surplus and augment his personal economic power. Here villagers did not develop into a sō and had little control over production, tax payment, or jurisdictional processes.[98]

The second type in Tabata's categorization was the most numerous in the capital region. Villages were organized into sō, but local warriors maintained strong leadership. In Kamikuze-no-shō, for instance, the proprietary agent (kumon) and the local warriors had a major voice in the sō. Police jurisdiction was first in the hands of the proprietor (Tōji), but it was transferred to local warriors as their power increased in the post–Ōnin War era. Local surplus seems to have passed to the proprietor and the local warriors. But the resolution of disputes concerning irrigation remained a prerogative of the village in the fifteenth and sixteenth centuries.[99]

The third type of village and the type with the greatest political power was the sō village, whose self-governing features extended to payment of taxes, local control of surplus, and police jurisdiction. Tabata cites Okushima as the "purest" sō form and concedes that sō like it were very scarce. In the thirteenth and fourteenth centuries Okushima villagers fought against what they considered illegal taxation by the proprietary agents (gesu and *azukaridokoro*). The sō structure emerged in the 1340s out of the villagers' struggle against the local authorities. The sō's growth was therefore proportionate to the degree of political authority it was able to expropriate from the local agents.[100]

If Imabori is characterized using Tabata's criteria, its sō would fall somewhere between the second and third types. Imabori villagers held extensive control over production, irrigation, and the disposal of the surplus. They developed their own irrigation facilities, expanded cultivable land, and, in the late medieval era, channeled local surplus where they wished. Documents do not reveal the presence of strong local warriors, but in their stead, financially powerful merchants or myōshu may have had a major voice within the sō. In contrast to Okushima, Imabori did not develop a collective tax-paying system. Because the local agents posed no great threat to the villagers, there was no serious attempt to appropriate their prerogatives. The local agents (zushi and kumon), in any case, seemed to have worn two hats, participating in the sō's accumulation of financial assets by contributing to the coffers of the shrine.

Imabori sō's local jurisdiction expressed itself most commonly in the form of regulations with penalty clauses. Sixteen sets of regulations have survived from the two centuries (1383 through 1582) before Hideyoshi's surveys.[101] The changing emphases in the regulations over the years reveal the patterns of growth in the sō's authority within the community.

Before the mid-fifteenth century, the sō directed its efforts exclusively toward keeping ceremonies in order and maintaining the shrine premises. In the 1380s and 1390s, the sō regularized the system of appointing heads of ceremonies.[102] At the beginning of the fifteenth century, it established punitive measures for those negligent in financial or service obligations to the miyaza.[103] The offenders were barred from participation in the za, a measure suggestive of the dominant position the sō had secured by this time. The sō's increasing financial assets perhaps explain the new confidence. From the period between 1314 (the date of the earliest surviving sales slip) and 1403 (the year this set of regulations was issued), more than 40 sales and commendation records have survived. Shrine land increased from 3 *tan* 300 *bu* in 1335 to over 5 *chō* in 1403.[104]

Regulations of 1425 introduced fines (of 300 *mon*) for violations and further punishment for repeat violators: exclusion from the za for generations to come. The sō also broadened its jurisdiction from ceremonial matters to the physical area surrounding the shrine. It dictated the following rules: "(1) do not close the wooden shutter of the prayer hall at your own discretion; (2) do not beat the drum at your own discretion; (3) do not dry your personal items [perhaps, dry grain] or gamble in front of the shrine buildings; (4) do not place boards [to reserve seats on the ground] at your own discretion."[105]

Matters concerning ceremonies concurrently increased in complexity as outside figures, such as the hijiri, came to be involved (by 1451),[106] as the shrine association split into east and west za (by 1488),[107] and as the senior and the junior members of the za formed two separate interest groups (by 1582).[108] All these changes required the sō's attention and the issuing of pertinent rules.

The protection and management of the sō's natural resources—trees, seedlings, firewood, mulberry leaves—became a new focus of written regulations in 1448[109] and remained a theme through the rest of the

Imabori documents. In imposing penalties, the sō observed and reinforced gradations in the offenders' status by imposing differentiated punishments.[110] In 1502, the sō formulated, in addition, differentiated punishments for the misuse of sō resources according to the tool employed; as mentioned above, the highest fine was assigned to the offense committed with a broadax and the lowest for the offense executed without a tool.[111]

The sō's jurisdiction also extended to broader aspects of the community, less immediately connected to its own operations than were the miyaza and the sō forest. For example, it regulated the relationship of the community to outsiders by instituting measures to keep the latter out. Occurring first in 1460, such measures grew more restrictive as time went on.[112] The desire to promote intracommunity peace and order probably lay behind the closed-door policy. The rising population, the physical and social mobility of commoners and warriors, and the general confusion of the Warring period may have stimulated this desire. Internally, the sō sought to eliminate the common causes of social disorder by repeatedly proscribing gambling and visiting brothels.[113]

The sō issued an array of rules that demonstrated its economically rational organizational character. For instance, money was the solution prescribed by the sō in 1489 for settling disputes about the borders between sō land and private land. The sō also imposed a standard fee (3 percent of the sales price) for houses being sold, at the threat of expulsion from the sō in the case of noncompliance. Those concealing the sales price were also to be punished.[114] Finally, more immediate and practical problems—such as the wearing home of someone else's sandals—also drew the sō's attention; sandal borrowing evoked a regulation setting forth a small fine.[115]

The content of these regulations reveals the parameters of the sō's self-governance. Imabori's regulations were incidental rules, written to adjust concrete situations of immediate and long-lasting relevance. By no means did they provide comprehensive coverage of all aspects of village life. Conspicuous among the areas that went untouched was the handling of serious crimes, such as arson and murder. Imabori set no specific guidelines in judging criminals, unlike Sugaura, which, in 1461, established written rules requiring supporting evidence, elimination of personal bias, and consultation among all za members.[116] Nor, as far as we know, did Imabori actually arrest or punish criminals, unlike Hine-no-shō, where villagers cut down local thieves, along with their family members, during the famine of 1504.[117]

The regulations embodied no explicit "legal" principles but emphasized order, first only in the ceremonial realm but increasingly in the larger community as well, and promoted the authority of the sō in the very enactment of its regulations. Many regulations probably developed into quasi-customary laws as they came to be issued repeatedly over the centuries.

Imabori was by no means an archetypal sō of medieval Japan. It did not follow some of the notable practices associated with communal rule, including collective payment of taxes and maintenance of the local jurisdiction over crime. Nonetheless, the documents of the Imabori sō point up certain characteristic elements that give historical significance to the phenomenon of the sō villages. Despite the obvious gradations among its members, the sō was a collectively organized, consensus-based structure that accommodated normal, legitimated resistance to proprietary control and, at the same time, served as the medium for proprietary control over local community order.

Recent literature on peasant culture has shown renewed interest in "everyday forms of peasant resistance—the prosaic but constant struggle between the peasantry and those who seek to extract labor, food, taxes, rents, and interest from them."[118] Echoing Marc Bloch, who emphasized "patient, silent struggles stubbornly carried on by rural communities,"[119] James C. Scott has reevaluated the historical significance of the more flamboyant, open, organized peasant activities. In line with Scott's theme, Imabori (and other Tokuchin-ho villages) waged no open rebellion against the proprietor throughout the medieval period. Estate residents found persistent pressure against the proprietor sufficient for protecting their interests. The sō's collective stratagems won the residents what they desired: accumulation and expansion of surplus, unencumbered access to the commons, and a political organization with a firm economic base and the authority to manage the local social and economic order. Quietly resisting what seemed to be unreasonable proprietary demands with such measures as collectively written grievances, the sō found no need to openly oppose its master. Although not a legal entity, as many communities were in the West,[120] the sō was a permanent institution, grounded in the perpetuation of routinized but strictly defined ceremonial procedures. Its collective strength outlived generational changes; its technique of prosaic resistance gained results as long as its economic base was secure.

The lack of a need to openly defy authority was buttressed by a conciliatory attitude on the proprietor's part. Instead of draining local resources dry, the proprietor chose to permit a degree of local self-governance and to maintain close ties with the villagers. While it naturally sought its own aggrandizement, it found benefits in forgoing a share of the profits from the land to support the activities of its local daughter shrine, Jūzenji. Because the shrine was the village's social and political center, with the power to enforce community order, the proprietor's grant of an occasional tax exemption for its support meant a capital investment in local community welfare—a governing technique of considerable refinement. The sō community, emerging with explicit approval from the proprietor, therefore fostered a lord-peasant relationship that was characterized by "sincere performance of mutual obligations" rather than "a brutal outbreak of hostility on both sides."[121] But the relational dynamics between Imabori and Enryakuji must be assessed from a wider perspective. We shall need to expand our analysis to the activities of the Honai merchants' sō and its network of commercial enterprises, for which Imabori provided the social base. The region's commercial sector and the involvement of Honai merchants in that world will be the focus of the next two chapters.

CHAPTER FOUR

Village Links with the Outside

THE DEVELOPMENT OF sō villages manifested and stimulated the rapid economic expansion of late medieval Japan, visible at the local level in the sō's ability to retain and utilize a greater volume of agricultural surplus. As the overall growth in farming affected the marketing sector, expansion in the volume and intensity of exchange in an ever-larger variety of commodities also increased the opportunities for commercial profits for enterprising commoners.[1] The Tokuchin-ho residents quickly seized the moment, responding to the new challenges that, for them, lay within arm's reach at the market town of Yōkaichi and on the major roads intersecting it. Manipulating circumstances to their great advantage, they evolved into a group of enterprising traders dealing in a variety of commodities in a large number of markets, often with sufficient clout to oust competing merchants.

In Japan's merchant history, the Honai merchants came to occupy a special place; they are often called the Ōmi merchants, a term that holds a certain luster in Japan today because many of modern Japan's entrepreneurs come from Ōmi (now Shiga). The Ōmi merchants were the successful merchants of the Tokugawa period with home bases in Ōmi (especially Gamō, Kanzaki, and Echi counties), who became nationally known for their fair, frugal, well-disciplined, and enterprising business practices. The term "Ōmi merchants" became current only after the documents ceased to mention the Honai merchants at all. But to many historians, the Honai merchants are the quintessential—but medieval—model of the Ōmi merchants.[2] These medieval merchants of historical renown, then, are the subject of our inquiry. This chapter will attempt to shed light on some aspects of their background; the following chapter will trace the pattern of their rise to eminence.

Commodity Circulation

Merchants were not free agents in late medieval Japan, inasmuch as "productive and distributive activities [did not] depend on buying and selling or the concept of economic efficiency" per se—a pattern found in many premodern societies.[3] Instead, politically inspired, "artificial" factors influenced what, where, and how the merchants could trade, undermining the potentially "natural" distribution pattern shaped by the factors related to supply and demand. Befitting the dictum of Karl Polanyi, Conrad M. Arensberg, and Harry W. Pearson that "the economy was embedded in the maze of social relationships,"[4] the Japanese merchants' success ultimately depended, not on such "economic" factors as the competitiveness of their goods vis-à-vis the final consumer, but rather on their ability to shape and cultivate the kind of social and political relations suitable for promoting the most advantageous "artificial" patterns of distribution. The Honai merchants were successful precisely because they excelled in this art.

The pattern of commerce in this era was fundamentally linked to the decentralized political structure in which multiple authorities—old and new—competed over the country's economic resources. Increasingly particularistic control exercised by each authority over each commodity, market, and road directly reflected this fragmented condition. But the practice of political control over nonagricultural economic sectors itself was age old, finding its origin in the centralized state system of the ancient period.[5] What was the nature of this control, and how was it transformed over half a millennium? An outline of this development will help to clarify the late medieval patterns of commodity circulation and the mode of trade adopted by entrepreneurial merchants.

The centralized government of the seventh and eighth centuries sought to control the country's economic resources and to regulate supply and distribution systems. It sponsored irrigation projects, developed land, allocated land to people, and collected taxes in kind, as well as set up metropolitan markets to exchange tax rice and other items to meet the demands of the capital's population. Government officials, who often had exclusive knowledge of high-level continental technology, operated certain workshops in the provinces, overseeing the production of quality handicrafts, which were then sent to the capital for state-controlled distribution.

By the tenth century, with the deterioration of the equal allotment program, reclamation projects increasingly fell into the hands of regional elites. Assuming the previous prerogatives of the state, these local developers obtained direct rights to the reclaimed land. But because they lacked the political influence to protect their new rights, they tended to commend a portion of their rights to prominent figures and institutions at the center. These acts of commendation underlay the trend toward the privatization and fragmentation of land rights that matured into the shōen structure. Central proprietors—including En-ryakuji—came to amass a large number of holdings in addition to the stipendiary and other tax-exempt land previously granted to them by the central government.

This new pattern contrasted with the earlier pattern in which the state held concentrated power over production, supply, and distribution. In shōen with hierarchically divided land rights, however, the absentee proprietor's hold over the local processes of production or division of labor tended to be weak, undermined by the direct control exercised by the local lords and the cultivators themselves. Largely responsible for this weakness was the land accumulation pattern; proprietors had been only passive recipients of commended rights to profits in the first place.

In lieu of direct control over local production processes, proprietors sought to assure the supply of necessary goods by, in a sense, buying out the services of artisans and purveyors with grants of tax-exempt land. To obtain goods not provided through this channel, they also set up new markets or sought to extend control over existing markets, which would then be tailored to meet their specific needs.

Proprietary involvement in the market economy intensified in the late Kamakura and Muromachi periods, the era that saw the rise of the sō village. General economic growth certainly played a part here, but equally important was the progressive attenuation of the proprietary hold on the agricultural sector. The rising level of productivity brought little increased benefit to the central authorities, for surplus tended to pass into the hands of local agents or upper-level peasants (myōshu), decreasing the relative percentage, if not the absolute quantity, channeled to the top. The kenmon's response to this situation was to participate actively in the commercial sector. By the late thirteenth century, proprietors found that the increased level of general commodity flow offered them a viable opportunity to diversify income and supplement the decreasing level of profit from agriculture. To tap into this new source, proprietors staked out claims to various facets of distribution—commodities, roads, markets, and so on—while concurrently forming patron-client relationships with specific groups of traders; the patron protected the rights of the traders with political power and social prestige, while the clients supplied goods and paid dues. Enryakuji, Honai's proprietor, for instance, set up seven toll stations along the west bank of Lake Biwa. Because each station was managed by a different organization within the temple, passing boats—whether commercial boats or boats transporting taxes—were required to pay a toll at every one of the stations. Only client groups with a proven toll-exempt status could duck payment. The profit for the collector was tremendous; in one year, one of the toll stations amassed 1,200 *kan* in cash.[6] Needless to say, the temple set up barriers at other points along the lake and inland.[7]

Meanwhile, manifesting the trend toward greater decentralization, local powers were also busy seizing the new economic opportunities that arose from the thirteenth century onward; they took control of trade and marketing, despite their lack of prestige and traditional authority.[8] Thus central and regional powers together affected the distribution pattern; they set up local markets and toll stations, charging dues and collecting tolls.

For the merchants of medieval Japan, then, impositions and restrictions at various points in their travels were an unavoidable fact of life. The situation worsened in the sixteenth century as the growing localism of the Warring period transformed commerce into an extension of the battlegrounds. The degree to which the authorities harassed merchants is vividly illustrated in the following case of barrier construction in the early 1500s.

The statement of the case comes from the Goka Merchants Federation, a group of merchants who were apparently the Honai merchants' competitors at this time. They described the situation in the early 1500s concerning the Kurihan-kaidō, the sole road connecting Imazu, on the lake's western shore, to Obama, on Wakasa Bay.

The Kutsuki family set up a barrier at Hosaka on behalf of the bakufu, but the Goka Merchants Federation petitioned and it was removed. Subsequently the merchants forwarded gifts. This was followed by the erection of a new barrier at Hosaka, [this time] by the Noto family. The merchants petitioned again and it was removed. As before, they forwarded gifts [to the Noto family]. At Ōsugi, the Awaya family set up a barrier on behalf of the bakufu, but it came to be removed through the efforts of Kutsuki's vassal named Iida Shinbei. Gifts were forwarded for this as before. A new barrier was set up at Hosaka by the Yokoyama, but it was taken down after the [Goka merchants'] petition. As before, gifts were forwarded. In 1498, the Hosaka barrier was reerected by an agent, named Tago Shinbei, of the Etchū family, but through the efforts of Tagoyasu, it was removed. Gifts were sent as before. In 1512, Kamisaka Sōzaemonnojō and Katsurada Yashichirō erected a new barrier at Oiwake, but this turned into an armed confrontation and the barrier was set on fire. Subsequently through Aeba Ōinosuke's mediation, and after we submitted horses, swords, and 36 *kan* in cash, the barrier was [finally] taken down.[9]

The number of barriers erected and reerected on this one road at Hosaka, Ōsugi, and Oiwake during the fifteenth and sixteenth centuries was prodigious. Here all barriers were set up by locally prominent warrior families. The Kutsuki, Noto, Yokoyama, and Etchū were branch families of the Sasaki and served as the area's jitō. The Awaya were the vassals of the deputy shugo of Wakasa Province, named Takeda, and Kamisaka and Katsurada were powerful families of Sakata County, in Ōmi. How did merchants deal with the situation? To have the barriers taken down, the organized merchants sometimes relied on connections, almost always forwarded gifts, and in one instance used outright violence.

The presence of barriers may not have altered the direction of commodity flow per se, since the Kurihan-kaidō provided the sole approach to Wakasa Bay from Imazu. However, the tolls may have discouraged passage by isolated merchants, thereby reducing the volume of merchants and commodities. The barriers tended to select the type of merchants who could use the road: merchants with large organizational strength, good connections, and group dynamism. The presence of barriers may also have fostered a tendency for specific commodities to travel particular roads, handled by a given set of toll-exempt merchants. Many barriers were short-lived, however, since they succumbed to the protests of local residents, merchants, or other authorities seeking to set up competing barriers.[10] Even in dismantling a barrier an authority usually made a profit, for gifts usually followed a plea for its removal. Ironically, in their attempts to beat the system, merchants also perpetuated the restrictive marketing system; they could conveniently apply such restrictions to competitors while guarding their own rights. Taking the credit for the removal of barriers, these merchants later sought to claim the road as theirs and to keep other merchants from using it. The act of removing the barriers gave the groups a proprietary right to the road and served as a basis for prohibiting road use by encroaching merchants.[11] Thus what was initially an obstacle in the end turned into an asset for enterprising merchants.

Some obstacles to the free flow of trade were not a product of intentional manipulation by the authorities or merchants. For instance, circumstantial road hazards (probably common in the Warring period) played an important part in diverting distributive channels, perhaps cutting off merchants from the most direct route for transporting a given commodity. Such was the problem encountered in the sixteenth century by the Edamura Merchants Collective, the sole distributor in Kyoto of the highly desired Mino paper. When an increase in military tensions paralyzed the section of road that connected Kyoto with the center of Mino paper production, Edamura merchants were forced to procure it elsewhere. But Edamura's new business conduct interfered with the interests of other merchant groups—the Honai Merchants

Collective in particular—which then retaliated. The ensuing conflict greatly weakened the Edamura merchants' previously unshaken dominance in the sale of this particular commodity, as will be detailed in the chapter to follow.

In these ways commodity distribution was bound by various layers of restrictions and rights. In this age of a rising economy with highly regulated mercantile opportunities, restricting others' rights and expanding one's own became the cardinal rule for commercial success. Both merchants and political authorities played this game, sometimes in collaboration, at other times with one as the other's pawn. But the ultimate goal of merchants was to survive and prosper in their complex environment. They therefore developed, as we shall see, forms of organization that would maximize their leverage in manipulating vertical social links as well as in penetrating market frontiers. The Honai merchants, in particular, built up two sources of strength. The first was the merchant sō, a collective and horizontal organization of the merchants in the four gō of the Lower-ho that greatly bolstered their competitiveness in planning and executing winning stratagems. The second was the patronage of Enryakuji, a commercially inclined kenmon with considerable authority and power, without which the execution of these stratagems would have been quite impossible. We will discuss how they turned their organizational strength and political connections into actual commercial profits in the next chapter. But our first task is to clarify the social and economic position of the Honai merchants by examining their origins, forms of organization, and relationship to the markets.

Medieval Merchants

Occupational categories in Japan were ill defined and quite flexible until the end of the sixteenth century, when the unifying powers began correlating commoners' occupations with rigidly and legally defined status categories. Therefore, *shōnin,* or merchants, in premodern Japan made up a diverse group, including urban- and rural-based, full- and part-time traders. Perhaps most typical were those like the Honai merchants, part-time traders and part-time cultivators. In fact, before the mid-fifteenth century the Honai merchants called themselves hyakushō, a term associated with being agriculturalists. Later they differentiated the terms *hyakushō* and *shōnin* to suit the context, suggesting, perhaps, an increasingly stronger consciousness of separate occupational categories as they engaged in both kinds of work.

As traders, however, they were not all similar or equal; they fit into differing categories that expressed their level and strength of organization, relationship to the authorities, and mode of trading.

The Origins of Medieval Merchants

Whence did the merchants come? In a predominantly agrarian but increasingly commercialized society, how inclined were rural peasants to get involved in the rising market economy? These questions, of scholarly interest for many times and places, have recently developed into a focus of intense debate. James C. Scott delineated the "moral peasant," who, chiefly concerned with the maintenance of security (i.e., subsistence), produced for markets only when self-sufficiency fell below the acceptable cultural level.[12] The "rational peasant" proposed by Samuel L. Popkin, on the other hand, was a risk taker who turned to markets for investment opportunities.[13] Evaluated against these two models, the Honai merchants appear to have embodied, at different chronological points in their development, characteristics associated with both types. In accordance with Scott's interpretation, the inability to maintain self-sufficiency in rice production may have induced Honai residents to turn to the market in the first place. By the fourteenth century, however, the lives of Tokuchin-ho residents were directly intertwined with the workings of a major market nearby, in the fashion of Popkin's schema. The market's proximity brought the residents into early contact with its mechanisms, which aided in transforming them into a group of rational and profit-oriented merchants. Furthermore, access to a network of markets in a broader region, connected by well-developed communication routes, augmented their mercantile outlook.

In examining the connection between the peasantry and markets, the major area of interest to Japanese historians since the 1930s has been, more specifically, the question of class formation: the emergence of the merchant class from the agricultural order of the shōen system. The main actor to be examined has been the myōshu stratum of peasants, who were increasingly likely to serve as a human link between agriculture and commerce. Just as these two sectors of the economy lacked a clear distinction, the myōshu as agriculturalists were easily assimilated into the newly expanding commercial structure. A variety of increasingly complex and nuanced arguments have emerged in this regard, though by no means resolving the question. The brief review of the literature that follows attempts to show how an answer is developing.

The place to begin is the prewar scholarship of Toyoda Takeshi and Shimizu Mitsuo, who, each in a different way, set the foundation for the discussion. To Toyoda, commercial practices growing out of the shōen economy fell under the control and supervision of the shōen proprietor and the warrior managers (jitō). Myōshu were responsible for the rise of commerce primarily in the peripheral regions, where such control was more diffused. In the capital region, the proprietary influence overrode the myōshu's enterprising character. There a combination of other factors stimulated market formation: demand and consumption by the shōen proprietors and the management of the agricultural and manufacturing sectors as well as the distribution of commodities by the small-peasant class—as opposed to the myōshu class. Likewise, while the peripheral regions saw the rise of the myōshu-type merchants, with their roots in the land, the capital region was dominated by itinerant merchants, who were anchored in the metropolitan area or its entrepôts.[14]

The role of the myōshu in stimulating shōen-based commerce was more direct and explicit in Shimizu Mitsuo's work. In the latter part of the Heian period, as the greater intensification of cultivation channeled surplus produce into the hands of a group of peasants, the peasantry came to be fragmented into two distinguishable classes: cultivators and myōshu. It was the myōshu who transformed surplus into commercial capital and stimulated the formation of rural markets. In consonance with his fundamental thesis that production and the daily life of medieval peasants took place outside the framework of the shōen, Shimizu emphasized the irrelevance of the economic structure fostered by the proprietor to the promotion of rural commerce. For Shimizu it was the "progressive" quality of the myōshu that advanced the local commercial economy.[15]

Postwar scholarship, built upon the interpretations of Shimizu and Toyoda, continued to stress the role of the myōshu. Methodologically, however, there was a new emphasis on the detailed analysis of land registers. Behind this trend lay Ishimoda Shō's influential work, *Chūseiteki sekai no keisei,* in which he assiduously analyzed the internal class structure of the shōen in order to understand its overall social and economic dynamics.[16] Along these lines, Sugiyama Hiroshi, for example, studied Niimi-no-shō (Bitchū Province) and found that those holding myōshu rights to land parcels of various sizes were the merchants who lived in the markets in the shōen. But commercial development in this estate rested on the combined interests of the proprietor (the temple Tōji), the shugo, the jitō, and the myōshu until the end of the fifteenth century.[17]

It was also in the postwar decades that the Imabori documents came to be examined in detail. As mentioned earlier, prior to the publication of the critical work by Wakita Haruko in 1960, many scholars, including Kumada Tōru, labored over local land registers, seeking the class origin of the local merchants. This process led to the confirmation of the rise of myōshu-cum-merchants with the breakdown of the old myō units of taxation in the late fourteenth and early fifteenth centuries.[18]

Following the lead of Kumada Tōru, other scholars also identified the new myōshu class with the class of merchants while elaborating and modifying the theme. Sasaki Gin'ya, for instance, espoused the idea of a pyramid-shaped organizational structure among the Honai merchants, while Kanamoto Masayuki stressed the horizontal relationships within the group.[19]

The publication of the work by Wakita Haruko in 1960 gave a new twist to the prevailing lines of argument. It may be recalled that Wakita brought to general attention the crucial limitations of the local sources, the sō documents showing the holdings of the shrine. Unlike the registers compiled by shōen proprietors, the sō documents in no way reflected the overall class character of the residents and certainly not the connection between the possession of land and the growth of the merchant class. The land registers in the Imabori collection, which dealt with no more than 15 percent of the total cultivated area, did not provide sufficient evidence to fully confirm the hypothesis that merchants were once myōshu peasants.[20]

Although Wakita conclusively invalidated the methodology previously used to examine the class structure in Tokuchin-ho, an additional piece of evidence nonetheless tended to confirm a link between the myōshu and the Honai merchants. The Honai merchants' appeal to Enryakuji, dated 1427, contesting a claim of the Obata merchants was duly signed by "[Honai] myōshu hyakushō."[21] The appeal testifies, then, that in the first part of the fifteenth century, the Honai merchants were represented by the myōshu in communicating with the proprietor. It also demonstrates that at this time, these merchants regarded themselves first and foremost as myōshu and only secondarily as merchants. The division of labor had not developed to the point of segmenting society into discrete occupational categories. The local elites were involved both in agriculture and commerce.

Merchants in Trade Associations (Za)

Best known among Japan's medieval merchants are those organized into za, a form of trade association whose linguistic origin is "seat" (as in miyaza, shrine association), a meaning expanded to imply "a seating order" or "the right to a seat."[22] The merchants in each trade association collectively possessed the right to a "seat" in markets, where they could set up stalls and sell their commodities. Their strategic goal was the expansion of their commercial rights—to distribute greater volume (and often varieties) of commodities at a greater number of markets. Some za merchants were known for their exclusive right to deal in a specific commodity over a wide region.

In their collective organization and exclusive goals, the za resembled guilds or *Zunfts* of medieval Europe. But there were some fundamental differences as well. As Toyoda Takeshi points out, the Japanese za was heavily dependent on the patronage and protection of an authority for the maintenance of its trading rights and privileges.[23] Unlike the Western guilds, which stood for urban liberty in opposition to the traditional relations with authority, the Japanese za was a direct product of the shōen system, still embedded in the characteristically hierarchical ties between subjects and proprietors.[24]

A notable characteristic of medieval trade associations, then, was their close tie with their sponsoring institutions. This feature suggests elements of historical continuity from the earlier, noncommercial form of za, which Wakita Haruko calls the service za.[25] The service za, dominant in the late Heian period, was specific to the capital region, and it mainly purveyed labor to the patron, for carrying palanquins, for example, or maintaining the shrine premises. In return for their service, the members of the za received tax-exempt land. The tie binding the service za to the patron was personal in nature. In comparison, the relationship between the commercial za—the type more relevant to the Honai merchants—and the patron was more economic in character; the za paid dues to the proprietor in return for protection and privileges, such as exemption from tolls and market fees.[26] Axiomatic to both types of za, however, was their dependence on the authority for measures of economic relief and protection.

The commercial za became prevalent starting in the late fourteenth century. One could be found in nearly every major trading center.[27] Despite their links to the authorities, the commercial za was not created by the authorities but arose from below. Merchants with a history—whether actual or fabricated—of dealing in a particular product at a certain market came to form a za for that specific product and at that market. To protect their trading rights and to enhance the social status of their organization, these merchants leaned on the prestige of their patron.

In documents we recognize za merchants by their territorial name as well as by the specific commodity they traded—paper, salt, or fish, for example. There seems to have been no convention as to the number of za (that is, the number of commodities) a particular merchant group could deal in. Some were known for only one za, while others had a great many. Records show that the Honai merchants had za for cloth, salt, paper, and, later, horses. In contrast, one of the Honai group's competitors, the Yokozeki merchants, seems to have had a cloth za only.

The right of a za to occupy market seats in the late fifteenth and sixteenth centuries tended to be specific to each market, each market being under the control of a specific political authority. This pattern reflected the increase in the number of markets and in the number of authorities seeking revenues from commercial sources. Although the Honai merchants had a salt za, they could not trade in salt at every market. The developing norm was for each merchant group to make arrangements for each market and for each commodity severally.

Some za merchants had a home market—Yokozeki merchants had Yokozeki market; Edamura merchants, Edamura market, for instance. But they traded at other markets as well, as their goal was expansion. Conversely, a large market, such as Uji Yamada of Ise Province, had no "home" merchants but accommodated outside za merchants dealing in as many as twelve commodities: tofu, iron kettles, oil, utensils, hemp, sake, fish, malt, paper, rice, cloth, and prepared sardines.[28] The goal of organized medieval merchants was to penetrate as many markets as possible with a wide range of goods.

The Honai Merchants

The Honai Merchant Collective was composed of merchants from the Field Side, the lower four gō in Tokuchin-ho. They traveled in a group, some with packhorses and some on foot. Many carried a pack-staff on their shoulders with a load at each end.[29] They were also armed, for violent altercations with other merchant groups were frequent, as the next chapter will illustrate.

The precise number of Honai merchants for any given time is unknown, but a mid-fifteenth-century count of Imabori merchants found 34.[30] Assuming some 60 to 80 households in the village as a whole,[31] less than half the adult male population was listed as merchants on this occasion. In practice, the merchant collective of Honai must have represented a substantially larger number of persons, and it seems possible that nearly all village males engaged in commerce at some time and in some capacity.

Internally, the Honai merchants were ranked into horse-owning merchants (*uma-no-shū*) and foot merchants (*kachi-no-shū*). This distinction was formalized by rules and regulations. A regulation estimated to date between the late fifteenth and early sixteenth centuries prohibited foot merchants from carrying goods on horseback for one generation. Violation of this rule would lead to confiscation of the merchandise by the Honai merchants' sō.[32] Although not strictly ruled out, status mobility was discouraged by the Honai sō. This was obviously an attempt to ensure the dominant economic position of the more wealthy as well as stabilize, by extension, the local political and social structure they dominated. The regulation also points up the desire to maintain a numerical balance between the two groups. Another regulation with probably a similar intent stipulated that on commercial expeditions one of every two merchants had to go on foot.[33] The Honai merchants may have found that, in order to maximize profits, it was important to minimize the cost en route by limiting the number of horses and thereby the amount of feed consumed and, occasionally, the payment of tolls levied on pack animals. Another reason for the numerical restriction might have been to assure an appropriate balance between the number of available hands at markets and the quantity of goods carried.

These regulations tell us of a desire for balance, but not the actual ratio between the two groups. The following piece of evidence suggests that merchants with mounts were in the majority, however. In 1454, 34 Honai merchants traveled to Ise, a major Honai trading area. En route, at a shrine near Kōzubata, they paid fees for the privilege of harvesting wisteria (used to make eating utensils) from a hill behind Fujikiriyama Shrine. On the payment record, a total of 22 people were listed as having horses and 12 as being on foot.[34]

How the ownership of horses (or oxen) related to the possession of land or what role it played in determining one's position within the local class or status structure are important questions for which documentation is inadequate to answer. Most scholars, including Wakita Haruko, however, assert that horse (or oxen) owners held a dominant position in both the Honai sō and the Imabori sō.[35] This suggests a social structure that was top-heavy and that paralleled the shape suggested by the miyaza organization. Expanding the question further, we might inquire into the relationship between the horse-owning merchants and the myōshu peasants. It may be recalled that it was myōshu hyakushō who appealed to Enryakuji in the commercial dispute of 1427. Can we assume that they were horse-owning merchants? Conversely, can we assume that foot merchants were not of myōshu status? These are questions for which there are no ready answers. The available evidence is too thin to definitively equate the two seemingly upper-level local groups: myōshu and horse owners. But it is a tempting hypothesis.

As a group, the merchants from Tokuchin-ho were known generally as the "Honai merchants" but often as well as by terms indicating commodity-specific groups within the collective, such as the "Honai cloth za merchants," or the "Tokuchin-ho salt merchants."[36] Such nomenclature should not be taken to imply internal divisions along commodity lines, however. It was commonly used to emphasize to outsiders the Honai merchants' right to deal in that commodity, especially in the context of trials.

Because the Honai merchants' original trading sphere stretched over the Suzuka Mountains in the direction of Ise, they were also known as yamagoe ("over-the-pass") merchants. The organizational structure of the yamagoe merchants is little understood, but from a 1518 expense account we know that in the sixteenth century they included merchants from Yōkaichi (specifically, Kanaya) and Mitsuya (located in Haneda-no-shō) in addition to those from Nakano, Imazaike, Kobochizuka, Koimazaike, Hebimizo, and Imabori in Tokuchin-ho. These merchants were grouped by village, each of which paid dues to a collective entity (confusingly) called "the *shō*." Here, Imabori was unique in that it collected dues "from the shō" instead of paying dues into it, reflecting its superior, managerial position over the other units of the yamagoe shō.[37]

In addition to the village-based fee, each individual over-the-pass merchant submitted fees—not to the yamagoe shō—but to the yamagoe sō. The functional difference between the sō and the shō is unclear. We may speculate that individuals made up the sō, and villages, the shō. Imabori and its merchants seem to have assumed a leadership role in both, probably collecting fees as well.[38]

The yamagoe sō promulgated internal codes to regulate the members' behavior. Most of the regulations were aimed at increasing competitiveness by promoting frugality, avoiding risk, and protecting the sō's reputation. To be frugal, each yamagoe merchant was to take one stove and one horse. If there were two merchants, one was to go on foot. To avoid risk, the use of credit was prohibited.[39] To protect the sō's reputation, "regardless of right or wrong, anyone who draws a sword and injures another at a market" or "who draws a sword or carries a stick and beats people or gets involved in fights on the road or at ports" was to be prohibited from trading. To establish credibility, "anyone who gets complaints about an insufficiency of goods after closing a sale at a market" was also forbidden to trade.[40]

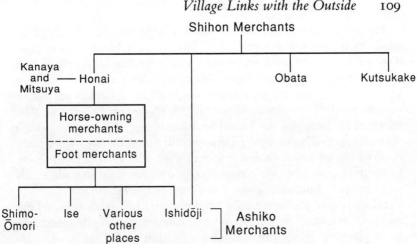

Fig. 2. Organization of the Honai merchants.

The Honai merchants were also a part of a larger federation called the Shihon ("four original") Merchants Federation. This federation included merchants from Tokuchin-ho, Obata, Kutsukake, and Ishidōji (see Figure 2). In function, they were all over-the-pass merchants; they traded to and from Ise by way of the Happū-kaidō and the Chigusa-kaidō.[41] Although the four merchant groups traveled the same routes, there is no evidence of collaboration. Indeed, far from working together, the Honai merchants engaged in violent disputes with Obata and Ishidōji merchants. Why did they carry a collective identification tag? The Shihon Merchants Federation was an umbrella for those Ōmi merchants who had the right to trade in Ise. It served as a license once they were in the region over and beyond the mountain pass.

Ashiko Merchants

At the bottom rung in the Honai merchants' organization were the *ashiko* ("leg children"), who lived outside Tokuchin-ho. Higuchi Setsuo characterizes them as itinerant merchants subordinate to and lower in social status than the za merchants. Ashiko served as assistants to the za merchants, carrying their merchandise and giving a hand in selling and buying at markets. They also traded, independently or in small groups, in villages scattered between market towns; and despite the implication of their name, they often did so on horseback.[42] They probably carried a proof of affiliation that gave them the same exemption privilege at toll barriers as the one held by the za merchants. For this prerogative, they submitted an annual fee (usually 400 *mon* per group) to their parent za merchant group.

The Honai merchants subordinated a large number of ashiko in many locations. The nature of the affiliation varied from case to case. Two ashiko groups about which we know more than we do others will serve as contrasting illustrations. The first group was from Ishidōji, a village located about 4 kilometers southeast of Tokuchin-ho and, it may be recalled, a member of the Shihon Merchants Federation. The relationship between the Honai merchants and the Ishidōji ashiko was complex. The vertical relationship between the two apparently evolved out of Ishidōji's defeat in a dispute with Honai. In the early fifteenth century, the two groups fought over the right to trade in salt and seaweed. Enryakuji judged in favor of the Honai merchants in 1418, thereafter prohibiting the Ishidōji merchants from encroaching on Honai's rights.[43] By the late fifteenth century, the Ishidōji merchants were pledging an exclusive ashiko affiliation with Honai; they acknowledged the receipt of four horses from Honai and the reciprocal obligation to submit 400 *mon* of annual dues (nengu). Honai also had the authority to define the volume of goods to be carried by Ishidōji on each trip: no more than two loads per horse or eight loads altogether.[44] Finally, Honai interfered with Ishidōji's attempt to expand its marketing sphere; upon Honai's request in 1528, the Rokkaku shugo's vassals denied Ishidōji entry into the Yokozeki and Mabuchi markets.[45]

The second group of ashiko lived in Shimo-Ōmori, a village in the Upper-ho with better irrigation and thus higher agricultural productivity than villages in the Lower-ho. Initially the Shimo-Ōmori ashiko had been associated with both Hebimizo and Imabori, but sometime in the early sixteenth century they limited their affiliation to Imabori. Apparently, Shimo-Ōmori had been paying an ashiko fee of 400 *mon* each to Hebimizo and Imabori. Under the new arrangement, Shimo-Ōmori paid 800 *mon* to Imabori and nothing to Hebimizo, probably because Imabori had become dominant in the Honai Merchants Collective. Instead of keeping the doubled fee, Imabori in turn forwarded 400 *mon* to Hebimizo. In 1535, Imabori settled accounts with Hebimizo once and for all by giving the latter a vegetable plot 4 *semachi* in size and canceling the annual payments.[46] Thus, Imabori in a sense bought the exclusive right to the Shimo-Ōmori ashiko.

The ashiko of Ishidōji and Shimo-Ōmori differed greatly in their manner of affiliation with the parent merchant group. For the former, the relationship of subordination derived from a defeat in a dispute, and the affiliation was exclusively with Honai merchants. Apart from this vertical tie, Ishidōji and Honai were both equally recognized as members of a larger federation of Ise-bound merchants. In contrast, Shimo-Ōmori's affiliation was not with Honai but specifically with Hebimizo and Imabori, and the ashiko paid fees separately to each of them until Imabori became their sole "parent" sometime in the sixteenth century. How Shimo-Ōmori came to have a group of ashiko in the first place eludes us. But we can speculate that the relationship between Imabori and Shimo-Ōmori was one of utilitarian dependency between an expanding merchant group in need of assistants and nearby peasants in search of a secondary source of income.

In addition to these two groups, the Honai merchants' ashiko, according to one undated list, numbered some 143 persons spread over 36 places in Ōmi and nine places in Ise, all within about 8 kilometers of Tokuchin-ho and along the three major roads to Ise—strategic locations for transporting merchandise. These ashiko were called "horse [*uma*] ashiko" and carried "seaweed, salt, and 110 other items" to and from Ise and to other areas where the Honai merchants held marketing rights[47] (see Map 4).

Some ashiko residing in Ise Province were also affiliated with the greater Shihon Merchants Federation. Apparently, the Honai merchants were not always aware of the number and whereabouts of their ashiko. In an apparent response to an inquiry by Honai concerning the distribution of ashiko, an Ise man believed to be Honai's trade associate listed eighteen men residing in eleven places in Ise. This number, according to his statement of the mid-sixteenth century, "had been reduced by about 30 since the time of my grandfather."[48]

The large number and wide distribution of ashiko serving the Imabori, Honai, and Shihon merchants testify to the scale of the Honai merchants' commercial endeavors. At the same time, they reveal the significant role ashiko played in the structure of medieval commerce. They were certainly not unique to Honai; Owaki merchants, for instance, had six ashiko living in Takebe,[49] and the Goka Merchants Federation, Honai's major competitor in the sixteenth century, had ashiko whose status as such derived from a "traditionally established right [*yuisho*]."[50]

Needless to say, ashiko were not their own free agents. The restrictions that applied to their parent za merchants also applied to the ashiko, just as the established rights of the former were the source of the latter's trading privileges. In the aftermath of a victorious dispute with the Obata merchants in the fifteenth century, for instance, the Honai merchants had an authorization from the deputy shugo (Iba) to confiscate goods carried by the Obata merchants' ashiko in case of a violation of marketing territory.[51]

The ashiko merchants differed from the za merchants in a number of ways. Unlike the za merchants, ashiko were known by their individual

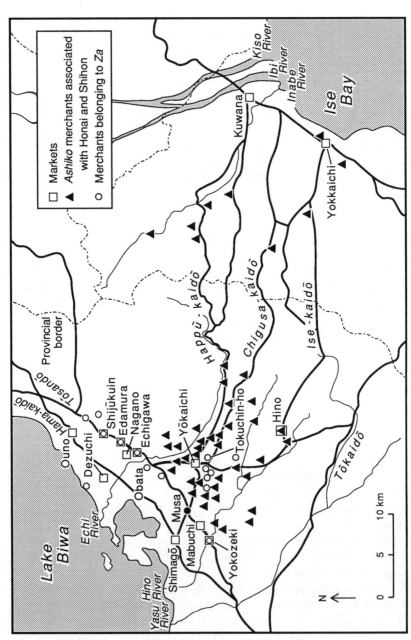

Map 4. Markets and merchants in eastern Ōmi. Adapted from *YS*, II: 354–55, fig. 30.

Legend:
- □ Markets
- ▲ *Ashiko* merchants associated with Honai and Shihon
- ○ Merchants belonging to *Za*

names and locations, not just by their territorial identity. When they traveled, they probably did so independently, or perhaps in small groups of two or three, again unlike the za merchant collectives. The za, with its political connections, dominated the markets, while ashiko served as distributing agents in nonmarket villages, thereby permeating the lower tiers of the economy still uninfiltrated by more direct political influences. How ashiko and the parent merchant group divided (if they did) the commercial profits has gone, alas, undocumented. At any rate, ashiko constituted a crucial component not only in the Honai merchants' entrepreneurial organization but also in the overall structure of the medieval economy.

Markets

Markets (*ichi*) of medieval Japan were rarely continuous institutions. They were, instead, periodic, held at regular intervals, typically three times monthly. Japan's periodic markets began to appear frequently in the eleventh and twelfth centuries and quickly multiplied during the thirteenth.[52] As in other parts of the world, these markets tended to develop where people gathered and relative safety prevailed. Areas in front of temples and shrines were favored early on for the exchange of goods. People also tended to bring salable items to the space around an estate's administrative offices or to points of collection for tax grain. Nodes of transportation, such as major road intersections or river fords, naturally invited commercial exchange.[53]

In the vicinity of Tokuchin-ho along the Tōsandō, a major thoroughfare leading to the capital, some of the markets originated as travelers' stopping places (*shuku*). Such was the case with Shijūkuin, Echigawa, and Shimagō,[54] although other stopovers, including Owaki and Musa, did not turn into markets.[55] The growth of Yokozeki market depended on its peculiar geographical situation. Yokozeki was located where the Tōsandō crossed the Hino River. Before the days of permanent bridges, Yokozeki provided boats or temporary bridges to travelers and charged transport fees.[56] The market grew here, where people had to stop, where they congregated and waited for passage across the river.

The economic and social functions of markets were many and varied. People bought items not produced at home and sold items with exchange or cash value. Medieval market towns provided a setting in which to socialize with acquaintances or observe people of different classes and statuses. They also offered a great deal in the way of entertainment. Itinerant lute (*biwa*) players may have plucked and sung, drawing onlookers' imaginations into famous scenes of the past. "Sacred" female singers may have sat on their straw mats spinning out fantastic tales of hell to stimulate the religious awe of passersby, while a monkey dance may have brightened the day for many others.[57] Finally, markets expressed the relationship of exchange between this world and the world beyond. Markets were a junction of two realms, the secular and the sacred, a point of temporal and spatial connection. The term *ichi,* which stands for both "priestesses" and "markets," metonymically joined the two worlds and symbolically assured the continuum between the two. Priestesses regularly intoned prayers at ceremonies held at markets, giving a concrete expression to the hope for the perpetuation of this continuum.[58]

For medieval villagers, then, markets served as the locus of tremendous opportunity and excitement outside their immediate microcommunity. Yōkaichi proved to be no exception for the residents of Tokuchin-ho.

The Market Town: Yōkaichi

The fundamental factor contributing to the growth of the Honai merchants was local geography, which placed the residents within intimate reach of the major channels of distribution. Imabori had two roads connecting it to markets near and far. One began just behind the shrine and led northward to Yōkaichi. About 200 meters west of the shrine ran another road, which led straight north and south. Both of them were called Ichi-michi, or Market Road. By the mid-fourteenth century the second had become the most important road in Imabori. It acquired the names Nishi-ōmichi ("big road to the west") and Ise-michi ("road to Ise"), which together denoted its location in Imabori, its breadth, and its ultimate destination, as the name Ichi-michi suggested its linkage to a market.[59] Tokuchin-ho residents traveled Ichi-michi regularly to attend nearby markets; for the Honai merchants, it was the first leg in their journeys to meet commercial challenges in the surrounding regions (see Map 3).

A short walk north on Ichi-michi, for 2 kilometers or so, brought an Imabori villager to Yōkaichi, the market adjoining Tokuchin-ho. Literally "the day 8 market," Yōkaichi was a periodic market set up on the eighth, eighteenth, and twenty-eighth of each month. As the years passed, it was held with greater frequency. We know that by 1749, it was held on the days of the month ending in 8 or 2. In 1881, it began to be held on the days ending in 2, 5, or 8, that is, nine times a month.[60]

The exact date of origin for Yōkaichi is unclear. Yōkaichi's own history holds that the market was established as early as 665, though there is no documentary evidence to support such a claim.[61] We know that it predates the mid-thirteenth century because the *Genpei seisuiki,* a war tale completed in the 1240s, mentions Yōkaichi.[62] The establishment of Yōkaichi undoubtedly preceded the rise of the Honai merchants.

More controversial than the date of origin is its precise location.[63] Scholarly dispute has focused on the account appearing in the *Genpei seisuiki.* Responding to a call to arms by Minamoto Yoritomo in 1180, Sasaki Shirō Takatsuna was hurrying on foot from Kyoto to Izu, but en route he confiscated a horse from one Kinosuke, a traveler heading to "Yōkaichi in Owaki, Gamō County."[64] This short phrase located Yōkaichi inside Owaki, which contradicted the historians' general opinion that Owaki and Yōkaichi were separate territorial units. Nakagawa Senzō resolved the inconsistency by asserting a transfer of "the day 8 market" out of Owaki to what came to be known as Yōkaichi at a later time.[65] Others eschewed attaching much meaning to the *Genpei seisuiki* entry and simply attributed the statement to the greater contemporary fame of Owaki.[66]

Evidence found in the Imabori documents, however, adds further complexity to this problem, for it shows Yōkaichi to overlap territorially with two estates: Tokuchin-ho to the south and Takebe-no-shō to the north.[67] After combining this information with the phrase in the *Genpei seisuiki* and reexamining the map, one arrives at the conclusion that Yōkaichi was situated at the junction of a number of territorial units under various authorities: Tokuchin-ho and Takebe-no-shō under Enryakuji, Kaki-no-misono under the Konoe family, and Owaki-gō under the Rokkaku. Moreover, Yōkaichi straddled two administrative districts—Gamō and Kanzaki counties. Finally, it was situated at the meeting place of two different agricultural worlds: the wet-rice culture of Kanzaki County and the dry-legume culture of Gamō County.[68]

Yoshida Toshihiro has reinterpreted the theoretical significance of this situation. To him, the overlapping locational character of Yōkaichi signified a concrete spatial manifestation of muen (separation from worldly norms; nonattachment), a concept, already mentioned in Chapter 2, that is of crucial importance in understanding medieval Japanese society. Geographical locations characterized by muen had unclear political and territorial affiliations and were often situated at the borders of territorial units. Such places, according to Amino Yoshihiko, tended to attract people and eventually to grow into medieval towns.[69] According to Yoshida, building his interpretation on Amino's theory, Yōkaichi was a place of muen, a space lacking clear political affiliation to any one authority.[70] The location of Yōkaichi, at the intersection of a number of different borders, indeed seems to have fostered the growth of a market. Yōkaichi was a market that grew up "naturally," in accordance with the economic and social needs of the local people, in contradistinction to the "artificial" markets planned by authorities.

The major market within a radius of 7–8 kilometers, Yōkaichi was a conveniently located common social and economic space, shared by residents of various territorial and political affiliations.[71] It was a center of commodity circulation, source of artisanal talent, and locus of capital accumulation. Merchants from various places had stalls at Yōkaichi. Imabori documents mention merchants from Obata and Yokozeki (located on the Tōsandō) and, of course, Tokuchin-ho.[72] But access by others is suggested by the passage in the *Genpei seisuiki*. Merchants and artisans initially gathered there on market days only, but by at least the mid-fifteenth century they had established themselves permanently, turning Yōkaichi into a town of merchant and artisan settlements. One area called Kanaya ("metalsmith area"), which overlapped with Tokuchin-ho, was particularly known for its blacksmiths.[73] Two smiths of Yōkaichi, probably residing in Kanaya, cast the bell for Imabori's Jūzenji shrine in 1484.[74] Permanent occupational specialization was clearly taking place and was transforming the urban landscape.

Talent found in Yōkaichi was often exported to areas beyond. Two builders from Yōkaichi erected a shrine in Mabuchi, west of Yōkaichi on the Tōsandō. In reaching out to other areas, local artisans sometimes collaborated with artisans in other market towns. A carpenter of Yōkaichi and a carpenter of Musa, as well as three helpers—two residing in Yōkaichi and another in Hino—built a holy palanquin for the same shrine in Mabuchi in 1493.[75]

Wealth and capital accumulated in Yōkaichi, at least among some resident merchants. A piece of indirect evidence testifies to this. In 1492, a fish merchant's home in Yōkaichi was broken into by a leading warrior in Ashikaga Yoshitane's army. The warrior searched the house and seized and carried away 500 *kanmon* in cash to his headquarters in Azuchi.[76] Such a large sum of money clearly implies prosperity. Needless to say, communities served by Yōkaichi benefited from its economic and human resources.

Outbound and Beyond

A network of communication routes made Yōkaichi accessible in a number of directions. Two roads led to the lake and, via its passage by water, to western Ōmi and, beyond, to Wakasa Province. Before reaching the lake, these roads merged with the Tōsandō, at Obata to the north and at Musa to the south. The Tōsandō tied eastern Ōmi to Echizen and Mino provinces in the north and east, as well as to Kyoto in the southwest.

Two other roads extended toward the eastern mountain range, which marked the provincial border between Ōmi and Ise. One was the Happū-kaidō, which ran alongside the Echi River, over the mountains and down through Ise Province. Its destination was Kuwana, a major port and market town near Ise Bay. Another road out of Yōkaichi traversed Tokuchin-ho (where it was called Ichi-michi, Nishi-ōmichi, or Ise-michi, as mentioned above) and split into the Chigusa-kaidō and Ise-kaidō. Of these two, the Chigusa-kaidō roughly paralleled the Happū-kaidō, and both offered direct but steep access to Ise; going over the Suzuka mountain pass into Ise required an ascent of 900 meters over about 25 kilometers. The Ise-kaidō, in contrast, provided a more circuitous approach to Ise Bay, but one with two advantages. It passed through Hino, the only major market on the Ise side of Yōkaichi. It also provided a less strenuous though more lengthy approach to Ise: taking the Ise-kaidō to Hino, the traveler went southward (instead of eastward) and met the Tōkaidō, which crossed the pass at a low elevation of 300 meters. While the distance to Kuwana was approximately 50 to 55 kilometers on the Happū-, Chigusa-, and Ise-kaidō, this last approach was over 70 kilometers long. From the viewpoint of Tokuchin-ho merchants, the traffic on the lakeside routes differed considerably from the traffic on the interior routes. The geographical distribution of markets vividly reflected this difference (see Maps 4 and 5).

Regional Markets

The mountainous hinterland of Tokuchin-ho, with its sparse population, supported only one market, Hino, between Tokuchin-ho and Ise. In comparison, the lakeside, an important supply route for the capital region, hosted a number of markets, both along the Tōsandō and closer to the lake (along the Hama-kaidō, in part). These markets were differentiated in status. According to early-sixteenth-century information, Nagano market, located about 12 kilometers from Yōkaichi on the Tōsandō, was called the "parent market [*oyaichi*]." It was probably the very first market to be established in the region, and it subsequently provided a model for organizing business and merchants. According to the same source, a magistrate of Echi County (Tairō Narikiyo) constructed Nagano market to be like Miwa market, located

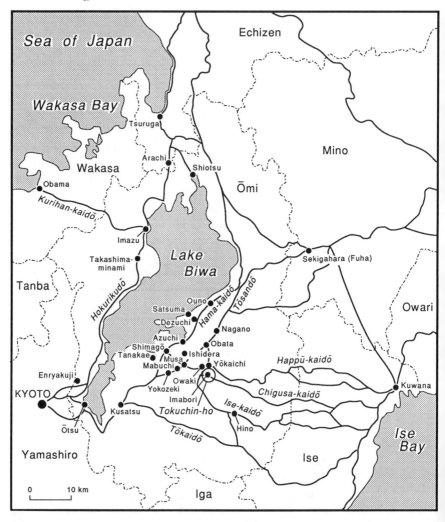

Map 5. Major roads in Ōmi Province. Adapted from *YS,* II: 369, fig. 32.

in Yamato Province and known to be Japan's earliest. Although not necessarily reliable, a reference to its construction in the ancient period suggests the length of Nagano market's history. Nagano was a "day 1 market," meeting on the first, eleventh, and twenty-first of each month.[77]

Nagano market opened on the eleventh day of the first month each year with appropriate ritual observances. The ceremonies were intended to invite good fortune and reinforce the structure of privilege and obligation in which participating merchants were involved. Seated in an assigned order and dressed in formal outfits, the merchants with stall privileges (za merchants) decorated the market with pine ornaments and paid respect to the market deity, or *ichigami*.[78] At Miwa, Nagano's possible model, a similar ceremony took place on the sixth day of the first month.[79]

In contradistinction to the "parent market," markets on both sides of Nagano along the Tōsandō were called the "new markets" (*shin'ichi*). Echigawa was to the south; Edamura and Shijūkuin to the north. New markets crowded the Tōsandō, situated at intervals of less than 3 kilometers. They undoubtedly emerged in the late medieval period, when commercial traffic along the Tōsandō flourished.

Additional markets in the region included Ouno and Dezuchi, near the lake along the Hama-kaidō. Situated side by side, Mabuchi and Yokozeki markets were to the south of Obata and Musa on the Tōsandō. Shimagō market was located only a few kilometers away from Mabuchi but across the plain, on the Hama-kaidō.[80] Markets were dense along the 20 kilometer stretch of the lake's eastern coast. Being set away from the Tōsandō itself, Yōkaichi held a unique position; while benefiting from the volume of traffic, Yōkaichi had the advantage of being the sole gateway to Ise (see Maps 4 and 5).

The density of markets on the lake's eastern plain raises questions about their survival and, consequently, the nature of the economic organization in which the Honai merchants operated. Classic central-place theory posits that the relative location, size, and hierarchical arrangement among markets are determined in proportion to the level of demand, which is based on the distribution of population and competitive relations within the market economy.[81] How do we explain the presence of so many markets at such close intervals? Was the regional demand high enough to support them all?

Sources give no information on the regional population or level of demand. But a combination of several other factors helps to explain this proliferation. First, the periodicity of markets—"day 1" at Nagano, "day 5" at Echigawa, "day 8" at Yōkaichi, for instance—allowed a far greater density in market distribution than continuous markets would have allowed, as G. William Skinner has pointed out.[82] By staggering the market days, competition for the region's net demand was reduced, for each market could attract a percentage of potential buyers.

Second, in terms of sales, most markets were open only to recognized merchant groups, which handled an approved set of commodities. Therefore, each market made available only what the market's za merchants handled. Fulfillment of one's consumption needs may have required visits to more than one market, to purchase salt at market A and cloth at market B, for instance. Even if the market authority desired the sale of a greater variety of commodities, this was not always possible, because restrictions on other aspects of distribution—such as road use or the procurement of goods—were also in play.

Third, irrespective of market forces, consumer demand, or the convenience of the merchants, the fragmented authority structure of the late medieval period tended to foster a profusion of markets. Each political authority sought to incorporate a market into its sphere of control in order to have its own supply station and to accrue income in the form of market dues collected from merchants. The proliferation of markets alone, therefore, did not necessarily reflect the net volume of commodities in circulation or the level of demand for commodities. Classic central-place theory needs to be modified to take political circumstances into account in addition to the periodicity of market days. At any rate, these centers of trade were the structural medium through which the za merchants engaged in the act of trade. Whether concentrated or dispersed, they represented the physical target indispensable for the merchants' economic goal.

The rise of Tokuchin-ho residents to the status of successful merchants happened in a period of burgeoning economic expansion that offered new commercial opportunities to people of all classes—central political authorities, provincial warriors, and villagers alike. The Honai residents' background proved highly suited to the seizure of these opportunities. The proximity of a major market and well-developed transportation routes, combined with the paucity of agricultural yields, induced their involvement in the market economy. The proprietor, mercenary in its own right, no doubt encouraged the development of this alternative occupation for revenue purposes of its own.

Merchants found the path to success a complicated one, for they were not free to trade as they desired. The structure of commerce largely meshed with the decentralized political order, in which major and minor authorities all regulated various aspects of commodity circulation to their own advantage. The wide-scale involvement of authorities resulted in a pattern of distribution often arranged in accordance with their motives, rather than one that reflected the existing structure of supply and demand. Markets and transportation routes easily fell under the control of authorities who sorted out "their" merchants from others and manipulated commodity movements through the mechanism of patronage and exclusion.

Resourceful merchants confronted this situation less by fighting it than by assimilating into it. They functioned as a lower extension of the mechanism of political control over commerce by serving a patron as za merchants. Following this strategy, rural residents organized themselves into collectives with high internal solidarity, inducing the authorities to grant certain mercantile prerogatives. Only through group solidarity and careful organization could merchants—with no political prestige of their own—work with the authorities to reshape the restrictions to their own liking. The structure of the Honai merchants' organization included various layers of affiliations—including the subordinate ashiko—that served to augment their entrepreneurial power. Relying on the collective discipline and strength that derived from the sō, the Honai merchants successfully accommodated to the late medieval commercial structure with its complex, shifting political nuances. How they managed their relations with rising or declining authorities, and how they competed with rival groups similar to themselves, forms the subject of the next chapter.

CHAPTER FIVE

The Assertion of Commercial Interests

THE HISTORY OF the Honai merchants is a shining example of a commercial success story in premodern Japan. Starting from a modest base, the Honai merchants carved out their territorial niche bit by bit. A key to their success was their keen awareness of the prevailing political and social values that shaped commercial practices. Adapting themselves to these values and re-creating them in their own language, they circumvented restrictions and overcame competitors that lay on their path.

Central to their entrepreneurial activities was the series of disputes and accompanying adjudication processes that always—at least according to the papers they preserved—ended in their favor. Dating from the first quarter of the fifteenth through the late sixteenth centuries, the records of disputes and subsequent resolutions delineate the Honai merchants' concrete goals and strategies, their interactions with the authorities and the values and principles underscoring their expansionist outlook. The records also bring into relief the changing social and political climate, which greatly tested these merchants' perspicacity and adaptability.[1]

The Honai Merchants' Mode of Operation

In the presence of frequent warfare, under conditions where naked military force wielded the greatest material power, late medieval Japanese society tenaciously held onto a brand of traditionalism that honored established practice and ancient prestige tied to the kenmon, the proprietary institutions in the capital.[2] Speaking in a modern context, Clifford Geertz has suggested that the replacement of an old political order by a precarious new one accentuates the need "for a new symbolic framework in terms of which to formulate, think about, and react to political problems" and that this need for a framework takes the form of a search for an ideology, including some variety of re-constructed traditionalism.[3] Faced with extreme decentralization and an accompanying sense of disorientation, late medieval Japanese also sought to justify their actions in the traditionalist vocabulary, which may have provided an illusion of stability and continuity. Honai's patron, a kenmon of stature, dating back to the Heian period, was both a source and a defender of traditionalist values. In their own proud words, the Honai merchants were the "merchants of the kenmon,"[4] who operated in a tradition-based niche to advance their commercial goals.

The tenacity of traditionalism in mercantile activities expressed itself most vividly in the contemporary term *yuisho,* whose meaning ranged from "lineage" and "legacy" to "historical precedent." In its contemporary usage among merchants, *yuisho* contrasted with *shingi* (innovation) and implied a socially recognized tie between a merchant group and a particular market, marketing region, commodity, or, perhaps, transport route. Merchants with yuisho enjoyed trading rights in those areas that were well established and thus legitimate. Conversely, merchants without yuisho committed the social crime of "innovation" in seeking to expand their trading sphere. A record of past practice justified today's trading activity; history legitimated the present.

Had the logic behind yuisho overridden all other norms and values, the commercial world and merchant society would have frozen into a status quo. Strict adherence to the dictates of yuisho would have eliminated the possibility of a new crop of merchants gaining marketing shares, or even of an old group expanding its practice. In actuality, of course, the expanding economy of the age proved flexible and accommodating to the rise of upstarts. Political situations in which authorities competed over commercial profits also promoted continual readjustments in the distribution of rights. In one way or another, the market economy accommodated newcomers and new claims. But in so doing, it upheld the prevailing rhetoric of yuisho; paradoxical as it may seem, newcomers won trading rights by proving they possessed yuisho. What mattered in the end was the rhetoric or appearance of acceptable "realities"—however obtained—not the actual track record of the merchants. The Honai merchants' success, which depended greatly on their ability to build up yuisho, only too clearly illustrates this point.

For the Honai merchants, a series of disputes with other merchant groups was a primary means of enhancing their commercial "legacy." Favorable resolution by the authorities endorsed their new commercial prerogative and produced a set of documents that clearly spelled out the newly acquired yuisho, powerful evidence to be reserved for future use. To begin with, however, it was necessary for them to create a conflict that required a trial and to ensure a winning verdict. How did they accomplish these objectives?

Their first concrete step was to overstep their existing trading boundaries. With their merchandise in hand, the Honai merchants entered a marketing region hitherto closed to them, an act of transgression that naturally provoked the area's established merchants. To the latter, Honai's gesture deserved a punitive response—usually, in such cases, the confiscation of the infractors' cargo. Once this reaction was elicited, Honai was master of the situation; the seizure of such goods created victims out of the violators, who now had a reason to complain to a higher authority.

At this juncture, Honai leaned on its most valuable asset: a patron powerful enough to function as the ultimate source of justice and partial enough to assure the victory of its client merchants. To demonstrate the legitimacy of their claim and to facilitate the work of the judging authority, the Honai merchants prepared impressive documentation to support their case. Such documentation provided facts and fiction, both equally valuable in legitimating Honai's claim and providing the basis for the verdict. Finally, an upward flow of gifts ensured the economically beneficial exchange between the patron authority and the client merchants. Winning cases tended to accumulate further winning cases; each victory pushed back the limits of commercial prerogatives.

In the early phase of Honai's history, when its legacy was still thin, the merchants (and perhaps their patron also) relied heavily on forged documents to demonstrate their established rights. A medium commonly adopted by fifteenth- and sixteenth-century merchants,[5] forgeries provided the users the desired yuisho by creating fictitious past practices or historical ties to a powerful traditional authority. The Honai merchants forged at least half a dozen documents. While all were effective, one among them stands out by virtue of its power, long-lasting prestige, and breadth of application; it literally changed the course of local history.

This was an imperial decree dated 1157, purportedly issued by Goshirakawa (1127–92), an emperor who retired after less than three years, then ruled from behind the throne for 21 more. The document in question bears the alleged right handprint of Goshirakawa in black ink and confirms the Honai merchants' right to trade in horses in all directions. Although its date of issuance coincides with Goshirakawa's reign as an incumbent emperor, the decree was usually called an *inzen* (retired emperor's decree) and, only occasionally, a *senji* (an emperor's decree), probably because Goshirakawa was more powerful and better known historically as an *in* (retired emperor). To any knowledgeable eye, the document is a readily detectable forgery, exhibiting many points of irregularity when compared with the proper inzen format.[6]

A certain amount of contradictory evidence shrouds the origin of the inzen. The earliest possible reference to it dates from 1418, the time of Honai's first recorded dispute (with Ishidōji), during which an arbitration statement mentioned an "imperial authorization [*chokukyo*]," though without specifically naming it.[7] In the subsequent dispute, the opposing Obata merchants made suggestive remarks concerning the origin and possession of the supposed imperial decree. According to their statement of 1426, the inzen had been held collectively by the merchants of the region—apparently from Tokuchin-ho and beyond—in a shrine in Owaki (where the Rokkaku had their headquarters). But it had been lost. Now, the inzen being in its possession, Honai was claiming to be the "chief [*sōryō*]" merchants group. Obata presented the case thus, but argued that even if the lost *inzen* had been discovered, its finder would still have no grounds for such a claim.[8]

From this statement we learn that an inzen of some type (authentic or otherwise) had existed in the area sometime in the past. It was meant to grant privileges to merchants located in a region broader than Tokuchin-ho, extending at least to Owaki and Obata. While Obata contested the way the inzen was used to bolster Honai's relative position among merchants, it never questioned the authenticity of Honai's inzen.[9]

Beginning with this dispute, the inzen came to certify a range of "established" trading rights the Honai merchants previously had not held in fact. The document's power emanated from its type (inzen) and from its author (Goshirakawa), both of which conveyed ancient prestige of the highest grade and served as a sure vehicle for impressing medieval minds. As disputes unfolded one after another, the Honai merchants drew on this piece of evidence to gain an upper hand; and each victory added greater credence to the inzen, as the disputes described below will demonstrate.

It is well to remember, however, that in and of itself, the forged inzen was just a piece of paper. It gained life and vitality only through the process of adjudication and an adjudicator's willingness to accept it as winning evidence. The Honai merchants could not have been more fortunate in this regard. In late medieval Japan, as Chapter 1 has indicated, a number of authorities could act as arbitrators of commercial disputes. In Ōmi, until about the beginning of the sixteenth century, Enryakuji had jurisdiction over commerce, with the Muromachi bakufu intervening from time to time; thereafter the Rokkaku and their vassals performed this function. Internally, Enryakuji was split into a number of contending factions, each of which sought to mediate disputes involving its client merchants. The capacity to adjudicate was a barometer of relative political importance and rested in the hands of the more powerful. It greatly benefited the Honai merchants that the political influence of their patron, Higashitani of Tōdō (one of the three divisions of Enryakuji), surpassed that of other temple organizations. Disputes involving Honai—especially in the early years of precedence building—came to be resolved through the mediation of priests from Higashitani. By the time the Rokkaku and their vassals gained greater jurisdictional power, the Honai merchants had already established their fame as the group backed by the inzen. Their traditional prestige had become a social reality, recognized by other merchants and authorities alike.

The inzen held unquestioned power for a century, until Honai had a temporary falling out with the Rokkaku in the 1550s. Though the Rokkaku and the Higashitani priests suspected the authenticity of the inzen, they did not explicitly reject its traditional value. Even so, after the falling out, Honai abandoned the use of the inzen altogether. Recognizing that times were changing, Honai's new strategy was to compensate for the loss of its old trump card with a grandiose gift-giving scheme to woo the adjudicating authority.

The Disputes

From the 1420s to the 1570s, a decade before Nobunaga's entry into Ōmi, the Honai merchants engaged in more than a dozen disputes of greater or lesser consequence. In all but one of these the Honai merchants were on the offensive. They initiated each conflict to establish a "legacy" for yet another new trading sphere. They cast their nets with the aim of true expansionists, and they won favorable results. While Honai's offensive strategy remained broadly consistent throughout, each dispute had its unique traits; each was a product of specific circumstances that reflected the strength and status of the Honai merchants relative to other groups as well as to the political and economic conditions of the time. The sequence of major disputes illuminates the process of Honai's rise and its adjustment to a complex and shifting political climate.

Establishing the Foundation: A Border Dispute
with the Obata Merchants (1425–1427)

As the first major stage in Honai's expansion, this dispute was by far the most important in establishing its yuisho. Fittingly, it was also the most elaborately conceived, carefully prepared, and astutely executed. Honai's immediate goal was simple: the dissolution of the marketing boundaries that had hitherto confined it. Its opponent was a group of Obata merchants with marketing rights to a region Honai apparently considered its frontier at this time.

The Honai and Obata merchants, the latter located on the Tōsandō not too far from Yōkaichi, were both client merchants of Enryakuji. But they did not share a patron. Two different organizations within the Tōdō section of the temple—Higashitani and Minamitani—supported the Honai and the Obata merchants respectively. As the events unfolded, it became apparent that the merchants' dispute was also a conflict within the temple.

A dozen or so statements issued in the course of the trial by the competing merchant groups, their collaborators, and the adjudicating authorities bring many details to light. At the time of this dispute, various merchant organizations of eastern Ōmi still held relatively restricted marketing territories. The Honai and Obata merchants circulated the same commodity, cloth, but in two different areas, according to Obata's statement of 1426. The two groups' marketing territories were clearly separated by the Honai River, also called the Ikada River, a human-made sluiceway that ran between Yōkaichi and Nakano in Tokuchin-ho.[10] This boundary, set about 30 years earlier by an Enryakuji magistrate (*gofuku daikan,* presumably an agent and arbitrator specializing in cloth), confined Obata to the north and Honai to the south of the sluice.[11]

A peaceable division lasted until 1425, when the Honai merchants resolutely and repeatedly crossed the border. Outraged by the breach of agreement, the Obata merchants seized their rivals' goods—unknowingly performing according to the latter's script. The Enryakuji magistrates reacted to the Honai incursion and the Obata response calmly; they simply ordered Obata to return the confiscated goods and both parties to continue trading "harmoniously as before."

If maintenance of the status quo was the mediator's guiding principle, breaking it was Honai's goal. After more interloping, Honai appealed the case to its patron, the Higashitani priests. Honai's story was different from Obata's: it was Obata, not Honai, that had violated the border by moving south of the Honai River to confiscate Honai goods.[12] In anticipation of a trial, the Honai merchants prepared elaborate documentation. For them, this was to be a groundbreaking case, one that promised both immediate and long-range returns. Victory might open up an entirely new commercial region, including markets on the Tōsandō and possibly in areas beyond. Moreover, for the Honai merchants, who had won no major dispute before, this trial was the key to future victories. It was to be the first step in consolidating written evidence to legitimate and endorse their yuisho in the future. It is no wonder that the Honai merchants expended much labor in compiling and creating documents. A set of impressive pieces of evidence, many of them forgeries, including the inzen, now awaited presentation and evaluation.

In preparing documentation, it seems that Honai had two differing goals. One was to establish Honai's previous presence at various markets along the Tōsandō and beyond; the other was to discredit the claims of the Obata merchants. To accomplish the first, Honai necessarily relied on the art of forgery. The Honai merchants had not traded in those regions and thus possessed no evidence to support their claim. Two documents, dated 1345 and 1418 respectively, were created. The first of these was a spurious statement providing evidence of Honai's earlier, fictionally legitimated sales activity in the areas to the north of the Honai River. Addressed to the "salt sellers of Tokuchin-ho" and signed by the market magistrates of Nagano, Kawara (the same as Shijūkuin), and Hirakata (located farther north along the lake), it ordered "the payment of market dues twice annually as before" and assured "noninterference in trading [rights] even [if the Honai merchants had] no za." As so often happens with forgeries, it bore a nonexistent date, Jōwa 1.3.20; the Jōwa era did not actually begin until the twenty-first day of the tenth month.[13] The second paper also documented Honai's past payment of market dues in the amount of 50 *mon* to each market magistrate in Shijūkuin, Nagano, and Echigawa twice annually, in the seventh and twelfth months. This one was signed by the Honai merchants themselves.[14] The logic was that past dues payments proved that Honai had traded at these markets with the approval of the appropriate authorities.

Documents prepared to discredit Obata were more numerous and varied. Two of them were pledges purportedly signed by the Obata merchants themselves more than a century and a half earlier, in 1260 and 1265.[15] In these "pledges" Obata agreed to keep away from Ise and to trade only in the area north of the Honai River—a strange pledge to have been made at this time, since the Honai River, a sluice for irrigating Owaki, was not built until about 40 years later![16] They further conceded that their goods should be seized if they violated the agreement, another rather unlikely declaration from a group of merchants.

In addition to these self-imposed limitations on Obata, the Honai merchants sought to split the Obata group along the lines of the three geographical sections in Obata-gō: Shōden, Nakamura, and Inouda. Honai's tactic was to pit the villagers of Nakamura and Inouda against the main disputant, the Shōden villagers. Under Honai's pressure, the Nakamura and Inouda merchants joined in writing a condemnation of the Shōden merchants' action.[17] Keen-eyed historians may detect Honai's ruse with little difficulty. The handwriting in the accusation, dated 1426, is identical to that in the Obata pledges, dated 1260 and 1265, despite the century and a half that separated their supposed dates of creation. Without doubt, these were produced by one person, probably in one sitting. Only the signatures of Inouda and Nakamura merchants were in different hands. Honai had apparently pressured them to sign after the text had been drafted.[18]

The Honai merchants thus promoted their rights to trade at markets along the Tōsandō by asserting their past payment of market dues. They set their opponents up as villains who had broken a century-old pledge. Internal dissent among the Obata merchants served to confirm that the Obata Shōden group was in the wrong.

The concrete evidence for Honai's established marketing practice and for Obata's incursions, contained in this set of papers, was given further credence by the prestigious inzen, which, we may recall, granted the Honai merchants the right to trade in horses in all directions. Although the inzen named horses as the commodity to be traded, it was employed to empower its possessor to trade in all kinds of goods. The Honai merchants' 1427 assertion sums up their claim: "[We have] traded in all four directions from ancient times without any interference. [Despite this fact,] Obata closed the north side of Tokuchin-ho by making a new claim. We request a judgment of the priests' assembly [of Higashitani] that will put a stop to this offensive act."[19] Only four days later, Enryakuji transmitted the result of the adjudication to their magistrates (zushi and kumon) in Tokuchin-ho.

Along with the decision we learn the manner in which the case came to be adjudicated. Initially Enryakuji had dispatched an order through its envoys (shisetsu) requesting the shugo's intervention. But the shugo advised that the envoys representing each of the disputants meet to work out a resolution. Although a date was set for the meeting, Obata's envoy, presumably a member of Minamitani, failed to appear. Having submitted no supporting documents at that time (although it had done so earlier and had also included a complaint about Honai's possession of the inzen), Obata was declared the loser. Honai was to trade as before and report to the temple authority should Obata make any new claims.[20]

Honai's arduous labor in compiling evidence won solid returns. Before this dispute, the number of markets accessible to Honai was extremely limited; the only major market to the south of the Honai

River was the Hino. Despite Honai's ability to acquire goods in Ise, it held few channels to distribute them. This victory opened up an approach to the territory north of the Honai River, including many markets located on the Tōsandō. Although the right to cross the border did not guarantee the right to sell at these markets—because of particularistic regulations at each market—this was clearly a necessary first step to expansion. Furthermore, equally important to Honai's future was the precedent that the judgment set for the documentation involved. Although in fact Honai had won by default, the verdict implicitly certified the authority of its papers. These included the inzen, which from this point on would serve as a guarantee of whatever prerogatives the Honai merchants chose to seek. Through official recognition of its authenticity and power, the inzen was transformed into Honai's symbol of status and prestige. Honai's patron priests also gained concrete benefits: a 3 *kan* gratuity[21] and probably other undocumented gifts along with—most significant of all—the great future potential of their merchant clients.

The handling of the dispute reflected the relative strength of the patrons within the temple. Perhaps because Honai was the party favored by the more influential of the two temple authorities, its documentation far outweighed what Obata had prepared. Indeed, Honai and Higashitani might well have collaborated in drawing it up. Even if Obata's envoy had made an appearance, there was probably little chance for the verdict to have been different. The promptness with which the decision was reached also suggests the possibility of a prearranged verdict that only awaited the submission of the documentation necessary to support it.

The process of adjudication also reveals the particular form that Ōmi's political triangle took at the time. The relationship between Enryakuji—at least its Higashitani section—and the shugo was extremely harmonious. This was an era in which the Rokkaku were seeking to cultivate the support of the temple in the face of the Kyōgoku opposition, which was supported by the bakufu. When Enryakuji asked the shugo to adjudicate, the latter deferred to the former instead of taking this opportunity to expand its authority.

A year later, when there was another small incident between the Honai and Obata Shōden merchants, the Rokkaku's magistrates reported, in language of considerable partiality, that the Shōden merchants had been aggressive once again, and urged Enryakuji, through the deputy shugo, Iba, to quell this offensive behavior.[22] Thus, not only their patron but also the shugo backed the Honai merchants, probably because of the greater political influence of Higashitani compared with that of Minamitani.

Seeking Monopoly Rights: A Dispute with the Yokozeki
Merchants over Honza Status (1463–1464)

Organized merchants identified by their za held greater rights to sell certain commodities in certain regions or markets than their non-za counterparts. But there were further status gradations among za, expressed in such terms as *honza* (original za) or *shinza* (new za). About three decades after the conflict with Obata, the Honai merchants were at odds with the Yokozeki merchants over who held the status of honza. What did it mean to be honza merchants? What was the essence of this dispute, and what was at stake? Historians are not altogether clear on these points, but Toyoda Takeshi sees the honza as a trade association whose monopolistic rights and exemption from tolls were originally certified by its patron—the estate proprietor—in return for tax and service obligations.[23]

For Honai and its rival, Yokozeki, honza was a name to be sought after. They probably equated honza status with unchallengeable security in trading rights. The merchants of Yokozeki, a market on the Tōsandō, described themselves as honza with dues obligations to the Konpon Chūdō unit of Enryakuji. On the basis of this status, Yokozeki felt justified in seizing Honai merchants' goods. Honai denounced Yokozeki's act and claimed to be the honza itself.

Extant documentation on this case is spotty. Only the decisions have survived. Petition or rebuttal statements written by the plaintiffs and defendants themselves—a rich source of background information— are lost. Nonetheless, we find that the Honai merchants had been trading in cloth in a way that represented an encroachment on the activities of the Yokozeki merchants. Yokozeki eventually confiscated Honai's cloth, laying the groundwork for a trial. Resolution of this dispute involved a number of decision-making authorities whose relative power and interrelations are not entirely clear to us. The progression of decisions and counterdecisions, at any rate, provide a sense of competition and cooperation among various units in the temple, the bakufu, and the shugo, as well as among particular—probably influential—individuals.

A series of complicated steps preceded the final resolution of the case. The case was initially handled by the temple's *heirōshū,* a group of priests of unknown organizational affiliation who secluded themselves to meditate over the verdict. The heirōshū upheld the status quo, just as Enryakuji's cloth magistrate (gofuku daikan) had done in the previous dispute: "Because Honai and Yokozeki both hold cloth za they should continue trading as before, keeping to the previous marketing territories."[24] Not surprisingly, this decision displeased Honai and Yokozeki alike. The point of contention was not the cloth za, which they both held, but rather the status of honza. Each of them sought to outdo the other, not to be equal.

But it was not only the merchants who opposed the decision. The Higashitani priests, who viewed Honai as "having the force of the argument," were similarly displeased.[25] Meanwhile, a new twist placed Honai at a disadvantage. Only eight days after the first decision, probably as a result of Yokozeki's lobbying, a certain priest named Hōdōbō issued a decree of a "private nature," negative for Honai, which overrode the heirōshū decision.[26] We learn of this from a Higashitani statement that adamantly advised the nonacceptance of this decree.

In the month that followed, the situation worsened for Honai. Yokozeki apparently sought a new judgment from yet another source—the bakufu, according to an Enryakuji statement—and won a more favorable verdict. This turn of events outraged the Higashitani priests, who accused the Yokozeki merchants of having extorted an official decree.[27] About a year later, in 1464, the bakufu's magistrates ordered the shugo to terminate Honai's claim to honza status, which, according to the bakufu, was impairing Yokozeki's fulfillment of its obligations to the Konpon Chūdō.[28] The Higashitani priests then moved to invalidate the bakufu's statement by dispatching their own order to the deputy shugo, Iba Sadataka. In it, they argued in Honai's favor: Honai held the status of honza with a certificate of firm proof, while Yokozeki was making new, unsupported claims.[29] Two months later, what would become the final verdict in this dispute firmly denounced Yokozeki's act while supporting Honai's claim. The decision traveled through the various command channels, over to the bakufu, which by then had dramatically reversed its earlier position—perhaps owing to pressure from Enryakuji. The bakufu declared:

Re the Honai merchants, as well as the dues and services pertaining to cloth: our previous order to terminate the new claims of Honai merchants was based on false assertions made by Yokozeki merchants that the latter owed dues on cloth and services to Konpon Chūdō. Although we accused the Honai merchants of asserting a new claim, the inzen and other documents of proof demonstrate that it is the Yokozeki merchants who falsely claim to be the honza.[30]

The bakufu sent an order to both the shugo, Rokkaku Takayori, and to Higashitani's estate agent (zassō). The shugo's magistrates in turn sent the message to the deputy shugo, Iba,[31] who subsequently relayed it to two other vassals of the shugo located near Tokuchin-ho with the order to have the Yokozeki merchants return the confiscated goods to their Honai owners.[32] Both the priests and the deputy shugo informed the Honai merchants directly, reconfirming their right to trade in cloth.[33]

As a result of this dispute, Honai firmly secured its rights to market cloth, although the resolution failed to support its honza status. Instead, Honai's claim was supported by its possession of the inzen, which accorded it a privileged status. Yokozeki, without a paper of equivalent value (and a patron of comparable stature), was denounced as the "new claimant."

Though this was hardly a defeat, the outcome of this dispute did not award Honai the tangible marketing rights it desired. It endorsed Honai's rights to set up markets to deal in cloth, but it did not prohibit Yokozeki from doing the same. Honai's rights, which came to be certified through the network of jurisdictional channels, were not described as those of honza status. In the end, then, although Honai did not lose, the dispute left the two groups on a par—at the same point from which they had started. Neither specifically was the honza, and both had the right to continue trading. Unsatisfactory as these terms might have been to the contending parties, they probably reflected the current level of demand at the markets, which accommodated a growing number of suppliers. The concept of preferred rights originally associated with the term *honza* was perhaps showing signs of wear in a widening economy.

As a side effect, the outcome of this dispute established the enormous value of the inzen. The document had been recognized as valid proof of the Honai merchants' rights and status by all the upper-level institutions of the medieval political structure. Now the inzen's power of precedent pertained to disputes judged by any authority, significantly increasing its potential force in future disputes.

Because the resolution of the dispute did not remove the source of friction between the two merchant groups, they continued to treat each other as enemies. Within half a year Yokozeki seized Honai's goods a second time, leading once again to the issuance of decrees. The shugo's magistrates again contacted Iba Sadataka, the deputy shugo,[34] who in turn notified the Honai merchants. Both the shugo and the deputy shugo assured Honai's freedom to repossess the goods that had been confiscated "despite Honai's unquestionable right to set up markets everywhere in the province."[35] But still the antagonism simmered, and in 1501 a really major conflict erupted.

Setting Up Shop: A Marketing Dispute with the
Yokozeki Merchants over Cloth (1501–1502)

Three and a half decades later Honai and Yokozeki were still seeking to eliminate each other. As earlier, the preresolution phase of events does not survive in our documents. The nature of the resolution in this case was different, however, reflecting the changing economic and political conditions in the province. Japan had gone through the Ōnin War, which left Kyoto in ruins and the countryside divided into even more parcels with local military rule. The point of contention—which earlier had been the merchants' za status and the rights it embodied—acquired a new dimension, centering on the privilege of setting up shop at each market. Because a different authority controlled each market, conflict was particularized and resolved separately for each market.

The trend toward increasingly specific marketing rights was symptomatic of a general transformation: the intensification of political decentralization at the expense of the great central institutions—the shōen proprietors and the bakufu (both in Kyoto). One dimension of this trend was the growing control of regional warriors (*kokujin*) over commercial practices, including the rights and obligations pertaining to regional markets. In Ōmi, the relative strength and independence of the Rokkaku's vassals further enhanced their control.

The first in a series of confirmations of Honai's market rights came in the tenth month of 1501 from a Rokkaku vassal, Kunori Kazuhide, who apparently was in charge of the Mabuchi market.[36] Honai's rights as detailed in this statement were more extensive than in any of the other statements that would follow. Kunori emphasized that Honai had been the cloth-trading honza since ancient times and that Honai had not only the right to trade at Mabuchi but also the privilege of exemption from market dues. In view of the 1460s decision in which honza status was not explicitly awarded to either Honai or Yokozeki, Kunori's statement seems unjustified. The location of Mabuchi, however, serves to explain the decision. Mabuchi was the first major market to the north of Yokozeki on the Tōsandō and the first market that the Honai merchants going south past Yōkaichi came to. If Yokozeki merchants controlled cloth trading at the Yokozeki market, the Mabuchi market may have been seeking to compete with its neighbor.

This step by Kunori prompted the Yokozeki merchants to go on the warpath. In the fourth month of the following year, Yokozeki seized Honai's goods at the Shimagō market,[37] but on the strength of the inzen, the deputy shugo and a local warrior (named Shimagō Hidetsuna) proceeded to confirm Honai's rights.[38] Hino was a third location where the two merchant groups had been fighting, and there also the official declared that "they were both cloth merchants."[39] At Yōkaichi as well, both Yokozeki and Honai were confirmed in their right to sell cloth.[40]

In this way, the Honai merchants, on the basis of the inzen, expanded their rights to trade in cloth at nearby markets on the lakeside and in the hinterland. Honai's right was cited separately for each market. But the basis for the market-specific right continued to be the inzen, which had become a certificate of comprehensive prerogatives. In its broad application, the inzen was similar to honza status and served, in the absence of the latter, as the basis for Honai's generalized rights.

Honai's expansion into cloth trading was made possible by the way markets generally permitted sales by more than one merchant group. In the present case, possible exceptions were the Yokozeki market, the home base of Honai's opponent, and Mabuchi, Yokozeki's immediate neighbor. Opening a market to several merchant groups reflected an expansion in the volume of trade, at least in the cloth sector.

Securing Transportation Routes: A Road Dispute with the Goka Merchants (1528–1529)

The next frontier for Honai after its successful expansion along the Tōsandō lay to the west, on the other side of Lake Biwa. The new target was Obama, a port market in Wakasa Province facing Wakasa Bay. Exactly when the Honai merchants began traveling to Wakasa is unknown, but by 1502 they had encountered opposition—in the usual form of a confiscation of goods—from the merchants of Takashima-minami market, on the lake's western coast. In an apparent response to Honai's plea, Kunori Kazuhide, the Rokkaku vassal who had previously confirmed Honai's rights at the Mabuchi market, ordered the return of the goods, because "Honai had established its precedent" for this transport route.[41]

The dispute of 1528 was basically a continuation of this quarrel. However, it took a more elaborate form, involving a federation of merchant groups from a number of locations: merchants from Obata, Satsuma, Hatsusaka, Tanakae, and Takashima-minami, who made up the Goka Merchants Federation, together with merchants from Minami-Koga and Kita-Koga and the teamsters (*bashaku*) of Imazu. For Honai, the ultimate target was the marketing territory, but the object of contention was road access—passage on the Kurihan-kaidō ("9.5 *ri* road"), which connected Imazu, on the lake's western shore, to Obama.

Among the opposing groups, the Obata merchants were the main spokesmen. A century had passed since the major dispute between Obata and Honai in the 1420s. Despite their defeat then, the Obata merchants had thrived. Theirs was the only merchant group recognized as part of both the Shihon Merchants and Goka Merchants federations, whose combined marketing territories stretched from Ise Bay to Wakasa Bay.

The petition prepared by the Obata merchants and their allies argued the case from the standpoint of yuisho and Honai's violation thereof.[42] First of all, they pointed out, the Kurihan-kaidō was controlled by Takashima-minami, Kita-Koga, Minami-Koga, and Imazu. Honai's passage on this road to markets in Wakasa was unprecedented. It was therefore a violation of great magnitude because no one, not even the descendants of the Goka merchants, would go against the rules of yuisho. Even the far-flung ashiko of the Goka Merchants Federation, who peddled their wares in remote villages, observed the yuisho. The petition asked, "On what grounds are the Honai merchants basing their claim? Honai merchants are people who received the inzen and the Sanmon's [Enryakuji's] certification in ancient times. But this is no basis for trading as they wish [today]." Rather, according to the petition, "merchants were to differentiate trading rights at each port and market in each province. Even if merchants dealt in many items, each item had to be negotiated separately with the respective za. Whether selling in markets or not [i.e., on village roads], this distinction had to be made. Such was the old truth in the commercial world."

At this point in the petition the Obata merchants listed examples of trading patterns based on yuisho.

Ise-bound trade via the Happū-kaidō and Chigusa-kaidō was called the Shihon because Ishidō, Honai, Obata, and Kutsukake merchants [i.e., the Shihon Merchants Federation] participated in it. The merchants of Satsuma, Hatsusaka, and Tanakae did not. It was false that the Honai merchants had a precedent for traveling to Wakasa. [Instead of securing commodities in Wakasa] they bought dried food from the merchants of Obata and Satsuma [on the eastern side of the lake] and sold it at markets, but not beyond Echigawa to the north.

Obata then sought to establish Honai's lack of yuisho for using the Kurihan-kaidō by emphasizing Honai's absence from the incidents involving the construction and removal of barriers there: "Many major conflicts arose concerning the Kurihan-kaidō in the past. Takashima-minami market, Kita-Koga, and Minami-Koga took care of the expenses incurred for the gifts. Honai merchants knew nothing of these conflicts [and thus have no right to access]." This accusation was buttressed by a statement (already discussed in Chapter 4) listing the names of those who set up barriers and the costs of having them abolished.[43]

Despite Obata's energetic opposition, the verdict issued by the shugo magistrates in 1529 showed unwavering support for the Honai merchants. The verdict indicated that the decision was based on two factors: (1) "the inzen and other supporting evidence"—despite Obata's denunciation of the certificates that were in Honai's possession— and (2) "the unquestionable precedent for Honai's passage along the Kurihan-kaidō."[44] Honai's traditional rights were thus confirmed by virtue of their actual past use of the road and by virtue of the written proof attesting to this right, namely the inzen. As for the Goka merchants, they not only lost the case but—to add insult to injury—had to pay a stiff penalty of 50,000 *hiki* (500 *kan*) "for having sought cooperation from an official in Obama to oppose the Honai merchants, which must be paid promptly."[45]

Despite the open doubt cast by the Obata merchants on Honai's documentation, the shugo determinedly upheld Honai's efforts to cultivate new territory. The timing of this dispute explains the course that the shugo, Rokkaku Sadayori, took. Only a few months after the resolution of the previous dispute, in 1501–2, an open conflict ensued between the shugo and the deputy shugo, Iba Sadataka, which lasted until the latter's death in 1520. Taking this opportunity, Rokkaku Sadayori sought to ensure for himself the jurisdictional authority previously undermined by strong vassals, as illustrated by the resolution process in the dispute of 1501–2.

Sometime before the conflict, Rokkaku Sadayori had planned the course that this dispute was to take. An undated statement from a vassal of the shugo (Takeda) of Wakasa Province to a vassal of the Rokkaku shows that the two shugo agreed to "allow both parties [the Honai and the Goka]" to use the road. Apparently Sadayori's agent had forwarded some 50 pieces of sushi to Takeda, a gift of food that induced agreement.[46] Sadayori's plan was thus not to exclude the Goka from the Kurihan-kaidō, which would have been impossible anyway, but rather to demonstrate the force of his authority vis-à-vis both his own vassals and the prominent local interests.

After the issuance of the verdict, Honai set about retrieving goods that had been confiscated by the opposing merchants. Apparently the goods had been left at Imazu. Honai requested mediation by two Imazu merchants named Nobushige and Nobusada, who apparently succeeded in returning the goods, and who, for their troubles, subsequently received gifts.[47]

Finally, because this trial turned out to be an unusually costly one, the Imabori section of the Honai merchants' sō requested a financial contribution from the Imabori village sō. The former received some aid from the latter after promising not to use this case as a precedent for similar future contributions.[48]

Throughout these disputes, a variety of authorities judged in favor of Honai, endorsing the validity of the inzen and disregarding its specificity, its reference to horse-trading rights alone. Yet the inzen's litigious force, based on the society's respect for the principle of ancient prestige and medieval precedent in abstraction, could not hold indefinitely. The Warring period was at its height in Japan; there were new rationales for the expansion of political power and the reorganization of society, including the commercial sector. The emerging principles and practices would help to unite the country under one political system and one hegemon within the next half-century. In these changing conditions, the power embodied in the inzen finally drained away, as the Honai merchants would find in their next dispute. Crippled by the loss of their traditional asset, they would be forced to seek an alternative path to commercial survival.

On the Defensive: Pressure from the New Horse Traders (1550–1551)

The dispute of 1550–51 stands out in Honai's history. For once, the Honai merchants did not initiate the dispute; they were accused instead. Moreover, their symbol of traditional prestige—the inzen—came under fire. Finally, the authorities were against Honai from the start. In this dispute, the Honai merchants came closest to tasting defeat.

A confirmation decree issued by the shugo's magistrates to the province's established horse traders sparked this conflict. It endorsed their commercial rights and simultaneously called for the termination of horse trading by new claimants.[49] Responding to this order, established horse traders of the province pressured Honai (whom they viewed as a new claimant) to deal through them in buying or selling horses or oxen.[50] Honai confronted this challenge in the way it knew best: by appealing to a higher authority on the strength of the inzen. But Honai's appeal to the shugo met a clear rejection. The shugo viewed "horse trading to fall outside the limits of Honai's trade privileges," despite its possession of the inzen, which specifically certified none other than its horse-trading rights.[51]

We do not know whether the Honai merchants had traded in horses or oxen before this time, although we do know that they possessed them. From the authorities' viewpoint, however, Honai had no yuisho in horse trading; after all, Honai's accumulated trial evidence did not include one case dealing with horses. In this tight spot, the Honai merchants pursued their traditionalist strategy with a daring discursive innovation: they created an origin-myth dating back to Emperor Goshirakawa to enhance the group's self-definition.

Merchants of this ho have engaged in commerce as the purveyors for Hie Ninomiya Shrine from ancient times up to the present without any change. During the time of Retired Emperor Goshirakawa, notices were posted everywhere stating, "There is a serpent that rises out of Sarusawa Pond in the Southern Capital [Nara], and it is causing much grief to the people. Anyone who subdues this snake will receive a reward."

In response, one of our merchants, Bōtarō of Nakano by name, came forward after considering the matter. He broke off a stalk of bamboo, shaved it thin, and made the point as sharp as a spear. Then, donning a formal robe and holding the spear firmly in his hand, he went to the side of the pond. Thereupon the snake appeared and swallowed him up. As Bōtarō was being swallowed alive, he stabbed through the snake's side, abandoned his outer robe, and jumped out. Getting hold of the snake's neck, he dragged it down to its death.

The scarlet hue that the pond turned could not be concealed, and Bōtarō received both fame and honor. As a reward, the area between the far side of Nara Temple [Kōfukuji] and Kasuga Plain was designated pasture for Honai's horses. This news reached the imperial presence, and Bōtarō was summoned to Kyoto. There he was presented with an imperial edict [*rinji*] bearing the emperor's handprint. The edict stated, "As a reward to you merchants for subduing the serpent, you may freely engage in buying, selling, and riding horses without any hindrance, including tolls and services in various provinces."

By thus explaining the origins of their prestigious status, the Honai merchants reinterpreted their past and gave new meaning to their present. They then proceeded to address the concrete problem before them.

We are merchants affiliated with kenmon that do not trade for mere private ends, and are exempt from all levies, not only on horses and oxen but on all goods. But as though addressing other ordinary people, the horse traders [*hakuraku-chū*] told us in this ho that we must buy and sell horses and oxen through them. We hereby appeal [to you to confirm] that we are the original merchants and that the imperial edict of the Hōgan era [1156–59] specifically proclaimed [our rights regarding] horses. Based on this, the result of the deliberations of 1529 [in the dispute with the Goka Merchants Federation] was clearly in our favor.[52]

With the shugo's support now apparently withdrawn, Honai beseeched their original patron institution for favor. This was a sensible step, because Enryakuji was still a formidable economic force in the capital, despite its centurylong absence from dispute arbitration. Enryakuji responded to Honai's call, presumably for economic reasons, and sought to ensure a positive resolution by appealing to bakufu magistrates on Honai's behalf.[53]

Exactly how Enryakuji's appeal shaped subsequent developments went largely undocumented. We know, however, that the eventual outcome was a surprising victory for the Honai merchants. They were referred to as the "horse-trading za" by the shugo, to whom they had forwarded a gift of 1,000 *hiki*.[54] Thus with the help of their original patron along with the aid of cash, the Honai merchants were once again successful.

But why, before the fortuitous reversal, had Honai lost the shugo's favor? The sources provide no direct hint, but Honai's defeat was symptomatic of the changing times. By 1549, the Rokkaku had established the country's first politically inspired *rakuichi* ("free market"). Located in Ishidera at the foot of Kannonji Castle, the rakuichi was the shugo's instrument for consolidating domainal commerce, partly by attracting merchants unaffiliated with traditional za.[55] Although outside Ishidera the Rokkaku continued to honor traditional privileges, this innovation—a model that would be followed by other warrior magnates, including Oda Nobunaga—signaled an entirely new era with a new set of principles for merchant organizations. It is possible that the Honai merchants had become a target of this new policy; perhaps the shugo was seeking to promote the merchants who had gathered at Ishidera by deterring outside competitors.

Reflecting the shifting political climate, moreover, Honai's patronage by the Higashitani priests was also showing signs of weakening: the priests for the first time cast doubt on the reliability of the inzen. "Although we would like to check the original of the imperial decree," they explained to the shugo's agent, "lack of time makes this impossible. Would you please examine it carefully and let us know later if you have any suspicions about it?"[56] Still unwilling to commit itself, Honai's patron institution nonetheless placed the age-old trump card in a new light of suspicion. It seems that the content and the meaning of the inzen had faded into a distant memory; it had been, after all, nearly a century since Higashitani was directly involved in Honai's dispute resolutions. Honai's new and embellished narrative about its origins perhaps was meant to convince its patron as much as the shugo.

This mistrust for the inzen meant flagging support for the prestige claimed by the Honai merchants. It is true that no one actually questioned authorization deriving from the kenmon itself or explicitly rejected Honai's ties to the kenmon. But the life of the inzen was now over, and the Honai merchants were thrown into a new phase of commercial competition.

The horse-trading dispute marked a watershed in Honai's trial history. There was a sudden need for innovations in winning jurisdictional favors. Faced with a crisis of no small magnitude, the Honai merchants contemplated their past achievements. In 1552, the year following the conflict, they compiled a list of four memorable dates from the past. The earliest date listed was Ōei 35 (1428), the year the first dispute with Obata was finally won with the use of many forgeries; the second date, Kanshō 5 (1464), was for the honza dispute with Yokozeki; the third, Bunki 1 (1501), was for the renewed conflict with Yokozeki; and the most recent, Taiei 8 (1528), was for the dispute with the Goka merchants. Next to these dates, the author marked what appears to be the number of years that had elapsed since each event: 125, 88, 52, and 32 (an error in subtraction for 24) respectively.[57]

We can only speculate on the precise motive behind this act of recollection. Did the Honai merchants wish to know the frequency of disputes in the past century and a quarter? Were they reminiscing over former days of rising prosperity? Were they analyzing their fortune in accordance with some mythological cycle? At any rate, their reflections on the past may have made it clear that to sustain their commercial position, they now had to adopt a different strategy. Assertion of their mythical past and ties with the kenmon now held little sway.

On the Warpath: A Dispute with the Edamura
Merchants over Paper (1558–1560)

Honai lost little time before launching another trade war, a contest marked by a departure in strategy. The most significant development was the unprecedented role of money and warriors in shaping the course of events. The inzen, of course, was not employed.

Honai's new strategy was much more congruent with the contemporary political atmosphere. While espousing a rhetoric of traditionalism tied to the capital's force of prestige, the rising warrior magnates, the daimyo, were nonetheless seeking to thoroughly reshape the country's economic and political order. Some had already issued domainal laws (*bunkoku hō*) on their own authority; others clearly contemplated doing the same. These men of the new age were carving out regional hegemonies. Honai's connection with a twelfth-century aristocrat now seemed clearly outdated. A materialist and rational strategy would be in keeping with this general trend.

Before initiating the dispute, the Honai merchants consolidated subordinate (hikan) ties with the shugo's vassals, numbering ten or so. The political circumstances of the 1550s made these connections meaningful to both parties. The years 1556 and 1557 marked a period of escalation in the war between the Rokkaku and the Chigusa in Ise Province. The Rokkaku required a reliable merchant group with the ability to meet the material needs of their troops. The opportunity was ideal for the Honai merchants, who had established trade rights on the Ise-bound route. By provisioning the Rokkaku army, Honai could strengthen its political leverage and try to expand its commercial prerogatives.

The location of this military campaign made the shugo dependent on the people of Tokuchin-ho in more ways than one. In addition to the merchants' services, labor was requested from every resident male. In 1557, the shugo sent an emergency order for corvée service to every household in Tokuchin-ho, demonstrating in the process an attitude of ample goodwill and conciliation. To make the request more palatable compensation in the form of wages was promised. To ensure results, the shugo's magistrates dispatched the orders to the local agents of Enryakuji, the zushi and kumon, as well as to Enryakuji itself. With assurances from Enryakuji that this request was an urgent measure "not [meant] to set a precedent for the future," all Honai men complied. Those "who had returned temporarily for provisions or because of injuries or a [normal] guard change" were the only exceptions.[58]

In the course of this recruitment drive, Tokuchin-ho villagers came to have ties to more than a dozen prominent vassals of the Rokkaku and their subvassals. Although it is entirely unclear as to what these ties meant in practical terms, the manner in which they were established shows the villagers' keen awareness of the vicissitudes of political life: they directed their individual affiliations to individual vassals. By avoiding a concentrated focus on just one or two warriors, the villagers diffused the alliance, maximizing the benefits of political association while minimizing the risk of a warrior's hegemonic control over the area or of collective incrimination in case of one warrior's downfall.[59]

The consolidation of such relationships prepared the Honai merchants for their ultimate goal: paramountcy over the Ise-bound routes. In this scheme, the specific target was the Edamura Merchants Collective, the monopolistic supplier of Mino paper, which came to be highly prized in the mid-fifteenth century.[60] This was paper produced and sold in Ōyada, Mino Province, a mountainous area wedged between two rivers, and a shōen under the proprietorship of Hōjiin, a temple in Kyoto.[61] The Edamura merchants, under Hōjiin's patronage, controlled the supply link along the Tōsandō between Ōyada and cosmopolitan Kyoto. They held the privilege of toll exemption for the transport of paper and the monopoly on its sale in Kyoto. In return, they paid regular dues to Hōjiin. The Muromachi bakufu endorsed these rights on several occasions.[62]

By the mid-sixteenth century, however, the Edamura merchants were selling paper not only in Kyoto but also in their home province of Ōmi, situated conveniently between Mino and Kyoto. Although their formal monopolistic marketing rights did not include Ōmi, they nonetheless received authorization from the shugo there to confiscate the paper of other merchants should the latter encroach upon their territory.[63]

The process of distributing paper grew more complicated over time and led to an inevitable clash between the established paper sellers of Edamura and the ambitious Honai group, which continually diversified and expanded its commodities and sales regions. One cause of the growing complication was beyond the control of the merchants, however: an increase in military tensions was paralyzing the section of the Tōsandō between Ōyada and Edamura. When the points of production became inaccessible, the Edamura merchants were forced to procure paper wherever they could, including locations in Owari, Echizen, and Ise provinces.[64]

The Edamura merchants explained their new method of paper procurement in the following terms. Merchants of Mino delivered paper to three trading posts (shuku) in Kuwana (in Ise Province). Edamura merchants purchased paper at these posts regularly. But sometimes dangers on the trip from Mino to Kuwana prevented the delivery of paper, and at other times the quantity delivered did not meet the Edamura merchants' needs. Under these circumstances, the Edamura merchants availed themselves of the backup stock held by Kuwana merchants.[65] After purchasing the paper, they carried it on the Ise roads (Happū-kaidō, Chigusa-kaidō, or Ise-kaidō) over which Honai claimed privileges. Despite all the readjustments, the Edamura merchants apparently fell into trouble with their patron. In 1553, Hōjiin began to complain about the reduction in income caused by other merchants' encroachment of Edamura's prerogatives.[66] Later developments suggest that the encroachers—not explicitly named in these grievances—were most likely the Honai merchants.

To the Honai merchants, Edamura's new business conduct represented outright intervention. They perceived themselves as holding an unshaken dominance over the Ise-bound routes and in the port market of Kuwana, although Kuwana was generally known to be a free port, where theoretically anyone could trade. In 1518, Honai claimed not only to have procured paper at Kuwana but also to have wholesaled it at no fewer than fourteen Ōmi locations, including Edamura, Echigawa, Yokozeki, Takashima, and Sakamoto, "since ancient times."[67] Honai declared that Edamura was "stealing/buying [*nusumi-kau*]" paper from the Kuwana post that belonged to the Honai merchants.[68]

The Honai merchants also argued that since ancient times, they had held the exclusive right to transport thirteen items on the Ise roads: three types of seaweed, all kinds of birds, all kinds of fish, sesame, Ise cloth, clayware, salt, wooden bowls and utensils, cotton, hemp, and, of course, paper. In case of violations by other merchants, the Honai merchants had the right to confiscate their cargoes immediately. The implied target was undoubtedly the Edamura merchants carrying paper on the Ise roads.[69]

In fact, the Honai merchants were unconcerned with Edamura's prerogatives in Kyoto or in any other region outside Ise and Ōmi. Honai's challenge to Edamura focused on one goal: to monopolize the distribution of paper from Ise by barring Edamura from the Ise-bound roads and from the key supply stations (shuku) in Ise. The conflict developed over the rights to procure and transport paper, not the right to market it.

The specific tactic Honai used was to delegitimize Edamura's travel on the Ise-bound roads. An appeal dating from the fifth month of 1558 focuses on three points.[70] The first was the claim that more than twenty years before, Edamura had "borrowed" the road to Ise from Honai. This claim implicitly constructed the historical assertion that Honai "possessed" the road and that Edamura did not. To lend a touch of credibility, the petition explained the circumstances of this borrowing in intimate detail, spelling out the names of men who came to negotiate with Honai and even describing their interactions on matters unrelated to the road.

When Mt. Inaba was attacked, the Mino-kaidō came to be blocked. An Edamura man named Hachirō sent a merchant to Shinzaemonnojō of Kobochizuka [in Tokuchin-ho], who is a vassal of Lord Gotō, and pleaded to borrow the Ise road from Honai. We leased him the road for twenty days and had him sign an agreement. After that, three Edamura men, Busshin Tarōemon, San'emon, and Hachirō himself, came to show their appreciation. They submitted 2 *kan* to the Honai merchants and 300 *mon* to Shinzaemonnojō of Kobochizuka. The Edamura men stayed here overnight. The following morning, they wanted to take a look at our sea bream knife. So Saemonkurō of Imazaike [in Tokuchin-ho], who is a vassal of Lord Kojima, demonstrated the knife. Matazaemonkurō spent 200 *mon* [unclear, but perhaps for buying a fish to use the knife on]. In this way, we treated them well, and there should be no argument about this.

Thus Honai constructed the traditional position of Edamura: it was an unauthorized user of the Ise-bound road and was fully cognizant of that fact. Nevertheless, the Edamura merchants abused their privilege of using the borrowed road, thereby justifying the Honai merchants' confiscation of their goods. According to the petition, Edamura sent an apology and gifts to Honai, actually admitting its own misconduct. As before, the petition furnished the names of all the men connected with the incident, emphasizing especially the vassal ties between the Honai men and the Rokkaku warriors.

In the tenth month of 1536, Edamura's Matazaemon carried paper over the Ise road to a shuku named Itaya in Yuzurio [a place in Ōmi on the Happū-kaidō]. We seized this cargo there. Those who were involved in this act were

> Matazaemonnojō of Imazaike, vassal of Lord Onsue
> Shinzaemonnojō of Kobochizuka, vassal of Lord Gotō
> Wakazaemonnojō of Imazaike, vassal of Lord Awaji
> Shinzaemonnojō of Hebimizo, vassal of Lord Fuse-atarashikurōdo
> Chayazaemonnojō of Imazaike, vassal of Lord Shibawara-atarashi
> *Tarōzaemon of Imabori, vassal of Lord Gotō
> *Okuzaemonnojō of Imabori, also a vassal of Lord Gotō
> *Ihyōe of Imabori, also a vassal of Lord Gotō
> *Fukuishizaemonjirō of Imazaike, vassal of Lord Mikami
> *Sakontarō, vassal of Lord Shibawara-higashi

Those with * marks have since died.

Those listed above seized Edamura's cargo. Then Edamura apologized right and left through the intermediaries of the officials at the Yamanouchi barrier. So the matter was settled. Edamura then brought a gift made up of five barrels of five types of goods to us. From the men at the barrier, we also received two barrels of three types of goods. These added up to seven barrels. In addition, Hanashige Shichirōhyōe of Tabika [a place in Ise near the Ōmi border] also came to express appreciation to the officials at the Yamanouchi barrier. The gift was received at the place of Shinzaemon [nojō], vassal of Lord Fuse-atarashikurōdo, in Hebimizo. Honai merchants went to the monastic office [anshitsu] of Hebimizo's shrine, where these barrels were kept, and received the sake.

The Honai merchants went on to describe yet another incident of a similar nature: the confiscation of Edamura's goods at Kuwana in 1553 and the subsequent apology delivered by Edamura. According to the petition, this third incident occurred when a battle kept the Edamura merchants from their regular passage on the Mino road. When Edamura resorted to the unauthorized use of the Ise road, the Honai men took retaliatory action by seizing the Edamura cargo. Once again, a list was given of the Honai men involved in the seizure along with the names of their warrior masters. As before, apologies from Edamura followed the confiscation, and after the intermediaries received a gift from Edamura, the matter ended.

By combining mention of the repeated abuse of road privileges with the constant delivery of apologies, the petition sought to establish the fundamental illegitimacy of Edamura road use. Yet Honai was hardly acting alone in trying to discredit Edamura. A close examination reveals that the petition was written in collaboration with a Rokkaku vassal and was also forwarded to a Rokkaku man.

Under the circumstances, the odds were heavily against the Edamura merchants. They nonetheless issued a rebuttal about four months later, seeking to convey the impression that Honai was falsifying facts. Edamura, for one thing, knew nothing about the renting of the Ise road for twenty days. Besides,

> when a public matter such as [borrowing the road] comes up, we decide by holding a conference and signing a statement collectively. A decision of one or two persons would not lead to an actual act. Moreover, the elders, who are now as old as 90 years old, do not remember a thing about signing a loan agreement with Honai to borrow the road. The three [Edamura] people mentioned in Honai's statement have all died. Thus Honai seems to be saying whatever it wishes.

However, Edamura did not entirely deny using the Ise road. Its stated reason for using the road was different from Honai's version. According to Edamura, a seizure of cargo and thirteen horses by "evil bands [*akutō*]" on the Mino road had forced its merchants to use the Ise road. Edamura said Honai had not seized any goods in 1536. Matazaemonnojō (called Matazaemon in Honai's earlier statement), whose goods had purportedly been confiscated, had since died. Honai was simply perpetrating a hoax because it knew that neither Edamura nor Honai could verify the incident. The Edamura sō knew nothing of the incident with Matazaemonnojō.

Edamura's rebuttal showed its understanding of usage rights to be remarkably different from Honai's. Edamura argued that the Happūkaidō was traveled by various merchants of Japan. How, then, could Honai have the power to close it to the Edamura merchants, who had used it on numerous occasions? The seizure at Kuwana was even more unreasonable; Kuwana was a free port, open to all merchants. In fact, Edamura merchants traveled anywhere that paper might be sold.[71]

As appeal followed appeal, new details were introduced. Additional claims by Honai included monopoly rights on the passage of various goods, including paper, on the Ise road.[72] Moreover, Honai also asserted an ancient right to wholesale paper at fourteen major markets all around Tokuchin-ho, including the village of Edamura. According to Honai, the Edamura merchants had been in a position to purchase paper from Honai since time immemorial![73]

In making these assertions, Honai held an unshakably secure position. In addition to its various vassal connections, it was in a patron-client relationship with Gotō, the shugo's magistrate (to whom Honai paid a fee twice annually) and with two officials in Ise (to whom it forwarded annual fees in the amounts of 4 *kan* and 320 *mon* respectively).[74]

In 1560, the shugo's magistrate (bugyōnin) issued a verdict that, as expected, awarded victory to the Honai merchants and accused the Edamura merchants of "making new claims."[75] An order to block the flow of Edamura paper immediately followed these deliberations.[76] Money in various amounts traveled from Honai to its associates and partners on both sides of the border. The shugo's magistrate received a "magistrate's fee [*bugyōsen*]" of an unrecorded amount.[77] Honai delivered as much as 2,000 *hiki* in cash to each of two men in the Rokkaku camp.[78] The collaborating authors of the petition (Tsujimura and Tani) also recorded gifts being dispensed to other unnamed men in the amounts of 200, 100, and 50 *kan*. As if to admit the shadiness of these operations, they directed that the receipts be torn up.[79] Two other Rokkaku men (Furuhata and Taira) wrote a "congratulatory thank-you note" implying obvious collaboration.

Regarding the recent paper dispute between our side and Edamura over the use of the Ise road, you have troubled yourself with [i.e., sent gifts to] the shugo, sent 120 *kan* to Fuse, gifts to Awaji, Miyagi, and [gifts] to the two of us as well. It is matter for congratulation that everything, both public and private, has been cleared up.[80]

For the Honai merchants, this dispute ended as the most elaborate and most expensive in their history. It involved a large number of people of various social ranks in two provinces as well as tremendous material resources. They succeeded in thoroughly buying out the significant people, from the shugo's magistrate down to the lower ranks in the vassal structure. The pattern of cooperation at all levels was scarcely a secret, and indeed the dispute was regarded as a joint project of both warriors and merchants. "Our side" in the above note shows the togetherness all too vividly. In the end, the Honai merchants eliminated the Edamura merchants from the Ise-bound routes. After the dispute was settled, Honai carried greater weight in the Ōmi-Ise traffic but a much lighter purse at home.

For historians, this intricate dispute with copious documentation provides a valuable picture of commercial practices in Japan's Warring age, when political and military conditions considerably influenced the movement of merchants and commodities as well as the strategies that merchant groups adopted. Although at its point of origin, Mino paper was distributed efficiently—the production center was also a wholesale market held at regular and frequent intervals—the quantity of available

Mino paper in the central sales region, Kyoto, was determined by what the sole supplier was able or willing to disburse, irrespective of demand. But the supplier's monopoly was not universal. It held sway only within the geographical limits of the patron's political prestige and only for as long as that prestige lasted. Edamura's client relationship with Hōjiin, therefore, did not guarantee its monopolistic privilege in mid-sixteenth century Ōmi, the time and place that saw the rise of different sets of authorities and brought opportunity to the Honai group.

In the age of military dominance and turmoil, circumstantial road hazards, in addition to intentional manipulation by the authorities or their client merchants, played a large part in diverting distributive channels. The Edamura merchants were forced to find an alternate, more lengthy route when the most direct route became unavailable. Thus, once the Tōsandō was blocked, Mino paper reached the consumer through a variety of distributive links. The first carrier was a group of Mino merchants who transported it from Ōyada to Owari, Ise, and Echigo provinces. At each destination, they dropped the paper off at an affiliated post (shuku) that served as the wholesale depot and as an entrepôt for middle-distance trading. The same post most likely served as a local retail shop, while merchants who purchased paper there probably wholesaled it once again or retailed it at other market towns. The division between wholesale and retail transactions was ambiguous at this particular link in the chain.

The Honai merchants, in the usual manner, cited precedents centuries old for their use of the Ise-bound roads, making it difficult for the Edamura merchants to refute that claim. The Honai merchants sought to exclude others, not from using the Ise roads, but from carrying specific commodities—a long list of them—on the roads. The Edamura merchants' marketing rights did not come into question. Instead, Honai's attack sought to cut off their supply source and distribution channel. Needless to say, the outcome for the Edamura merchants was the same: no merchandise, no sale.

Occurring after the inzen had been discredited, this dispute took on a clearly different character from the earlier ones. In this post-inzen period, the Honai merchants adopted a strategy relying on money and alliances. The sō of Tokuchin-ho promoted broadly based vassal connections with the shugo's men. To consolidate these ties, they forwarded generous sums of money. The collapse of the inzen's efficacy ushered in a new era in which Honai's approach was unabashedly utilitarian. Though being practical and materialistic was not completely new, in the past Honai's practical economy had been adorned by tradition and myth—those subjective guarantors of ancient and medieval realities. However, the late medieval period was drawing rapidly to a close, leaving in its wake a set of outdated values.

The story of the Honai merchants and their commercial expansion can be used to illustrate the changing economic structure and concomitant political transformation of decentralized Japan. During the century and a half in which the Honai merchants made great headway, their greatest resource was their awareness of the connection between authority and profit and their consequent flexibility in adjusting to a changing political climate. Honai was a good client for each of the authorities that was influential in the region at each historical moment.

Broadly speaking, Honai's commercial sphere developed in two stages. First, Honai succeeded in abolishing the significance of the original marketing border (the Honai River) and gained access to the marketing region directly connected to the cosmopolitan center of consumption, Kyoto (disputes 1, 2, 3). This development took place within the framework of a still-prospering shōen system, in which the country's commodities flowed mainly to the capital.

As regional powers began to displace Kyoto, their material needs also began to replace the concentrated consumption needs of the capital. Concurrently, interregional communication routes took on an ever-greater significance as the provincial military authorities launched incursions into each other's territories. Such was the military background for the disputes in the second stage (disputes 4 and 6), which focused on the interregional transportation routes—the Kurihan-kaidō and the Ise roads. The importance of the roads was borne out by the way these disputes proceeded: even if trading at a particular destination was the crux of the issue for the merchants, documents prepared for consideration by the warrior authorities addressed the problem in terms of road use.

Honai's progress was both quantitative and qualitative. As it expanded territorially, its retail trade became a wholesale trade, and the commodities it handled became much more diverse. These advances were made possible by Honai's adaptability to extremely fluid regional politics. When the Honai merchants saw a falling off of support (dispute 5), they quickly cultivated new patrons without damaging the old ties. The move from client status under Enryakuji to client status under the shugo's vassals and under the shugo himself was accomplished without making enemies anywhere within this maze of authorities. Bribes played a significant role, and they amounted to handsome sums after the demise of the inzen's power.

In 150 years of achievement, the Honai merchants displayed all the wisdom and skill that would later gain "Ōmi merchants" their reputation. The organizational fortitude embodied in the sō and the discipline manifest in their regulations doubtless promoted their meticulous style of doing business. Their ingenuity in cultivating relationships, in adjusting to changing times, and in redefining themselves mythologically remains impressive in our century. Their considerably high level of literacy and keen awareness of historical progression doubtless contributed to their tremendous resourcefulness. But as change swept across the country under the influence of the unifiers, the social and economic position of the Honai merchants underwent a grave and monumental transformation. This is the story that marks the end of Honai's gilded age.

CHAPTER SIX

Reorganization from the Top

THE GROWTH OF collective organizations, such as the sō, was characteristic of the decentralized political order of the late medieval period. In the absence of hegemonic rule, the sō villages equipped themselves with their own governing apparatus, accumulating shrine land and solidifying the economic base for communal autonomy. As long as the country's manifold divisions persisted and each political authority hung in precarious tension with all the others, commoners found ways to consolidate their own strength and form systematized structures. The merchant collectives held the field as long as the authorities were vying with each other for survival and dominance—both of which greatly depended on the resources that commoners could offer. The strength of the sō—the sō of the village and the sō of the merchants—was founded on the decentralized political system.

In the late 1550s, the Honai merchants forged an alliance with influential men in the shugo's camp and succeeded in securing monopolistic trade privileges. However, just as the Honai merchants were greasing the Rokkaku's palms in exchange for a further extension of their long prosperity, the age of decentralization was slipping into decay. The stronger daimyo were absorbing the weaker. A tide of unification was sweeping the country. Japan was about to enter a new age governed by new rulers according to different principles. What transformation awaited our villagers? This chapter deals first with the impact of the reorganization instituted by Oda Nobunaga and his successor, Toyotomi Hideyoshi, and the villagers' response to the changes. It then considers the transformation that the sō underwent, and the continuities it maintained, against the background of administrative reorganization implemented by the Tokugawa. Faced with a series of new situations, in what ways did the local population seek to develop a new meaning for their indigenous communal structure? How did state and society oppose, accommodate, or otherwise interact with each other to give the "autonomous village" its final shape?

Commerce and Land Under Nobunaga and Hideyoshi

The process of unification affected Tokuchin-ho directly in a number of ways. Geographically, Ōmi was a buffer between the three unifiers' home provinces and Kyoto, the focal point of unification. Kyoto had been the center of the kenmon and, as the home of the bakufu, the imperial court, and estate proprietors, was still the pinnacle from which political legitimacy radiated. Despite political decentralization, Kyoto and its environs continued to be the point of confluence for much of the country's long- and middle-distance trade. Many of the za merchants still regarded kenmon as their patrons and continued to trade in their interests. The dependency of regional economies and politics upon the center had not broken down through the long years of warfare among the daimyo families.[1] It is not surprising, then, that Oda Nobunaga viewed intervention in Kyoto as the crucial first stage in reorganizing the country's political and economic resources.

In these circumstances, Ōmi necessarily played a significant role. It became an important battleground for a number of decisive confrontations as the would-be hegemons pushed westward, absorbing and destroying their allies and foes. Tokuchin-ho's proximity to major thoroughfares must have brought home the news about troop movements, provisioning requirements, and the results of each clash of arms. To the unifiers, defiance or compliance on the part of the area's warriors and producers meant hindrance or accommodation of considerable impact. To safeguard their own positions, villagers probably maintained a close vigil over the ups and downs of the power struggle.

In 1568, Kannonji Castle, the Rokkaku's military headquarters, which had stood since the fifteenth century, fell to Oda Nobunaga's forces. In hindsight, this victory comes as no surprise; Nobunaga had prepared for it for several years by tempting many of the Rokkaku's vassals with the guarantee of a fief in exchange for their cooperation. The collapse of the castle secured Nobunaga more allegiant followers, the shugo's prominent vassals.[2] Two years later, the Rokkaku resurfaced and joined in the provincewide resistance against Nobunaga, together with Enryakuji, their old rival Azai, some adherents of the Ikkō sect, and some local peasants.[3] Fortune granted no favors, however; the political life of the Rokkaku was over.[4] In the following year Nobunaga had the particularly defiant monastic complex of Enryakuji razed.[5] Honai's century-long patron and the family of its less entrenched warrior lord—Enryakuji and the Rokkaku—became nothing more than a recent memory, and Honai itself a political orphan.

Still, the fact of a new hegemon did nothing to reduce the strategic importance of eastern Ōmi. Although a new political structure supplanted the old, Tokuchin-ho villagers could gaze in the usual direction when speaking about their new lord. Ten years after the fall of Kannonji Castle, Nobunaga chose to build his own lavish castle at Azuchi, a mere 2 kilometers west of Kannonji and the old archery fields of the Rokkaku,[6] thus supplanting 400 years of the Rokkaku's hereditary influence. He made the lakeshore his home and the geographical hub of his newly acquired military and political supremacy. The extinction of the traditional authorities and Nobunaga's presence in Azuchi foreshadowed unprecedented changes for the region's microcommunities.

Nobunaga's political and military accomplishments were sufficiently flamboyant to suit his new gilded castle in Azuchi. He asserted hegemony by formulating his rule into a universalistic framework of *tenka* ("under heaven").[7] He destroyed or absorbed warrior enemies and manipulated the imperial court by force as well as law,[8] but he grasped control more slowly and cautiously at society's lower levels. Commoners were the material foundation of society, as indispensable as the food they raised. In terms of their productive capacity, commoners were more precious than the elites and therefore warranted careful handling.[9]

The records of Tokuchin-ho reveal that Nobunaga's control over villagers was fundamentally economic. He was interested in grain from the land and goods from the villagers. Yet the village economy was inextricably tied to its social, religious, and local political structure. The new policies of exchange and extraction set by Nobunaga, then, had many implications that went beyond the economic aspect of village life.

Commerce

Reorganization of the merchants in eastern Ōmi began under the Rokkaku, long before Nobunaga took over. We saw that as early as 1549 the shugo promoted a rakuichi (free market) at the foot of his castle in an attempt to nullify traditional za privileges and to place the region's commercial resources under his immediate control. The Honai merchants were ordered to trade there under threat of punishment for noncompliance. They were to be transferred to a district within Ishidera named after them: Honai-chō. Because this order bears no date, we do not know when Honai-chō was set up or when the directive was issued.[10] The physical movement of the Honai merchants after the order also went unrecorded. To what extent was this measure enforced? We know that at least until 1560 the Honai merchants continued to use Imabori as their home base; they left records at Jūzenji Shrine concerning, for instance, the dispute of 1550–51 with the horse traders and that of 1558–60 with the Edamura paper merchants.

Still, the historical significance of the proposed relocation is profound. This was the first recorded instance in Japan of a conscious economic policy to divide village populations along social and occupational lines. Some villagers would be full-time merchants living in castle towns, and others, full-time cultivators living in villages. A precursor to the more elaborate and complete separation of functional groups enforced under subsequent rulers, the Rokkaku's measure was concerned strictly with the movement of merchants. The relationship between warriors and the land received no attention, for instance. Only under Hideyoshi in the 1590s would samurai come to be separated from the land completely and relegated to castle towns. The incomplete division of functional categories was reflected in the city plan of Ishidera. Unlike in castle towns of Tokugawa times, samurai, merchants, and peasants were dispersed in clusters throughout Ishidera without the systematic separation of one occupational group from another.[11]

With its besiegement in 1568, Kannonji Castle became defunct as the area's political and commercial center. What happened to Ishidera and its merchants at that point is unknown. But since Nobunaga began to construct his castle in Azuchi in 1576,[12] the same general region remained the center of commerce. For those previously trading in Ishidera, relocation to Azuchi, which was not far away, might have secured similar commercial opportunities with little disruption.

In the sixth month of the following year, Nobunaga issued a thirteen-article code regulating the castle-town residents.[13] Historically known as the classic *rakuichi rakuza* set of regulations,[14] it nullified za privileges and various levies within the town, discontinued tolls, required all passing merchants to stop over, and ordered all horse trading to take place within Azuchi. To further attract merchant capital via moneylenders, it guaranteed no cancellation of debts (tokusei, or "virtuous rule").[15] Those newly relocated to Azuchi would be free of any incumbrances or obligations imposed by their former patrons or superiors. These and other articles promoted the town's growth, one aspect of which was the expansion of merchant settlements.

The regulations were more ideal than practicable, however. The greatest difference between the regulations and their implementation was in Nobunaga's treatment of the za merchants. Instead of eradicating the institution of commercial za, he sought to usurp the authority to issue seals of confirmation to the za. In other words, his attack was on the previous patrons of the za—mostly the members of the kenmon—not on the za merchants themselves. Quite contrary to the stated regulation, Nobunaga took care to protect the most renowned za merchants in order to reap their profits. Protection was extended, for example, to the oil za of Takebe and to our own Shihon Merchants Federation, the name by which Tokuchin-ho merchants were known in Ise.[16]

Ironically, the piece of evidence that shows the continued existence of the Honai merchants under Nobunaga also provides one of the last glimpses of their activities. In 1578, the Shihon Merchants Federation received a request from Takigawa Kazumasu, a vassal of Nobunaga in Ise. According to Takigawa, the Shihon merchants had delegated their trading rights in Ise to certain "amateur" (*shirōto*) merchants. The latter were to submit regular dues to Takigawa. However, some other amateur merchants began encroaching upon the prerogatives of the Shihon's surrogates, impeding the flow of income to Takigawa. He therefore requested that the Shihon merchants firmly command their amateurs to pay dues as before.[17]

This document brings to light elements of continuity and change that hung in an uneasy balance in the world of commerce at this time. On the one hand, the Shihon Merchants Federation still held, at this late date, the publicly recognized authority—built upon its traditional prestige—to issue commands to merchants in Ise. In contradistinction to the days of the disputes with the Edamura merchants two decades earlier, Honai's involvement in the Ise-bound trade seems to have fallen to the status of an absentee proprietorship—it farmed out trade rights. The Honai merchants remained at home, conferring on newer and "lesser" merchants the privileges and obligations of trading in Ise. This delegation of authority was vulnerable, however, to the defiance of merchants who did not follow established customs. For instance, it is easy for us to imagine that the guarded privilege of using certain stopover points for warehousing was, as we saw in the dispute with the Edamura merchants, no longer observed. Nobunaga's endorsement of the Shihon merchants' za privileges did not amount to a right to keep newer merchants from invalidating their traditionalist claims in the outdated commercial system. Recorded instances of other similar incidents[18] testify that the tension between the old and the new was becoming pervasive.

It is against this background that the Honai merchants disappear from local records. As to what became of them, we can only speculate.

Perhaps they moved to Azuchi and traded there as full-time urban merchants. Perhaps they became an element in the famous Ōmi merchants of the Tokugawa period. Perhaps they lost in the competitive war as new merchants made inroads and carved out trading sectors not bound by traditional restrictions. We do know that some traders—whom we recognize by name—continued to live in their home villages: three men from Imazaike who had participated in the earlier dispute with Edamura (1558–60) had acquired by 1583 the status of owner-cultivators.[19] At any rate, by the 1580s the term "Honai merchants" was an anachronism.[20]

As Japan's medieval age ended, then, this prototypical medieval merchant group also faded into oblivion. Just as the Honai merchants had always claimed, they were indeed "the merchants affiliated with the kenmon."[21] When the kenmon disappeared, so too did the Honai merchants, and the residents of Tokuchin-ho became a full-fledged, land-based peasantry. It was not long before Hideyoshi, in his consolidation of the new realm, legally tied peasants to the soil, forbidding them to engage in commerce or wage labor.

Land

The rural population on Enryakuji's estates must have found the total demise of the proprietary institution utterly shocking. For the villagers of Tokuchin-ho this development had grave consequences. Put in economic terms, the eradication of the traditional patron foreshadowed a new and unpredictable tax-collecting structure outside the long-entrenched relationship of patronage and obligations. The fall of the religious center on Mt. Hiei also meant that the complex system that integrated all the subsidiary shrines had lost its centripetal force. Local shrines were now independent agencies without the structural links that had tied them to the home of the Tendai sect.

Directives dispatched by Nobunaga's officials concerning local landholding began to reach Tokuchin-ho in 1575. Their dispatch was not a sudden impulse. Before putting a torch to Enryakuji in 1571, Nobunaga sought to win fiscal sway over the temple's vast landholdings through nonviolent means. First he investigated their income potential by ordering each village within the shōen to submit its putative yield.[22] Commensurate with his position as the country's overlord, he then claimed title to the land and certified the temple's possession of land rights under his vermilion seal. Accompanying this gesture was an order to his agents to collect taxes from Enryakuji's holdings.[23]

What percentage of the local yields Nobunaga intended to seize at this time is unclear, but we know that he was proceeding with caution;

while he expropriated Enryakuji's profits in practice, he continued to recognize its proprietorship in name. From 1572 on, however, having destroyed the temple, Nobunaga had free rein to collect taxes in full from lands recently taken from under their traditional proprietary umbrella. One practical problem that remained was the presence of the customarily untaxed shrine land, ardently guarded by the incorrigible village residents. Abolition of tax-exempt shrine land, therefore, constituted a logical step within Nobunaga's larger scheme to rule over the country's entire productive resources.

Two directives from 1575, issued by Nobunaga's close vassals (Shibata Katsuie[24] and his subordinate) to the lower four gō of Tokuchin-ho show one kind of village-lord interaction typical of this period. One statement informs us that sometime in the recent past Nobunaga had "confiscated" the shrine land of the lower four gō. In the words of Nobunaga's agent, this confiscation was not a grave matter but had resulted in the collection of "a small amount of tax." The response of the villagers to this sudden imposition was not benign. They pointed out the invalidity of the taxation by claiming "there is no precedent for this." Their grievances bore fruit, and the new samurai authority rescinded the order, guaranteeing that the shrine property would be free of tax in the future.[25]

This conciliation on the part of Nobunaga's officials turned out to be a short-lived victory for the villagers. Initially, the new authorities, who were outsiders, astutely avoided igniting local unrest. To them, the peasants must have appeared well organized and quite volatile. Eventually, however, Shibata Katsuie reassigned a large portion of the shrine land to himself, although he was still careful not to take all of it.[26]

Some harassment accompanied the effort to command greater obedience from the villagers. In the late 1570s, just about the time the shrine land became an issue, Nobunaga accused the villagers of Imabori, Hebimizo, and Kobochizuka of complicity in the anti-Nobunaga struggle of 1570, which had included the Rokkaku, Enryakuji, and the peasants of Takebe-no-shō. Honai's strategic location and previous close ties with both the shugo's men and the temple probably gave reason for this accusation. Whatever the cause, a charge made by the head of the country's largest military force must have posed no small threat to the local people. In an attempt to avoid the worst of all possible outcomes, the villagers were naturally more amenable to the new demands, including those made on the shrine land. We know little about the details of the accusation and its outcome, except that a subsequent investigation cleared the villagers of the charge.[27]

From the outset, the notice of confiscation foretold an ominous change for the community. Shrine holdings were the foundation of all the community's social and religious ties. They had been accumulated through centuries of piecemeal donation, purchase, and land development; they were managed through the painstaking efforts of the sō. Abolition of the tax exemption on shrine land meant a destruction of corporate assets consolidated over more than 200 years and the reversal of a historic local achievement. In terms of social practices, the confiscation of shrine land threatened the perpetuation of ceremonial activities and maintenance of the shrine building itself. Confiscation could well destroy the communal funds needed for the shrine's symbolic and structural continuity. Under the circumstances, the villagers' grievances, if not their will to resist, must have been deep and real. Ultimately, though, villagers had little control over the destiny of their land. The last remaining shinden list from Imabori's Jūzenji shrine dates from 1566.[28]

At this juncture in Tokuchin-ho's history, villagers were faced with more than the loss of the communal treasury, however. A new kind of relationship with a political authority, one that was more arbitrary and distant, was clearly in the making. In the past, the Rokkaku had consulted Enryakuji before exacting any new dues; they had even expressed apologies. In the new age, rational and nonparochial ways of managing land eroded the legitimacy built upon custom. During a decade or so the force of precedent would be destroyed as the unification program swept across the country with new vigor under Nobunaga's successor, Toyotomi Hideyoshi.

Nobunaga was assassinated in 1582. Hideyoshi wasted little time in avenging his lord and then destroying the lord's vassals who were now his rivals. These included Shibata Katsuie, Nobunaga's ally-vassal in Tokuchin-ho. Having cleared out his competitors in eastern Ōmi, Hideyoshi set about systematizing his tax-collection program, making it even more rational and efficient than that of his predecessor. Hideyoshi's cadastral surveys were to compress the traditional multilayered landholding system into one layer. Each parcel would be placed under one person only, who would hold the exclusive rights and obligations attached to it. Taxes would be assessed on the basis of the mura (village), a new and uniform administrative unit replacing the old designations, such as gō. The mura would then apportion obligations among its landholders.

In the sixteen years between 1582 and 1598, Hideyoshi succeeded in implementing his reform program over the entire length of the country.[29] Tokuchin-ho experienced some of its earliest applications. A

series of local records from this period illustrates the gradual maturation of the program in successive surveys and its local impact.

Before tracing the records of the surveys and local reactions to them,
it is well to emphasize the radical nature of Hideyoshi's program. Its
proposed reorganization of land rights completely defied the traditional pattern of landholding in at least two ways. First, before the
survey, land parcels embodied a number of overlapping land tenures
(shiki), some defined as the right to the harvest, or *tokubun-ken,* and
others as the right to cultivate, or *kōsaku-ken,* all providing a set rate of
profits. By the late sixteenth century, a villager's social status had only a
tenuous correlation to the type of land tenure he (or she) held, unlike in
the early medieval period, when various "rights" were hierarchically
arranged to correspond to the social status of the holder. One person
now often held any number of these rights pertaining to any number of
parcels. For example, one Dōsen of Imabori held tokubun-ken to six
different plots but also held the kōsaku-ken to another parcel, whose
tokubun-ken was listed under someone else's name.[30] Actual "ownership" of land was a slippery issue.

Second, the attempt to simplify tax collection by basing it on administrative mura also ignored the medieval landholding pattern, in which
many rights were no more confined within a mura than were the social
interactions of the people. For example, residents within and without
Tokuchin-ho frequently donated land to the shrine of a village ("gō" in
those days) other than his or her own. Territorial borders in no way
served to arbitrarily restrict the flow of people or yields from plots of
land.

Tokuchin-ho documents do not disclose the exact process by which
the surveys defined and reorganized these rights. We can be relatively
certain that an arbitrary selection process imposed by outsiders caused
some difficulties among villagers, especially to tokubun-ken holders,
who had the most to lose. In another Ōmi village, for example, a
certain Yoroku who possessed a tokubun-ken had granted cultivation
rights to three peasants. On the ·eve of the survey, he forced the
peasants to guarantee in writing the following agreement: they would
refrain from selling the land without Yoroku's approval, and even if
they were designated the title holders in the survey records, Yoroku
could confiscate the parcels if needed.[31]

This type of insecurity among villagers is not recorded for our area.
All we see are the consequences as the traditional hierarchy of tenures
was streamlined into a single dimension of ownership. But the system
came to allow cultivation by outsiders (either owner-cultivators or

landlords) who owed a specified amount of tax in the village where the land was located. At least 22 men from Hebimizo cultivated land in Imabori.[32] A pattern of commuting (or renting out to tenants) was apparently common; in another Kinai village, close to 60 percent of the title holders resided outside the village.[33]

By the sixth month of 1583, Hideyoshi's land survey project was well under way in Tokuchin-ho. Implementation of his program progressed in several stages, growing more systematic as the years went by. During the first phase, the surveys still depended on the cooperation of local people in assessing and reporting putative yields. While employing this method, Hideyoshi, suspecting underregistration, required complete reports from both cultivators and his own vassals. In an order thought to date from the autumn of 1583, Hideyoshi's vassal Asano Nagayoshi (later Nagamasa) demanded that the cultivators (hyakushō) of Gamō County report all parcels that for one reason or another had gone unregistered in the past. Anyone evading this order was to be judged severely.[34]

Two registers of the earliest surveys, in Imazaike, survive; they date from 1583 and 1584. Even a brief comparison of the two registers indicates a systematic improvement in the survey technique, format, and style from one year to the next.[35] The first had the cover title "Honai Imazaike." By adhering to the name Honai, the cadasters upheld the traditional shōen-based framework. At this juncture, assessed yields were recorded in an uneven fashion, by both the traditional and the emerging standard units of measure.[36] By the following year, not only the new standardized measure but also the quality-based grading system for land values—superior, medium, and inferior—had been established. The register's cover now read "Gamō County Imazaike-mura survey record."[37] The shōen terminology had been abandoned. The term *mura* now defined all villages in Japan as a uniform administrative category, replacing any variations, such as gō.[38]

Accompanying the improved survey technique was a considerable increase in the recorded cultivated area. The second survey "discovered" close to 10 *chō* of land, a 45 percent increase over the previous calculation. Woods and forests of different types, including one called the "shrine's woods," received fresh attention, generating the increase in land area. This, however, did not translate into a marked increase in the total putative yield for Imazaike—up only 3.6 percent, from 210.06 *koku* to 217.67. Meanwhile, people of nonpeasant origins—samurai and priests, for instance—came to be eliminated from the list and their holdings categorized as having "no owner." A greater number of

Imazaike residents (79, up from 71) were listed, as were a smaller number of outsiders (17, down from 22; they lived in Nakano, Hebi-mizo, Imabori, and Koimazaike). Finally, the sō was designated the biggest holder, exceeding the next in line by about threefold.[39]

For Imabori, unlike Imazaike, only fragments of survey records have survived. But it is evident that Imabori villagers anticipated the surveys with anxiety and resolve. The sō discussed the situation, resigned itself to the idea of change, and decided on ways to deal with it to cause minimum disruption to the community. The three-article regulation drafted by the Imabori sō in the seventh month of 1583, a few months prior to the first survey, clearly illustrates this attitude of collective resolve: Those listed on the register shall have the right to discuss matters concerning the survey;[40] once the ownership of land is decided, do not covet other people's land; landholding peasants who make trouble will be ostracized.[41] Faced with a shakeup whose impact would probably surpass that of any past change, the sō sought to avoid internal friction and promoted, above all, social cohesion and "one-mindedness" among its members.

The loss of the 1583 survey records for Imabori makes it impossible to examine the registry in detail. But the sō expressed grievances over three conditions: the taxation rate (presumably too high), the supple-mentary taxes (presumably high and without precedent), and the mea-suring cup (presumably too large). Their complaints crystallized into a collective protest: the sō's 90 members cosigned an oath.[42] The oath read: "If the three points above are not reconciled after our appeal, we will all leave our homes and refuse to accommodate [Hideyoshi's order]. Anyone not acting in accordance with this pledge shall be excluded from the sō." The outcome of the survey made the villagers realize the extent to which their burden had been increased since the previous era. Enryakuji not only had tolerated the considerable extent of shrine land but also had taxed rather superficially, at least on dry fields. The shugo had imposed few demands on Honai villagers, and when he did, he acted unobtrusively through the temple. The new situation must have seemed ominous. In pressing their position, sō members employed a time-tested form of peasant protest—the threat to abscond and leave the arable land untended.

A statement by Hideyoshi, estimated to date from the third month of the following year, 1584, testifies that villagers indeed resisted the new imposition. Addressing his vassals, Hideyoshi expressed concern over "the disappearance of the Ōmi cultivators who protested the survey" and deferred the payment of currently owed taxes until the following autumn "if it is difficult [for the cultivators] to pay now." He further urged the local vassals to open new land for cultivation in order to increase not only the net yield but also the land available to cultivators.[43] To Hideyoshi, the flight of cultivators signified a grave problem. At a practical level, the area's agricultural resources were going to waste, halting the flow of incoming taxes. In terms of his political authority, unrest among the peasantry indicated a failure to govern the country's most important productive sector.

The result of the second survey in Imabori was submitted in the ninth month of 1584.[44] By then, some significant changes were discernible. Imabori village had come to be administratively—not physically—divided into two sections, estimated to yield 280 and 260 *koku* respectively, and was placed under two different agents. It is speculated that this was the division that the Tokugawa bakufu later adopted when it enfeoffed Imabori to two daimyo: Date of Sendai and Ii of Hikone.[45]

One month after the survey results were available, the Imabori villagers wrote another pledge. This pledge displayed a radically different tone from the previous one. Instead of noting grievances, the villagers promised cooperation: to abide by the newly determined boundaries and to report what they possessed down to the last grain and the last *sen* (of cash). They promised to report any field that might be opened after the completion of the survey and not to confuse the land rankings for the purpose of lowering taxes. They pledged not to befriend magistrates or bribe them. An incident of gift giving or the receipt of magistral leniency (in return) would be immediately reported upon discovery.[46]

What caused this sudden change in the villagers' attitude, the switch from protest to accommodation? Asao Naohiro speculates that this pledge was a response to a renewed order by Hideyoshi to conduct yet another survey intended to increase the village's putative yield.[47] The demonstration of compliance was meant to suggest the villagers' goodwill and, thus, the lack of a need for another survey. Other scholars read coercion in the statement; villagers wrote this pledge under duress in response to pressure from Hideyoshi's cadastral officials.[48] A third possible explanation is that the Imabori villagers drafted the pledge for internal use—to minimize friction within the community—not for showing to the authorities. There was probably a general fear that the surveys, especially in their assignment of cultivators to holdings, would cause intravillage antagonism. Some villagers may have already sought to bribe magistrates in order to be listed as cultivators or to have their putative yields underestimated. Villagers must have known that officials gave occasional favors to those who "served loyally during the survey"; for instance, one Jōsai of a nearby village received a tax exemption on his residential plot.[49] With villagers now competing with one another, the sō had ample reason to warn against the purchase of favors, a divisive act harmful to the community.

Whatever the reason, no subsequent protest was recorded, although the Imabori sō continued to write mutual pledges that displayed the collective resolve to receive fair treatment.[50] Hideyoshi conducted large-scale cadastral surveys throughout Japan in 1591. These included a third examination of Tokuchin-ho.[51] In preparation, Imabori's local representative submitted a putative yield of about 540 *koku* (for the entire village) based on the harvest of the year before.[52] This putative figure decreased to 526 *koku* in 1591[53] and stabilized at about 506 *koku* throughout the Tokugawa period,[54] a constancy usually attributed to administrative difficulties, not productive stagnation.

The Surveys and the Question of the Independent Peasant

In reorganizing the country's taxation system, Hideyoshi intended to create a social and economic order that was simpler and more governable than what had previously existed. He envisioned a two-tiered structure of agricultural producers and nonproductive urban consumers that eliminated the intermediate levels of landholders and tax collectors. Registration of land under the name of the person actually cultivating it sharpened the bureaucratic penetration of Hideyoshi's rule into the countryside.

Historians have given much attention to Hideyoshi's surveys. Some have argued that they promoted the growth of an independent small peasant class for the first time in Japanese history. The argument emphasizes the correlation between the title to the land, the right to its productive capacity, and the obligation to pay dues on it, which now converged in one person. This system ended the era in which peasants' rights and obligations had been subsumed under the authority of the idle recipients of shares. Simultaneously, the new independence of the peasantry was aided by the migration of warrior peasants and merchants to castle towns, which left more land rights available to the cultivators.[55]

To what extent was this state of affairs true for the peasants of old Tokuchin-ho? Did they become a group of economically independent cultivators, free of personal subjugation? The extant records from Imazaike and their examination by Miyagawa Mitsuru illuminate these questions.[56]

To investigate the nature and degree of "independence" gained by the "small peasants" of the postsurvey period, Miyagawa compared a set of survey-related documents. One was the cadastre (*kenchichō*) listing putative yields by plot and cultivator's name; the other document was the register of individual holders (*nayosechō*) and their property holdings, including land parcels and houses. The former was useful for the outside tax collector, who only needed to know the sum total of tax obligations for the mura. The latter was used by the village head, who needed to keep track of who owed how much in the village.

Miyagawa looked at two questions in particular: whether the size of the landholding was sufficient for the economic independence of the peasant and whether peasants with land titles were clear of personal servitude to others.

His investigation regarding parcel size demonstrated that in Imazaike and other nearby areas, over 50 percent of the parcels were under 3 *tan,* a size essentially insufficient for subsistence once tax was subtracted. In large villages in Japan's peripheral regions, such small parcels constituted a lower percentage of the landholdings (as low as 14 percent).[57] This meant that the majority of owner-cultivators in Imazaike were neither economically or personally independent. For them and for peasants of other central regions, a need existed to find additional means of livelihood. Some became tenants, submitting their labor to a local notable.[58] The availability of secondary occupations, such as fishing on Lake Biwa, for Sugaura villagers, or forestry, for Yamabe (Settsu Province) villagers, alleviated the general dependence on agriculture.

What this finding suggests is that despite the drastic reorganization of landholdings, there was much continuity in local economic patterns. For those villages with established nonagricultural occupations, the small size of holdings was not a new condition resulting from the surveys of the 1580s but had been a characteristic of the area for centuries. Very few people, before or after the surveys, would have been economically independent based on their landholdings alone. For Tokuchin-ho residents, the key to the local economy was the change in the structure of their source of nonagricultural income—commerce.

How was the local economy affected by the disappearance of the Honai merchants in the 1570s? Without this social link to a market economy, did the region shrink into isolation? Quite the contrary was true. Yōkaichi doubtless continued to benefit from the traffic centered around the country's largest cities, all located within a radius of perhaps 65 kilometers in the Kinai region.[59] During the tumultuous era of Nobunaga and Hideyoshi, the prosperity of Yōkaichi never abated, despite the near disappearance of other noncastle market towns in Ōmi Province. Perhaps Yōkaichi profited from the demise of the smaller market centers, brought about by the trend toward greater specialization and commercialization.[60] In addition, the failure of other towns to obtain permission from the authorities to reestablish their markets allowed Yōkaichi to remain the province's vital center of goods and communication throughout the Tokugawa period.[61] Yōkaichi residents claimed that their good fortune was due to the power of their Market Deity. A record dating from the early 1600s states that Nobunaga ordered Yōkaichi's Market Deity to be transferred to Azuchi. But the residents deceived him and dispatched Sannō Deity (a deity associated with Enryakuji) instead. Because of this hoax, merchants failed to patronize Azuchi, continuing instead to trade at Yōkaichi; the Azuchi market deteriorated, and Yōkaichi prospered.[62]

As in earlier days, Yōkaichi distributed ocean products from Ise, Wakasa, and the new town of Osaka; added to these were various agricultural products, including tea and dye.[63] Tokuchin-ho residents, therefore, never lost their close access to the commercial center and the network that it was part of. Although they were peasants in the Tokugawa status order, they were not cut off from an important center of exchange or (probably) from urban material privileges. The residents could count on supplementary local income associated with commercial activities centered on Yōkaichi.

The precise economic activities of the peasants of this area went unrecorded. But there is evidence that they engaged heavily in cash-crop production. The proximity of the market may have stimulated the production of crops with a high market value. Tea production, which had begun before the sixteenth century, picked up rapidly during the early Tokugawa period. A record from 1673 shows that the area of Tokuchin-ho controlled by the Date daimyo (parts of Kobochizuka, Hebimizo, Imabori, Nakano, Imazaike, Koima, and Kanaya) paid taxes in the form of tea at the rate of 5 *kanme* of tea to 1 *koku* of rice. Local tea came to be distributed widely; from Yōkaichi it was transported north and west to such ports as Obama and Tsuruga. By the early eighteenth century, 98 percent of the total cultivated area in Nakano village was planted in tea.[64]

Miyagawa proceeded next to examine the question of house ownership and its relation to land parcel size to shed light on the pattern of personal dependency among the peasantry. About 50 percent of the landholders in Imazaike owned houses.[65] Miyagawa speculated that those without houses lived with locally influential figures who took them in as servantlike subordinates. Others might have been part of a large, blood-related (real or pseudo) household.[66]

What was the correlation between land size and house ownership? The Imazaike registry of 1584 lists 76 cultivators, 35 with and 41 without houses. Of those without houses, 32 held parcels of 2 *tan* or less, and none held parcels larger than 6 *tan*. For the house owners, land parcel size varied from 10 *tan* to as little as a fraction of 1 *tan*. In fact, land parcels of less than 1 *tan* were distributed evenly among owners and nonowners of houses.[67] Those without houses, then, tended to hold small parcels, but house owners did not necessarily hold large parcels. A small parcel size did not necessarily mean the lack of a house.

What does the foregoing suggest about the livelihood of the new "owner-cultivators"? Did Hideyoshi's cadastral survey in fact create a new class of independent peasants in Tokuchin-ho? Our findings are inconclusive, partly because some villagers also owned or cultivated land in other villages, whose registries did not survive. The available information also paints a complex picture in which the crucial variables were not just land and houses within the village borders. Factors related to larger market forces also came into play.

Nonetheless, it can be said in summary that those without houses held little land and probably were in some type of dependent status. Holders of small parcels with no house, then, were probably not "independent" peasants. Those with houses, on the other hand, often held sufficient land to be economically and personally independent. Those with houses and little land probably depended on non-agricultural sources of income, perhaps producing handicrafts for the nearby market. The social structure of Tokuchin-ho after Hideyoshi's cadastral survey retained elements of ambiguity; not all registered peasants were actually independent, and it appears unlikely that all landowners were full-time peasants.

Reorientation of the Sō

The unification program of Nobunaga and Hideyoshi gave a severe jolt to the local landholding pattern, whose basic shape had not changed over the previous 300 years. The shrine's fisc—the economic base of the communal bond—was perhaps most heavily hit. Confiscation of the shrine land also undermined the sō's function as the manager of corporate assets. But the new ruler did not undermine the importance of the sō as a local political organ—for a good reason.

Within the new hegemony, the presence of a local collective organization such as the sō represented both a potential source of rebellion and a means through which to penetrate the foundation stratum of society, where its productive forces lay. The sō villagers were highly accustomed to decision-making processes, fairly literate, and well experienced in implementing rules and regulations for the common good. The community had a cohesive organization, which emphasized acting "of one mind." The local network of communication was developed, and information flowed smoothly. From the ruler's viewpoint, this collective force could be good or bad; it could turn rebellious, or it could serve to mediate the new and alien rule. The obvious strategy was not only to nip the sō's bud of rebellion but also to absorb the sō into the larger political structure. How did the hegemon accomplish this task?

Several stages were necessary for the reorientation of the sō. First, Hideyoshi's allies near Tokuchin-ho sought to integrate themselves into the local community by making grants of land, a practice familiar to warrior lords and their vassals. Two outsiders, whose names— Tanaka Hisazō and Kajimura Nagaemonnojō—suggest their warrior background, commended plots of land to Imabori's Jūzenji shrine in 1589.[68] We know that they were outsiders because the sō responded to their commendations by writing a receipt for the first time in its history, using ample honorifics. The commendations doubtless pleased the villagers; they were the first instances of commendation in decades, and the shrine sorely needed contributions at this point.

Land commendation won Tanaka Hisazō the trust of the community. By 1591, he was more than an ordinary community member; he was the signatory representing the collective body of the sō. In the same month of 1591 that a survey was in progress, the Imabori sō prepared a two-part pledge. It was signed by the "Imabori sōbun," represented by Tanaka's seal; after the seal came the names of 74 sō members and a majority of their signatures.[69] The first item in the pledge stipulated that if any cultivator absconded, the three households in front and the two on either side of the offender's residence would pay his or her tax instead. The second promised that in case the sō members' petition to the cadastral magistrate was rejected and they decided to flee, they would act of one mind and all depart together.

The pledge asserted the sō's collective potential in two mutually contrasting ways. The first item guaranteed to uphold the responsibility of the village at large in fulfilling an obligation to authority. The second provided for the abrogation of such obligations if the authority failed to meet certain minimum conditions decided by the sō (which in this instance are unknown to us). The collective responsibility toward authority coexisted with the power to bargain and protest.[70] The members of the sō thus agreed to sanction each other's behavior and to act as the community's police, preempting the need for outside intervention. Obviously, this system was beneficial to the authorities, but it also gave the villagers a means by which to perpetuate autonomy in local governance. Through the efforts of a local ally, Hideyoshi thus succeeded in transforming the sō into a structure of collaborative control, without denying it an option for resistance.

Arbitrary Impositions

Under the Rokkaku, emergency taxes and services were not unknown in Tokuchin-ho. But Hideyoshi's rule brought an impost of an unprecedented nature. Hideyoshi had been planning to conquer China since the 1580s. In 1591, when Korea denied Hideyoshi safe passage to China, he began preparations for invading Korea. His vassal daimyo were ordered to mobilize men to construct a forward base in Hizen, Kyushu, and to fight in Korea.[71]

The first step in the preparations involved a survey of labor power, ordered in the third month of 1592 throughout the 66 provinces. The surveyors were to register and count the men and the women, the old and the young, and the households in each village. Classificatory designations such as "servant," "townsperson," and "peasant" were added to applicable names. In Imabori the 75 households were also grouped by categories of services: 29 households were eligible for corvée levies, 5 households that were dependent servitors of samurai families were exempted, and 41 households headed by a priest, nun, or widow were likewise exempted.[72] A comparison of this list with the sō's pledge of the year before[73] reveals a sudden increase in the number of widows and priests. Only 38.6 percent of the villagers fell in the draftable category. Obviously many villagers sought to avoid conscription by naming a nondraftable person as the household head. The list was largely a fiction. Only 36 names are identical on the two lists.

In the twelfth month of 1592, the Imabori sō received a written conscription order.[74] It stipulated, among other things, the departure of four conscripts within eight days and their arrival at the site of the forward base (Nagoya in Hizen Province) before the end of the year. It also prescribed the quantity of rice to be submitted by the sō: 8.5 *koku* now and 7 *koku* next fall. The term of service was to be one year.

Corvée duty of one full year in Kyushu must have seemed an onerous task not only for the drafted male but also for his household, which would lose a main source of labor. Ultimately the burden of conscription must have fallen on the sō, which was obligated to cultivate the lands of those households left with inadequate labor. The sō was also ordered to submit rice, whether to feed its own conscripts or others.[75] The country's many communities were forced to sacrifice much for the sake of one man's grandiose vision. Their sacrifices were a by-product of the unification; villagers could appeal to no other authority to counter Hideyoshi.

As the residents of old Tokuchin-ho came to be labeled "peasants," they bore far more restrictions from authorities than they had in medieval times. Now they were registered and bound to the land. By law, geographical mobility was disallowed. Also by law, though undocumented in our area, they were forbidden to arm themselves or practice commerce. Taxation was imposed more rationally and on greater stretches of land, leaving less room for flexibility.

Change and Continuity Under Tokugawa Rule

In 1591, Hideyoshi enfeoffed Ōmi land worth 90,000 *koku,* including Tokuchin-ho villages, to Tokugawa Ieyasu, whose territorial base was in the Kantō area, around Edo.[76] Ōmi was Ieyasu's only holding outside eastern Honshu, and the grant was intended to provide for the expenses associated with his regular sojourns in Kyoto.[77] At this time Hideyoshi did not foresee what the future held for Ieyasu. When Hideyoshi died in 1598, Ieyasu became the effective overlord of the Ōmi region. To consolidate his position in the eyes of the population, Ieyasu immediately conducted his own survey of the villages.[78]

At the level of the countrywide power struggle, Ieyasu pursued a pacification policy by seeking to control both friends and foes alike. The celebrated battle of Sekigahara opened the way in 1600 for thoroughgoing institutional reform. At once he began confiscating enemy domains and granting fiefs to his major allies. Eventually the greater part of Ōmi Province went to his most trusted vassals, the *fudai,* while the Tokugawa themselves controlled important nodes of transportation.[79]

In 1601, Ieyasu apportioned a large segment of the villages—now legally defined as mura—in the lower four gō of old Tokuchin-ho to Date Masamune of the Sendai domain. At this juncture, Imabori was split and about one half went to Date.[80] The remainder of Imabori was enfeoffed to Ii Naotaka, daimyo of Hikone, in 1617.[81] This division did not signify that the mura was geographically split up. Imabori retained its physical integrity; only the putative yield and the sphere of bureaucratic administration was divided. Other mura in the region fell under the control of a number of daimyo, reflecting the Tokugawa plan for diffusing authority in this key central region.[82] The productive capacity of the mura was translated into components of the daimyo domains enfeoffed by the shogun, the supreme ruler of the entire country.

The Tokugawa village was the smallest administrative unit in the new centralized order. This order assumed a clear-cut hierarchy of functional groups that would uphold both the political supremacy of the samurai class and the productive obligations of the farming class. While the physical distance of the samurai from the land enhanced their bureaucratic character, it also restricted them from direct intervention in village affairs. With minimal involvement of the urban bureaucrats, the primary producers paid taxes and kept local peace and order. Despite a large number of peasant uprisings (*ikki*),[83] recorded especially in the latter part of the Tokugawa period, the Tokugawa village on the whole was an administrative success that helped to perpetuate more than two centuries of relative stability.

In this context, the question of how the Tokugawa mura operated has long interested historians. Matsumoto Shinpachirō, for one, gave an answer in the 1940s that has since become classic: the self-governing, familylike quality of the earlier village worked in conjunction with the goals of the state headed by the "despotic feudal hegemon."[84]

While the basic outline of this argument has endured the test of time, its very strength and credibility, ironically, have impeded empirical investigation of the precise link between local, pre-Tokugawa forms of village structure and the new mura.[85] The pattern of transformation at the local level involved the complex interaction of different forces— old and new, local and central—each of which underwent continuous reshaping in processes of adaptation, modification, and reproduction.

The Sō and the Tokugawa Village

The establishment of the Tokugawa shogunate inaugurated extensive political restructuring at higher levels. This affected local communal organizations, including the sō. We can easily evaluate the degree of this transformation by comparing the quantity and quality of sō documents from Imabori before and after the tide of unification struck the area. The 300 years before Nobunaga's rise saw the accumulation of around 800 documents. The three decades under Nobunaga and Hideyoshi left about 50, many of them concerning surveys. In the 268 years of the Tokugawa period (1600–1868) we find only 95 documents, a number that suggests a radical disjuncture.[86] Conspicuous by their absence are records related to merchants and shrine land. The villagers were now functionally and legally classified as peasants. The past glory of the area's merchants lived on only in communal memory. The removal of shrine land—corporate assets essential to financing a multitude of communal projects—reshaped the village into a Tokugawa village, marked by the lack of collective assets upon which to build an independent social, religious, or political organization. In Tokugawa times, the sō held only land that lacked an officially recognized cultivator; landholding primarily obligated the sō to pay taxes. Operating without a solid economic base derived from commerce or land, the Tokugawa village's so-called autonomy was necessarily limited. It was autonomous only within the framework of the ordained, standardized state administrative structure.

The sō's archival importance was drastically reduced in yet another way. In the new political structure, the sō was no longer virtually the sole record-keeper of the village. Because the sō did not represent the village in an administrative sense, many aspects of record keeping fell outside its purview. The village officials issued and kept documents in their public capacity apart from the sō. Our examination of the Tokugawa mura therefore must depend heavily on documents kept by other agencies.

However, Imabori's sō documents dating from 1600 on nonetheless bear witness to the unbroken role of the sō in managing certain crucial aspects of community life. They are similar to some of the document types of medieval origin—land sales records, village regulations and ordinances, records of intervillage disputes, and records related to certain ceremonies. What did these elements of continuity signify in the context of the new political structure?

The sō played a vital function in a political order that distinguished two realms—the outer, public, and bureaucratic realm and the inner, local, and private realm. The newly imposed hierarchy of administrative offices helped to separate formal from informal modes of control. The guidelines set by the daimyo (or shogun) were formal, while the authority and power of the sō over local social and political processes were informal—although the two modes often and necessarily converged.

In their outer structure, Tokugawa villages were largely uniform. But many of the mura's new administrative mechanisms were built upon indigenous human and institutional resources, making possible much variation within the specified structure. Daimyo and samurai, who were physically, politically, and socially outsiders to the mura, had minimal involvement in local affairs. To the lord, the mura was fundamentally a collective unit of taxation and an independent jurisdictional entity—for bringing suits, for signing contracts, for possessing property, and for carrying on financial transactions.[87]

Beneath the administrative overlay, residents of old Tokuchin-ho kept alive the terms and concepts associated with earlier centuries. Though the name Tokuchin-ho went out of use and each gō was now called a mura, the local people continued to regard the lower four gō, for example, as a geographical division of vital significance. The split between the upper and lower sections remained because it directly touched upon the villagers' daily lives; it reflected the contrasting agricultural conditions and often identified claims to the region's commons. Nor did Imabori's administrative division affect the cohesion of Imabori as a communal entity. Solutions to problems in Imabori-mura often required the cosignatures of both headmen (*shōya*), indicating the communal coherence and unity of purpose of the two sections.[88] The influence of this administrative division on the shape of the Imabori sō, moreover, was minimal. The sō remained a mura-wide unit, represented by about 70 signatures in 1639, for example, a number not significantly different from the number in earlier times.[89] It was still centered on the Imabori shrine and its shrine association. Deities specific to the village were worshiped by all. The kannushi, or priest, was the primary spokesman for the sō, and his name often led the list of sō members in endorsing sō-initiated pledges.[90]

The success of the Tokugawa village depended on the fine interplay of the outer and inner realms. Essential to the smooth functioning of the new rural political order was the work of informal local organizations and their acceptance of the public structure as a viable framework within which to operate.

Village officials. The public, administrative realm operated under the government's agents, who were appointed from among the local population. The agents included a headman, or shōya, and his delegate, a *yokome* or *kimoiri*, though the titles themselves varied from one domain to another. In Imabori-mura, there was a shōya and a yokome or kimoiri for each of the administrative sections. Although the formal offices of shōya and kimoiri were strictly Tokugawa institutions, the titles themselves emerged during the era of Hideyoshi's surveys. As early as 1591, bearers of these titles represented Kobochizuka village in defending the boundaries of their commons.[91] The list of Imabori households submitted to Hideyoshi in 1592 also included one man whose name was capped by the notation for shōya.[92]

In the Tokugawa period, these men became the leaders of the public, political realm created by the centralized government. Their official status carried with it formal responsibilities that had been nonexistent in the pre-Tokugawa village. The headman in particular represented the village vis-à-vis the lord and was accountable for the village's fulfillment of its state-ordained functions. He was a mediator between the ruling institution and its subject population and was the chief vehicle for disseminating the lord's orders. The scope of his duties extended from overseeing tax collection and household registration to bringing lawsuits on the village's behalf. If the village's tax payment fell short of the assessed figure, it was the headman who had to make up the difference. If a villager's daughter wedded an outsider, the headman had to make certain that this population movement was duly registered. The appearance of his name and title on many village documents—a deed of land transfer,[93] an appeal to the lord,[94] and village codes,[95] for example—illustrates the importance of the headman in Tokugawa village affairs.[96]

Because these official positions accorded their bearers legitimacy and social prestige, they were often coveted; but the evidence for our region suggests the reverse. In 1738, the incumbent headman of Nakano village submitted a request to resign, citing "poverty" as his reason. Apparently Nakano village had been suffering excessive turnover in the office of headman. The village considered increasing the salary.[97] But according to the villagers' statements, many in Nakano were quite impoverished. It was difficult for them to contribute toward officials' salaries; the domainal government had initially paid the salaries, but the burden had been gradually passed on to the shoulders of the villagers themselves.[98] It was true that the headman received some material compensation for his work, such as a salary and exemption from taxes and corvée duties, as well as social recognition and visibility both in and out of the village. But here obligations apparently outweighed the privileges. He was required to finance his own trips to the domainal capital to carry on public duties, for instance.[99] It is no wonder that an impoverished man—by his own admission—would have encountered trouble fulfilling the office satisfactorily.

After the resignation of the headman, following the custom observed in this area, the village held an election. A man in his 50s who had served as an otona (elder) previously and thus was familiar with administrative matters received the largest number of votes. This change was duly reported to a higher authority.[100]

While the office of headman was a relatively novel creation from above, the holder of the title came out of the local or inner sphere. In administering the village, outer elements came to be juxtaposed with indigenous elements. For one thing, the elders—an institutional legacy from the pre-Tokugawa sō[101]—provided the pool of talent from which officials came to be chosen. In the above case, the newly elected headman had been an elder. The office of kimoiri in Nakano was assigned, on an annually rotating basis, to two men among the village's ten elders.[102] Several elders and sometimes a "head hyakushō" (*hyakushō-dai*) often signed important documents alongside the officials.[103] The actual running of the Tokugawa village thus depended greatly on the human and structural resources developed in the earlier centuries of communal rule.

The registration system. A Tokugawa institutional innovation that undoubtedly aided the local officials' ability to oversee the activities of villagers was the family registration system (*shūshi ninbetsu*), enforced in connection with the governmental ban on Christianity. Starting in 1645, in the aftermath of the Shimabara Disturbance,[104] the bakufu ordered families to register themselves at a temple (*dannadera*). The temple then certified the registered family's lack of a tie to Christianity. It also arranged funerals[105] and other ceremonies in return for donations (*fuse*).[106] Family registration grew more systematic by the 1660s and became an effective way to keep track of village households. The name, sex, age, occupation, birth, marriage, divorce, death, and transfer of household members (servants included) all came to be recorded.

In complying with the bakufu's new registration system, people had to choose a temple. As with many other facets of village life, a communitywide decision, not individual choice, was the norm in our region. Of 58 sample villages in the environs of Yōkaichi, 34 villages had exclusive affiliation with one temple.[107] Imabori, along with Nakano, Shibawara, and Kami-Ōmori, were affiliated with two temples. The location of one's residence influenced the pattern of affiliation. Imabori's Renkōji, which was not established until 1713,[108] came to serve the vast majority of Imabori residents, while Fukumeiji, located in Hebimizo and dating from 1591, served a few residing on the village's outskirts.[109]

The pattern of villagewide affiliation was less prevalent in the country at large. According to Takeda Chōshū, it was more common for one village to host multiple temples of various schools, the villagers being divided into a number of patronage (*danna*) groups, or parishes. He speculates that kinship, neighborhood, and class relations may have shaped such groupings.[110] The simplicity of the registration pattern in the Yōkaichi region may reflect the strength of communal cohesion, which tended to override other considerations.

The newly imposed family registration system and its ramifications bring into relief the pattern of transformation in the social significance of religion. In pre-Tokugawa times, Imabori's shrine was the focal point of its social, religious, and political activities. The shrine housed both Shinto and Buddhist images and took broad care of local spiritual needs. Now this comprehensive role was segmented. The temple firmly bound the registrants financially through donations and tied them further to the country's governmental requirements. Worship of the dead was regulated, with an established schedule of commemorative ceremonies. Residential architecture even changed to include a room with an altar to accommodate a priest and guests on those ceremonial days.[111]

Before the seventeenth century, village temples and shrines were amorphous religious centers not necessarily adhering to one doctrine. Despite Imabori's counterexample, they often existed independently of any larger doctrinal center. Nor were priests necessarily distinguished from lay people; many held an ambiguous semipriest, semilay status. But the new regime sought systematization of the entire religious order, demanding strict definition and clarification of all its aspects, including doctrinal affiliation and the status of priests.[112] The Tokugawa government's measures to track and record the populace through the temples naturally led to a great surge in their number. Only ten of 73 temples located in Gamō and Kanzaki counties had existed before unification.[113]

In our region, registration brought the eclipse of the Tendai school of Buddhism. Notwithstanding the area's long association with Enryakuji—the estate proprietor and the center of the Tendai school—the most popular doctrinal school locally was now Pure Land Buddhism. The devastation Enryakuji had suffered at the hands of Nobunaga probably contributed to the Tendai school's unpopularity; although the school recovered under Hideyoshi and Ieyasu, it did not achieve the status and importance it had had in the medieval period. In 1584, Toyotomi Hideyoshi ordered the reconstruction of Enryakuji and solicited donations from various daimyo, including Ieyasu. Subsequently, Hideyoshi revived the cloisters in Sakamoto by granting a stipend of approximately 1,500 *koku,* which Ieyasu increased to 5,000 *koku.* All the buildings were rebuilt between 1624 to 1643. Even though Enryakuji regained some prestige during the Tokugawa period, aided partly by this new economic security,[114] its branch temples still failed to prosper as the lineage, or patron, temples. It seems that the Tendai-school temples were more important to the fortunes of a community than to the well-being of a lineage or ancestor, for they collaborated easily with Shinto shrines to celebrate local deities.[115] In Yōkaichi, four of seventeen temples were Tendai temples, but only two of them had registrants, totaling a mere 76 families (out of 979 households accounted for).[116] There were nine Pure Land temples, including Imabori's Renkōji and Hebimizo's Fukumeiji.[117]

Meanwhile, local shrines such as Jūzenji continued to hold a meaningful place in the villagers' lives and in the seasonal cycles of the village. The shrine association remained intact, and local deities—now called *ujigami*—thrived.[118] Natural signs of spiritual forces, such as the Field Deity and the Mountain Deity, doubtless continued to inform the landscape. Centuries-old ceremonies, such as the coming-of-age ceremony and the promotion-to-otona ceremony, or Kechi, brought spiritual security by elevating one's socio-religious status or purifying one's body and soul. Despite the lowered profile of Enryakuji, villagers continued to celebrate deities originally associated with Hie Shrine— such as Sannō and Jūzenji.

This is not to suggest a placid continuity. The price participants paid for the ceremonies was considerably reduced, for example. In the fifteenth century a fee of 1 *kan* or more for the coming-of-age ceremony and 350 to 500 *mon* for otona ceremonies was standard. In 1585, the Imabori sō accepted a payment of 300 *mon* "without sake" for a certain Iwa's coming-of-age ceremony. In 1698, the coming-of-age ceremony was 2 *to* of rice for everyone. Similarly, an otona ceremony of 1587 or 1691 cost only 100 *mon*, or 2 *to* of rice, to each participant.[119] It seems that the shrine's activities were promoted within the framework of a reduced economy of scale commensurate with its material assets.[120]

The five-household group (gonin-gumi). Despite the new formalized mechanisms of control, governance of the mura was substantively entrusted to the villagers themselves. An institution of mutual surveillance, usually called the *gonin-gumi*, or "five-household group," was important in this regard. Ideally, each gonin-gumi consisted of five households, two adjoining each other and three facing, which were collectively responsible for one another's conduct, the fulfillment of tax obligations, or any legal transactions, such as the sale of property. Outside the family (*ie*), it was the minimal and, socially, the most powerful collective unit that—ideally—fostered the state ideology of a docile and productive peasantry. The institution promoted mutual dependence, cooperation, and consensus while strongly discouraging dissent. The members helped each other during the busy agricultural seasons, promoted technological education, helped to alleviate financial difficulties, discouraged mobility, and expelled or otherwise punished controversial persons.[121] Sometimes gonin-gumi also took the responsibility for registering people at a temple.[122]

The principle behind the gonin-gumi had emerged at least by Hideyoshi's era. During the surveys, for example, the system of mutual responsibility among three families had been endorsed by the Imabori sō.[123] In the formalized Tokugawa structure, the idea of local social control became important in local governance throughout the country, although its implementation showed little uniformity—it was universal in the shogun's lands but less so in daimyo domains.[124] The particular form it took also varied from one domain to another, even from one village to another, probably influenced by prior local conditions.

A brief comparison of Imabori's gonin-gumi with Nakano's allows us to assess the varying patterns of transformation in local systems before and after unification. In Imabori, probably because of the powerful role played by the sō, the five-household group of mutual surveillance was never formalized as a stable feature of community rule.[125] A preexisting structure of social control and a tightly knit communication system preempted the need for other policing organizations. The formal institutions of mutual security promoted by the Tokugawa shogunate found a local surrogate in the sō of Imabori.

In contrast, Nakano had gonin-gumi with a concrete and substantive function that increased in authority after the mid-seventeenth century. Initially, Nakano residents were divided into six divisions (*kumi*) composed of an unknown number of members divided according to the location of their residences (in the northeast, for instance). In 1658, a ten-household group was introduced, followed in 1659 by the creation of the five-household group. Until 1669, all village members or the sō signed collective pledges and regulations. After the late seventeenth century, however, the communal rights to sign such documents came to be vested in the chiefs of the five-household groups. Sometimes a large number of household heads also signed the documents, but these names were listed below the names of the chiefs of the five-household groups.[126] The indigenous social system of Nakano, composed of the villagers at large, was rapidly being subsumed under the formal structure.

The contrast in the function and significance of the gonin-gumi of Imabori and Nakano might be examined in combination with other factors that distinguished the two villages. Compared to the Imabori sō, the Nakano sō was perhaps less developed and less structured in medieval times. The absence of a meeting hall in Nakano, a problem noted in 1664 by the domainal government, which required a place for public announcements,[127] confirms this point. The survival pattern of documents tends to support our speculation. In the medieval period, the relative importance of Nakano within Tokuchin-ho must have been minimal. The Nakano sō's archival collection attained a fraction of the level of Imabori's. But Nakano village records from the Tokugawa period survived in large numbers, demonstrating the strength of the public and outer aspect of village governance.

Through formal reorganization, the mura was transformed into a political entity in the full sense; each villager was a vital component of

the governing body, linked through the institution of a mutual surveillance team, which in turn was organized and supervised by officials
who at once answered local needs and the lord's demands. This collec-
tivistic quality of the Tokugawa village was built upon the legacies
of the past, especially those of the sō. Past patterns informed each
Tokugawa village, yielding variations in the supposedly uniform mura
system.

Taxation

Fulfillment of taxes and services was by far the most important
function a mura played in the eyes of the government. The recognized
parameters within which this extractive relationship took shape rested
greatly on the acceptance of the traditional collective social organization. In the system of *mura-uke* (mura-wide payment), collection of
taxes became a responsibility borne by the village's entire body of
landholders. By entrusting the administration of tax payment to the
village, rulers also accommodated the village's inclination to promote
the communal interest through collective resolve. We may recall that in
confronting each new development in Hideyoshi's surveys, the Imabori villagers demonstrated concern and an ability to uphold internal
solidarity. In the Tokugawa period, a similar resolve to maintain a
degree of local self-determination persisted. When a new Date official
(*daikan*), Sama-no-shin, sought to impose added taxes on tea, mulber-
ries, and persimmons in 1616, residents of four villages in the old
Tokuchin-ho area[128] protested, saying that the sixteen years since the
enfeoffment of the area to Date Masamune had seen no precedent for
such taxes and that these villages, which had practically no paddy land,
could not withstand this new imposition. Because Sama-no-shin did
not heed the request to rescind the order, some residents moved out
while others carried the appeal to Date commissioners (*bugyō*) of higher
rank residing in Sunpu (present-day Shizuoka), Tokugawa Ieyasu's
place of retirement. After describing the predominance of dry farming
in this area, the villagers succinctly pointed out the illegitimacy of the
imposition on two counts: (1) no such practice existed in any of the
neighboring villages or counties and (2) no precedents had been set
under Hideyoshi or his successors, Hidetsugu, Ieyasu, or Date. In
response, the commissioners guaranteed the same level of taxation for
these Tokuchin-ho villages as for the neighboring regions and ordered
the residents to return.[129]

Far from quelled, the conflict climaxed with the visit of another Date
agent, Ishimoda, who had been staying in Edo. Outraged by the appeal
to Sunpu, he sought to nullify the new agreement and rounded up 25

peasants, neck-cuffed those who had journeyed to Sunpu, and burned down their houses. As for the taxes levied by Sama-no-shin, Ishimoda forced the peasants to sign a note of acceptance without changing the terms. Thirty households absconded as a result.

The fight continued. Residents found an opportune moment to protest the following year when different commissioners of the Date house accompanied the shogun, Hidetada, to Kyoto. Appealing directly to these commissioners, the residents reported more crimes committed by Sama-no-shin: (1) he had forced the peasants to accompany him to Kyoto with expensive horses and kept them for nine days instead of one, as promised; (2) he had violated the daughter of a village official in Nakano who, together with the daughter, was socially obligated to leave the village; (3) he had detained innocent peasants since the fifth month of the previous year and had imposed fines upon them. Consequently, they summarily requested Sama-no-shin's dismissal.[130]

Their complaint was heard. A new order issued three months later by the commissioners in Sunpu guaranteed that the village would be treated like neighboring villages and directed the absconding peasants to return. While silent on the issue of Sama-no-shin, the order recommended direct appeal to the commissioners in Sunpu in case of any future violation by governmental agents. It was addressed to the four shōya of the villages involved.[131]

The kind of collective bargaining that led to the final resolution of this conflict was a legacy of the medieval period, in which the sō—highly organized, literate, and aware of general political conditions—had resisted the untoward demands of higher authorities. In this Tokugawa incident, we see again the power of collectively signed words and concerted action. The demand for "comparable treatment" and the observations concerning precedent required a respectable knowledge of regional taxation and historical patterns. Behind the demand also lay the unspoken understanding that the lord and peasant maintain some degree of balanced reciprocity; the former had the obligation to observe custom and to recognize the right of the latter to appeal in cases of its violation. The peasants' signatures on the *ukejō,* a letter acknowledging the type and rate of tax being imposed, symbolized the ideal that taxation was to be based on mutually agreed-upon terms—despite its actual exploitative character.

In practical terms, were Tokugawa peasants better or worse off than medieval peasants? It is impossible to compare meaningfully the actual rates of taxation from before and after unification. In the old Tokuchin-ho region now administered by the Date, the basic taxation rate was established on the basis of the survey of 1602 and remained practically the same throughout the next two centuries. For Imabori, the yield determined in 1602 was a reduction in what had been determined by Hideyoshi's officials in the 1590s. For Ōmi Province, there was a 7.1 percent increase from 1591 to 1602.[132] The other domainal lord, Ii, conducted periodic surveys for every village in his fief. Despite this attention, the putative yield hardly changed after the survey of 1602. It seems that reexamination merely reconfirmed the previous judgment.[133] Stagnation in the tax rate allowed local accumulation of some cultivated land unlisted in the registers. A Nakano regulation of 1638 suggests that this was possible. Signed by 107 men, it stipulated no disclosure of matters regarding "secret paddies [*onden*], even to wives and children."[134]

Apart from the land tax, which became systematized and predictable after the surveys, villagers were faced with other forms of impositions. Particularly onerous was the requirement that horses and porter services be purveyed to Yōkaichi, an officially designated post station in Tokugawa times.[135] Yōkaichi, which had served as a major source of local economic growth and as the center of exchange for goods and information, now became a liability for sixteen surrounding villages, including those in old Tokuchin-ho. We lack details regarding the service offered by an "assisting village" (*sukegō*) to a post station in this region, but the duties expanded and intensified in proportion to the ever-increasing rate of transportation on major roads.[136] A grievance issued by Nakano, Imazaike, Hebimizo, and Kanaya in the mid-nineteenth century reveals that these villages had been serving two post stations (Musa and Minakuchi, in addition to Yōkaichi) and had become too impoverished to serve any longer.[137] Besides assisting the post stations, these villages were sometimes levied emergency imposts, such as contributions toward the expense associated with the passage of Korean ambassadors on nearby roads.[138] Despite the ability to accumulate a surplus, villagers in the Tokugawa mura met harsh requirements for service.

The Sō in Intervillage Disputes

The first century of the Tokugawa period witnessed a large number of intervillage disputes. The nature of the sō's involvement in these disputes is an important barometer of the sō's status and its relationship to the larger political order. But before investigating the sō's role, we need to understand why disputes were frequent.

The transformation in the political structure and in economic relations ushered in an assortment of changes in social values and in people's consciousness. One dimension of change was the evolution of the concept of "private" property at the village level. Several processes nurtured this trend. The land surveys clearly designated property holders, making who owned what clear for everyone. This was a shift from the earlier concept of overlapping landholding rights. A title holder came to be fully and unambiguously associated with a piece of land. The land surveys also clarified the territorial borders of mura. Just as individual cultivators won clear titles and obligations to their parcels, so each mura gained clearly defined territorial rights to a distinctly mapped region. Each mura acquired an awareness of its separateness from its neighboring villages, strengthening the proprietary notion of private territory. "Individualization" of persons and villages thus developed, fostering the idea of exclusive rights to "private" communal property.

Two factors were juxtaposed against this trend and tended to promote an atmosphere of conflict among villages. First, the surveys and the tax reforms reduced the net quantity of commons available for use, including sō land. Therefore, the mura's claims to natural resources intensified. Second, land surveys demarcated village borders and cultivators' plots, but they did not put nontaxable land—the commons—through the same rationalization process. They neither identified which community had claims to which commons nor outlined the borders of the commons. Because the commons yielded no direct revenue to high-level authorities, they fell outside the restructuring from above of landholding relations under the new regime.

It was against this background that the sō frequently became embroiled in both intra- and intervillage disputes, which almost always concerned natural resources. For the sō, this concern had been a focus of its activities since its inception, and after Nobunaga's time, it continued to issue regulations. But the orientation of the regulations had changed somewhat; the sō's authority and responsibility had expanded to include a broader surveillance of the non-sō land, as the following example demonstrates.

A set of regulations from 1599 stipulated a penalty of 1 *to* of rice for harvesting someone else's crop by hand, 5 *to* of rice for damaging irrigation drains, and double that penalty for destroying fields worked by animals. These applied to non-sō land. As for the sō forest, harvesting grass or cutting trees cost a fine of 2 *to* of rice.[139] By 1626, the penalty for similar offenses would inflate tenfold, from 1 *to* to 1 *koku* of rice.[140]

When intervillage disputes occurred, it was the sō that took charge for as long as the dispute's resolution remained in local hands. In conflicts the sō demanded unity of purpose and action under threat of expulsion from the village. Some disputes turned violent, and the

Hebimizo sō, for instance, resolutely demanded martial services from the residents. In 1625, the sō guaranteed that the family—parents or children—of anyone who collapsed (died?) at the scene of fighting would receive not only exemption from tax obligations but also 2 *koku* of rice as compensation; as for the injured, the sō would fulfill his services and cultivate his land.[141]

About eight years after this regulation was drafted, Hebimizo villagers prepared themselves for a dispute with Imabori over an irrigation ditch. The elders of Hebimizo village (still the core members of the sō) demanded that everyone follow their orders under threat of expulsion from the village. No one was to be so eager, however, as to act in haste before receiving orders from the elders. Anyone who happened to be outside the village was to return to the place in dispute at the sound of the drum. Adjustments similar to those of 1625 were promised for the dead or injured.[142]

In these ways the sō commanded and protected the villagers in disputes. But when a dispute called for arbitration by domain-level officials, the sō relinquished its authority to the shōya and his subordinates. The shōya and yokome were probably important members of the sō. But on documents meant for bureaucratic channels, they signed with their official titles, not in the sō's name.[143] For Imabori, which was divided into two administrative spheres, shōya of both sections signed.

The following illustration comes from documents handed down through successive village heads in Hebimizo. It shows what types of dealings were beyond the sō's authority.

In 1677 (at the latest) there began a dispute between the seven mura of the former lower-four-gō area and Fuse, a village southwest of Tokuchin-ho and under Ii (Hikone) authority, over the use of Nunobiki Terrace. The trial went through many stages, lasting until 1705. The crux of the problem was the use of the commons located on Nunobiki Terrace. According to the villages of the Lower-ho (including Hebimizo and Imabori), the commons were for their exclusive uses. One day, however, men of the Lower-ho were confronted by men from Fuse while harvesting grass.[144] The confrontation escalated to the point of violence. Each group accused the other of having entered the area to steal a thousand pine trees. The Lower-ho set up a camp on Nunobiki Terrace to defend its land, but Fuse sent in 140 to 150 armed men to scare away those in the camp.[145]

The Lower-ho finally appealed to the domainal officials. Bakufu (Kyoto *machi bugyō*) investigators were sent from Kyoto to examine the situation. They found, among other things, that each of the disputants called the area in question by an entirely different name—as though two different places existed, with one claimed by each party. But a closer examination proved that the two place names indeed referred to the same spot. Finally, based on records and maps drawn up earlier by domainal officials, the claims of the Lower-ho villages were upheld, ending a complicated dispute that had lasted for almost two generations.[146]

Throughout the trial process, the sō as an organization had no official role. It was the shōya of each village who signed documents. On occasion, the elders (*toshiyori*) also signed, but without any mention of the sō. We can speculate that within each village, the sō probably organized and directed the strategy for pursuing the dispute. But on public records, the sō was devoid of political authority. What the sō did inside the villages was separated from what appeared in bureaucratic documents.

The local system of the village, whose vital component was the sō, came to occupy a sphere independent of the official vocabulary. Although the sō managed local social and political processes, the hierarchy of administrative offices constructed by the state gave it no official recognition. The administrative structure separated formal from informal, relegating the sō to the latter realm. As we have seen, the smooth operation of the formal structure rested heavily on the work of informal local organizations. But the power and authority of the latter were confined to the local realm, with no channel of formal communication with the central powers. This was a great difference from the medieval pattern, in which the sō was the de facto and de jure representative of the village community.

Social Control by the Sō

Tokugawa rule retained a considerable degree of the old local social and political structure. Despite the reduced number of sō documents, the sō's normative function in the community, in particular, did not abate. Throughout the late medieval period, the Imabori sō had issued regulations in an attempt to impose communal standards of behavior. Many concerned the community's natural resources—forestland, grassland, water—while others concerned varied items from gambling to wearing someone else's sandals (both were prohibited; for these and other regulations, see Appendix B). In the new era, the sō continued to issue regulations. But as the following pages will reveal, they took on a more formalistic tone and were used to implement collective social control with greater severity.

Elements of continuity and change are evident in a regulation of

1588. It stipulated a reward for catching a thief stealing from paddies and fields. In this case, the amount of the reward was differentiated according to when the capture occurred—1 *koku* 5 *to* for the daytime and 3 *koku* for the night. To avoid anyone's mistaking an innocent passerby for a thief, carrying rice seedlings through the village before six at dawn was also prohibited and was liable to the same punishment as theft.[147] Repeating the old practice, the sō employed precise language for the terms of punishment. The difference was that the status-differentiated punishments of medieval times had now been totally eliminated. All villagers were now subject to the same measures.

For enforcing community order, collective governance relied ultimately on the force of negative social sanctions and ostracism as before. Ostracism was always a powerful mechanism of control for an agrarian community in which survival depended on an exchange of labor or the sharing of common resources, such as water for irrigation or forestland for fertilizer and building materials. In the Tokugawa political order, ostracism was incorporated into the formalized state mechanism of control as one ideological component of the five-household groups. Where mobility was legally forbidden, the consequence of expulsion from a community was indeed grave, much more serious than in a society that permitted geographical and occupational fluidity (as Japan had done before Hideyoshi's time).

A single example will suffice to illustrate the power of negative sanction. One night in 1639, someone stole unhulled rice seeds. After this crime had been reported to the sō, it was decided that the villagers would cast ballots to determine who the thief was. The man who received the most votes would be punished along with his parents, children, and wife. Anyone who did not cast a ballot would also be regarded as a criminal. Imabori's 68 household heads (all men) endorsed an oath to this effect.[148]

The immediate outcome of the tribunal went unrecorded,[149] but its implications for village society should be assessed from a broader standpoint. The incident reveals that the village had created its own jurisdictional system in which each member held equal power to judge his neighbor's behavior. No legal principle guided the voters' judgment. The question of partiality was not even raised. It is not difficult to imagine how an institution of collective justice such as this one could instill a value system based on fear. In this situation the way to avoid trouble was to keep a low profile, foster mutual goodwill, and blend in.

Once labeled as a dissident or a troublemaker, there was little one could do to save oneself. In 1639, one Chōbei caused problems for the sō by blocking the village's watercourse. As a result, the sō stipulated that "anyone associating with him, even secretly, shall be forever regarded as a criminal, even if Chōbei is later forgiven."[150] Chōbei was thereby expelled from the network of human communications that made up the village's working community. Even if he continued to live in the physical village, he was finished as a village member. The rigidity of the Tokugawa social order in general added greater significance to alienation from the web of human intercourse in the community.[151] A "democratic form" of justice replaced the status-based form; it was a powerful means of promoting the fundamental virtues of conformity and compliance.

In the Tokugawa period, the sō was an informal local organization that played a vital role in reinforcing the type of value system encouraged by the state. But the sō was not the sole agency that sought to regulate the lives of residents. The domainal government also issued series of regulations. How did the official codes differ from the sō codes? Codes issued by the public and outer institution show, instead of disjunction, a striking resemblance to the kinds of prohibitions set down by the sō earlier. The domainal injunction of 1674 forbidding travelers to linger in a village was an echo of Imabori regulations of 1460 and 1566, which stated: "Do not allow a traveler to stay in the village."[152] Repeated Tokugawa proscriptions against gambling and fighting[153] were familiar themes in earlier Imabori regulations. Of course, these injunctions were based on common sense as well as custom. The domain was not necessarily imitating the earlier sō codes; late medieval warrior houses had also issued injunctions against fighting, for instance.[154] But the sō doubtless had an important influence in regularizing these rules into a type of "formalized customary law." Tokugawa government inherited and incorporated elements of the social practices nurtured by the sō. In so doing, the state sought to establish a legal structure consonant with local conditions and easily accepted by all.

This is not to say, however, that the lord's governance consistently upheld the familiar and customary interest of the people. In 1658, Date officials issued a nine-item injunction, including one item banning local credit associations, or tanomoshi. It may be recalled that in medieval times, the tanomoshi functioned as a local communal banking system to which all the members contributed and from which they received some form of dividend. The order was sent to the shōya, kimoiri, and head hyakushō of Nakano village.[155] About a month after the arrival of this order, the headman and his delegate received a pledge from the leaders of eleven household groups. To summarize their statement:

We should honor the lord's injunction against having a tanomoshi. But that would inconvenience everyone, including the smallest peasant. Borrowing and lending activities would cease; the payment of taxes [nengu] would also cease. Therefore we will continue to have a tanomoshi in secrecy. Should it be discovered, the villagers at large will appear [to face the lord], in order to ensure that the headman and the delegate will not be punished. We will explain that there has been no error on their part and apologize.[156]

The lord's law, issued in obvious violation of customary practice, led to collective and secret defiance on the part of the populace. In this area of dissonance, we see a clear point of friction between local systems and state control. Since the people resisted, the order from above lost any practical import. Far from being intimidated by the new rule, villagers responded to it with a resilience born of confidence in their own history of local social control.

The sō was formed on the occasion of the shrine's first steps toward holding landed property. The sō was largely a shrine-centered organization that developed to handle the community's economic, social, and political affairs. This orientation of the sō did not change drastically after the unifiers rearranged the country's authority and land structures.

The sō in the post-Nobunaga period continued to be associated with the shrine. It still managed ceremonies, collecting necessary expenses from participants, albeit in reduced amounts, perhaps reflecting the decline in the shrine's prestige as well as its property. The sō's connection with the shrine was also visible in the role of the head priest (kannushi), who tended to represent the sō in documents.

Despite its loss of economic power, the sō's political and social function remained locally important. But this importance was undermined by the new bureaucratic structure. The sō regulated the villagers' lives through the mechanisms of ostracization and expulsion, methods formally adopted by the Tokugawa ruling order. The sō developed into a powerful internal organization and demonstrated how a village might be run. Functionally, the sō was the primary agent of local governance. Structurally, however, it was placed outside the bureaucracy; no public status or authority was conferred upon the sō.

The removal of formal authority from the sō coincided with the creation of a new countrywide political order. The assignment of new village offices, which constituted the basic level of bureaucracy, diluted the administrative significance of the native institution and helped provide an aura of uniformity to the centralized structure of the Tokugawa bakufu. The Tokugawa shogunate established a powerful centralized state, carefully incorporating many elements of the local systems. Gradually the old local systems were modified and, in many cases, incorporated into the formal, outer state structure. If the sō had usurped state prerogatives centuries before, the Tokugawa gradually gained them back, absorbing what had become established prerogatives of the local systems.

Before unification, the sō villages had asserted collective responsibilities and privileges in order to govern themselves. The Imabori sō had run councils, improved agricultural production, and issued its own ordinances with punitive measures. The Sugaura sō had administered tax collection and judged criminal cases, for example. But the Tokugawa village was not simply a social unit from the past overlaid with a new administration. Unlike before, the Tokugawa villages were formally and administratively integrated into the larger state structure. Villages maintained political and social equilibrium, not as isolated islands, but as part and parcel of the state. In this major phase of social transformation, the old and the new interacted with each other, yielding a structure based on both continuity and development.

In a number of significant ways, the Imabori sō became localized and more inward looking in the Tokugawa period. In terms of membership, the sō had lost its most vital group: the Honai merchants, who had been the great carriers of outside information, goods, and values. In terms of political status, the sō no longer had a legitimate role in dealing with outside officials. Likewise, Jūzenji Shrine, the sō's physical center, was no longer attached to one of the central elite institutions; it had evolved into a strictly local and religious organization. Shrine land, the sō's economic foundation, was also taken away and transformed into a component of the ruling structure's taxable resources.

The change that had taken place in the role of the sō had its counterpart in the history of the inzen, the embodiment of the Honai merchants' origin and achievement. With the demise of the medieval order, the inzen lost its efficacy in the rational economic realm. Its essential value became religious, and it was placed in the shrine as a sacred object believed to cure illnesses. Until the 1920s, residents of Imabori and surrounding villages gathered regularly to worship the inzen.[157] Devoid of economic and political significance, the inzen rarefied into a source of supernatural power for the community alone. Similarly, the sō was transformed into a localized organization with little economic power and no official sanction to deal with the central political authority. Yet in their diminished spheres both the inzen and the sō structure retained their vitality down into our own century.

Conclusion

THIS STUDY OF an evolving community in Tokuchin-ho is long in chronological span but narrow in geographical scope. The region's history as preserved in local records rarely strays from the immediacy of the village and its people. But this close-up picture contains messages and implications that extend far beyond the horizon of the local society and affect our perspective on Japanese historical issues.

The sō village was a form of society distinguished by its highly communalistic character. Not a structural anomaly, however, it represented one possible variation within the broad spectrum of village types sharing traits fundamental to Japanese agrarian society. Commonality with other villages marked the sō village no less than did its distinctive features.

Medieval Japanese villages were a social institution without a legal status. No village, including the sō villages, received formal—written or spoken—recognition from the state or the lord. The physical outlines of a village and its social space mattered little to proprietary institutions, inclusively called the kenmon. The proprietors' interest was predominantly economic, defined by the boundaries of their estates, not by the boundaries of villages. The abundance of proprietary records regarding the payment of taxes (nengu) vividly contrasts with the scarcity of documentation regarding village life.

Technological and cultural factors tended to inhibit direct proprietary involvement in peasant society and village affairs. Rice-based agriculture had little use for continuous top-down supervision. Once irrigation was developed, rice production demanded delicate attention to soil preparation and cultivation on the part of the cultivator. If the possession of practical skills separated the peasant from the overlord, cultural differences also left a wide gap between them. The representatives of the kenmon, accustomed to the refinements of the capital, must have found the cultivators' world quite alien. Whether or not their estates produced rice, the aristocrats of the capital in their silken robes had little inclination to interfere directly in the peasants' social system. As Asakawa Kan'ichi notes, central proprietors never had home farms on their estates, in great contrast to their Western counterparts. Japanese peasants, free from supplying the kind of direct personal services known in the West, enjoyed "a great degree of personal freedom in the disposition of [their] plots"[1] and greater autonomy in shaping their own society. This was the social base on which the sō villages were built.

It can be granted that many estates came to have warrior masters who established themselves locally and exerted direct pressure on the residents in order to squeeze more revenues out of them. The sō emerged in such places as well. There, communal cohesion may have expressed itself most saliently through resistance to such pressure and in alliance with the more benign, absentee proprietor. The need to withstand the immediate challenge posed by the warrior could even have stimulated the growth of a collective rule more comprehensive and intense than that found in areas free of warrior intervention. The locally administered jurisdiction over crimes and the collective payment of taxes found in Sugaura point to this possibility. Regardless of the bothersome presence of a local warrior, village societies had a structural expectation for considerable freedom from top-down interference in communal life.

Formation of a community in Japan was a normal social process that was, unlike in the West, neither a special privilege nor a legal right to be discussed. Communalism in different outer forms—for example, assembly—required no explicit approval of the lord. Community in rural Japan was an ordinary social institution, as taken for granted as the need for irrigation to grow rice. The collective consciousness and the communal organization found in Imabori represented an elaboration on and intensification of this basic theme, not a departure from it. This communal social base partly explains the relatively low incidence of overt gestures of peasant protest (especially those accompanied by violence) in medieval Japan.[2] The strength and resilience underlying the rural culture accommodated meaningful resolutions at an earlier stage of conflict.

Our history of Tokuchin-ho is a history of a shōen as well as a history of sō villages. As it is commonly understood, the shōen system has come to represent the economic, political, and social order defined by an evolving hierarchy of proprietary arrangements primarily based on landed income. In Tokuchin-ho, however, no hierarchy of proprietorship was visible. For the lord, Tokuchin-ho was a source of commercial as well as agricultural income. Tokuchin-ho did not die as a result of changing proprietary arrangements, as many others did prior to the onset of the Warring period.

Admittedly, some features of Tokuchin-ho seem atypical, but those differences may be more illusory than real. The conventional view of the shōen system owes its insights largely to the documents kept in the proprietors' archives: mostly records of land rights and land taxes. On paper, commercial income mattered less; unlike the rights to land, proprietary rights to merchant groups evoked few outside threats, and there was no formal commercial tax to be recorded. If Enryakuji's records had survived intact and Imabori's records had not, our knowledge of the region might very well have been biased toward the landed income from Tokuchin-ho. The nonproprietary local records challenge our previous understanding of the shōen system by positing the possibility of distortion in the system's self-representation.

The productive components of Tokuchin-ho were mobile peasant-merchants. Apart from agriculture, they engaged extensively in trade, carried weapons, understood the political values of their time, and lobbied influential people. The proprietor upheld and brought to order the ambiguous and complex occupational status of its subjects by calling them either peasants (hyakushō) or merchants (shōnin), depending on the occasion.

This dual occupational status of the villagers colored the lord-subject relationship. As peasants, the residents were unqualified objects of expropriation; as merchants, they had more leverage vis-à-vis their superior. The pattern of medieval commerce, which demanded a collaborative arrangement between a holder of prestige and a carrier of goods, influenced the lord-peasant nexus of this relationship. In order to promote lucrative business relations, the proprietor was interested in coopting local organizations.

Beyond the immediate profits from commerce, this vertical alliance had the long-term effect of prolonging the life of the proprietary institution. While the kenmon's landed prerogatives in the country were gradually lost to the rising warriors, the symbolic power of the kenmon's prestige continued to be revitalized by the merchants. Skillful exploitation of the elite source of influence benefited the merchants and helped to keep alive the rhetoric of the medieval world order, on which the kenmon had staked so much.

Within the community, the borrowing of prestige from the kenmon tended to minimize potential conflict among villagers with differentiated interests. Because the prestigious connection enhanced the ranking of the village within the larger world, the entire community, even persons of lesser status, usually supported the sō and the merchants. Each member was a beneficiary, though to differing degrees, of concrete returns brought by the kenmon connection. This local utilization of the patron-client relationship tended to assuage the consequences of the usual split between upper and lower peasants.[3]

The shōen system, then, lasted much longer than is conventionally assumed. The ongoing recognition of kenmon-based prestige and the accompanying system of prestige-based legitimation in the world of commerce helped to sustain its economic viability. These factors also influenced the internal dynamics of the shōen community.

In the 1590s, with the shōen now gone, the occupational status of Tokuchin-ho residents was reduced to one unambiguous category: peasants, legally bound to the soil in terms of both physical mobility and occupational choice. Until then, their commercial practices had benefited from patron-client relationships nurtured in the decentralized atmosphere. Now the term of this evolution had clearly expired. But the impact of the local system instituted by these villagers would reach far into the future.

The organization of the medieval sō, interlocked with the structure of the shōen, promoted economic rationalism and group solidarity, shaping a social base for the later development of Japan's economy. The kind of rational economic outlook found in Tokuchin-ho—pragmatism in dealing with the authorities, with agricultural production, and with a collective social organization—spread throughout Japan as the structure of the sō became the basis for the efficient Tokugawa form of community governance. The sō's comprehensive local system fit perfectly into the Tokugawa order, where the political, social, and economic dimensions of rule were demarcated ambiguously at the state and local levels. The social and economic organization of the sō was a precursor of the later village system and later business relations. Using traditional symbols and medieval modes of operation, Tokuchin-ho residents nonetheless exhibited entrepreneurship in their appreciation of commercial profit. A talented, aggressive, ambitious, well-organized, fairly literate, and historically minded population, the villagers of Tokuchin-ho shaped the social forms that lay to hand as much as they were shaped by them.

Appendixes

The Origins of the Rokkaku Family

The Rokkaku family was a branch of the Sasaki family, whose genea-
logical background is complicated by discrepancies in the sources. The
Sonpi bunmyaku traces the line directly from Emperor Uda (r. 887–98).[1]
But an entry dated 1185.10.11 in the *Azuma kagami* suggests a greater
complexity in the way the lineage evolved. The entry shows that
Yoritomo granted the Sasaki estate (Sasaki-no-shō) to Sasaki Saburō
Naritsuna but directed Sasaki Sadatsuna to supervise the landholding.
Added to this entry is a notation that reads, Naritsuna "calls himself *hon*
[original]-Sasaki," and "Naritsuna and [Sasaki] Sadatsuna are not of the
same lineage."[2] Working out the discrepancies between the notation in
Azuma kagami and the genealogical table in the *Sonpi bunmyaku*,
Uwayokote Masataka has reconstructed the Sasaki lineage as follows.[3]

   Briefly, Uwayokote found that there were two different lineages in
the ancient period: one that traced its origin to Emperor Uda and
another, that of the entrenched local magnate Sasaki-no-yama-no-
kimi[4] who occupied the governorships (*dairyō*) of Gamō and Kanzaki
counties during the Nara and Heian periods. This second lineage was
of the hon-Sasaki family, which held the Sasaki shrine listed in the *Engi-
shiki* of the tenth century[5] and which had close connections with the
capital through the family's female members who served at the imperial court.[6] Emperor Uda's line was granted the Minamoto name in 936
in its third generation[7] and began to reside in Ōmi in its fifth generation. From this new base, it apparently consolidated its position, for it
began to exceed the rival line in rank, power, and prestige by the late
Heian and early Kamakura periods. Not to be outdone, the district
governor's Sasaki line now started to trace its origin to a Minamoto in
order to assert origins of greater central prestige. In turn, the Uda line
absorbed the genealogy of its rival in order to show a more impressive
local history for itself. At any rate, the two lines came to merge on
paper, and this was the version appearing in the *Sonpi bunmyaku*.

In the eighth generation, a member of the line of Uda (Tsunemasa, also called Tsunekata) served as both the head priest (kannushi) of the Sasaki's family shrine and the local administrator (gesu) of the Sasaki estate, an area overlapping the grounds of the old family headquarters in Sasakiyama. He also constructed the Owaki headquarters and started to call his family the Sasaki.[8] His grandson Hideyoshi married the daughter of Minamoto Tameyoshi, and in the Heiji Incident (1159) fought on the losing side, with Tameyoshi's son Yoshitomo. Defeat resulted in exile and the loss of property. For twenty years, Hideyoshi and his sons, including one named Sadatsuna, stayed under the care of Shibuya Shigekuni in the eastern province of Sagami. During this period, they grew close to Minamoto Yoritomo in Izu, subsequently becoming his loyal followers. In the wake of Yoritomo's victory in the Genpei War (1180–85), Sadatsuna and his brothers were appointed to a variety of shugo posts.[9]

In contrast, the hon-Sasaki family supported the Taira, who emerged victorious after the Heiji Incident, and did not rally to Yoritomo's side until the Taira had left the capital with their defeat certain. This difference in timing was evident in the quality of the rewards granted after the inauguration of the new regime. The Uda Sasaki family gained prestigious shugo posts in seventeen provinces, but the hon-Sasaki, who had delayed giving support to Yoritomo, received few military titles and continued to serve as the priests and administrators for the Sasaki shrine and estate. Eventually, the hon-Sasaki formed subordinate vassalage ties to the Rokkaku branch of the Uda Sasaki family, which came to flourish as the shugo house of Ōmi Province.[10]

The epoch following the establishment of the Kamakura bakufu was characterized by the reordering and realignment of the nation's warrior houses. The Jōkyū War of 1221, the first test of Kamakura strength, divided many warrior houses into opposing camps. In the Sasaki family, Sadatsuna and his heir, Hirotsuna, sided with Gotoba and fought against the fourth Sasaki son, Nobutsuna, who was on the bakufu side. With the bakufu's victory, Hirotsuna's line ended, while Nobutsuna gained stewardships (jitō-shiki) in several shōen in addition to the Ōmi shugo post.[11]

The death of Nobutsuna in 1242 prompted an inheritance dispute between the first son, Shigetsuna, and the third son (but principal heir), Yasutsuna. Yasutsuna inherited the shugo post and all the associated lands, whereupon Shigetsuna complained that, as the eldest, he should receive the holdings acquired by his father apart from the shugo title. Upon hearing of this dispute, the bakufu promptly seized the "extra" landholdings, arguing that they had come into the family illegally in any case. Ignoring all objections, the Kamakura bakufu was resolute in its stand, and the land was lost to the Sasaki.[12]

About this time, the family began dividing into several independent branches. The main line, headed by Yasutsuna, took the name Rokkaku after the location of Yasutsuna's inherited residence in Kyoto. The first son, Shigetsuna, came to be called Ōhara, after the Ōhara estate in Sakata County, where he was the jitō. The second son, Takanobu, was a jitō in Tanaka-gō, Takashima County. He thus began calling himself Takashima, but his line also came to be known as Kutsuki, since it branched into the so-called Takashima Seven—Etchū, Noto, Hirai, Nagata, Yokoyama, Tanaka, and Kutsuki. Finally, the fourth son, Ujinobu, started the Kyōgoku house, named after his inherited residence in Kyoto. This trend toward lineage division was not particular to the Sasaki but occurred all over the country. It also coincided with the bakufu's design to consolidate its hold over certain prominent warrior houses in the aftermath of the Jōkyū War. Accordingly, the Sasaki branches (Rokkaku, Ōhara, Takashima, and Kyōgoku) came to reside in Kyoto and formed their own ties to the bakufu under the supervision of its deputy there, the Rokuhara *tandai*.[13] The Rokkaku retained their dominant position among the branch lines for most of the medieval period but also faced stiff competition from the Kyōgoku, the line holding the other shugo post in Ōmi.

APPENDIX B

Sō Regulations

These regulations were written for internal use; many have incomplete sentences whose meanings are difficult to interpret. The *hashiuragaki* (marginal notations), made on the reverse of the document for quick reference after it was rolled up, are omitted from translation here with one, designated exception.

Doc. no. 357, Eitoku 3 (1383).1.4

Concerning the headship [*tō*] of the Kechi ceremony, Imabori-gō: new *za* members who have attended the *za* even once shall be appointed to the headship in accordance with the seating order.
For the headship of the Ninth Month Ninth Day ceremony, follow precedent.
  1. Paddy in Kōgatani belonging to the shrine should be assigned to the head of the Ninth Month Ninth Day ceremony.
  2. Concerning Sakonjirō and the headship of the Kechi ceremony: because he is inappropriate [*hibun*] to serve as the head [now], he will serve when the position rotates to him in the future.

Doc. no. 389, Ōei 4 (1397).6

The incumbent sexton [*shōshi*] shall not have to serve as the head of the Kō ceremony to assist with the monkey dance [*sarugaku*]. One mat each should be woven for the head of the Kō ceremony and for the sexton. Those items brought in by the shrine members [*ujiko*] from outside shall be offered to deities by the shrine priest [*kannushi*].

Doc. no. 33, Ōei 10 (1403).2

Concerning *za* obligations: those who fail to pay *za* fees shall not be part of the *za*.
  1. Myōamidabutsu, Shinjirō, Gorōjirō, Sukegorō, Kurōjirō, Hyōegorō, Hikotarō, Umatarō. Those who are of *mōto* [in-between] status shall take the lower seats even if they are three years senior.
  2. Those who are not paid up for each of the *za* obligations shall not occupy a seat [or, participate in the *za*].

198

Doc. no. 365, Ōei 32 (1425).11

Regulations stipulated by Imabori-gō *za* members:
  1. Do not close the wooden shutter of the prayer hall at your own discretion.
  2. Do not beat the drum at your own discretion.
  3. Do not dry your personal items [perhaps, dry grain] or gamble in front of the shrine buildings.
  4. Do not place boards [to reserve seats on the ground] at your own discretion.

Those who disobey these items shall be subject to a penalty of 300 *mon*. Those who continue to exercise private will [even after being penalized] shall be barred from the *za* for generations to come.

Doc. no. 369, Bun'an 5 (1448).11.14
  1. Those who do not come to the meeting after two beats of the drum shall be fined 50 *mon*.
  2. A penalty of 500 *mon* shall be imposed for cutting down forest trees and seedlings.
  3. A penalty of 100 *mon* shall be imposed for taking firewood [or leaves] and mulberry leaves.
  4. [Unclear. Kanamoto Masayuki speculates that it means "A 100 *mon* penalty shall be imposed for gathering cut trees." Nakamura Ken understands it to mean "When taking new persimmons, take only one."][1]

Doc. no. 327, Hōtoku 3 (1451).11.6

Regulations concerning the period of *ge*[2] [*ge* lasts three months from 4.16 or 5.16, during which time priests do not go outside]:
  1. A list of goods for the period of *ge* and the interim period between the residency of two *hijiri* [nonlocal religious specialists].
  2. These are half a set of bowls and a thin wooden tray. If any of these items becomes lost, the incumbent *hijiri* shall replace it. If there are any disagreements, a witness shall resolve the problem.
  3. Should there be any leftover rice or miso from the *ge* period, convert it into cash and buy bowls, etc.
  4. When the *hijiri* change places, hand over 5 *kin* of dregs [unclear; perhaps, of tea or firewood] and 2 *gō* of oil to the incumbent *hijiri*.

Thus the villagers [*murando*] have decreed.

Doc. no. 371, Chōroku 4 (1460).11.1

Regulations:
  1. Concerning ceremonies: 10 pieces of pickled meat [*hachinokasu*], 3 sweets, 5 *to* of *mochi* [sweet rice-cake] for the First Month Fourth Day ceremony; 5 *to* of *mochi* for the Ninth Month Ninth Day ceremony.
  2. The head of the Dō ceremony shall pound 1 *koku* of rice. Two sweets [unclear].
  3. [Unclear. Perhaps, The same person shall not hold the position continuously.]
  4. Do not let a traveler stay [in the shrine or, alternatively, in the village].

5. [Unclear. Perhaps, Do not cultivate a paddy just because it is clear of tax obligations.]
6. If an outsider, [do not] act like a villager by wearing an *eboshi* outfit and calling yourself a villager.

Doc. no. 370, Chōkyō 2 (1488).11.4

East *za:* 1 Buddhist priest.
West *za:* 1 Buddhist priest.
The above shall be exempt from various obligations. In addition, four elders [*otona musha:* elders in charge of the bow and arrow ceremony or, alternatively, elders of samurai status] shall be exempt.

Doc. no. 363, Entoku 1 (1489).11.4

Regulations set forth by Imabori residents [*jige*]:
1. Regardless of the size [or, the prestige] of the lineage, all shall deposit the proceeds from shrine land in the monastic office [*anshitsu*].
2. Salt, miso, and miscellaneous items shall be prepared by the priest [*kannushi*]. The *sō* shall pay the expense.
3. Firewood and charcoal belonging to the *sō* shall be used.
4. Rice brought to the hearth shall be kept by the *sō;* the *sō* shall then deliver 5 *shō* of rice to the priest [*kannushi*].
5. Do not let a nonvillager [*murabito nite naki mono*] use a house rented from the *sō.*
6. A house shall not be divided into two [in default of mortgage payments or alternatively, Do not rent two houses from the *sō*].
7. Do not allow an outsider [*tasho no hito*] to stay here without a local guarantor.
8. Disputes concerning boundaries between *sō* land and private land shall be settled by money.
9. For taking leaves or cutting trees in the *sō* forest, villagers [*murando*] shall lose *murando* status and non-*murando* shall be evicted from the village.
10. Rice for the Kechi ceremony shall be handed over on the eighth day of the tenth month.
11. Rice for the Ninth Month Ninth Day ceremony shall be handed over on the eighth day of the eighth month.
12. Do not keep dogs.
13. Do not serve as a middleman for a credit association [*tanomoshi*].
14. For the New Year's purification [*mushiro harai*] ceremony, the *sō* shall pay 1 *to* to the priest [*kannushi*].
15. For the monkey dances held in the second and sixth months, *sō* money in the amount of 1 *kan* shall be paid each time.
16. Those who sell houses shall pay 3 *mon* to the *sō* for each 100 *mon* of the sale price, or 30 *mon* for each *kanmon*. Any villager [*murando*] who breaks this rule shall be removed from the *za*.
17. Those who hide the sale price of a house shall be punished.
18. Do not pay out 3 *mon* [to the builders] for the sake that accompanies house construction.
19. Sons adopted after age seven cannot become *za* members.
20. Do not build a house to the east of the moat.

Doc. no. 375, Bunki 2 (1502).3.9

Items decided:
1. About rice cakes [*ine mochi*], wheat cakes [*mugi mochi*], and buckwheat cakes [*soba mochi*].
2. Those who stay overnight at a gambling party shall be fined 300 *mon;* those who eat things [perhaps the cakes mentioned above] shall be fined 100 *mon.*
3. As for the *sō* forest: [there is] a penalty of 100 *mon* for breaking branches and leaves by hand or collecting soil; of 200 *mon* for cutting [branches and leaves] with a sickle; of 300 *mon* for cutting [them] with a hatchet; and of 500 *mon* for using a broadax.
4. A 100 *mon* penalty shall be charged for [taking?] wheat roots, millet husks, or cowpea [*sasage*] vines.

In case of violations, if offenders are villagers [*jigenin*], they shall be forbidden to participate in the *za.* If widows or orphans, they shall be evicted from the village. The sale [of the house or, alternatively, of *mochi*] to outsiders shall be forbidden for generations to come.

Doc. no. 570, Eishō 1 (1504)

Tatsu-no-Matatarō	Removed from the *za* for non-payment.
Monbei	Removed from the *za* for non-payment.
Komajirō	Removed from the *za* for non-payment.
Kotorasaburō	Removed from the *za* for non-payment.
Wakaishitarō	Removed from the *za* for non-payment.
Kerikomaishi	Removed from the *za* for owing 200 *mon.*
Shōkōgaishi	Removed from the *za* for non-payment.
Gorōbei	Removed from the *za* for owing 4 *to* 6 *shō* in taxes [*nengu*].
Wakabeigorō	Removed from the *za* for owing 100 *mon.*
Kadonene	Removed from the *za* for owing 170 *mon* to the Third Day Kō [confraternity].
Umainujirō	Removed from the *za* for owing 1 *kanmon.*
Kakaemon	Removed from the *za* for owing 200 *mon.*
Wakaemon-nyudō	Removed from the *za* for owing 550 *mon.*
Uyojirō	Removed from the *za* for non-payment.

Eishō 1, Gyōbujirō, 38 *mon*★   Removed from the *za*.

                                                         ★Paid 38 *mon*.³

Thus decided.

Should the above seek to reenter the *za* in the future while still in arrears, [they should] compute the fees and pay [them] and contribute foot-cleansing sake [*ashi arai sake*] as before.

Doc. no. 374, Eishō 1 (1504).10.7

Regulations concerning *naoshi* items [rice and money offerings to the deities]:
  1. To become an *otona* [elder], those who own horses or oxen shall pay 400 *mon*, and all others, 300 *mon*.
  2. For the coming-of-age [*eboshi*] ceremony, each participant shall pay 500 *mon*.
  3. The head of the Dō ceremony serving in the year of the ox [the following year, Eishō 2] shall pay 2 *kan;* [the head] serving in the year of the tiger [Eishō 3], 1 *kan* 600 *mon;* [the head] serving in the year of the hare [Eishō 4], 1 *kan* 200 *mon*. [For the head serving] in the year of the dragon [Eishō 5] and thereafter, do not reduce [the payment] below 1 *kan*.
  4. In the year of the ox, the head of the Ninth Month Ninth Day ceremony shall also pay 2 *kan;* in the year of the tiger, 1 *kan* 600 *mon;* in the year of the hare, 1 *kan* 200 *mon;* in the year of the dragon, 1 *kan;* thereafter, no further reduction.
  5. In the year of the ox, the head of the Kechi ceremony shall pay 1 *kan* 200 *mon;* in the year of the tiger, 1 *kan;* in the year of the hare, 900 *mon;* in the year of the dragon, 800 *mon;* thereafter, no further reduction.
  6. There shall be no offerings made for the coming-of-age ceremony [unclear; perhaps, this year].
  7. Nobody shall become an *otona* this year [unclear]. Thus deliberated.

Doc. no. 372, Eishō 17 (1520).12.26

Items decided:
  1. Gambling is strictly prohibited at the various shrine halls and the monastic office [*anshitsu*].
  2. Those who have stayed at a house of gambling or prostitution shall not sit with the *za*, as stipulated before.
  3. Penalties concerning the *sō* forest:
       330 *mon* for cutting with a broadax.
       200 *mon* for cutting with a sickle.
       100 *mon* for breaking off [branches] with the hands or collecting leaves.
  4. Cutting grass or gathering soil in vegetable and other fields is forbidden.
  5. Tampering with any crop while pretending to be gleaning is forbidden.
Thus deliberated.

Doc. no. 347, Tenbun 23 (1554).12.11

Items decided by the Imabori *sōbun*:
  1. After the twentieth day of the twelfth month in the year of the tiger [the current year, 1554], we shall not perform coming-of-age [*eboshi*], *otona* [becoming an elder in the *za*], or other ceremonies [such as the Kechi,

Dō, or Ninth Month Ninth Day ceremonies]. The payments for these ceremonies shall be placed in the *sō*'s coffer this time. But this will not become a precedent for the future. If these ceremonies are resumed in the future, they shall follow the custom established in previous years.

[Signed] Imabori *sōbun*

Doc. no. 5, Kōji 2 (1556)

1. Overnight guests are forbidden.
2. For whatever reason, those without permission [or, a guarantor] shall not be allowed in [the village].
3. Any and all gambling is prohibited.
4. Fighting is prohibited.
5. The penalty for wearing someone else's straw sandals [*zōri*] shall be twelve sticks of charcoal in a bunch, and for wearing someone else's wooden footwear [*geta*], two 12-stick bunches of charcoal.
6. The new members are restricted from expressing opinions as the senior members' equals.

Thus decided.

Doc. no. 366, Tenshō 10 (1582).12.8

Rules stipulated by the *otona* [seniors] and *wakashū* [juniors] of the village:
1. As we have decided thus, there shall be no mistake in the future.
2. All matters concerning the village shall be decided through consultation, but the majority rules.
3. Those who violate the established rules and continue to disagree shall be punished by the *sō*.

Thus decided.

[Signed] *otona sōbun* [simplified signature]
[Signed] *wakashū sōbun* [kaō signature]

Doc. no. 467, Tenshō 11 (1583).7

1. Those listed on the register shall have the right to discuss [matters concerning the survey].
2. Do not covet other people's land. Once the owner is agreed upon, do not make different claims.
3. Should there be troublesome people among the landholding peasants [*hyakushō*], dissociate from them as the regulations stipulate.

[Signed] Imabori *sōchū*

Doc. no. 468, Tenshō 11 (1583).11.13

Items to appeal:
1. About taxation rates.
2. About supplementary taxes.
3. About the measuring cup.

If the three points above are not reconciled after our appeal, we will all leave our homes and refuse to accommodate [Hideyoshi's order]. Anyone not acting in accordance with this pledge shall be excluded from the *sō*. Thus it is decided.

[Signed] Imabori *sōbun* [90 names]

Doc. no. 462, Tenshō 12 (1584).10.1

Foreword to an oath written in awe of heavenly punishments:
1. We shall not alter the boundaries of county [*kōri*], estate [*shō*], and village [*gō*].
2. We shall report what each of us possesses at home and in the fields down to the last penny [*sen*].
3. During the survey, we shall report whenever there is leniency based on gifts in goods and cash. If leniency is being given [unclear], we shall report it without concealment.
4. After the survey takes place, we shall also report whenever there is new open land or newly planted paddies and fields.
5. We shall not lower the tax by intentionally confusing [the land-quality ranks of] superior, medium, and inferior.
6. We shall not befriend the magistrate or his agents and conceal this fact.
7. Should there be anyone who goes against these pledges and conceals it, that person shall have his or her relatives down to the women and children crucified. If the person continues to deceive even then, he or she will be subjected to all the heavenly punishments embodied in this oath.

Doc. no. 469, Tenshō 12 (1584).12.2

Items decided:
1. Concerning an appeal made to the official again conducting a survey.
2. We wish to request that the official submit as the formal figure the amount stipulated in either register, the one from this year or from last year.
3. We wish to demand that the total tax figure calculated by the two officials be consistent.

We act of one mind.

[Signed] Imabori *sōbun*

Doc. no. 367, Tenshō 16 (1588).7.11

Regulations stipulated:
1. Should anyone catch a thief stealing from paddies and fields, he or she shall receive a reward of rice in the amount of 1 *koku* 5 *to* if during the day and 3 *koku* if during the night.
2. The same applies to thieves entering homes.
3. If anyone carries rice seedlings and passes through [the village] before [after?] six at dusk or before six at dawn, she or he shall be subject to the same penalty [as a thief].

Thus we have decided.

[Signed] Imabori *sōbun* [*kaō* signature]

Doc. no. 368, Tenshō 18 (1590).10.6

Regulations stipulated:
1. Whoever does harm to the village or villagers shall be punished by the *sōbun* as soon as the act is heard of.

2. In discussing and deciding on various matters, majority rule holds. Those who do not participate in the decision making shall be treated as though they were criminals.

[Signed] Imabori *sōbun*
[Four names, two with *kaō* signatures]

Doc. no. 470, Tenshō 19 (1591).8.21

Regulations stipulated:
1. Concerning the tax rice ordered by the magistrate: having acknowledged the receipt of the order, three households on both sides of any villager who conceals anyone's flight shall pay the tax [*nengu,* that would have been paid by the fleeing peasant].
2. Concerning the survey records: should there be contradictory terms given by the magistrates, we shall petition; if the petition is not accepted and we the villagers flee, we are all of one mind to do so.

If anyone acts against these decisions, we will dissociate from him or her as pledged.

[Signed] Imabori *sōbun* [*kaō* signature]
[74 names, 48 with signatures]

Doc. no. 254, Keichō 4 (1599).5.10

Regulations stipulated:
1. [Unclear. Perhaps, A person shall be penalized if she or he is found to have damaged the irrigation ditch (that runs) from Shibawara to Imabori.]
2. Anyone who breaks by hand, gathers, or harvests [foliage] shall be penalized 1 *to.*
3. For damaging the irrigation outlet of the village paddy, 5 *to* in rice shall be charged.
4. For destroying land prepared with horses and oxen, twice that amount shall be charged.
5. As for the *sō* forest, anyone who harvests grass or trees shall pay 2 *to* of rice.

As we have decided on these regulations today, previous regulations are annulled. Anyone violating these rules shall be treated by the villagers as a criminal.

[Signed] Dōshō [simplified signature]
Imabori *sōbun* [*kaō* signature]

Doc. no. 247, Genna 3 (1617).12.27

Items stipulated:
1. If a house is transferred to one person, he or she shall fulfill all services and obligations. A retired person [*inkyo*] shall fulfill half the obligations [of a householder] up to age 60; after he reaches 61, his services end. This applies only to a retiree without an heir, however.
2. If a house is transferred to two persons, even if the recipients are young, there shall be no services or obligations [levied on the original householder].

3. [Unclear. Perhaps, If a household is separated from a retiree's household, then the obligations must be fulfilled.]

While these regulations are in effect in Imabori, be sure to abide by them.

[Signed] Imabori *sō's* priest-representative [*sō-dai kannushi*]

Doc. no. 255, Kan'ei 3 (1626).6.3

Items stipulated:
1. For harvesting grass in someone else's paddy, 1 *koku* of rice shall be charged as a penalty.
2. Breaking off branches and leaves by hand shall also invoke a penalty of 1 *koku*.
3. Breaking off branches and leaves in the *sō* forest will invoke the same penalty. Anyone violating these rules shall be driven out [of the village] by the *sō*.

Thus commanded.

[Signed] *sōchū*

Doc. no. 296, Kan'ei 16 (1639).8.21

Recently, Chōbei blocked a crucial spot [in the watercourse] in the village and caused problems for the *sō*. We have judged that this is a criminal offense and that the *sō* shall not associate with him. Anyone associating with him, even secretly, shall be forever regarded as a criminal, even if Chōbei is later forgiven.

[Signed] Imabori's priest [*sōbun kannushi*]
[72 names, 60 with signatures or seals]

Doc. no. 290, Kan'ei 16? (1639?).11.19

On the night of the eighteenth day of the eleventh month, it was reported to the *sō* that unhulled rice seeds had been stolen again. It has been decided that on the coming twenty-third day, we shall cast ballots. The person who receives even one more ballot than the others shall be incriminated along with his parents, children, and wife. Anyone not attending this vote on the twenty-third shall be regarded as a criminal and shall have no say about the matter.

[Names of 68 men, 66 with signatures or seals]

Doc. no. 291, no date (late 16th c.)

Regulations decided by Imabori-mura *sōchū*:
1. Should there be a criminal in the seven-household group [*kumi*], the group shall review this matter collectively and report to the *sō*.
2. Do not steal foliage from other people's land. Should anyone go over to another village [*gō*] and steal, his group shall go there and examine [the situation].
3. Do not harvest foliage in Miyabayashi or Atagoyama.
4. Violators of the rules concerning trees and leaves are subject to a penalty of 1 *to* of sake.
5. Any other forms of theft shall be judged accordingly. In addition, a thief staying [the rest is lost].

Doc. no. 870, no year.12.11

Concerning the meeting [*yoriai*] to be held on the thirteenth: come to the meeting after no more than two beats of the drum.*

 *[Later correction] Meet after four beats.

After this, [latecomers] are subject to a penalty of 2 *shō* of sake. Such persons shall not have any complaints about [this matter]. Thus commanded.

[Signed] *sōchū*

Regulations Concerning Merchants and Commerce

Doc. no. 600, Eishō 15 (1518).12.21

Regulations concerning trading stipulated in accordance with precedent:
1. Concerning *za* members: three packages of salt [should] make up one horseback load to be sold in Hino. Following precedent, relinquish one package if none of the three packages comes from over the pass [*yamagoe*, i.e., from Ise].
2. Daily visits to Kyoto are firmly forbidden. *Yamagoe* ("over-the-pass") merchants should take one stove and one horse. If there are two merchants, one should go on foot.
3. House servants [*ienoko*; meaning unclear] are strictly forbidden.
4. Trading on credit or with checks is firmly forbidden.
5. Horse-riding *yamagoe* merchants who do not stop at either Aidani or Kōzubata shall not return without profit.
6. *Yamagoe* merchants shall not buy up [*mukai gai*; meaning unclear] goods before reaching the destined market.

[Signed] Minami-gō [i.e., merchants of Imabori,
Hebimizo, Higashi-Kobochizuka]

Doc. no. 62, Taiei 7 (1527).5.4

Rules stipulated by the *yamagoe* ["over-the-pass"] merchants:
1. Regardless of right or wrong, anyone who draws a sword and injures another at a market shall be prohibited from trading.
2. Those *yamagoe* merchants who draw a sword or carry a stick and beat people or get involved in fights on the road or at ports shall be forbidden to trade over the pass for generations to come.
3. Anyone who gets complaints about an insufficiency of goods after closing a sale at a market shall be forbidden to trade.

Although there are regulations from before, we are setting these rules forth once again. In the future, be sure to abide by these regulations. Thus resolved.

[Signed] *yamagoe* merchants

Doc. no. 20, Kyōroku 2 (1529).12.4

During the trial over the use of the Kurihan-kaidō, we requested aid from the [Imabori] *sōbun*. In response, we received support to cover sake expenses. The members were very pleased. In the future, should there be trials over trading practices that result in expenditures, we will not take this as a precedent and make requests. For future reference, we hereby firmly resolve.

[Signed] Imabori-gō *sōchū* [*kaō* signature]

Doc. no. 64, Kōji 3 (1557).2.4

Those *yamagoe* ["over-the-pass"] merchants who do not make good their unpaid dues [*nengu*] before the second day of the third month shall be forbidden to go over the pass [to Ise]. The *sō* has decided thus.

[Signed] *yamagoe sō*

People owing dues: Genpachi, Wakamatsu, Shōkō Matsuchiyo, Miyauchibei Shinpatsu. Total, 35 *mon*.

Doc. no. 373, no date (late 15th to early 16th c.)

Decided items:

1. Foot merchants [*kachi*] shall not handle horse-carried goods for one generation. Any violation will result in the confiscation of [the violator's] goods by the *sō-shō* [Honai merchants' *sō*]. While staying at ports and market towns, they must observe this regulation. Thus ordered.

[Signed] Umagorō [simplified signature],
Shirōtarō [simplified signature],
Wakaemon-nyūdō, Sakonsaburō
[simplified signature]

Reference Matter

Notes

For complete authors' names, titles, and publishing data on works cited in short form in the Notes, see the Bibliography, pp. 257–71. The following abbreviations are used in the Notes:

CSS   Nakamura Ken. *Chūsei sōson shi no kenkyū: Ōmi no kuni Tokuchin-ho Imabori-gō*. Tokyo: Hōsei Daigaku Shuppankyoku, 1984.
GS   *Ōmi Gamō-gun shi*. 10 vols. Edited by Nakagawa Senzō. Shiga-ken: Shiga-ken Gamō-gun Yakusho, 1911–12.
int.   intercalary
YS   *Yōkaichi-shi shi*. 6 vols. Edited by Yōkaichi-shi Shi Hensan Iinkai. Yōkaichi: Yōkaichi-shi Shiyakusho, 1983–86.

All document numbers are from *Imabori Hiyoshi jinja monjo shūsei*, compiled by Nakamura Ken (Tokyo: Yūzankaku, 1981), except where another source is given.

Introduction

1. This cedar tree was 5 meters in girth and 70 meters in height when it was cut down for its lumber on July 23, 1944, by a governmental order during the Pacific War. The back of the photograph, taken then, is inscribed: "Note the grief on the faces [of the men lined up in front of the tree] just before the saw was placed on this sacred tree." The photograph is reproduced in *Imabori Hiyoshi jinja shaki*, locally compiled by Murata Sōkichi in 1973.

2. The celebration of the Mountain Deity takes place in the first month of the year, on the third day now, but on the seventh day in medieval times. It involves all the village men, who march to the site and share food and sake with the deity and each other. See Chapter 2 for a further discussion of this ceremony.

3. Anne Walthall has pointed out to me that the Imabori documents differ from village documents of the Tokugawa period in that they did not serve to mediate between commoners and the ruling lord.

4. Makino, *Buke jidai shakai*, p. 407.

5. It was believed that the document collection had remained untouched for centuries until Nakamura Ken's detailed scrutiny uncovered contrary evidence. *CSS*, pp. 130–32.

6. Cited as *GS*.

7. *Imabori Hiyoshi jinja monjo.*

8. *Imabori Hiyoshi jinja monjo shūsei.* Unless otherwise noted, all document numbers are from this collection. The shrine was originally called Hie Shrine. Here I have adopted the pronunciation locally used today. Accordingly, I have not romanized the title as *Imabori Hie jinja monjo shūsei.*

9. Cited as *YS*. Volumes 5 and 6 contain documentary sources.

10. *YS*, II: 3. Access problems are not unique to this region. In his investigation of miyaza in Wakayama Prefecture, Andō Seiichi was denied access to certain material because the local people claimed that the opening of the "black box," which contained the documents, would bring illness. Andō, *Kinsei miyaza*, p. 125.

11. Nakamura Ken, "Shin hakken," p. 14.

12. The economic growth of this era has been discussed by many scholars from various angles. For this section, I have relied on Satō, *Nanbokuchō nairan*, pp. 250–70; Kuroda Hideo, "Sengoku Shokuhōki," pp. 275–316. For more information on technological development, readers are referred to the eight-volume series *Kōza Nihon gijutsu no shakai shi*, edited by Nagahara Keiji and Yamaguchi Keiji.

13. Ishida, "Gōsonsei," pp. 45–49.

14. Satō, *Nanbokuchō nairan*, pp. 254–61. These local agents were usually warriors and were thus interested in using the commons as military training ground.

15. Including those explicitly named along with those that had similar characteristics but lacked the sō designation per se.

16. Some of the most famous sō villages, for instance, were located where the rice yield was inadequate and local income was supplemented by non-agricultural means. Sugaura and Okushima, two well known sō villages located on the northern and eastern shores of Lake Biwa, derived much of their income from fishing and forestry. Tokuchin-ho relied on commerce. On the other hand, a paddy-based economy supported the sō at Kokawa-dera's Higashi-mura, Tomobuchi in Kii Province, and at Iriyamada in Izumi Province.

17. Eisenstadt and Roniger, "Patron-Client Relations," p. 49. A fuller exposition of their argument can be found in their *Patrons, Clients and Friends.*

18. The kenmon constituted the group with high "social visibility," a term employed in Eisenstadt and Roniger, *Patrons, Clients and Friends*, p. 174, for example.

19. According to one of the "configurations of coalitions" mentioned in Eisenstadt and Roniger, "encapsulative policies" were adopted by central elites who allied with or coopted powerful local figures without interfering in local affairs. Ibid., p. 235.

20. Ishimoda, *Chūseiteki sekai.*

21. For the best historiographical treatment of feudalism and hōkensei, see Hall, "Feudalism in Japan." More recently, Germaine A. Hoston has unraveled and illuminated historical debates concerning the Asiatic mode of production, feudalism, and capitalism as they shaped Japanese history. See her *Marxism.*

22. Araki, *Bakuhan taisei.*

23. Kuroda Toshio, *Nihon chūsei hōkensei ron.* This is a collection of articles mostly written in the 1950s and 1960s. Nagahara Keiji analyzes and criticizes the historiographical treatment of feudalism from the 1950s through recent years in his "Chūsei no shakai."

24. Kikuchi, "Sengoku daimyō."

25. Kurokawa Masahiro, "Sugaura shō to sō," reprinted in his *Chūsei sōson no shomondai.*

26. To Ishida, however, mura kyōdōtai ("community") existed before the documentary appearance of the term *sō*, despite the lord's control over forests, rivers, irrigation, and/or police jurisdiction. Collective agricultural projects and shrine ceremonial activities served as evidence for the presence of this pre-sō form of kyōdōtai. Ishida, "Sō ni tsuite"; Ishida, "Sōteki ketsugō"; Ishida, "Gōsonsei." Ishida's view invited a number of responses. Hagiwara Tatsuo observed that the term *sōshō* remained in customary use in some areas even after the emergence of essentially sōson qualities there. Nakamura Ken demonstrated how in Tokuchin-ho, for example, the sōshō circumscribed the sōson geographically and the two forms overlapped from the fourteenth through the sixteenth centuries. Hagiwara, *Chūsei saishi*, p. 179; Nakamura, "Chūsei kōki no sonraku," p. 23.

27. See, for instance, Nakamura Tadashi.

28. For a recent concise summary of Japanese historiography on lord-peasant relationships, see Tabata, "Ryōshusei to sonraku kenkyū no genjō to mondaiten," in her *Chūsei sonraku no kōzō*, pp. 1–18.

29. Makino, "Chūsei makki ni okeru sonraku no ketsugō." Hagiwara adds that, owing to this structural continuity, the sō villages experienced little disruption at the hands of the unifiers. *Chūsei saishi*, p. 168.

30. For instance, the size and yield of taxed land, the effectiveness of collection agents and collection methods, and the appropriate acceptance of higher authority by cultivators.

31. Maki, "Chūsei makki," pp. 2–4. In Maki's reading, as villages became extricated from this historical anonymity, they came to possess their own system, independent of the shōen, despite the fact that village land remained under the shōen. The sō continued to mature, and by the Warring period it functioned as an exclusive self-defense organization.

32. Shimizu, *Nihon chūsei*. For a personal history of Shimizu—including political arrest (in 1943 by the wartime police for his progressive views) and a premature and solitary death in Siberia in 1947 (due to pneumonia)—and criticism of his works, see Fujitani.

33. A large portion of Nakamura Ken's various articles are collected in *CSS*.

Chapter 1

1. Doc. no. 1, Kōan 7 (1284).11.30: Sanmon shūgi gechijō.

2. The lake is presently 235.2 kilometers in length and 674.4 square kilometers in area. *Nihon chishi*, 13:32.

3. According to one source, Emperor Tenchi adopted the name Ōmi, descriptive of the lake's proximity to the capital, then located at Ōtsu on the lake's east side. The name was also meant to contrast with that of Tōtomi Province, the "far (from the) large river" province. *Ōmi no kuni yochi shi ryaku*, 1:7. Because a number of places were named Ōtsu, it is not certain, however, if Ōtsu the capital was in Ōmi.

4. *Kadokawa Nihon chimei daijiten*, 25: "Biwa-ko"; *Ōmi no kuni yochi shi ryaku*, 1:34–35. It mentions that for example in *Kaito shokoku ki*, published in Korea in 1471, the author Shin Sook Joo compared the shape of the lake to a lute.

5. From the northernmost section of the Suzuka Mountains to the southernmost end of Lake Biwa, the major rivers are Seri, Inukami, Echi, Hino, Yasu, Kusatsu, and Seta.

6. Concerning "hunting," W. G. Aston notes: "Any excursion of the Emperor's was called hunting. The hunt on this occasion was no doubt for medicinal herbs (kusurigari), for which this was the appointed day." Entry for the fifth day of the fifth month in the seventh year (668) of Emperor Tenchi's reign, in Aston, p. 288 n. 2.

7. "Poem by Princess Nukada when the Emperor went hunting on the fields of Kamau [i.e., Gamō] . . . ," song no. 20, in Levy, 1:48. Here is the Crown Prince's response (song no. 21, in ibid., p. 49):

> If I despised you,
> who are beautiful as the violet
> from the murasaki grass,
> would I long for you
> though you are another's wife?

8. Shiga-ken shi, 1: 15–16. YS, I: 320–39; Maruyama Yoshihiko, "Ōmi no kuni Tokuchin-ho Nogata," p. 695; Ashikaga, p. 1.

9. Ashikaga, pp. 1–3.

10. YS, II: 253. At Imabori, the elevation is about 130 meters.

11. Before Heian-kyō (Kyoto) became the capital in 794, the "capital," or the palace, moved with each ruling emperor. Before the Taika Reform of 645, 23 rulers of Yamato erected 31 palaces, all close to one another in the Asuka region. After that, the capital was in Naniwa from 645 to 654, in Asuka from 654 to 667, in Ōtsu from 667 to 671; in Asuka (Kiyomihara) from 672 to 694, in Fujiwara until Heijō-kyō (Nara) was finished in 710, in Nara until 784 (but temporarily moved to Kuni, then Naniwa, between 741 and 746), and finally in Heian-kyō in 794. See Hall, "Kyoto." Emperor Shōmu's (r. 724–49) plan to transfer the capital to Shigaraki is treated thoroughly in Cort, esp. chap. 2.

12. Shiga-ken shi, 1: 42; Miura Kaneyuki, "Rekishi," p. 26.

13. Toyoda and Kodama, 1:5.

14. Shiga-ken shi, 1: 41–42.

15. Miura Kaneyuki, "Rekishi," pp. 9–10. See Appendix A for the historical origins of the Rokkaku family.

16. Doc. no. 1, Kōan 7 (1284).11.30: Sanmon shūgi gechijō. This document exempts the payment of tax accrued in 1279 on account of the ongoing border dispute with Hata-no-shō.

17. Shiga-ken shi, 1: 28–29; Hieizan, pp. 56–58. Saichō, also known as Dengyō Daishi, was born in Furuichi-gō, Shiga County. Shiga-ken shi, 1: 28. In 813, Enryakuji also received imperial permission to build an ordination hall. At that time there were only three government-approved temples for ordination: Tōdaiji in Nara, Yakushiji in Shimotsuke and Kanzeonji in Tsukushi. Kageyama, p. 319. Buddhism in the Nara and Heian periods was closely connected to the interests of the state, symbolized by the title Saichō used for Enryakuji: Temple for the Pacification and Protection of the State. McMullin, Buddhism, p. 291 n. 19. Saichō's establishment of a Tendai school in the mountains was not characteristic of the Buddhism of the Nara period, which was urban. For doctrinal analysis of the Japanese Tendai school with emphasis on Saichō, see Hazama.

18. Fujiwara Tadahira and Fujiwara Morosuke, the founders of the imperial regent's line at court, were two of the important patrons. The fire occurred in 969. Kuroda Toshio, "Chūsei jisha seiryoku ron," p. 258; Tsuji, p. 2. Neil McMullin provides a detailed description of the involvement of Fujiwara Morosuke in "The Enryakuji." The role of Ryōgen is also analyzed in the same article.

19. Tsuji, p. 1; Hieizan, p. 4.

20. The buildings ranged from residences for the high-ranking priests to small storage sheds. Kuroda Toshio, *Jisha seiryoku*, pp. 132–33; McMullin, *Buddhism*, p. 21. McMullin counts 3,800 buildings in an area of about 20 square kilometers.

21. Hieizan, p. 191. The original building for Hieizanji, constructed by Saichō, became the Konpon Chūdō building of Tōdō. Ibid., p. 57.

22. Ibid., pp. 58–60. Neil McMullin examines the long-term and immediate causes of the schism, which he calls "one of the most important events in the history of the Tendai school of Buddhism, and of Buddhism in general in Japan" in his "The Sanmon-Jimon," p. 83.

23. Kuroda Toshio gives a penetrating analysis of separate but overlapping categories of internal conflicts based on the "public" structural divisions and "private" antagonistic relations in his "Chūsei jisha seiryoku ron."

24. Tsuji, p. 2.

25. McMullin, *Buddhism*, p. 298 n. 50.

26. McMullin emphasizes the doctrinal, ritual, and institutional amalgamation of Buddhism and Shinto in pre-Tokugawa Japan, warning against the misconstrued image, propagated by the scholars of later periods, that the two were separate entities. *Buddhism*, p. 8.

27. Kuroda Toshio, *Jisha seiryoku*, p. 156; Toyoda, *Nihon shūkyō seido*, pp. 44–49.

28. Hagiwara, *Chūsei saishi*, p. 252.

29. According to Kuroda Toshio, the practice of individuating the cross-identified deities began only in the eleventh century, despite the earlier attempts to attach Buddhist values to Shinto kami. Until the mid-ninth century an accepted theory was that Shinto kami protected Buddhism in a general sense. In the subsequent century Tendai teachings related to the multiple manifestations of the Buddha separate from his original body came to be adapted to Japanese conditions, allowing for the interpretation that kami generally were manifestations of the Buddha. This brought parity to the statuses of the indigenous kami and alien Buddhas and bodhisatvas. The final phase in the evolution of the theory of honji suijaku was the practice of identifying one particular Buddhist deity with a particular Shinto deity, as we see in the case of Enryakuji and Hie Shrine. See Kuroda Toshio, *Jisha seiryoku*, pp. 47–48. Also see his "Shintō in History." For a full historical discussion of honji suijaku, see Matsunaga.

30. Hieizan, p. 55.

31. Ibid. See Grapard, pp. 213–14, for a slightly different and fuller account. Ōmononushi is said to have been transferred to Ōtsu when the capital was moved there in 667 and to Sakamoto in 715.

32. Grapard, pp. 213–15.

33. Ibid., p. 215.

34. *Shiga-ken shi*, 1: 36; Hieizan, p. 60. Honji suijaku notions gave practical

advantages to the expansive goals of central religious institutions, for they incorporated prestigious aristocratic and imperial associations in explaining the origins of the temple and its affiliated shrine. Kuroda Toshio, *Jisha seiryoku*, p. 48. Allan G. Grapard provides fascinating segments of medieval texts explaining this rationale and analyzes them from structural viewpoints in Grapard, pp. 216–31.

35. It was a regular practice for Enryakuji priests to take part in all Sannō-related ceremonies at the Hie Shrine located in Sakamoto. Hieizan, p. 167.

36. Some smaller institutions welcomed the protective umbrella of the centrally connected powerful temple, but others were subjugated. The subsidiary institution could be one of an entirely different Buddhist school, such as the Gion shrine acquired by Enryakuji during Ryōgen's time. This so-called *hon-matsu* relationship was widespread by the twelfth century among all major institutions. Kuroda Toshio, *Jisha seiryoku*, pp. 155–56; McMullin, *Buddhism*, p. 21.

37. Hieizan, p. 60. Other incarnations included Shōshinji, Hachiōji, Kyaku-jin, and Sannomiya.

38. Those commonly involved in the lending activities were the *sansō* of the temple and the *jinin* of Hie Shrine. The former were usually married, low-ranking priests, while the latter characteristically held a tax-exempt status from the shrine in return for their services in ceremonial and managerial matters. Toyoda, *Chūsei no shōnin*, pp. 248–88. Topics related to jinin have attracted much attention from social historians in the recent past. See, for example, Ōyama, "Kugonin, jinin, yoriudo."

39. Oda, p. 110. The interest rate was about 2–5 percent monthly, according to Toyoda Takeshi. *Chūsei no shōnin*, pp. 289–90.

40. Toyoda, *Chūsei no shōnin*, pp. 288–91.

41. Amino, "Some Problems," p. 84.

42. Gay, pp. 104–5; Wakita Haruko, *Nihon chūsei shōgyō*, p. 279.

43. Wakita Haruko, *Nihon chūsei shōgyō*, pp. 276–90.

44. Kuroda Toshio classifies armed priests into four categories: *shuto* or sōhei (priest-warriors), jinin (service people), priests of branch temples and shrines, and common soldiers. *Jisha seiryoku*, p. 66. The term *sōhei*, commonly used by historians to refer to the militarized priests of all periods, came into actual use in the early eighteenth century. There was no specific term in the medieval period. The writings from the tenth century, when this type of priest began to make an appearance, call them by various names, including "shuto," "masked priests," and "the kind with polluted footwear." Ibid., pp. 29–32.

45. Toyoda, *Nihon shūkyō seido*, pp. 40–43.

46. Kuroda Toshio, *Jisha seiryoku*, pp. 63–66.

47. GS, II: 1–3.

48. YS, II: 18.

49. GS, II: 224; V: 14; VIII: 302; Yōkaichi-shi Shi Hensan Iinkai, ed., *Yōkaichi-shi shi hensan dayori* 15 (November 1983): 4. This sluice was called the Ikada River (*kawa*) or the Honai River. Although there is no documented instance of conflict between Tokuchin-ho (or Enryakuji) and the Sasaki over the water, residents of Namazue-no-shō, where the ditch began, apparently petitioned over the presumed reduction in their own water supply. The water that irrigated Tokuchin-ho was drawn at Ikeda. GS, V: 13–15.

50. *Taiheiki*, 2: 89. According to this entry, Tokinobu's troops included men

named Mekata, Iba, Kimura, Mabuchi, Hatano, Mano, and Hirai. Katsuyama Seiji groups the followers into three categories: Sasaki branch families, hon-Sasaki lines, and the others, including the Mekata, who traced their origin to the Fujiwara. See Appendix A and *Kusatsu-shi shi,* 1: 482–86.

51. Yokoyama, p. 77.

52. *Kusatsu-shi shi,* 1: 486–91; *YS,* II: 84–89, 131–36. For an example of a district-level shugo, see Doc. no. 743, Kagen 3 (1305).9.7: Azai kōri shugo shi kizu jikken jō an, in *Sugaura monjo,* 2: 44. For an illustration of this in English, see Doc. nos. 152–55 in Mass, *The Kamakura Bakufu,* pp. 167–68.

53. For example, villages in Hine-no-shō in Izumi Province, under the proprietorship of the Kujō family, experienced repeated incursions by the forces of the shugo (Hosokawa Masahisa). According to the diary of Kujō Masamoto, the proprietor who actually lived on the estate from 1501 to 1504, over 1,000 armed men on the shugo side invaded in the ninth month of 1501. About 200 villagers fought against them for six hours, injured 89, and forced them to retreat. There was only one death among the villagers. Entry for Bunki 1 (1501).9.23, in *Masamoto-kō tabi hikitsuke,* p. 140.

54. The hon-Sasaki family followed the Taira after Minamoto Tameyoshi's downfall. The Taira took over two levels of rights to income (*ryōke-shiki* and *azukaridokoro-shiki*) pertaining to Sasaki-no-shō. *YS,* II: 20.

55. *YS,* II: 42–44; entry for Kenkyū 2 (1191).3.29, in *Dainihon shiryō,* ser. 4, 3: 473–78; entry for Kenkyū 2 (1191).4.26, in ibid., pp. 492–507; entry for Kenkyū 2 (1191).4.30, in ibid., pp. 509–12; entry for Kenkyū 2 (1191).5.20, in ibid., pp. 587–89; entry for Kenkyū 4 (1193).3.12, in ibid., ser. 4, 4: 317.

56. Called *kayochō jinin,* these carriers belonged to Hie Shrine, located in Takashima County. In 1235, this shrine held 66 jinin, but Enryakuji wanted to replace seven of them with commoners of non-jinin status. The shugo Nobutsuna objected, because their replacement would reduce the fees he charged the jinin. In the sixth month, while Nobutsuna was away, the trouble escalated, because his son Takanobu, a jitō of Tanaka-gō in Takashima County, attempted to extract a levy for emergency services from the jinin. The jinin refused to pay, and the irritated priest-officials (*miyashi*) of Hie Shrine confronted Takanobu in person, leading to the brawl that resulted in a murder.

57. *YS,* II: 62–64; entry for Katei 1 (1235).int.6.26, in *Dainihon shiryō,* ser. 5, 10: 122–24; entry for Katei 1 (1235).int.7.23, in ibid., pp. 184–89; entry for Katei 1 (1235).int.7.26, in ibid., pp. 197–99; entry for Katei 1 (1235).int.7.29, in ibid., pp. 200–201; entry for Katei 1 (1235).int.8.8, in ibid., pp. 207–9; entry for Katei 1 (1235).int.12.12, in ibid., pp. 375–77; entry for Katei 2 (1236).2, in ibid., pp. 619–20; entry for Katei 2 (1236).6.9, in ibid., pp. 740–42; entry for Katei 2 (1236).8.28, in ibid., pp. 851–52; entry for Katei 3 (1237).6.30, in ibid., ser. 5, 11: 316–18.

58. *YS,* II: 158–64. A series of complicated interpersonal conflicts among the bakufu officials and the members of the Kyōgoku and Rokkaku branches preceded this measure. In part, Yoshimitsu was taking advantage of the weak position of Rokkaku Kamejumaru, who had become shugo in 1377 at age nine. A full list of hanzei land obtained by the Rokkaku from 1352 to 1409 can be found in Shimosaka, "Ōmi shugo Rokkaku-shi," p. 93, table 9.

59. Shimosaka Mamoru gives a thorough and penetrating analysis of Enryakuji shisetsu in his "Sanmon shisetsu."

60. *YS,* II: 165–67. This section of *YS* was written by Shimosaka.

61. *YS*, II: 167–68.

62. *YS*, II: 132. For examples of shugo kakikudashi, see Doc. no. 541, Eiwa 2 (1376).2.11: Ōmi no kuni Hayami Kawamichi-no-shō monjo utsushi, addressed to Mekata, in *Kyōō Gokokuji monjo*, vol. 2. Also see Doc. no. 603, Meitoku 2 (1391).8.23: Ōmi no kuni shugo kakikudashi, also addressed to Mekata, in *Mibuke monjo;* the document bears a *kaō,* a personal signature.

63. The Kyōgoku held various *shiki* (income rights) in shōen located strategically at the juncture of the Hokurikudō and the Tōsandō. Shimosaka contends that from around the Ōei era (1394–1428), the now-mature Rokkaku Mitsutaka (formerly Kamejumaru) began to show signs of resistance to bakufu orders. *YS*, II: 171–72.

64. *YS*, II: 171. For example, in an order dated Ōei 3 (1396).10.13, issued to Kyōgoku Takaaki, the bakufu complained: "The shugo has not clarified right from wrong, but has expropriated [the land] for himself [instead]."

65. On appointments to this position, see the entry dated Eikyō 6 (1434).8.23, in *Mansai Jugō nikki,* p. 604.

66. An entry dated Eikyō 6 (1434).8.29, in *Mansai Jugō nikki,* p. 606, states: "Enryakuji land was again seized by the *shugo-nin* [who were directed to do so]. It is said that is the reason for the *gōso* [violent protest involving the transfer of portable shrines]." Another entry, on 9.12 of the same year, states that "both Sasaki were dispatched to Ōmi to confiscate Enryakuji land completely. All of the land and water communication routes have been blocked. When [the shogun] heard that there was an opening, he repeatedly ordered that the gap be stopped. . . . [It was even said that] one third of Enryakuji's tax [nengu] receipts should be distributed among the peasants." Ibid., p. 608. See also *GS*, IX: 240–43.

67. Entry dated Eikyō 6 (1434).10.1, in *Mansai Jugō nikki,* p. 615. According to this entry, Enryakuji priests were arrested and no Enryakuji land was left. Entry for Eikyō 7 (1435).2.8, in *Kanmon gyoki,* p. 259. Shimosaka Mamoru, in *YS*, II: 176–85, asserts that the temple troops were led by the shisetsu.

68. *GS*, II: 385–86.

69. Entry for Bun'an 2 (1445).1.13 to Bun'an 3 (1446).9.5, in *Morosato ki,* cited in *YS*, II: 186–89; *GS*, II: 385–86; *YS*, V: 267.

70. *YS*, II: 190.

71. During Takayori's tenure as shugo, in the late fifteenth century, the same document format was used. *YS*, II: 196–97.

72. *GS*, II: 399–400. The citation, taken from *Ōnin ryaku ki,* appears on p. 399.

73. The shugo post was held by Hisayori until 1456, Kamejumaru (different from the earlier one by the same name) until 1458, Masataka until 1460, Kamejumaru until approximately 1468, Masataka until 1469. Then Kyōgoku Mochikiyo took over until 1470, the year of his death. Kyōgoku Magodōji held it until 1471, when the post was split between the north and the south and assigned to Kyōgoku Masataka and Rokkaku Torayasha respectively until 1473. In this year, Kyōgoku Masataka was granted the shugo title for southern Ōmi as well. Rokkaku Kamejumaru, later called Yukitaka and still later Takayori, regained the southern part at an unknown date and held it until 1490.

74. *YS*, II: 201–2. After this phase of the war, in the ninth month of 1470, Jinson, a courtier-priest, remarked that "Ōmi belonged to the Western [Ya-

mana] army." Entries for Bunmei 2 (1470).9.9 and 9.22, in *Daijōin jisha zōjiki*, 4: 489, 494.

75. *GS*, IV: 305–9.

76. Entry for Bunmei 7 (1475).8.10, in *Nagaoki Sukune nikki*, p. 585; *YS*, II: 207–9.

77. *YS*, II: 210. The bugyōnin hōsho issued by the bakufu to Rokkaku Takayori (Yukitaka) on the following dates survive: Bunmei 10 (1478).9.19, about Nariyasu-no-ho, which belonged to Gion Shrine; Bunmei 10 (1478).10.15, about Tane-no-shō, which belonged to the Koga family; Bunmei 10 (1478).10.23, about Nishiima-mura of Daitokuji Yotokuin; Bunmei 10 (1478).11.16, about "various places in Ōmi" held by Shōren'in.

78. Entry for Bunmei 13 (1481).10.8, in *Nagaoki Sukune nikki*, pp. 643–44; *YS*, II: 211.

79. Document dated Bunmei 14 (1482).int.7.28: Muromachi bakufu bugyōnin rensho hōsho an, in *Kutsuki monjo*, cited in *YS*, II: 212.

80. Entry for Bunmei 13 (1481).3.21, in *Nagaoki Sukune nikki*, pp. 634–35.

81. The entry for Chōkyō 1 (1487).7.23, in *Inryōken nichiroku*, states: "The vassals [*hōkōshū*] have appealed, saying that their primary landholding [*honryō*] in Ōmi has been seized by the Rokkaku. [As a result] some of them have starved to death. It is the vassals' wish that the shogun take punitive action. The shogun gave them a positive response [and] they presented his honorable self with a sword." Cited as doc. nos. 94–95, in *YS*, V: 293. This incident is described in *YS*, II: 213.

82. *YS*, II: 216.

83. Entry for Eitoku 3 (1491).11.18, in *Daijōin jisha zōjiki*.

84. *YS*, II: 224–25.

85. Yokoyama, pp. 81–82.

86. The shugo force was weakened when the Iba force was aided by Hosokawa Masamoto. Doc. no. 279, Bunki 2 (1502).10.15: Rokkaku Takayori shojō, in *Kutsuki monjo*, 1: 279.

87. *YS*, II: 229–37.

88. *YS*, II: 238–47; *GS*, IX: 614–16; Yokoyama, p. 85.

89. See the text and interpretation of the "Rokkaku-shi shikimoku" by Katsumata Shizuo.

90. *GS*, IX: 525–26.

91. Yokoyama, p. 83; *GS*, IX: 525–83.

92. Doc. no. 114, Kōji 3 (1557).7.5: Sanmon gakutōdai gechijō an.

93. Doc. no. 115, no year.7.7: Tokuchin-ho ryō satanin shojō an.

94. Miyagawa, "Gōson seido," p. 11; entries for Eiroku 11 (1568).9.13 and 14, in *Tokitsugu-kyō ki*, 4: 270. Those that turned on the Rokkaku were Gotō, Nagata, Shindō, Nagahara, Ikeda, Hirai, Kunori, Seta, Yamaoka, and seven others.

95. Fujiki with Elison, p. 172.

96. Hieizan, p. 64.

Chapter 2

1. Doc. no. 1, Kōan 7 (1284).11.30: Sanmon shūgi gechijō.

2. *YS*, II: 267.

3. *YS*, II: 267.

4. Nakamura Ken, "Muromachi," p. 5; Nakamura Ken, "Nōgyō," p. 149.

5. The following illustrate the use of "Tagata," "Nogata," "Kami-ho" and "Shimo-ho": Doc. no. 23, Eiwa 4 (1378). 10.1: Sanmon shūgi gechijō an; Doc. no. 319, Kakitsu 2 (1442).9.17: Tokuchin-ho Nogata Imabori sanden moku-roku; Doc. no. 42, no year.9.11: Sanmon shūgi gechijō an.

6. Doc. no. 354, Tenshō 17 (1589).3.23: Tanaka Hisazō tō shitaji kishinjō. Ho and shō cannot be clearly distinguished. In the ancient period *ho* designated a five-household group that (in theory) functioned as a workable unit of mutual surveillance. With the deterioration of the equal allotment system, those ho disappeared and a new kind appeared. The new ho were essentially private landholdings, an example being *benpo-no-ho,* set up by the government to provision temples and shrines. Yoshie Akio provides a thorough analysis of ho in the Heian period in his "Ho no keisei." Shimizu Mitsuo discusses the differences between ho and shō by focusing on origins and physical shapes: ho were reclaimed by the provincial governors for private use, while shō were developed under the supervision of local upper peasants (myōshu); ho tended to be non-paddy land hitherto neglected by the shōen proprietors; and ho lots tended to be small but contiguous, while shōen lots were generally large and often dispersed. Shimizu also found that one piece of land could be called either a shō or a ho depending on who controlled it, as in Yanase, a village in Kuroda-no-shō, in Iga Province. The land was a shō under Tōdaiji's control and a ho in the hands of a provincial governor, switching status and ownership three times in the eleventh and twelfth centuries. *Nihon chūsei,* pp. 64, 68–74.

7. In the broad sense, *hyakushō* meant agriculturalists in general—to distinguish them from the nonagricultural and wandering populations. In the narrow sense, it referred to a select group of elite rural residents in a given territory (such as a shōen) with, for example, the authority to communicate with the lord. Kuroda Hiroko states that in a late medieval sō, *hyakushō* referred to the majority of its members. *Chūsei sōson shi no kōzo,* p. 20. In English, Thomas Keirstead discusses "Hyakushō and the Rhetoric of Identity" in chapter 2 of his *Geography of Power.*

8. For a discussion of shiki, readers are referred to Cornelius J. Kiley's classic article, "Estate and Property in the Late Heian Period."

9. The gō under the Taika Reform was a unit comprising approximately 2,500 persons registered in 50 households that served as a unit of taxation based on available labor. Not a territorially defined unit, it embodied no specific spatial size or shape. In actuality, territorial boundaries for the gō remained amorphous, since the gō were joined by a series of commons for use by several neighboring gō. Kiyama, p. 218 n. 6. Questions related to "natural" and "artificial" categories form an important analytical scheme in Shimizu, *Nihon chūsei,* and Ono Takeo, *Nihon sonraku shi gaisetsu.* An excellent approach to the same question from a more clearly social-scientific perspective is found in G. William Skinner, "Cities and the Hierarchy of Local Systems."

10. Doc. no. 32, Ōnin 2 (1468).8: Sanmon gakutōdai seisatsu an. The organization of Tokuchin-ho villages in the medieval period is described in Tokugawa-period documents in connection with an ongoing dispute of medieval origin. See the documents dated Genroku 7 (1694).3.10 and Hōei 1 (1704) in a largely unpublished collection, currently known as *Hebimizo kuchō mochi-mawari monjo.* Scholarly opinions vary as to the precise number of gō that made

up this shōen. Maruyama Yoshihiko and Kanamoto Masayuki hold that there were eight gō in the Lower-ho alone. My interpretation, which differentiates the perceptions of the proprietor and the residents, supports the conclusion reached by Nakamura Ken. Maruyama, "Chūsei kōki shōen sonraku no kōzō," p. 5; Kanamoto, "Chūsei kōki ni okeru Ōmi no nōson," p. 254; Nakamura Ken, "Nōgyō," p. 149.

11. Ono Takeo, p. 20; *Ryō no gige*, p. 334.

12. Doc. no. 32, Ōnin 2 (1468).8: Sanmon gakutōdai seisatsu an.

13. This solicitation list recorded the names of the donors and the amounts of their contributions to the shrine. In another example, the officials of "the miyaza [shrine association] of Imabori-gō," not the officials of "the miyaza of Jūzenji Shrine," signed regulations concerning the use of the shrine premises and the drum. Doc. no. 362, Bunmei 6 (1474).12.13: Tokuchin-ho Imabori-gō kane kanjin hōga kyōmyō; Doc. no. 365, Ōei 32 (1425).11: Imabori-gō zasu shūgi sadamegaki an.

14. Doc. no. 573, Kenmu 4 (1337).12: Hikojirō tō rensho kishōmon an. The presence of local deities may imply a pattern of indigenous worship before the area's absorption into a shōen or, on the other hand, simply the people's propensity to associate all spatial categories, from large to minute, with some identifiable spiritual forces.

15. Doc. no. 574, Kenmu 2 (1335).11.10: Imabori shinden chūmon. The list originally showed entries amounting to 4 *tan* of tax-exempt shrine land. But the first part of the list was destroyed, and what remains today only shows 270 *bu* held by five people. They lived in the Lower-ho but not in Imabori (Hebimizo, Koimazaike, Imazaike, and Nakano). The parcels outside Imabori were located in Imazaike and Koimazaike.

16. For Higashi-mura, see Doc. no. 491, Eikyō 4 (1432).1.24: Imabori Heisaburōtō rensho hatake baiken; Doc. no. 518, Taiei 2 (1522).8.13: Kita Matatarō sonauchi baiken. For Shibawara's mura, see Doc. no. 402, Shitoku 1 (1384).7.10: Shibawara murando rensho hatake baiken. In *Imabori Hiyoshi jinja monjo shūsei*, Nakamura Ken interpreted this document as having been written in Hōtoku 1 (1449). This is a misreading of the characters *Shitoku* for *Hōtoku*. Two factors confirm that the former is correct. The *eto* (the zodiac sign in the sexagenary cycle) written under the era name (*kō shi* in this case) fits Shitoku 1. (For Hōtoku 1, the eto is *ki shi*.) Additionally, the first year of Hōtoku began on the twenty-eighth day of the seventh month. On the tenth day, the era name would still have been Bun'an 6.

17. For example, Nankōbō wrote in 1422 that he "discussed the matter concerning the wasteland with the mura." "Both of the mura," in another example, had *kannushi* (head priests of the shrines), who, along with three other men, expelled two merchants with disagreeable attitudes from their home villages. Doc. no. 410, Ōei 29 (1422).int.10.14: Nankōbō menjō; Doc. no. 608, Ōei 25 (1418).4.16: Ryōmura kannushi tō rensho ukebumi an.

18. According to Fukutake Tadashi, after the nineteenth-century reform of rural administrative units, the boundaries of these sixteenth-century mura lived on in the memory of the villagers. He asserts that the lasting importance of territorial definition is a "particularly Japanese characteristic, not to be found in other Asian countries, such as China and India," and that "membership in the village is a territorial rather than a socio-relational" one. Fukutake, p. 34.

19. Ikeda-no-shō, under the proprietorship of Kōfukuji, had a small terri-

tory, while Nata-no-shō, under the proprietorship of Renga'in and, later, Daitokuji, encompassed a large area alongside a river and was divided into upper (*kami*) and lower (*shimo*) sections. Each mura was administered separately by an agent of the proprietor. Nagahara, *Nihon chūsei shakai kōzō no kenkyū,* pp. 173, 175.

20. Document dated Genroku 7 (1694).3.10, in *Hebimizo kuchō mochimawari monjo.* The Upper-ho included Shibawara-nishi, Shibawara-minami, Shibawara-futamata, Shinashi, Shimo-Ōmori, Hirao, and Kami-Ōmori. For the Lower-ho we find Imabori, Hebimizo, Imazaike, Koimazaike, Kobochizuka, Nakano, and Kanaya.

21. For example, Doc. no. 20, Kyōroku 2 (1529).12.4: Imabori-gō sōchū sadamegaki. *Sōbun* or *sōchū,* which meant "the sō portion" or "among the sō members," denoted the sense of "the sō members at large."

22. Ishida, "Gōsonsei," pp. 40–41.

23. Maki, "Chūsei makki," pp. 7, 16–17.

24. Ishida, "Gōsonsei," p. 41; Hagiwara, *Chūsei saishi,* p. 176. According to Ishida, *sōryō,* or "chief (representative of the whole)," was used in *Hitachi no kuni fudoki* and *Harima no kuni fudoki,* local historical records of the early eighth century. In the Imabori documents, we also find *sōryō* (of merchants) and *sōmotsu* (a thing owned by everyone). Doc. no. 80, Ōei 33 (1426).7.4: Hiyoshi Ōmiya jinin Obata jūmin tō meyasu an.

25. To illustrate the existence of sō organizations: Hebimizo sōbun, Nakano sōbun, and Imazaike sōbun all made financial donations to Imabori's construction of Jūrasetsu statues in 1497. Doc. no. 316, Meiō 6 (1497).10.22: Jūrasetsu hōgachō. "Shibawara-gō sōchū" appears in Doc. no. 271, Tenshō 9 (1581).4.22: Fuse Mitsuyasu saikyo gechijō.

26. *Sōson,* therefore, is more a historian's term than a historical term. Another famous "sōson," Okushima, was called a sōshō by contemporaries.

27. As Saemonshirō and Sakonshirō did in 1520. Doc. no. 447, Eishō 17 (1520).11.23: Imazaike Saemonshirō tō rensho denchi kishinjō.

28. Doc. no. 230, Tenbun 21 (1552).1.23: Ju hatake kishinjō. Similarly, Kōjun commended a vegetable patch to Jūzenji Shrine and added: "This written proof of transaction shall not leave the sō." Doc. no. 426, Eishō 10 (1513):11.4: Kōjun saichi kishinjō.

29. The following incident serves to illustrate this point. Apparently, in 1408, a son, Hikotarō, left Tokuchin-ho (Honai) after a dispute with his father. Twenty years later, for unspecified reasons, the father (who lived in Koimazaike) and four other men (from Nakano, Imabori, and Kobochizuka, all among the lower four gō) pledged that Hikotarō would not be allowed to enter the "Honai sōshō" even if he had done no wrong. Doc. no. 37, Ōei 35 (1428).int.3.20: Koimazaike Shōkin tō rensho kishōmon.

30. For example, the regulations of this group called for the confiscation of goods by the sōshō in the event foot merchants violated the proscription against handling horse-carried cargo. Doc. no. 373, no date (late 15th to early 16th c.): Kachi sadamegaki. Outsiders also addressed the group as "Honai sōshō." In the course of a dispute, for instance, the Honai merchants received a letter from an ally so addressed. Doc. no. 17, 1529?.11.26: Imazu Izumiya Nobushige shojō.

31. Doc. no. 64, Kōji 3 (1557).2.4: Yamagoe sōchū sadamegaki an.

32. Doc. no. 9, 1535?.9.22: Shimo-Ōmori shōbaishū sōbun shojō an.

33. In 1581, the "lower-four-gō sō" and "Shibawara-gō sō" had a dispute over the communal use of a grass-cutting area, which was resolved by Oda Nobunaga's agent. Doc. no. 271, Tenshō 9 (1581).4.22: Fuse Mitsuyasu saikyo gechijō an. In another case, the "upper-four-gō sō" sent a request bearing its seal to Imabori-gō sō, soliciting flood relief. Doc. no. 929, no year.8.11: Kami-yon-gō sō shojō.

34. Doc. no. 20, Kyōroku 2 (1529).12.4: Imabori-gō sōchū sadame-gaki; Doc. no. 254, Keichō 4 (1599).5.10: Imabori sōbun okibumi; Doc. no. 367, Tenshō 16 (1588).7.11: Imabori sōbun okijō; Doc. no. 470, Tenshō 19 (1591).8.21: Imabori sōbun rensho sadamegaki.

35. Doc. no. 364, no date: Yon-gō sadamegaki an. Doc. no. 64, Kōji 3 (1557).2.4: Yamagoe sōchū sadamegaki an, also illuminates the relationship between the two sō. It sets forth a regulation concerning a fee for doing "over-the-pass" trading. Nakamura Ken found that three of the four men who signed this document were Imabori residents, suggesting the dominant role Imabori held among Honai traders. Nakamura Ken, "Mura okite," p. 238.

36. *CSS,* pp. 135–36.

37. Marc Bloch, *French Rural History: An Essay on Its Basic Characteristics.* Works by Carol A. Smith and G. William Skinner may be found, for example, in Smith, ed., *Regional Analysis.*

38. In fact, for most Japanese historians reconstruction of original village sites is a basic first step in examining local productive and power relations. To give but one example, Hattori Hideo analyzes the increasingly tighter control a newly migrated warrior family was able to exert on the economy of a shōen by mapping out the locations of water, residences, and paddies with differ-ent types of taxation obligations. See his "Kaihatsu, sono shinten to ryōshu shihai." For university students of medieval Japanese history, "walking the original land" is part of the normal course of their historical studies.

39. The 1873 map is currently kept at Yōkaichi City Hall. The map from 1695 is at Shiga University.

40. Yoshida Toshihiro's work has been particularly helpful in reconstructing Imabori's landscape. See his " 'Sōson' no tenkai."

41. Doc. no. 329, Kakitsu 2 (1442).10: Imabori Gyōbu sonau kishinjō; Doc. no. 538, Bunmei 5 (1473).12.24: Hebimizo Hyōe denchi baiken; Doc. no. 543, Entoku 2 (1490).12.26: Nishi Shirōhyōe denchi baiken; Doc. no. 427, Meiō 8 (1499).11.8: Shibawara Yamada Sanehisa nahatake kishinjō.

42. Doc. no. 545, Meiō 9 (1500).8: Higashi Gyōbutarō sounachi baiken.

43. Doc. no. 518, Taiei 2 (1522).8.13: Kita Matatarō sounachi baiken; Doc. no. 488, Kyōroku 1 (1528).12.15: Imabori Jirōemon sounachi baiken; Doc. no. 445, Tenbun 10 (1541).4.8: Chiku'un Jukei sounachi kishinjō; Doc. no. 478, Tenbun 12 (1543).3.5: Eijun tō rensho yashiki baiken; Doc. no. 476, Tenbun 12 (1543).3.23: Higashi Wakaemon yashiki baiken.

44. "Nishi-yashiki" appears in Doc. no. 318, Shitoku 1 (1384).11.26: Imabori-gō shinbata tsubotsuke; "Nishi-zaike" appears in Doc. no. 561, Ka-kitsu 3 (1443).12.23: Minami Suketarō hatada baiken. "Chaya yashiki" can be found in a number of documents including no. 547, Kanshō 2 (1461).1.8: Umajirō hatake baiken; no. 590-3, Kanshō 4 (1463).11.4: Imabori shinden osame nikki; no. 546, Eishō 7 (1510).6.9: Nakazaemontarō sounachi baiken; no. 591, Eiroku 4 (1561).11.4: Imabori-gō shinden osamechō.

45. Doc. no. 509, Bunmei 9 (1477).11.4: Goke Shōchin yashiki yuzurijō;

Doc. no. 493, Bunmei 14 (1482).12.29: Hyōe Saburō hatake baiken; Yoshida, p. 136. Doc. no. 403, Shitoku 3 (1386).3.6: Sakontarō tō rensho yashiki baiken, shows a house "to the east of Ise-michi" that was probably in the Central Cluster too.

46. Doc. no. 369, Bun'an 5 (1448).11.14: Shūgi sadamegaki an; Doc. no. 870, no year.12.11: Imabori sōchū okitegaki an. The penalty specified in the first document was 50 *mon* in cash; in the second, 2 *shō* of sake.

47. Some of these activities will receive fuller attention in the following pages. On prayers for rain, see Doc. no. 324, Bunmei 10 (1478).6.26: Shiba-wara da amagoi nikki. The monkey performance is the central topic in Ohnuki-Tierney, *The Monkey as Mirror*.

48. Miyaza have attracted much scholarly attention since before the Pacific War. Takamaki Minoru provides an excellent and thorough summary analysis of historiography on miyaza in his *Miyaza to sonraku*, pp. 3–102. In English, Winston Davis has treated the miyaza as a socio-religious monopoly in his "Parish Guilds and Political Culture in Village Japan." The historians' term *miyaza* represents a variety of contemporary terms, including *okonai, otou,* and *kō*. Higo, *Miyaza,* p. 78.

49. To Takamaki, only those shrine organizations with local initiatives should be called miyaza, whereas other historians have included under the "miyaza" label ritual systems organized by proprietors or local lords in which headships of ceremonies and other managerial responsibilities were imposed upon local residents. Such is the case, for example, with Higo Kazuo, who states that miyaza made their first appearance in documents in the early Heian period but became frequently mentioned in Kamakura times. Takamaki, pp. 54, 75–89; Higo, *Ōmi,* p. 443.

50. "Kokonoka no tō sashichō," in *Hebimizo-chō kyōyū monjo,* a continuous record from Einin 5 (1297) to Taishō 10 (1921).

51. Doc. no. 574, Kenmu 2 (1335).11.10: Imabori shinden chūmon.

52. Doc. no. 357, Eitoku 3 (1383).1.4: Imabori-gō kechi no tō sadamegaki an.

53. Doc. no. 370, Chōkyō 2 (1488).11.4: Otona sadamegaki an.

54. Doc. no. 317, Eiroku 9 (1566).12.1: Imabori-gō Jūzenji denbata nengu mokurokuchō.

55. Higo, *Miyaza,* p. 443.

56. Tsuboi, p. 264.

57. Doc. no. 349, no date: Kokonoka no tō yaku tō sakana shidaigaki.

58. Bourdieu, pp. 97, 190.

59. YS, II: 519–21.

60. Doc. no. 331, Eitoku 4 (1384).1: Kechi no tō tō irimotsu sadamegaki.

61. Ibid.; Doc. no. 349, no date: Kokonoka no tō yaku tō sakana shidaigaki; *Nenjū gyōji jiten, vide* "okunichi," p. 136; YS, II: 523–24, a section written by Itō Yuishin.

62. YS, II: 518; Doc. no. 326, no date: Kannushi gata e watasu nikki.

63. Doc. no. 429, Bunmei 14 (1482).11.16: Shinjōbō Shōsei denchi kishinjō; Doc. no. 590-2, Oei 23 (1416).11.9: Anshitsu da Nyohokyō dōjō kishin moku-rokuchō; YS, II: 519, 522.

64. The Imabori records give no account of the Paddy Deity. Apart from this belief in the transformatory character of the Mountain Deity, Miyata Noboru mentions a number of other fascinating beliefs. In northeastern re-

gions, more so than elsewhere, the Mountain Deity was seen as a deity of safe delivery. *Yama-no-kami* was a substitute term for one's wife as early as the Muromachi period. Although women shamans historically performed ceremonies for Yama-no-kami, gradually the idea of banning women (because of pollution) developed. (In Imabori today, only men can participate in related rituals.) See Miyata, pp. 40–72.

65. *YS*, II: 523. "Reading" the sutra in practice meant flipping through all the pages in one motion.

66. *YS*, II: 524–25; Doc. no. 235, Chōkyō 3 (1489).1.29: Daizenbō Sōshū denchi kishinjō; Doc. no. 213, Ōei 3 (1396).3.24: Umajirō hatake kishinjō.

67. *YS*, II: 525.

68. Toyoda Takeshi states that sumo was commonly performed in the fall and that the wrestlers were the heads of the ceremony. *Shūkyō seido shi*, p. 456.

69. *YS*, II: 525.

70. Originally a deity to aid in the construction of the Great Buddha of Tōdaiji in the eighth century, Hachiman came to be worshiped as a tutelary deity who protected the nation. Subsequently, Hachiman came to be affiliated with the Minamoto clan, first with the Seiwa branch but later with other branches as well. When the popularity of the deity increased among villagers in the medieval period, Hachiman was transformed into an agricultural deity, the protector of water especially. Many Hachiman shrines are built at or near the source of water. Toyoda, *Shūkyō seido shi*, pp. 515–28. For a concise summary in English of the evolution of Hachiman and its various appearances in statue form, see Kanda, *Shinzō: Hachiman Imagery and Its Development*.

71. *YS*, II: 526. Most of the registers for shrine land and many of the sō regulations were drawn up in the eleventh month. This, of course, required the sō members to meet and discuss matters.

72. Doc. no. 363, Entoku 1 (1489).11.4: Imabori jige okitegaki an; Doc. no. 355, Eikyō 6 (1434).1: Hatsu zaikeshū shussen nikki. According to Nakamura Ken, the performers of monkey dances invited to Imabori lived in Shimo-Ōmori, one of the Tokuchin-ho villages located in the Upper-ho. The performers formed a za that served the proprietary institution as well. "Sarugaku noh," pp. 3–4; later published in *CSS*, p. 513.

73. For example, Higo Kazuo emphasizes that "the miyaza was first and foremost an association of males. This [principle] was based mostly on our country's concept of purity and pollution. Men were pure and women were impure. Deities served by the miyaza were the purest of all, and therefore the miyaza had to be absolutely pure." *Miyaza*, p. 121. This observation, based on evidence from the late Tokugawa and after, needs to be modified for medieval times.

74. Toyoda, "Chūsei ni okeru jinja," p. 82; later included in his *Shūkyō seido shi*, p. 445.

75. Takamaki, pp. 260–63.

76. Doc. no. 331, Eitoku 4 (1384).1: Kechi no tō tō irimotsu sadamegaki.

77. Doc. no. 363, Entoku 1 (1489).11.4: Imabori jige okitegaki an.

78. Ibid.; Doc. no. 375, Bunki 2 (1502).3.9: Shūgi sadamegaki an.

79. See, for example, Takamaki, p. 212.

80. Amino, *Muen, kugai, raku*. This is by far the most influential work of the last two decades by a Japanese historian.

81. The people of muen are a fascinating topic that requires a monograph of

its own for full treatment. We might note here that beggars, or kojiki, were not necessarily poor, that the most famous of the hinin were grouped into powerful and influential collectives in Yamato and Yamashiro provinces and had strong ties to the imperial family, and that rōnin were numerous in the ancient and medieval periods. Murai Yasuhiko describes rōnin as "outsiders" in Murai, p. 67. An excellent treatment of the controversy surrounding the definition of *hinin* can be found in Kuroda Hideo, *Kyōkai no chūsei;* see esp. p. 155.

82. Doc. no. 33, Ōei 10 (1403).2: Za kuji sadamegaki an.

83. Nagahara, *Nihon chūsei shakai kōzō no kenkyū,* p. 272; *YS,* II: 435. The notion that mōto were not myōshu comes from an entry of 1482 in Jinson's diary (*Daijōin jisha zōjiki*): "those who were not myōshu, called mōto." Quoted in Toyoda, *Shūkyō seido shi,* pp. 464–65. We will discuss the question of myō and myōshu more fully in the following chapter.

84. For notations of "Myōami-myō," see Doc. no. 554, Meiō 2 (1391).12.24: Imabori Sakonjirō hatake baiken; Doc. no. 435, Ōei 25 (1418).4.29: Fujiwara Shōkonme tō rensho hatake kishinjō. The two documents are concerned with the same plots of land (described as 1 *tan* 20 *bu* of "field" land and one row in a "vegetable plot") within Myōami-myō. The southern edge of the field bordered the area cultivated by Myōami.

85. On the breakup of the myō, see Keirstead, "Fragmented Estates"; Keirstead, *Geography of Power,* esp. chap. 3.

86. Doc. no. 374, Eishō 1 (1504).10.7: Naoshimono sadamegaki an.

87. The sō reinforced this division by calling the two groups *uma-shū* ("horse people") and *kachi-no-shū* ("foot people") respectively. Doc. no. 339, Kyōtoku 3 (1454).6: Fujikiriyama kikori ninzū kyōmyō.

88. Doc. no. 33, Ōei 10 (1403).2: Za kuji sadamegaki an.

89. Takamaki, p. 213.

90. Doc. no. 391, Shōchō 1 (1428).8.3: Imabori otonashū rensho nahatake baiken; Doc. no. 370, Chōkyō 2 (1488).11.4: Otona sadamegaki an; Doc. no. 225, Eishō 2 (1505).8.23: Daizenji Sōshū shiryō kishinjō; Doc. no. 317, Eiroku 9 (1566).12.1: Imabori-gō Jūzenji denbata nengu mokurokuchō.

91. Such as the one in Kii Province in which the transfer of a seat to a daughter, previously cited, demonstrates the lineage-centered approach to za organization.

92. Takamaki, pp. 214–25.

93. *CSS,* p. 421. A man identified as a kannushi in a document dated 1418 appears in a document of 1428 as one of the otona. Doc. no. 608, Ōei 25 (1418).4.16: Ryōmura kannushi tō rensho ukebumi an; Doc. no. 391, Shōchō 1 (1428).8.3: Imabori otonashū rensho nahatake baiken. Today, Imabori's kannushi is chosen from among the eight otona for a one-year term. The position of shōshi is served, also for one year, by the eldest among the za members who are not otona. Upon completion of this service, the shōshi then becomes an otona. *YS,* II: 581.

94. *YS,* II: 579–80.

95. Hagiwara, *Chūsei saishi,* pp. 69–70.

96. *YS,* II: 579–80.

97. Doc. no. 5, Kōji 2 (1556): Imabori sō okitegaki an.

98. Doc. no. 366, Tenshō 10 (1582).12.8: Toshiyori wakashū okijō.

99. Doc. no. 374, Eishō 1 (1504).10.7: Naoshimono sadamegaki an.

100. Doc. no. 357, Eitoku 3 (1383).1.4: Imabori-gō kechi no tō sadamegaki an.

101. Doc. no. 371, Chōroku 4 (1460).11.1: Shinji sadamegaki an.

102. Takamaki, p. 212.

103. Doc. no. 357, Eitoku 3 (1383).1.4: Imabori-gō kechi no tō sadamegaki an.

104. Doc. no. 374, Eishō 1 (1504).10.7: Naoshimono sadamegaki an.

105. Doc. no. 570, Eishō 1 (1504): Za nuki nikki.

106. Ibid.

107. Doc. no. 351, Tenbun 18 (1549).12.13: Saemonjirō Mikka kō za ukebumi.

108. See, for example, Doc. no. 573, Kenmu 4 (1337).12: Hikojirō tō rensho kishōmon an. A similar pattern can be found in Okushima. Out of 97 murando in Okushima and the neighboring village (Kitatsuda) who signed a written oath in 1298, there were only three women, and all were nuns, that is, widows. Doc. no. 16, Einin 6 (1298).6: Ryō murando tō shatō ichimi dōshin rensho okibumi, in *Ōshima jinja, Okutsushima jinja monjo*, pp. 9–11.

109. Katō, pp. 207–8.

110. Though women held little institutional authority, there were some exceptions. Okushima's New Year ceremony was sometimes headed by women in the fourteenth century, according to Katō Mieko's findings. She found female names among the tō listed for 1324. Katō, p. 208.

111. Blacker, p. 368.

112. Katō, p. 209.

113. Doc. no. 318, Shitoku 1 (1384).11.26: Imabori-gō shinbata tsubotsuke; Doc. nos. 585-1 and 585-2, Bunmei 13 (1481).11.4 and Bunmei 14 (1482).11.4: Imabori shinden osamechō.

114. Doc. no. 362, Bunmei 6 (1474).12.13: Tokuchin-ho Imabori-gō kane kanjin hōga kyōmyō; Doc. no. 316, Meiō 6 (1497).10: Jūrasetsu hōgachō. An expense report for the kannushi, dated 1416, also shows the disbursement of 5 *shō* to the miko. Doc. no. 590-2, Ōei 23 (1416).11.9: Anshitsu da Nyohokyō dōjō kishin mokurokuchō.

115. Doc. no. 887: Hachizaemon miya makanai oboe. Even today in Shiga Prefecture (formerly Ōmi Province), women called ichi perform the *yu kagura*, or hot water ritual, before the formal ceremony. Their position is usually hereditarily transmitted. Harada Toshiaki, pp. 50–51.

116. Hori, *Minkan shinkō*, pp. 155–61.

117. Katō, p. 209.

118. Doc. no. 237, Kanshō 6 (1465).8.14: Chaya Torame hatake kishinjō.

119. Doc. no. 541, Jōji 5 (1366).12.21: Fukumatsume hatake baiken; Doc. no. 400, Eikyō 6 (1434).2.20: Kokurime hatake baiken.

120. Doc. no. 496, Chōroku 4 (1460).6.21: Hebimizo Sakontarō hatake baiken. It is difficult to estimate the extent to which women acquired land through inheritance, for the Imabori document collection reveals little of intrafamily property transmission patterns. In one record, a widow transmits a dwelling (*yashiki*) on 10 *semachi* of land to one Hyōesaburō. Their relationship is unknown. Doc. no. 509, Bunmei 9 (1477).11.4: Goke Shōchin yashiki yuzurijō.

121. Kawane Yoshiyasu, pp. 3–6.

122. Doc. no. 586-3, Eishō 7 (1510).12.19 and Doc. no. 317, Eiroku 9 (1566).12.1: Imabori-gō Jūzenji denbata nengu mokurokuchō.

123. Doc. no. 329, Kakitsu 2 (1442).10: Imabori Gyōbu sonau kishinjō; Doc. no. 488, Kyōroku 1 (1528).12.15: Imabori Jirōemon sounachi baiken.

124. Tabata, "Daimyō ryōgoku kihan," pp. 236–37.

125. Doc. no. 395, Eitoku 1 (1381).12.21: Emonjirō denchi baiken.

126. Doc. no. 511, Ōei 14 (1407).11.10: Emonsaburō tō rensho denchi baiken.

127. Doc. no. 616, Ōei 2 (1395).3.28: Akurime tō rensho denchi baiken. The main son (*chakushi*) or main daughter (*chakujo*) was the child most highly valued by the parents regardless of the birth order and was usually the primary beneficiary of the family's wealth. See Tonomura, "Women and Inheritance."

128. Doc. no. 316, Meiō 6 (1497).10: Jūrasetsu hōgachō. Five other women gave 100 *mon*, one gave 50 *mon*, and the donations of another 77 women ranged from 30 to 2 *mon*.

129. Doc. no. 362, Bunmei 6 (1474).12.13: Tokuchin-ho Imabori-gō kane kanjin hōga kyōmyō.

130. Doc. no. 468, Tenshō 11 (1583).11.13: Imabori sōbun rensho okibumi.

131. Doc. no. 8, Tenshō 20 (1592).3.18: Imabori-mura ie kazuchō an.

132. Doc. no. 375, Bunki 2 (1502).3.9: Shūgi sadamegaki an.

133. Entries for Bunki 4 (1504).2.16 and Eishō 1 (1504).3.26, in *Masamoto-kō tabi hikitsuke*, pp. 166–67, 169; *Izumi Sano-shi shi*, p. 143; Ishida, "Gōsonsei," p. 61. The thieves captured on 3.26 numbered either 6 to 7 people (Ishida's interpretation) or 67 people (Shibata's reading).

134. *CSS*, p. 373. The word *hijiri* means "holy man" or "sacred man" and originally referred to the reformers of institutionalized Buddhism and leaders of popular movements in Buddhism. Hori, "Hijiri," p. 128.

135. Hori, "Hijiri," p. 140. Hijiri of these periods also included itinerant performers of the popular arts, such as acting and playing symbolic music, and storytelling—"the forerunner[s] of [today's] indigenous Japanese dramatic and musical entertainments." Ibid.

136. Kuroda Hideo explains that hijiri began residing in village temples in the eleventh through thirteenth centuries. But in late medieval times, this practice became even more widespread. To Kuroda, documents left by the sō villages testify to the level of culture and literacy attained in the countryside. See his "Sengoku Shokuhōki," pp. 301–2.

137. *CSS*, p. 373.

138. Doc. no. 327, Hōtoku 3 (1451).11.6: Murando tō gechū sadamegaki an.

139. Doc. no. 316, Meiō 6 (1497).10: Jūrasetsu hōgachō.

140. The third largest amount, following 2 *kan* by Senryūan and 1 *kan* 100 *mon* by Saburōzaemon.

141. Goodwin, pp. 827–30, 840.

142. For example, Doc. no. 414, Ōei 28 (1421).4.13: Shukuei denchi kishinjō; and Doc. no. 423, Kyōtoku 3 (1454).8.3: Kinzōbō shukuei denchi kishinjō.

143. For example, the regulations drawn up by the sō in 1489 include an item regarding tanomoshi. Doc. no. 363, Entoku 1 (1489).11.4: Imabori jige okitegaki an.

144. Doc. no. 328, Ōei 32 (1425).12.27: Imabori Sakon hatake shichi nagarejō; *CSS*, pp. 372–73. The document's survival pattern tells us that the final destination of this land was the sō.

145. Miura Keiichi, "Chūsei no tanomoshi," p. 6. The term *tanomoshi* first appears in a Kōyasan document of 1275.

146. Miura Keiichi, "Chūsei no tanomoshi," p. 11.

147. Doc. no. 501, Ōei 17 (1410).12.25: Hebimizo Magosaburō denchi bai-

ken; Doc. no. 4, Ōei 23 (1416).12.26: Hebimizo Miyauchi tō rensho shishōjō; Nakamura Ken, "Baiken, kishinjō," p. 289.

148. *CSS*, p. 373.

149. Hagiwara, *Chūsei saishi*, pp. 21, 137.

150. Documents confirm the presence of shrine land in six of the eight gō in Tokuchin-ho. Other villages in the capital region typically had shinden. Maruyama Yoshihiko, "Chūsei kōki shōen sonraku no kōzō," pp. 30–31.

151. Doc. no. 574, Kenmu 2 (1335).11.10: Imabori shinden chūmon; Doc. no. 318, Shitoku 1 (1384).11.26: Imabori-gō shinbata tsubotsuke; Doc. no. 590-1, Ōei 23 (1416).11.4: Imabori sō shinden osamechō; Doc. no. 590-3, Kanshō 4 (1463).11.4: Imabori shinden osame nikki; Doc. no. 586-3, Eishō 7 (1510).12.19: Imabori Jūzenji denbata nengu mokurokuchō; Doc. no. 317, Eiroku 9 (1566).12.1: Imabori-gō Jūzenji denbata nengu mokurokuchō. Apart from these five, some 30 registers remain from the period 1335–1566. A table showing a complete list of these registers may be found in *CSS*, pp. 260–61.

152. A notation on the register of 1335 shows that the plots listed were specifically associated with *kariya* (temporary shelters for holy palanquins) and *kagura* (religious dances). Nakamura Ken, in *CSS*, p. 262, states that there were other shinden plots at that time. While this is entirely possible, I have been unable to find evidence suggesting or confirming it.

153. Doc. nos. 574, 318, 590-3, and 317; Fujiki, *Sengoku shakai*, pp. 38–39; Wakita Haruko, *Nihon chūsei shōgyō*, pp. 531–35. Fujiki's analysis is based on Sakamoto Michiyo's unpublished graduate thesis from Seishin Joshi Daigaku, 1971.

154. Doc. nos. 380 and 335, Bun'an 5 (1448).11.10: Sanmon gakutōdai tō rensho gechijō (an). When two documents are cited together, as Doc. nos. 380 and 335 are here, "(an)" indicates that one is a draft or a copy (*an*) of the other; the titles of the two documents are otherwise identical, and the content is nearly the same. For another illustration of Enryakuji granting an exemption, see Doc. no. 24, Bun'an 4 (1447).7.27: Sanmon shūgi gechijō.

155. Maruyama Yoshihiko, "Chūsei kōki shōen sonraku no kōzō," p. 23. Maruyama examined 118 sales and commendation documents to reach this conclusion.

156. Maruyama examined the shinden payment records between 1380 and 1550 and noted that records from 1380 to 1428 distinguish kajishi land from tax-exempt land. In the other eighteen records dating from 1460 to 1550, the two categories of profits are no longer distinguished. Ibid., pp. 29–30.

157. Fujiki, *Sengoku shakai*, pp. 38–39.

158. I counted 213 records, 93 concerning commendations and 120 concerning sales. Of the 120 sales records, 35 concern direct sales to shrines, the sō, or Imabori murando. Others are *tetsugi monjo*, that is, sales records that actually show previous transactions involving a parcel (or share) now being commended or sold to the shrine. Sometimes the sō added a notation on the outside of such a document to mark the transfer of interest to the shrine. Nakamura Ken's count is slightly different: 123 sales records and 81 commendation records. *CSS*, p. 355.

159. Doc. no. 522, Ōei 32 (1425).3.26: Imabori Matajirō denchi baiken; Doc. no. 428, Ōei 33 (1426).2.18: Imabori Genpō shitaji kishinjō. The parcel bordered a field to the east, a sō paddy belonging to Hebimizo to the west, land owned by Fuse Shin-dono but cultivated by Sakontarō of Hebimizo to the south, and land cultivated by Rokurōtarō of Hebimizo to the north.

160. Doc. no. 400, Eikyō 6 (1434).2.20: Kokurime hatake baiken.
161. Doc. no. 498, Ōan 8 (1375): Sakonshirō nahatake kishinjō.
162. Doc. no. 412, Eishō 10 (1513).11.4: Higashi Wakabei denchi kishinjō.
163. Doc. no. 609, Bunmei 14 (1482).4.29: Matajirō hatake kishinjō; Doc. no. 431, Kyōroku 2 (1529).3.12: Shōden'an Eihō sounachi kishinjō; Doc. no. 230, Tenbun 21 (1552).1.23: Ju hatake kishinjō; Doc. no. 225, Eishō 2 (1505).8.23: Daizenji Sōshū shiryō kishinjō.
164. Doc. no. 542, Tenbun 8 (1539).7.2: Gen'emon nahatake baiken; Doc. no. 384, Tenbun 8 (1539).7.2: Tokuzaemon nahatake baiken; Doc. no. 394, Tenbun 14 (1545).3.14: Kikuchiyo sounachi baiken; Doc. no. 393, Tenbun 15 (1546).2.12: Imabori Sukeemonnojō hatake baiken; Doc. no. 376, Tenbun 19 (1550).3.24: Imazaike Kishun sounachi baiken.
165. Doc. no. 420, Bunmei 15 (1483).10.11: Shinjō hatake kishinjō.
166. Doc. no. 359, Bunmei 2 (1470).3.20: Shinjō hatake kishinjō; Doc. no. 421, Eishō 16 (1519).11.5: Daitsūan Eiken sounachi kishinjō; Doc. no. 360, Bunmei 7 (1474).10.7: Shinjōbō Seisei hatake kishinjō.
167. Doc. no. 522, Ōei 32 (1425).3.26: Imabori Matajirō denchi baiken; Doc. no. 428, Ōei 33 (1426).2.18: Imabori Genpō shitaji kishinjō; Doc. no. 437, Eikyō 3 (1431).11.13: Dōsen hatake kishinjō; Doc. no. 329, Kakitsu 2 (1442).10: Imabori Gyōbu sonau kishinjō; Doc. no. 450, Bunmei 6 (1474).3.23: Imabori Sakon nahatake kishinjō; Doc. no. 212, Bunmei 11 (1479).11.4: Sakunin Jirōemon denchi kishinjō; Doc. no. 229, Bunmei 18 (1486).4.23: Hyōbu kō Seishū nahatake kishinjō; Doc. no. 445, Tenbun 10 (1541).4.8: Chikuun Jukei sounachi kishinjō.
168. Doc. no. 429, Bunmei 14 (1482).11.16: Shinjōbō Seisei denchi kishinjō.
169. Doc. no. 449, Bunmei 12 (1480).11.4: Higashi Jirōemon nahatake kishinjō.
170. Doc. no. 444, Ōan 3 (1370).3: Ryōmitsu hatake kishinjō; Doc. no. 216, Ōei 27 (1420).2: Shōin hatake kishinjō; Doc. no. 219, Kakitsu 2 (1442).1.25: Imabori Eichin hatada kishinjō; Doc. no. 217, Bun'an 3 (1446).9.21: Imabori Dōmyō shitaji kishinjō.
171. Doc. no. 436, Shitoku 1 (1384).2.10: Sakontarō tō rensho hayashi kishinjō.
172. Doc. no. 620, Kakitsu 2 (1442).10: Imabori Higashi-zaike Gyōbu hatake kishinjō.
173. Doc. no. 215, Ōei 26 (1419).12.18: Sakon hatake kishinjō.
174. Doc. no. 417, Ōan 5 (1372).11.21: Ajari Gensai denchi kishinjō.
175. Doc. no. 224, Bun'an 4 (1447).11.14: Shōshū hatada kishinjō.
176. Doc. no. 225, Eishō 2 (1505).8.23: Daizenji Sōshū shiryō kishinjō.
177. For land originally held by outsiders, see, for example, Doc. no. 416, Kōan 2 (1362).12.8: Shūsan no gobō hatake kishinjō; Doc. no. 395, Eitoku 1 (1381).12.21: Emonjirō denchi baiken; Doc. no. 616, Ōei 2 (1395).3.28: Akurime tō rensho denchi baiken; Doc. no. 515, Ōei 9 (1402).12.13: Nishimura Matagorō denchi baiken; Doc. no. 483, Ōei 15 (1408).12.3: Kobochizuka Dōbutsu denchi baiken. For land located outside Imabori, see Doc. no. 407, Ōan 4 (1371).int.3.24: Yorimune hatake baiken; Doc. no. 395, Eitoku 1 (1381).12.21: Emonjirō denchi baiken; Doc. no. 379, Eikyō 10 (1438).12.24: Hyōesaburō denchi baiken; Doc. no. 378, Bun'an 5 (1448).12: Shinato Myōshō sounachi baiken; Doc. no. 205, Kyōtoku 4 (1455).3.6: Imabori Dōritsu butsuden kishinjō; Doc. no. 377, Bunmei 11 (1479).1.26: Imabori Sakonjirō denchi baiken.

178. They lived in Hebimizo, Nakano, Koimazaike, and Imazaike.
179. Doc. no. 318. Fifteen out of 40. There are obvious interpretive differences. Nakamura Ken counts fourteen outsiders, and Maruyama Yoshihiko counts eleven. See CSS, p. 81; Maruyama, "Sōyūden ni tsuite," p. 305.
180. Doc. no. 402, Shitoku 1 (1384).7.10: Shibawara murando rensho hatake baiken. This plot was said to be the "private land [shiryō]" passed down among the Shibawara murando. Three men, representing the three mura in Shibawara, signed this deed of sale.
181. Doc. no. 590-1, Oei 23 (1416).11.4: Imabori sō shinden osamechō.
182. The shinden register of 1561 also shows six outsiders, that is, 5 percent of the total of 118 holders. Doc. no. 591, Eiroku 4 (1561).11.4: Imabori-gō shinden osamechō.
183. Doc. no. 574, Kenmu 2 (1335).11.10: Imabori shinden chūmon.
184. Doc. no. 590-1. It is extremely difficult to calculate the precise figure for outside land listed in the registers. It is often impossible to tell whether or not the locational description noted there pertains to Imabori or elsewhere. Kōgatani, for instance, was a paddy area including land in both Imabori and Shibawara. Land on "the Shibawara road" could mean a plot in either Imabori or Shibawara adjoining that road. The figure cited here, therefore, is an approximation.
185. Doc. no. 529, Ōei 27 (1420).12.11: Myōshin tō rensho denchi baiken; Doc. no. 607, Eikyō 8 (1436).4.15: Imabori Gyōbu nahatake baiken; Doc. no. 379, Eikyō 10 (1438).12.24: Hyōesaburō denchi baiken; Doc. no. 378, Bun'an 5 (1448).12: Shinato Myōshō sounachi baiken; Doc. no. 422, Hōtoku 2 (1450).4.13: Kyōnotono tō rensho denchi kishinjō; Doc. no. 205, Kyōroku 4 (1455).3.6: Imabori Dōritsu butsuden kishinjō.
186. Doc. no. 586-3, Eishō 7 (1510).12.19: Imabori Jūzenji denbata nengu mokurokuchō.
187. Miyake, "Kyōdōtai no denshō to kosumorojii."

Chapter 3

1. About 9 chō of shrine land, according to the 1566 register, calculated against about 54 chō of land recorded at the time of Hideyoshi's surveys in the 1580s. The percentage of shrine land would be 17, but the 9 chō included land located outside Imabori as well.
2. Water contains all the nutrients rice needs for its healthy growth. Bray, p. 9.
3. Ibid.
4. Dana Robert Morris states that farmers resisted rice cultivation in the first few centuries A.D., preferring less labor-intensive crops, such as millet. See his "Peasant Economy in Early Japan, 650–950" for an extensive discussion of the rice economy; see esp. p. 28.
5. Cited in Kelly, p. 76.
6. CSS, p. 230; Nakamura Ken, "Nōgyō," p. 49. This is suggested by a 1332 record of Myōōji, a temple in Shinashi. Yoshida, p. 124.
7. GS, V: 15.
8. Yoshida, p. 124.
9. Nakamura Ken, "Nōgyō," p. 150. Doc. no. 1022, Meiji 11 (1878): Honai mura mura genjō chōsagaki, describes the poor water conditions in Imabori.

10. Doc. no. 709: Imabori mura kokudaka oboe. We know the approximate date of this document from its handwriting, which is the same as for Doc. no. 699, a cadastral survey of the 1580s. This is pointed out in *CSS*, pp. 189, 192 n. 7. The document mentions approximately 25.7 *chō* of fields and 25.9 *chō* of paddies. By the late nineteenth century, paddy land had increased to 51.4 *chō* and fields had decreased to approximately 4.7 *chō*, while the total acreage remained nearly the same. This figure does not include forestland. See Doc. no. 1022, Meiji 11 (1878): Honai mura mura genjō chōsagaki.

11. Miyagawa, *Taikō kenchi ron*, 2:21.

12. Doc. no. 30, Kakitsu 2 (1442).10.5: Sanmon gakutōdai gechijō. "New paddies located in Kōgatani" are noted in the following sales and commendation records: Doc. no. 517, Eiwa 4 (1378).3: Hebimizo Shami Dōshō tō rensho denchi baiken; Doc. no. 501, Ōei 17 (1410).12.25: Hebimizo Magosaburō denchi baiken; Doc. no. 218, Meiō 8 (1499).4.13: Imabori Jōjun denchi kishinjō.

13. Higashi-mura in Naga County, Kii Province, was under Kokawadera proprietorship. Document dated 1296.12.27, in Hōgetsu, pp. 340–41. Hōgetsu attributes the pond building to the few upper-level residents. But after a more thorough examination of related documents, Kuroda Hiroko concludes that it was the sō's communal effort that brought about the "pond-construction period." See Kuroda Hiroko, esp. pp. 125–28.

14. Hagiwara, *Chūsei saishi*, pp. 171–73. Four villages were involved in this dispute. At some later date, three of the four arranged to share water in the ratio of 4.4:2. Today this arrangement is symbolically upheld by three oblong stones, which spatially divide the approach to the gate of Mamioka Shrine (the home of the villages' miyaza) into a wide and a narrow segment. The inhabitants of the villages with the rights to four parts in ten enter through the wide segment, while those of the other village must walk through the narrow segment. See the photograph of the gate and the stones in ibid., p. 752.

15. Doc. no. 505, Kanshō 1 (1460).12.15: Eishin hatake baiken.

16. Doc. no. 265, Kōji 1 (1555).12.3: Chaya mae hori kajishi chūmon.

17. Doc. no. 26, Chōroku 4 (1460).2.15: Imabori-gō jigenin rensho ukejō an.

18. The record is silent on how the sō's use of the ditchwater might be measured. Doc. no. 43, Tenbun 20 (1551).4.18: Kannushi Dōsen shishōjō an; Doc. no. 44, Tenbun 20 (1551).4.18: Imabori Emontarō shishōjō; Nakamura Ken, "Nōgyō," p. 152.

19. Before the mid-fifteenth century, waterways demarcating land parcels were typically described as *kawa*, or rivers.

20. Nagahara, *Gekokujō no jidai*, pp. 103–7.

21. "Daikaito," "Kaito-kita," "Nakakaito-kita," "Shinmaikaito," and "Nakakaito" can be found in the following documents: no. 224, Bun'an 4 (1447).11.14: Shōshū hatada kishinjō; no. 544, Entoku 3 (1491).12.12: Imabori Fukuemonjirō nahatake baiken; no. 606, Eishō 7 (1510).6.9: Nakazaemontarō sounachi baiken; no. 551, Eishō 10 (1513).11.1: Yūkei sounachi baiken; no. 537, Taiei 5 (1525).10.28: Saruemontarō sounachi baiken.

22. Makino, *Tochi oyobi shūraku*, pp. 149–52.

23. For example, the residents of Hine-no-shō, Izumi Province, were forced to defend themselves against the incursions of local and outside samurai. But there the village lacked enclosing ditches. Shibata, "Chūsei shōmin," pp. 340–41.

24. Doc. no. 1, Kōan 7 (1284).11.30: Sanmon shūgi gechijō; Doc. no. 2, Shōan 3 (1299).12: Enryakuji Higashitani Butchō o shuto sojō an. The victims in this incident were described as "Tokuchin-ho residents." We cannot be certain whether the property of Imabori villagers was damaged.

25. Miyake, pp. 59–60.

26. Doc. no. 371, Chōroku 4 (1460).11.1: Shinji sadamegaki an.

27. For example, "Do not allow an outsider to stay here without a local guarantor," in Doc. no. 363, Entoku 1 (1489).11.4: Imabori jige okitegaki an; "Overnight guests are forbidden," in Doc. no. 5, Kōji 2 (1556): Imabori sō okitegaki an.

28. Doc. no. 363, Entoku 1 (1489).11.4: Imabori jige okitegaki an.

29. The location of vegetable plots might read "in front of Higashi-mura" or "to the north of Nakakaito," for example, suggesting their proximity to the encircling ditch. Doc. no. 445, Tenbun 10 (1541).4.8: Chikuun Jukei sounachi kishinjō; Doc. no. 606, Eishō 7 (1510).6.9: Nakazaemontarō sounachi baiken. The inconsistent correlations between the traditional units of measurement and *semachi* can be seen in shinden payment records. For example, "4 *semachi* = 2 *tan*" in one place in a document and "2 *semachi* = two thirds of a *tan*" in another. Doc. no. 576, cited in *CSS*, p. 241.

30. The first appearance of *shinmaikaito* can be found in Doc. no. 551, Eishō 10 (1513).11.1: Yūkei sounachi baiken.

31. Doc. no. 421, Eishō 16 (1519).11.5: Daitsūan Eiken sounachi kishinjō.

32. Doc. no. 541, Jōji 5 (1366).12.21: Fukumatsume hatake baiken; Doc. no. 540, Ōan 6 (1373).11.4: Gyōbu hatake baiken.

33. Doc. no. 517, Eiwa 4 (1378).3: Hebimizo Shami Dōshō tō rensho denchi baiken; Doc. no. 501, Ōei 17 (1410).12.25: Hebimizo Magosaburō denchi baiken; Doc. no. 218, Meiō 8 (1499).4.13: Imabori Jōjun denchi kishinjō.

34. Doc. no. 538, Bunmei 5 (1473).12.24: Hebimizo Hyōe denchi baiken.

35. Doc. no. 23, Eiwa 4 (1378).10.1: Sanmon shūgi gechijō an.

36. Doc. no. 590-1, Ōei 23 (1416).11.4: Imabori sō shinden osamechō.

37. Doc. no. 590-2, Ōei 23 (1416).11.9: Anshitsu da Nyohokyō dōjō kishin mokurokuchō.

38. Doc. no. 219, Kakitsu 2 (1442).1.25: Imabori Eichin hatada kishinjō.

39. For example, the regulation of 1502 mentions mochi made of buckwheat and wheat in addition to rice, as well as millet husks and cowpea vines. Doc. no. 375, Bunki 2 (1502).3.9: Shūgi sadamegaki an.

40. Doc. no. 450, Bunmei 6 (1474).3.23: Imabori Sakon nahatake kishinjō. This land yielded income worth 1 *kan* 500 *mon* to the sō according to the commendation statement. It had been sold several times earlier, certainly in 1438 and 1470. The sales price depreciated over the 30 years, from 12 *kanmon* to 7 *kan* 500 *mon*. Ibid., Doc. no. 475, Eikyō 10 (1438).10.3: Seichin nahatake baiken; Doc. no. 492, Bunmei 2 (1470).10.22: Seishū nahatake baiken.

41. For example, Doc. no. 534, Bunmei 11 (1479).2: Imabori Hyōetarō hatake baiken; Doc. no. 233, Bunmei 17 (1485).11.8: Shinjō nahatake kishinjō; Doc. no. 544, Entoku 3 (1491).12.12: Imabori Fukuemonjirō nahatake baiken; Doc. no. 537, Taiei 5 (1525).10.28: Saruemontarō sounachi nachi baiken.

42. Nakamura Ken, "Nogyō," p. 154.

43. Kurokawa Masahiro, *Chūsei sōson no shomondai*, p. 189.

44. Doc. no. 32, Ōnin 2 (1468).8: Sanmon gakutōdai seisatsu an. This prohibition pertained to an area called Okino.

45. Doc. no. 246, Taiei 5 (1525).3.2: Sanmon gakutōdai gechijō.

234 Notes to Pages 81–84

46. Doc. no. 541, Jōji 5 (1366).12.21: Fukumatsume hatake baiken; Doc. no. 409, Bunmei 9 (1447).11.16: Wakaishi hatake baiken; Doc. no. 519, Hōtoku 3 (1451).8: Sanmon Gakutōdai Jōshun tō rensho hatake baiken; Doc. no. 509, Bunmei 9 (1477).11.4: Goke Shōchin yashiki yuzurijō; Doc. no. 562, Bunmei 14 (1482).11.3: Imabori Chūan Genchō mori baiken.

47. Doc. no. 369, Bun'an 5 (1448).11.14: Shūgi sadamegaki an; Doc. no. 363, Entoku 1 (1489).11.4: Imabori jige okitegaki an; Doc. no. 375, Bunki 2 (1502).3.9: Shūgi sadamegaki an; Doc. no. 372, Eishō 17 (1520).12.26: Shūgi sadamegaki an.

48. Doc. no. 363, Entoku 1 (1489).11.4: Imabori jige okitegaki an.

49. There are many explicit and implicit references to the sō's ownership of houses. The regulations of 1489 include an item prohibiting non-murando from renting houses from the sō. Many notations for "yashiki [residential structures]" remain on the sō's land register; see, for example, Doc. no. 591, Eiroku 4 (1561).11.4: Imabori-gō shinden osamechō.

50. Doc. no. 375, Bunki 2 (1502).3.9: Shūgi sadamegaki an.

51. Doc. no. 363, Entoku 1 (1489).11.4: Imabori jige okitegaki an.

52. Doc. no. 375, Bunki 2 (1502).3.9: Shūgi sadamegaki an. Such concern was widespread in medieval villages. In Kanaya, a neighboring village, a regulation dated 1430 prohibited the cutting of trees and grass, the keeping of horses and oxen, or the removal of soil from riverbanks. The sō charged offenders a fine of 300 mon. Ōmi Kanzaki-gun shi kō, 2:86.

53. Keirstead, "Fragmented Estates," p. 314.

54. This list of myō units fortunately survived among the documents kept at the local shrine. Doc. no. 129, Kakitsu 3? (1443?).10.13: Okushima onshō myōmyōchō, in Ōshima jinja, Okutsushima jinja monjo. According to Watanabe Sumio, the myōshu presumably managed these myō units in rotation, a pattern, called the bantō system by historians, that was prevalent in the shōen of the capital region. Cited in Maruyama Yoshihiko, "Chūsei kōki shōen sonraku no kōzō," pp. 8–9.

55. Uejima, p. 122.

56. Doc. no. 528, Kannō 2 (1351).3.14: Kōkai hatake baiken.

57. Doc. no. 416, Kōan 2 (1362).12.8: Shūsan no gobō hatake kishinjō.

58. Doc. no. 407, Ōan 4 (1371).int.3.24: Yorimune hatake baiken.

59. Doc. no. 494, Shitoku 3 (1386).4.29: Imabori Sakonnojō hatake baiken.

60. Doc. no. 23, Eiwa 4 (1378).10.1: Sanmon shūgi gechijō an.

61. Doc. no. 475, Eikyō 10 (1438).10.3: Seichin nahatake baiken.

62. Three surveys, dated 9.17, 9.18, and 10.19, survive and show that the paddy land totaled 13 chō 6 tan 120 bu. Shinden that yielded no tax to Enryakuji occupied 1 chō 8 tan 240 bu—a figure excluding the kajishi-type shinden (which yielded profits to the shrine in addition to bearing proprietary taxes) and the shinbata, which constituted a large percentage of the shrine holdings. Doc. no. 319, Kakitsu 2 (1442).9.17: Tokuchin-ho Nogata Imabori sanden mokuroku; Doc. no. 474, Kakitsu 2 (1442).9.18: Tokuchin-ho Nogata sanden torichō; Doc. no. 323, Kakitsu 2 (1442).10.19: Tokuchin-ho Nogata Shimo-ho Imabori-gō Jūzenji ta tsubotsuke.

63. Doc. no. 30, Kakitsu 2 (1442).10.5: Sanmon gakutōdai gechijō. Another area mentioned is "paddy associated with Fuse located in the Lower-ho." The name Dankōbō suggests that this myō might have been a tax-exempt salary field for an Enryakuji priest. CSS, p. 304.

64. Doc. no. 234, Bun'an 3 (1446).6.17: Dōmyō shitaji kishinjō; Doc. nos. 519 and 525, Hōtoku 3 (1451).8: Sanmon Gakutōdai Jōshun tō rensho hatake baiken; Doc. no. 205, Kyōtoku 4 (1455).3.6: Imabori Dōritsu hotokeda kishinjō; Doc. no. 592-1, Tenbun 22 (1553).8.1: Umemotobō onmyō sasage osamechō; Doc. no. 317, Eiroku 9 (1566).12.1: Imabori-gō Jūzenji denbata nengu mokurokuchō.

65. Maruyama, "Chūsei kōki shōen sonraku no kōzō," p. 8.

66. Yoshida, "'Sōson' no tenkai," p. 132 n. 48.

67. Doc. no. 371, Chōroku 4 (1460).11.1: Shinji sadamegaki an.

68. Doc. no. 23, Eiwa 4 (1378).10.1: Sanmon shūgi gechijō an.

69. Doc. no. 574, Kenmu 2 (1335).11.10: Imabori shinden chūmon; Doc. no. 442, Enbun 2 (1357).10.20: Imabori shinden chūmon; Doc. no. 405, Ōan 3 (1370).10.10: Imabori shinden chūmon.

70. Doc. no. 35, Kakitsu 2 (1442).11.21: Sanmon shūgi gechijō. Apparently, at the time of the survey, residents of Hebimizo, Imabori, Shibawara, and Shinashi demanded tax-exempt shrine land. Enryakuji granted 1 *tan* to each of the four gō exempting 2 *tan* of the land listed in each of the two registries. *CSS*, p. 472.

71. Doc. no. 500, Kōryaku 1 (1379).10.25: Shibawara Zenni denchi baiken; Doc. no. 513, Eikyō 7 (1435).2.24: Tomomitsu hatake baiken; Doc. no. 429, Bunmei 14 (1482).11.16: Shinjōbō Shōsei denchi kishinjō; Doc. no. 319, Kakitsu 2 (1442).9.17: Tokuchin-ho Nogata Imabori sanden mokuroku; Doc. no. 323, Kakitsu 2 (1442).10.19: Tokuchin-ho Nogata Shimo-ho Imabori-gō Jūzenji ta tsubotsuke.

72. Doc. no. 335, Bun'an 5 (1448).11.10: Sanmon Gakutōdai gechijō an.

73. Doc. no. 36, no year.10.17: Imabori Hebimizo hyakushō tō mōshijō an.

74. Matsumoto, pp. 362–63.

75. Kurokawa Masahiro, *Chūsei sōson no shomondai*, p. 53.

76. Ibid., p. 28.

77. *CSS*, pp. 301–3.

78. Nakamura Ken gives a comprehensive overview of the works of these scholars in *CSS*, pp. 12–47.

79. Miyagawa, "Nōmin to jizamurai," p. 7.

80. Ibid., pp. 4–6.

81. Wakita Haruko, "Chūsei shōgyō no tenkai—Ōmi no baai," in her *Nihon chūsei shōgyō*, esp. pp. 527–36.

82. Doc. no. 42, no year.9.11: Sanmon shūgi gechijō an.

83. Doc. no. 602, Kanshō 4 (1463).12.12: Tokuchin-ho myōshu hyakushō tō gonjōjō an.

84. Doc. no. 82, Ōei 34 (1427).12.19: Honai myōshu hyakushō tō meyasu an; Doc. no. 85, no year.11.18: Honai myōshu hyakushō tō meyasu an.

85. Doc. no. 483, Ōei 15 (1408).12.3: Kobochizuka Dōbutsu denchi baiken. A water-use fee was charged only on Kōgatani land. In some cases, a special plot (*iryō shitaji*) was set aside to support the payment. A plot of unknown size was "attached" to a paddy (210 *bu* in size) in Kōgatani and was to yield 2 *shō* to the proprietor for water use. Doc. no. 517, Eiwa 4 (1378).3: Hebimizo Shami Dōshō tō rensho denchi baiken.

86. Doc. no. 490, Ōei 33 (1426).12.10: Hebimizo Umatarō nahatake baiken.

87. Doc. no. 427, Meiō 8 (1499).11.8: Shibawara Yamada Sanehisa nahatake kishinjō.

88. *CSS*, p. 96. Maruyama Yoshihiko has interpreted the term to mean "water-use fee," which Nakamura refutes. Maruyama, "Ōmi no kuni Tokuchin-ho Nogata," p. 686. The term appears in the following documents: no. 539, Enbun 4 (1359).11.14: Hosshimaru hatake baiken; no. 550, Enbun 6 (1361).3.10: Dōbutsu tō rensho hatake baiken; no. 511, Ōei 14 (1407).11.10: Emon Saburō tō denchi baiken.

89. Doc. no. 548, Bun'an 5 (1448).1.26: Sakon Saburō tō rensho hatake baiken. A *chōfuda* ("encumbered paddy") appears to be the northern border for the parcel being sold.

90. Doc. no. 2, Shōan 3 (1299).12: Enryakuji Higashitani Butchō o shuto sojō an; Doc. no. 3, no year.4.20: Sanmon shisetsu rensho shojō.

91. Hōgetsu, pp. 336–37.

92. Doc. no. 32, Ōnin 2 (1468).8: Sanmon gakutōdai seisatsu an.

93. Doc. no. 29, Kōji 3 (1557).4.7: Ni yo Wakasa tō rensho ukejō; Doc. no. 39, Eiroku 1 (1558).5.20: Sanmon shūgi gechijō; Doc. no. 10, Eiroku 1 (1558).12.17: Sanmon gakutōdai gechijō.

94. This is the previously mentioned case in which Misono men had not only entered the area but also brought in Nomura men to cut grass, while Takebe residents also cut grass, claiming to have purchased this land from Misono.

95. Doc. no. 246, Taiei 5 (1525).3.2: Sanmon gakutōdai gechijō; Doc. no. 250, no date: Honai hyakushō tō mōshijō an. Giving gifts during dispute resolution was a common custom in other shōen as well. During a border dispute in the mid-fifteenth century, one Sugaura elder emphasized the importance of sending gifts to "people in Kyoto" as well as maintaining unity among the villagers. Doc. no. 628, Bun'an 6 (1449).2.13: Sugaura sōshō gassen chūki, in *Sugaura monjo*, 1: 280–84. The resolution cost Sugaura 200 *kanmon* in cash, 50 *koku* of rice, and 50 *kan*'s worth of sake.

96. Shiga, "Sonraku to kendan," p. 19.

97. Tabata, "Chūsei kōki."

98. Ibid., p. 79.

99. Ibid., pp. 79–80.

100. Ibid., pp. 80–81.

101. This does not include eleven sets issued between 1583 and 1639, three without precise notations for dates, and five pertaining to Tokuchin-ho merchants. These regulations are all translated in Appendix B.

102. Doc. no. 357, Eitoku 3 (1383). 1.4: Imabori-gō Kechi no tō sadamegaki an; Doc. no. 389, Ōei 4 (1397).6: Imabori sōchū shūgi sadamegaki an.

103. Doc. no. 33, Ōei 10 (1403).2: Za kuji sadamegaki an.

104. Wakita Haruko, *Nihon chūsei shōgyō*, p. 529, table 15. In 1384, shrine land already amounted to nearly 10 *tan*.

105. Doc. no. 365, Ōei 32 (1425).11: Imabori-gō zasu shūgi sadamegaki an.

106. Doc. no. 327, Hōtoku 3 (1451).11.6: Murando tō gechū sadamegaki an.

107. Doc. no. 370, Chōkyō 2 (1488).11.4: Otona sadamegaki an.

108. Doc. no. 366, Tenshō 10 (1582).12.8: Toshiyori wakashū okijō.

109. Doc. no. 369, Bun'an 5 (1448).11.14: Shūgi sadamegaki an.

110. Doc. no. 363, Entoku 1 (1489).11.4: Imabori jige okitegaki an.

111. Doc. no. 375, Bunki 2 (1502).3.9: Shūgi sadamegaki an. Such variations in laws are not unique to medieval Japan. Similar patterns—differences according to the social status of the offender and the victim and according to the

weapons or methods used—can be found, for example, in Kabylia, studied by Pierre Bourdieu. See Bourdieu, pp. 16–17.

112. Doc. no. 371, Chōroku 4 (1460).11.1: Shinji sadamegaki an.

113. Doc. no. 365, Ōei 32 (1425).11: Imabori-gō zasu shūgi sadamegaki an; Doc. no. 372, Eishō 17 (1520).12.26: Shūgi sadamegaki an; Doc. no. 5, Kōji 2 (1556): Imabori sō okitegaki an.

114. Doc. no. 363, Entoku 1 (1489).11.4: Imabori jige okitegaki an.

115. Doc. no. 5, Kōji 2 (1556): Imabori sō okitegaki an. This regulation must be understood in a Japanese context, where people remove their sandals before stepping on indoor floors.

116. Doc. no. 227, Kanshō 2 (1461).7.13: Sugaura sōshō okibumi, in *Sugaura monjo*, 1:89–90. Children could inherit the possessions of the expelled or executed offenders. Doc. no. 226, Bunmei 15 (1483).8.10: Sugaura shō jige hatto okibumi, in ibid., pp. 88–89.

117. Entries for Bunki 4 (1504).2.16 and Eishō 1 (1504).3.26, in *Masamoto-kō tabi hikitsuke*, pp. 166–67, 169. Villagers acted in accordance with the regulations issued by their lord. In 1501, when the proprietor, Masamoto, came to live on the shōen in order to reduce warriors' incursions, he immediately decreed that all thieves stealing over 3 *sen* in cash were to be executed. Masamoto himself upheld his order the following year by executing a priest who stole. Since his order failed to specify who would carry out the executions, villagers could punish criminals as rightfully as the shōen agents. Villagers followed the proprietary will, except that they interpreted their rights liberally, using the principle of joint responsibility to justify executing a thief's family members as well. The author of the diary, Masamoto-kō, expressed regrets over the extent of the punishment. Entries for Bunki 1 (1501).4.6 and Bunki 2 (1502).1.26, in ibid., pp. 18–19, 74–75.

118. Scott, *Weapons*, p. xvi.

119. Bloch, p. 170; Scott, *Weapons*, p. xvi.

120. Bloch, p. 173.

121. Ibid., p. 170.

Chapter 4

1. Japanese scholarship on medieval commercial activities is abundant and varied. Wakita Haruko, for example, focuses on the changing economies of villages and cities, as well as the transportation network that tied the economy together, in her "Muromachiki." In English, see her "Wider Perspective." Koizumi Yoshiaki, esp. pp. 123–36, gives an overview of economic advances. Also see Sasaki Gin'ya, *Chūsei shōnin ryūtsū*; and Toyoda, *Chūsei Nihon no shōgyō*. A good English summary is provided by Toyoda and Sugiyama.

2. Fukuo Takeichirō, "Ōmi shōnin zen shi," p. 545.

3. A condition noted for "many areas and many periods." Neale, p. 218.

4. Polanyi, Arensberg, and Pearson, p. 242. The quote encapsulates one of their central themes.

5. The following paragraphs owe their inspiration to Kamiki, pp. 170–73.

6. Tsuji, p. 16. The collection of tolls was based on a number of factors: the volume of goods, the type of commodity, a flat fee or percentage, the occupation of the traveler, his or her means of transportation, and so forth. See the list prepared by Gay, p. 93.

7. For example, there were toll barriers at Katada, Funaki, Okushima, Sakamoto, and Suruga. Toyoda, *Chūsei no shōnin,* pp. 316–23.

8. Unlike the kenmon, which could manipulate commerce from a distance through client artisans and merchants, the extent of control imposed by the local powers was more direct and geographically more limited.

9. Doc. no. 138, 1529?.6.7: Nanboku Koga shussen jōjōgaki an.

10. Toyoda, *Chūsei no shōnin,* pp. 398–425.

11. This was the basis of the dispute between the Goka merchants and the Honai merchants, which will be elaborated on in the next chapter. See Doc. no. 110, 1529?.6.7: Obata shōnin mōshijō.

12. Scott, *The Moral Economy.*

13. Popkin, *The Rational Peasant.*

14. Toyoda, *Chūsei Nihon no shōgyō,* pp. 102–8. The section on these pages was originally published in 1937.

15. Shimizu, *Nihon chūsei,* pp. 52–60.

16. Ishimoda, *Chūseiteki sekai.*

17. Sugiyama, pp. 218–40. The section on these pages was originally published in 1951.

18. Kumada Tōru argued further—mistakenly, in an effort to emphasize their "progressive" character—that the emergence of these merchants helped to destroy the traditional commercial structure, whose pillar was the za with its attendant privileges. Other scholars corrected this error. Sasaki Gin'ya argued that the Honai merchants were indeed za merchants, not a group that had usurped the za privileges, as Kumada had argued. Kumada, "Jiyū shijō"; Sasaki, *Chūsei shōhin ryūtsū,* pp. 379–98, originally published as an article in 1958.

19. Sasaki Gin'ya, *Chūsei shōhin ryūtsū,* esp. pp. 393–98; Kanamoto, "Chūsei Ōmi shōnin."

20. Wakita Haruko, *Nihon chūsei shōgyō,* pp. 527–36, a section originally published in 1960.

21. Doc. no. 82, Oei 34 (1427).12.19: Honai myōshu hyakushō tō meyasu an; Doc. no. 85, 1427?.11.18: Honai myōshu hyakushō tō meyasu an.

22. See Yamamura, "Za," for an overview of za from the standpoint of economic history. For a summary and analysis of the debate concerning the definition of za, ongoing since the early part of this century, see Toyoda, *Za no kenkyū,* sec. 1, chap. 1, originally published as an article in 1934.

23. Toyoda, "Japanese Guilds," p. 79.

24. Endō, pp. 2–4. Endō also points to the rural and closed nature of the economy under the shōen system in which the za operated. His observation rocked the scholarly world, which had tended to draw parallels with the West. But it was also criticized for having failed to consider the za of the capital, that is, those outside the shōen framework. See Toyoda, *Za no kenkyū,* p. 5.

25. Service za and entrepreneurial za are the two categories of za in the classification scheme developed by Wakita Haruko, who elaborates on the scheme worked out by Akamatsu Toshihide for noncommercial and commercial za. Wakita, "Cities in Medieval Japan," 40; Wakita, *Nihon chūsei shōgyō,* chap. 3; Akamatsu, "Za ni tsuite." Gay, pp. 81–89, describes the development of za in Kyoto along the lines of Wakita's analysis.

26. The nature of the relief the service za enjoyed is hotly debated. While agreeing with Wakita's categorization scheme, Amino Yoshihiko rejects her

argument that *kugonin* and jinin, who performed service-za functions, held an exclusive and unitary affiliation with a patron kenmon and were thereby protected against public (governmental) taxation. Amino believes that purveyors were taxed by the government beginning in the late Heian period. He explains that this was part of the government's attempt to control the nonagricultural population. Public taxation of the service groups, according to Wakita, began in the late Kamakura period. Amino's dating of governmental control over these people differs from Wakita's by some 200 years. Amino, *Hinōgyōmin to tennō*. For Amino's critique of Wakita, see pp. 223–38.

27. Toyoda gives examples of lumber za in Kamakura, oil za in Hakata, fish za in Settsu Imamiya, and others. *Za no kenkyū*, pp. 76–77.

28. Sasaki Gin'ya, "Rakuichi rakuzarei," p. 177.

29. Doc. no. 567, Tenbun 20 (1551).12: Honai shōnin tō gonjōjō an.

30. Doc. no. 599: Honai Imabori-gō shōnin kyōmyō. The dating of this document has become a major issue, although the disagreement is over a difference of ten years or so. Nakamura Ken dates it to the Kyōtoku era (1452–55), and Kanamoto Masayuki, to the Kanshō era (1460–66). *CSS*, pp. 193–201; Kanamoto, "Chūsei Ōmi shōnin." Because this document was left out of the Imabori document collection at the Tokyo University Historical Archive, it received no scholarly attention until Kanamoto's discovery of it in the late 1950s among the originals kept at Shiga University.

31. In 1583, the Imabori sōbun had 90 signatories. Doc. no. 468, Tenshō 11 (1583).11.13: Imabori sōbun rensho okibumi.

32. Doc. no. 373, no date: Kachi sadamegaki.

33. Doc. no. 600, Eishō 15 (1518).12.21: Minami-gō shoshōbai sadamegaki an.

34. Doc. no. 339, Kyōtoku 3 (1454).6: Fujikiriyama kikori ninzū kyōmyō.

35. Wakita, *Nihon chūsei shōgyō*, p. 542.

36. Doc. no. 170, Chōroku 2 (1458).2: Tokuchin-ho Nogata shōnin gonjōjō an, shows that merchants came from the Field Side, the Lower-ho. "Honai cloth za" appears in Doc. no. 100, Bunki 2 (1502).5.11: Takebe mandokoro Naohide shojō; "Honai salt merchants," in Doc. no. 103, Ōei 34 (1427).12.11: Minamoto Kazusada shojō an.

37. Doc. no. 65, Eishō 15 (1518).11.1: Yamagoe nengu sen sanyōjō.

38. In 1557, four men owed payments and were given approximately one month's notice to pay. According to a regulation issued in the same year, those owing payments were forbidden to engage in the Ise-bound trade. Doc. no. 64, Kōji 3 (1557).2.4: Yamagoe sōchū sadamegaki an.

39. Doc. no. 600, Eishō 15 (1518).12.21: Minami-gō shoshōbai sadamegaki an.

40. Doc. no. 62, Taiei 7 (1527).5.4: Yamagoe shūchū okitegaki an.

41. Doc. no. 112, no date: Goka shōnin mōshijō an.

42. Higuchi, p. 52.

43. Doc. no. 127, Ōei 25 (1418).8.21: Sanmon shūgi gechijō an.

44. Doc. no. 1018, Entoku 3 (1491).12.13: Ishidō shōnin sōchū ukebumi utsushi.

45. Doc. no. 57, Taiei 8 (1528).7.5: Kurita Sakyōnosuke Sadamasa tō rensho shojō.

46. Doc. no. 9, Tenbun 4? (1535?).9.22: Shimo-Ōmori shōbaishū sōbun shojō an; Doc. no. 68, Tenbun 2 (1533).10.5: Shimo-Ōmori shōbaishū rensho

shojō; Doc. no. 278, Tenbun 2 (1533).12.19: Yōkaichi Shinbei tō rensho ukejō; Doc. no. 66, Tenbun 4 (1535).5.13: Hebimizo-gō murando rensho ukejō. I owe the interpretation of this complicated relationship to Nakamura Ken; see *CSS*, esp. pp. 432–38.

47. Doc. no. 595: Tokuchin-ho kaisō tō uma ashiko kyōmyō.

48. Doc. no. 67, no year.12.2: Niugawa Tarōbei shojō.

49. Doc. no. 135, no year.12.17: Takebe Tsuneyasu shojō. Here, the six men were called *yoriko* instead of ashiko.

50. Doc. no. 112: Goka shōnin mōshijō an.

51. Doc. no. 91, Eishō 1 (1504).12.13: Iba Dewa-no-kami Sadataka gechijō an.

52. Toyoda, *Chūsei Nihon no shōgyō*, pp. 111–12.

53. Toyoda, *Za no kenkyū*, pp. 11–12. The section cited, "Nihon chūsei no shijō oyobi za," was first published in 1943. Toyoda lists Uji Yamada, Tennōji, and Saidaiji markets in Nara as examples of markets that developed in front of shrines and temples. Markets in Niimi-no-shō in Bitchū Province and Onyū, near Tara-no-shō, in Wakasa Province developed around shōen. Sakamoto, Hyōgo, Sakai, Yodo, and Uji were markets at transportation nodes.

54. Doc. no. 103, Ōei 34 (1427).12.11: Minamoto Kazusada shojō an; Wakita Haruko, *Nihon chūsei shōgyō*, p. 562.

55. *GS*, VIII: 112–15.

56. *GS*, VIII: 222, 294.

57. We can observe such scenes in many scrolls from the medieval period. Barbara Ruch has described the lively "jongleur" of medieval Japan in "Medieval Jongleurs and the Making of a National Literature." Ohnuki-Tierney discusses the history of the monkey performance from an anthropological perspective.

58. The widespread belief that markets served as a window to the other world was vividly manifested in the attitude of ancient and medieval people toward rainbows. Katsumata Shizuo has found that people felt compelled to set up a market where a rainbow—a bridge connecting the two worlds—was seen. "Baibai," pp. 183–85.

59. The first documentary use of "Ichi-michi" is in Doc. no. 550, Enbun 6 (1361).3.10: Dōbutsu tō rensho hatake baiken. "Ise-michi" appears in Doc. no. 480, Ōei 27 (1420).11.20: Keichin hatake baiken.

60. Kitamura, p. 10. Many markets began to be held six times a month after the Ōnin War of the 1460s and 1470s. Toyoda Takeshi gives an example of paper merchants going to Ōyada, in Mino, for procurement on the days ending in 3 or 8, that is, six times a month. *Chūsei no shōnin*, p. 472.

61. *YS*, II: 355. This information is in an unpublished Ichigami shrine document from much later.

62. "Sasaki uma o tori gekō no koto," in *Genpei seisuiki*, pp. 686–89, esp. p. 687.

63. *YS*, II: 345–48.

64. *Genpei seisuiki*, p. 687.

65. *GS*, V: 576–78.

66. For example, Yoshida Toshihiro in *YS*, II: 346.

67. "Tokuchin-ho Yōkaichiba" appears in Doc. no. 407, Ōan 4 (1371).int.3.24: Yorimune hatake baiken. But at least in the sixteenth century, it is clear that Tokuchin-ho lacked control over marketing in Yōkaichi. See the order issued by a Takebe agent in 1502 regarding the right to set up a cloth

market there. Doc. no. 100, Bunki 2 (1502).5.11: Takebe mandokoro Naohide shojō. Sugimura Yutaka first pointed out that Yōkaichi was part of both Tokuchin-ho and Takebe-no-shō in "Honai shōnin," p. 44.

68. *YS*, II: 346.

69. On the theory of muen, see Amino, *Muen, kugai, raku*. The theory of muen postulates that overlapping territorial units converged in the other-worldly realm as well.

70. This discussion of the connection between muen and markets is in *YS*, II: 347, in a section written by Yoshida Toshihiro. Our understanding of the medieval perception that markets connected this world with the spiritual realm strengthens Yoshida's argument.

71. *YS*, II: 347.

72. Doc. no. 100, Bunki 2 (1502).5.11: Takebe mandokoro Naohide shojō; Doc. no. 101, Shōchō 1 (1428).12.9: Obata hyakushō rensho shojō.

73. Today, Kanaya's shrine holds a certificate of exemption from tolls and taxes dated 1233. *Ōmi Kanzaki-gun shi kō*, 1:973–74. Many of the extant documents, such as this one, concerning the tax-exemption privileges of black-smiths are regarded as forgeries. The majority of "blacksmith documents" were issued by the Kurōdo-dokoro in Kyoto and are dated from the Tenpuku (1233–34) or Nin'an (1166–69) eras. Many are copies of certificates addressed to the Matsugi family, an influential blacksmith house in Kawachi Province which subordinated a large number of artisans. Toyoda Takeshi introduces this documentation problem in his *Chūsei Nihon no shōgyō*, pp. 495–508. Amino Yoshihiko elaborates on it in *Hi-nōgyōmin to tennō;* see esp. pp. 509–38.

74. Doc. no. 361, Bunmei 16 (1484).10.28: Kōshō meibun an. The smiths were called "*daiku* [greater craftsman]" and "*shoku* [lesser craftsman]." Their names were also recorded: Gorōhyōe and Hyōetarō.

75. *Kanzaki-gun shi kō*, 1: 988–89.

76. Entry from Entoku 4 (1492).4.6, in *Inryōken nichiroku*, 5: 2258. The culprit, Uragami Norimune, was participating in a punitive expedition sent by Ashikaga Yoshitane against Rokkaku Takayori, and he was based in Azuchi's Jionji. *YS*, II: 349; V: 294, doc. 94. To invite such an attack, the fish merchant must have been in some way connected to the Rokkaku.

77. Doc. no. 110, 1529?.6.7: Obata shōnin mōshijō an; *Ōmi Echi-gun shi*, 3: 143–44. The Miwa market developed at the location of the former Tsubaichi, a prominent market mentioned in the *Nihon shoki*. It held its opening ceremony on the sixth day of the first month. *Ōmiwa-chō shi*, pp. 65–67, 145–47.

78. Doc. no. 110, 1529?.6.7: Obata shōnin mōshijō an. It was a common practice for markets to set up market deities to assure prosperity. *Ōmi Hino-chō shi*, 2:353.

79. *Ōmiwa-chō shi*, pp. 145–47.

80. *YS*, II: 352–57.

81. Skinner, "Marketing and Social Structure in Rural China."

82. Skinner gives a concise analysis of the advantages offered by periodic (in contrast to daily) markets in ibid., pp. 10–12.

Chapter 5

1. Much of the content of this chapter was included in my article "Forging the Past."

2. Two examples are the influence of the Jōei Codes, the law codes of the

Kamakura bakufu, on the *sengoku* law of the late sixteenth century, and the persisting political value of the imperial seat. See the penetrating argument of Katsumata Shizuo with Collcutt in their "The Development of Sengoku Law," pp. 101–24.

3. Geertz, p. 221.

4. Doc. no. 567, Tenbun 20 (1551).12: Honai shōnin tō gonjōjō an.

5. Toyoda lists some examples of forgeries in his *Chūsei Nihon no shōgyō*, pp. 503–4. Nakamura Ken asserts that many forgeries written during these centuries co-opted imperial family members as the signatories—for example, Bifukumon'in chō kudashibumi for Arakawa-no-shō, and Gokomatsu-tennō rinji for Yamakuni-no-shō. See his "Gimonjo no kōyō." The fabrication of documents was regarded by the court, the bakufu, and military houses alike as a grave offense, requiring formal punitive measures. The Honai merchants were in fact committing a criminal act in forging documents, punishable by the laws of the Muromachi bakufu or of the Rokkaku family. The penalties set by the Rokkaku were particularly severe: death or banishment. It is questionable how often such sanctions were actually carried out. See my "Forging the Past," pp. 71–73, for a fuller discussion of the regulations against forgery.

6. For example, the absence of a signatory and an issuing office as well as the striking irregularities in the opening and closing phrases. For a detailed discussion of the inzen's content and various ways to detect forgeries, see my "Forging the Past," esp. pp. 74–78.

7. Doc. no. 127, Oei 25 (1418).8.21: Sanmon shūgi gechijō an.

8. Doc. no. 80, Ōei 33 (1426).7.4: Hiyoshi Ōmiya jinin Obata jūmin tō meyasu an.

9. According to the laws of both the Kamakura and the Muromachi bakufu, it was a penal offense to label an authentic document a forgery. This may have been the reason for Obata's silence on the question of the inzen's authenticity. See my "Forging the Past," pp. 72–74.

10. *GS*, VIII: 302. Sasaki Yoritsuna built this sluice in 1307, drawing water from the Echi River in order to develop Owaki-no-shō.

11. Doc. no. 80, Ōei 33 (1426).7.4: Hiyoshi Ōmiya jinin Obata jūmin tō meyasu an.

12. Ibid.; Doc. nos. 81, 87, and 89, no year.4.19: Sugie shojō.

13. Doc. no. 94, Jōwa 1 (1345).3.20: Ichi bugyōnin rensho satajō.

14. Doc. no. 111, Ōei 25 (1418).4.1: Nonogō shōnin tō ichitsuryō mōshijō an.

15. Doc. nos. 168 and 169, Bun'ō 1 (1260).3.15: Obata shōnin rensho ukejō an; Doc. nos. 74 and 75, Bun'ei 2 (1265).11.8: Obata Heiroku tō rensho ukejō an.

16. *GS*, VIII: 302. See also n. 10, above.

17. Doc. nos. 76 and 77, Ōei 33 (1426).12.11: Hōnin tō rensho ukejō (an); Doc. no. 78, Ōei 33 (1426).12.11: Shimo nigō Obata shōnin rensho ukejō an.

18. The close examination of the original document that resulted in this analysis was made by Nakamura Ken. See his "Honai shōgyō no tenkai katei," p. 218.

19. Doc. no. 82, Ōei 34 (1427).12.19: Honai myōshu hyakushō tō meyasu an.

20. Doc. no. 79, Ōei 34 (1427).12.23: Sanmon shūgi gechijō.

21. Doc. no. 99, Ōei 34 (1427).12. Honai Nogata hyakushō yōto okurijō.

22. Doc. no. 83, Ōei 35 (1428).int.3.2: Kiyotada hōsho.
23. Toyoda, *Chūsei no shōnin*, pp. 491–96.
24. Doc. nos. 141 and 143, Kanshō 4 (1463).6.3: Konpon Chūdō heirōshū shūgi gechijō (an).
25. Doc. no. 142, Kanshō 4 (1463).6.11: Sanmon gakutōdai gechijō.
26. Ibid.
27. Doc. no. 144, Kanshō 4 (1463).7.26: Sanmon Higashitani gakutōdai gechijō.
28. Doc. nos. 857 and 858, Kanshō 5 (1464).7.13: Muromachi bakufu bugyōnin rensho hōsho an.
29. Doc. no. 145, Kanshō 5 (1464).9.2: Sanmon Higashitani shūe kotogaki an.
30. Doc. nos. 146 and 150, Kanshō 5 (1464).11.12: Muromachi bakufu bugyōnin rensho hōsho an. This change in the position of the bakufu to comply with that of Higashitani fits Kuroda Toshio's theory regarding the inner cohesion of the kenmon. It posits collaboration—not conflict—among the top-level powers for mutual survival. Kuroda, "Chūsei no kokka to tennō."
31. Doc. no. 147, Kanshō 5 (1464).11.12: Ōmi no kuni shugo bugyōnin rensho hōsho; Doc. no. 154, Kanshō 5 (1464).11.14: Ōmi no kuni shugo bugyōnin rensho hōsho an.
32. Doc. no. 155, Kanshō 5 (1464).12.4: Iba Sadataka gechijō an.
33. Doc. nos. 156 and 157, Kanshō 5 (1464).11.14: Sanmon gakutōdai gechijō; Doc. no. 160, Kanshō 6 (1465).12.12: Iba Sadataka jungyōjō an.
34. Doc. nos. 152 and 158, Kanshō 6 (1465).6.5: Ōmi no kuni shugo bugyōnin rensho hōsho (an); Doc. no. 159, Kanshō 6 (1465).6.14: Ōmi no kuni shugo bugyōnin rensho hōsho an.
35. Doc. no. 160, Kanshō 6 (1465).6.12: Iba Sadataka jungyōjō an.
36. Doc. no. 104, Bunki 1 (1501).10.5: Kunori Kazuhide shojō.
37. Doc. no. 106, Bunki 2 (1502).8.10: Iba Dewa-no-kami Sadataka gechijō an.
38. Doc. no. 106, Bunki 2 (1502).8.10: Iba Dewa-no-kami Sadataka gechijō; Doc. no. 163, Bunki 2 (1502).8.10: Iba Dewa-no-kami Sadataka jungyōjō an; Doc. nos. 164 and 166, Bunki 2 (1502).8.10: Shimagō Hidetsuna shojō (an).
39. Doc. no. 107, Bunki 2? (1502?).4.29: Nishikōri Ukyōnosuke shojō an.
40. Doc. no. 100, Bunki 2 (1502).5.11: Takebe Mandokoro Naohide shojō.
41. Doc. no. 109, Bunki 2 (1502).9.2: Kunori Kazuhide shojō.
42. Doc. no. 112: Goka shōnin mōshijō an.
43. Doc. no. 138, Kyōroku 2? (1529?).6.7: Nanboku Koga shussen jōjōgaki an.
44. Doc. no. 22, Kyōroku 2 (1529).7.3: Ōmi no kuni shugo bugyōnin rensho hōsho an.
45. Doc. no. 15, Kyōroku 2 (1529).11.10: Ōmi no kuni shugo bugyōnin rensho hōsho an.
46. Doc. no. 50, no year.5.17: Awaya Ukyōnosuke Tsunetaka shojō. Nakamura Ken points out the relationship of this document to the trial in his "Honai shōgyō no tenkai katei," pp. 235–36.
47. Doc. no. 17, Kyōroku 2? (1529?).11.26: Imazu Izumiya Nobushige shojō; Doc. no. 18, no year.9.17: Imazu Izumiya Nobusada shojō; Doc. no. 19, no year.3.19: Imazu Izumiya Nobusada shojō.
48. Doc. no. 20, Kyōroku 2 (1529).12.4: Imabori-gō sōchū sadamegaki.

49. Doc. no. 47, Tenbun 19 (1550).3.26: Ōmi no kuni shugo bugyōnin rensho hōsho an.

50. Doc. no. 49, no year.12: Bō shojō an; Doc. no. 567, Tenbun 20 (1551).12: Honai shōnin tō gonjōjō an.

51. Doc. no. 49, no year.12: Bō shojō an.

52. Doc. no. 567, Tenbun 20 (1551).12: Honai shōnin tō gonjōjō an.

53. Doc. no. 343, no year.12.12: Yūsō shojō an; Doc. no. 49, no year.12: Bō shojō an.

54. Doc. no. 46, no year.12.28: Sasaki Yoshikata shojō.

55. Doc. no. 108, Tenbun 18 (1549).12.11: Ōmi no kuni shugo bugyōnin rensho hōsho an. This historically famous decree was addressed to the Edamura merchants, ordering them to confiscate goods transported by non-za merchants in Mino or Ōmi outside Ishidera. Perhaps it suggests the shugo's recognition of Edamura's right to trade in paper at the expense of Honai; Honai would later reverse the situation.

56. Doc. no. 343, no year.12.12: Yūsō shojō an.

57. Doc. no. 253, Tenbun 21 (1552): Sōron nendai oboe.

58. Doc. no. 601, Kōji 3 (1557).4.7: Sanmon gakutōdai gechijō an; Doc. no. 113, Kōji 3 (1557).7.5: Ōmi no kuni shugo bugyōnin rensho hōsho an; Doc. no. 114, Kōji 3 (1557).7.5: Sanmon gakutōdai gechijō an; Doc. no. 115, no year.7.7: Tokuchin-ho ryōsatanin shojō an.

59. Doc. no. 115, no year.7.7: Tokuchin-ho ryōsatanin shojō an. Nakamura Ken believes that these ties were temporary, arranged to facilitate the Rokkaku's mobilization in this particular exigency. *CSS*, p. 487. Miyagawa Mitsuru asserts that since each village had ties with a number of vassals, each vassal conversely had followers in a number of villages. He goes on to speculate that such ties were not necessarily feudal in nature nor involving the exchange of fealty and land. The absence of hegemonic control over a village by any one Rokkaku man also tended to weaken the Rokkaku's domainal hold. "Gōson seido," p. 10.

60. Paper was produced in Mino Province as early as the beginning of the eighth century. Ono Kōji, pp. 2, 25. See also *Gifu-ken shi*, 3:598.

61. Doc. nos. 183 and 184, Tenbun 21 (1552).12.24: Muromachi bakufu bugyōnin rensho hōsho an. By 1469, the Ōyada market was held six times a month. Ono Kōji, pp. 42–45. See the entry for Ōnin 3 (1469).3.12, in *Dainihon shiryō*, ser. 8, 2: 675, for evidence of the submission of dues by Edamura merchants to Ōyada's proprietor, Hōjiin, six times a month. Hōjiin was a monastery in Keiaiji, a temple complex in Kyoto. *GS*, V:645.

62. Doc. no. 182, Onin 3 (1469).3.12, Doc. no. 183, Bunmei 14 (1482).9.8, and Doc. no. 184, Tenbun 21 (1552).12.24: Muromachi bakufu bugyōnin rensho hōsho an; Wakita Haruko, *Nihon chūsei shōgyō*, pp. 554, 570 n.26.

63. Doc. no. 108, Tenbun 18 (1549).12.11: Omi no kuni shugo bugyōnin rensho hōsho an.

64. Doc. no. 201, Eiroku 1? (1558?).9.26: Edamura sōchū mōshijō an.

65. Doc. no. 188: Edamura shōnin mōshijō an.

66. Doc. no. 195, Tenbun 22 (1553).4.11: Muromachi bakufu bugyōnin rensho hōsho an.

67. Doc. no. 200, Eiroku 1 (1558).12.11: Honai shōnin mōshijō an.

68. Doc. no. 191, Eiroku 1 (1558).12.8: Honai shōnin ukebumi an.

69. Doc. no. 140, Eiroku 1? (1558?).11.17: Honai shōnin mōshijō an.

70. Doc. no. 594, Eiroku 1 (1558).5.19: Honai shōnin mōshijō an.
71. Doc. no. 201, Eiroku 1? (1558?).9.26: Edamura sōchū mōshijō an.
72. Doc. no. 140, Eiroku 1? (1558?).11.17: Honai shōnin mōshijō an.
73. Doc. no. 200, Eiroku 1 (1558).12.11: Honai shōnin mōshijō an.
74. Doc. no. 140, Eiroku 1? (1558?).11.17: Honai shōnin mōshijō an.
75. Doc. no. 192, Eiroku 3 (1560).9.16: Ōmi no kuni shugo bugyōnin hōsho an.
76. Doc. no. 194, no year.6.24.: Fuse Mitsuo tō rensho shojō an.
77. Doc. no. 175, no year.9.15: Yoshidera Tadayuki uketorijō.
78. Doc. no. 176, no year.10.20: Fuse Mitsuo shojō an; Doc. no. 177, no year.2.27: Mikami Kototada shojō an.
79. Doc. no. 202, Eiroku 4 (1561).3.22: Tani Yotsugu tō rensho satajō.
80. Doc. no. 186, no year.2.12: Furuhata Sadatsugu tō rensho shojō an.

Chapter 6

1. Asao Naohiro, "Heinō bunri," p. 40.
2. According to the diary of a Kyoto courtier, Yamashina Tokitsugu, the new followers of Nobunaga included men whose names were familiar to Tokuchin-ho residents: Gotō, Hirai, and Kunori, for instance. They were prominent vassals of the Rokkaku who had signed the Rokkaku Codes the previous year. YS, III: 17.
3. For example, peasants of Takebe-no-shō, Tokuchin-ho's northern neighbor. Residents of Imabori, Hebimizo, and Kobochizuka were later accused of having joined the rebellious force. Doc. no. 124, Tenshō 6 (1578).8.20: Onchūgen Iwa shojō.
4. Rokkaku Shōtei and Yoshiharu, father and son, left some traces of their activities after this date, however. Their last fight against the unifier took place in 1574. The names of Rokkaku family members appear sporadically in later diaries in reference to, for instance, tea ceremonies. The last heir died in 1681, ending the line. YS, III: 33–34.
5. According to Shinchō kō ki, Nobunaga resorted to this action because Enryakuji's priests refused to side with him against the Azai and the Asakura, who were allowed to take refuge in the temple compound in exchange for the return of previously confiscated temple land. Imai, p. 81.
6. GS, III: 383.
7. See Katsumata with Collcutt, pp. 101–24, for a discussion of the concept of "public" rule (of which tenka was one manifestation) as it developed among the daimyo and the unifiers. Herman Ooms also discusses Nobunaga's ideological goals in his Tokugawa Ideology.
8. See Fujiki with Elison, pp. 149–93.
9. But Nobunaga considered rebellious peasants "not worthy of account." Fujiki, "Tōitsu seiken," p. 36.
10. Doc. no. 56: Ōmi no kuni shugo segyōjō utsushi. An accurate city plan of Ishidera including the precise location of Honai-chō is not extant. Kobayashi, "Kannonjijō," pp. 231–33.
11. Kobayashi, "Kannonjijō." See McClain, Kanazawa, which discusses the use and development of urban space in a castle town by historical stages from 1583 on.
12. Earlier, in the fourth month of 1567, Nobunaga had built a castle town

in Kano, Mino Province. There he had guaranteed the tax-exempt status of every resident merchant. Imai, p. 77.

13. Document dated Tenshō 5 (1577).6, in *Hachiman-chō kyōyū monjo*. Cited in *Shiga-ken Hachiman-chō shi*, 2: 109. This well-known document has appeared in many secondary works, for example, Sasaki Gin'ya, "Rakuichi rakuzarei," p. 205.

14. Imai, p. 77.

15. Throughout the medieval period, cancellation of debts by various authorities was a common practice. Lending agreements commonly included the phrase "This debt agreement will continue to have force even if a tokusei is issued." In English, Delmer Brown deals with tokusei in his "The Japanese Tokusei of 1297."

16. Wakita Osamu, *Kinsei hōkensei*, 2:117–26.

17. Doc. no. 72, Tenshō 6 (1578).9.1: Tomita Kazumasa ukejō an. The message was addressed to the Shihon merchants, not the Honai merchants, because the matter was related to the Ise-bound trade.

18. Another document from the same year reveals a similar circumstance. The sō of Imazaike, part of the Honai collective, appealed to Honai's yamagoe merchants concerning negligence in the payment of dues by their ashiko. Doc. no. 997, Tenshō 6 (1578).10: Imazaike sō shojō an.

19. Tenshō 11 (1583).7.7: Gōshū Gamō-gun Honai Imazaike kenchihyō, in *Imazaki Onjōji monjo* (unpublished ms. in the eishabon form at Tokyo Daigaku Shiryō Hensanjō). This survey record shows Yojirō, Matazaemon, and Chayazaemon to be holders of 2 to 7 tan of fields. Yojirō appears in Doc. no. 139, Eiroku 3? (1560?).11.9: Honai shōnin mōshijō an; Chayazaemon and Matazaemon, in Doc. no. 594, Eiroku 1 (1558).5.19: Honai shōnin mōshijō an. In all cases, they are members of the Honai Merchants Collective (*shōninchū sōbun*).

20. Other well-known merchant groups similarly stepped into historical obscurity around this time. Kosodeya of Fuchū, Echizen Province, is one example. Catering to Kitano and Kamo shrines in Kyoto, it specialized in long-distance trade between the capital and Echizen. The possible direct causes for its disappearance are the demise of its patron shōen proprietors and Nobunaga's destruction of Fuchū in 1575. Aoyagi, pp. 64–65.

21. Doc. no. 567, Tenbun 20 (1551).12: Honai shōnin tō gonjōjō an.

22. The first estimate submitted is dated Eiroku 11 (1568).10.14. In *Kagamiyama-mura Hashimoto Sayū jinja monjo*, in GS, III: 355.

23. Document dated no year.12.23, in *Kagamiyama-mura Hashimoto Sayū jinja monjo*, in GS, III: 363. Enryakuji appealed to the court concerning Nobunaga's confiscation of land in 1569. Imai, p. 81.

24. Shibata Katsuie had been enfeoffed Tokuchin-ho and other Enryakuji land in Gamō County after the destruction of the temple. YS, III: 38.

25. Doc. no. 1014, Tenshō 3 (1575).8.10: Shibata Katsuie shojō utsushi; Doc. no. 1015, Tenshō 3 (1575).8.20: Katō Jirōsaemon satajō utsushi. Five days after issuing the first directive to Tokuchin-ho, Shibata Katsuie led an expedition against the Asakura in Echizen Province. Katō took over Shibata's function in the latter's absence. Copies of these documents remain in the largely unpublished *Nakano kyōyū monjo*.

26. Doc. no. 1014, Tenshō 3 (1575).8.10: Shibata katsuie shojō utsushi.

27. The accusation focused on the villagers' participation in the resistance

movement mobilized by the adherents of the Ikkō sect to aid the allied armies of the Azai, Asakura, and Rokkaku in 1570. The investigation took place eight years after the purported incident. Doc. no. 124, Tenshō 6 (1578).8.20: Onchūgen Iwa shojō.

28. Doc. no. 317, Eiroku 9 (1566).12.1: Imabori-gō Jūzenji denbata nengu mokurokuchō. At that time the total value of shrine land equaled 7 *kan* 261 *mon* in cash and 7.730 *koku* in rice measured in "large units" (*ōmasu*) and 17.642 more *koku* measured in "small units" (*komasu*).

29. Sasaki Junnosuke, p. 50.

30. Doc. no. 317, Eiroku 9 (1566).12.1: Imabori-gō Jūzenji denbata nengu mokurokuchō.

31. Sasaki Junnosuke, pp. 54–55.

32. For example, see Doc. no. 471: Hebimizo Imabori desaku chigaime sanyōjō.

33. Mizumoto, pp. 98–99.

34. Document dated 1583?.11.2 in *Mabuchi-mura Iwakura kyōyū monjo*, in *GS*, III: 595–96, addressed to Gamō-gun myōshu hyakushōchū. Which Gamō County villages besides Mabuchi received this order is unknown. No matter how systematic or thorough, errors and mismeasurements were fundamental to the land surveys conducted by Hideyoshi and by his Tokugawa successors. Philip C. Brown points this out in his "The Mismeasure of Land."

35. Entries for Tenshō 11 (1583).7.7 and Tenshō 12 (1584).11.16, in *Imazaki Onjōji monjo*.

36. Before Hideyoshi, the size of a *masu* (measuring cup) varied greatly not only from one region to another but even within one village. People in the Imabori area, for instance, used "lord's *masu*," "tea house *masu*," and many other *masu* named after a person or place before the "Kyō *masu*," associated with Kyoto, replaced them all. This shift took place at the time of Hideyoshi's nationwide surveys in 1591. Hideyoshi also adopted a more easily calculated measurement for land size while retaining the original terminology. For instance, 1 *tan* equaled 300 *bu* under Hideyoshi instead of 360 *bu*. "Large," "medium," and "small," which had meant 240 *bu*, 180 *bu*, and 120 *bu* respectively, now meant 200 *bu*, 150 *bu*, and 100 *bu*. Despite these steps toward standardization, however, much regional variation still remained in the Tokugawa period.

37. Miyagawa, *Taikō kenchi ron*, 2:52–53; *YS*, III: 72–73.

38. The mura appeared as a unit of political control for the first time under Nobunaga in a 1575 record in which he tried to abolish the shrines' ownership of land in several Honai villages. A letter of compromise delivered by Nobunaga's vassals to five Honai villages called each village a mura instead of a gō. Doc. no. 1015, Tenshō 3 (1575).8.20: Katō Jirōsaemon satajō utsushi.

39. The sō held 29.2 *koku*, and Jirōsaemon, the next largest holder, 9.7 *koku*. The sō held about 16 percent of the total area (not to be confused with yield) listed. *YS*, III: 75–79.

40. Miyagawa Mitsuru interprets this clause to mean "those whose names are on the list shall cultivate." *Taikō kenchi ron*, 2:24.

41. Doc. no. 467, Tenshō 11 (1583).7: Imabori sōchū sadamegaki an.

42. Doc. no. 468, Tenshō 11 (1583).11.13: Imabori sōbun rensho okibumi. Ten of the 90 names listed were without signatures, however.

43. Doc. no. 463, Tenshō 12? (1584?).3.19: Toyotomi Hideyoshi shuinjō

utsushi. The addressees were Miyagi Nagatsugu and Mori Heikichi, local warriors who had been prominent probably since the days of the Rokkaku.

44. Doc. no. 459, Tenshō 12 (1584).9.2: Imabori-mura kenchichō hyōshi.

45. Nakamura Ken, "Sōson monjo no seikaku," p. 207; Doc. no. 459, Tenshō 12 (1584).9.2: Imabori-mura kenchichō hyōshi. The front cover of one of the two registers shows a yield of 260.848 *koku.*

46. Doc. no. 462, Tenshō 12 (1584).10.1: Imabori-mura hyakushō kishōmon an.

47. In *YS,* III: 69.

48. *GS,* III: 598.

49. Document dated 1583? 1584?.6.26, in *Okayama-mura Funaki Nishikawa Ikutarō-shi monjo,* in *GS,* III: 603–4. Hideyoshi's agent who granted this exemption to Jōsai was the man who compiled Imabori's register of 1584.9.2. Doc. no. 459, Tenshō 12 (1584).9.2: Imabori-mura kenchichō hyōshi.

50. For example, Doc. no. 469, Tenshō 12 (1584).12.2: Imabori sōbun sadamegaki an. In this document, the sō pleaded to have the upcoming survey canceled and to have future taxes calculated on the basis of the surveys done either the previous year or that year. It also promised to satisfy the collection requirements of the two agents.

51. It is probable that the actual survey was conducted by vassal-officials of Tokugawa Ieyasu, who had been enfeoffed the old Tokuchin-ho area in the seventh month of 1590. *YS,* III: 80.

52. Doc. no. 458, Tenshō 18 (1590).9.17: Imabori-mura sashidashi an.

53. Doc. no. 456, Tenshō 19 (1591).8: Imabori-mura sashidashi an.

54. Nakamura Ken, " 'Sō 'oboegaki," p. 120. When Hideyoshi enfeoffed 90,000 *koku* of land in Omi to Tokugawa Ieyasu on 1591.4.22, Imabori's putative yield was listed as 526.75 *koku.* The yields in *koku* for other Tokuchin-ho villages were listed as follows: Higashi-Kobochizuka, 333.6; Nishi-Kobochizuka, 581.7; Hebimizo, 464.57; Koimazaike, 101.4; Nakano, 303.0; Imazaike, 336.18; Kanaya, 177.54. *GS* III: 619–20. Also see Horikawa, p. 31.

55. Asao Naohiro, "Toyotomi," p. 161; Miyagawa, *Taikō kenchi ron,* 2: 24.

56. The documents were published by Miyagawa Mitsuru in his *Taikō kenchi ron,* 3: 218–49.

57. Miyagawa, *Taikō kenchi ron,* 2: 28–29.

58. Thomas C. Smith has noted that in the central, more economically advanced areas, tenancy developed more extensively and earlier than in the "hinterland[s] of villages where subsistence farming still held sway and men had yet to feel the first sharp tremors of change emanating from the towns." To him, the contrast was a matter of differential rates of economic development. The pattern found in the Kinai was to be found later in other areas. This is a sustained theme of his *The Agrarian Origins of Modern Japan.* The quotation appears on p. 4.

59. Ibid. Smith states that the population of four Kinai cities (Kyoto, Fushimi, Osaka, Sakai) totaled about 400,000.

60. To borrow Skinner's language, Yōkaichi may have developed into an intermediate market town, subordinating "the ring of standard markets immediately surrounding the city." Although Skinner's work describes "a shift from standard to higher-level markets in the course of modernization," I speculate here that the same pattern may be applicable to other instances of economic expansion. Skinner, "Marketing," p. 215.

61. Obata's request was rejected in 1718 but was recognized in 1799 with the condition that trading there would not interfere with the schedule and activities at Yōkaichi. *Shiga-ken shi,* 3: 627.

62. *YS,* III: 406–7.

63. Kitamura, pp. 5–9.

64. Kawai, p. 64; *GS,* V: 58–61. "Tea field" appears frequently in commendation or land sales documents of earlier dates, for example, Doc. no. 544, Entoku 3 (1491). 12.12: Imabori Fukuemonjirō nahatake baiken. The term "tea house measuring cup [*chaya masu*]," one of many measuring cups used in Imabori, also suggests the importance of tea cultivation. See, for example, Doc. no. 518, Taiei 2 (1522). 8.13: Kita Matatarō sounachi baiken. Ready access to markets probably also promoted handicraft production. Medieval documents allude to local involvement in metalwork and wooden wares. We find no similar evidence from the post-Hideyoshi era, but the villagers—with or without the Honai merchants—probably traded actively in Yōkaichi at least. The local habit of close involvement with the market nexus and its larger economic system would not die easily.

65. From 49 percent to 61 percent, depending on the year. Miyagawa, "Gōson seido to kenchi," p. 15, table 3; or Miyagawa, *Taikō kenchi ron,* 2: 26, table 4.

66. Miyagawa, *Taikō kenchi ron,* 2: 30–33.

67. Ibid., p. 31, table 5.

68. Doc. no. 354, Tenshō 17 (1589). 3.23: Tanaka Hisazō tō shitaji kishinjō. The Imabori sō acknowledged the receipt with Doc. no. 455, Tenshō 17 (1589). 3.27: Imabori sōbun kishin shitaji ukejō an. Tanaka is the surname of a collateral branch of the Rokkaku. See Appendix A.

69. Doc. no. 470, Tenshō 19 (1591). 8.21: Imabori sōbun rensho sadamegaki.

70. A similar acknowledgment of collective responsibility can be found in pledges written by other sō. The Ōmori sō, for instance, wrote in 1588 that it would meet obligations neglected by absconding individual villagers. *YS,* III: 100.

71. Berry, pp. 208–9.

72. Doc. no. 8, Tenshō 20 (1592). 3.18. Imabori-mura ie kazuchō an.

73. Doc. no. 470, Tenshō 19 (1591). 8.21: Imabori sōbun rensho sadamegaki.

74. Doc. no. 125, Tenshō 20 (1592). 12.6: Jōshun tō rensho karafu sadamejō, issued by samurai who were probably Hideyoshi's local agents.

75. Hideyoshi was revolutionary in the way he provisioned his soldiers. Instead of requiring each soldier to take care of his own subsistence, he made it a policy to feed his fighters. This eliminated the need to live off the land in enemy territory, an important factor in securing the support of local peasants. Kuroda Hideo, "Sengoku Shokuhōki," p. 287.

76. *GS,* III: 619–21.

77. *YS,* III: 102.

78. *GS,* III: 622–23.

79. For instance, Ieyasu confiscated the domain of Ishida Mitsunari, located around Hikone (Sawayama Castle) and worth 195,000 *koku.* Of this amount, 150,000 *koku* went to Ii Naomasa, a fudai daimyo. *YS,* III: 102.

80. *GS,* IV: 305.

81. *GS*, IV: 256–57.

82. Yōkaichi-shi Shi Hensan Iinkai, ed., *Yōkaichi-shi shi hensan dayori* 18 (March 1984): 4. There were no fewer than fourteen fief holders in the present-day area of Yōkaichi. As for Imabori, 300 *koku* went to the Hikone domain and 200 *koku* to the Sendai domain. Document dated Genroku 7 (1694).3.10, in the unpublished *Hebimizo kuchō mochimawari monjo.*

83. Recently, there has been a surge of literature on peasant rebellions in the Tokugawa period. Conrad Totman provides a review and a bibliography in English on the Tokugawa peasantry; see his "Tokugawa Peasants: Win, Lose, or Draw?"

84. Matsumoto, p. 344, in a chapter originally published in 1942. His argument is built upon the work of Makino Shinnosuke, *Buke jidai shakai.*

85. As recently noted by Nagahara Keiji and Kozo Yamamura, "the political and institutional changes that transformed the war-torn country into the unified Tokugawa (*bakuhan*) system" has gained considerable scholarly attention. See their "Shaping the Process of Unification," p. 77. This gap in our knowledge is in one sense associated with the usual problem of chronological segmentation in academia. Medievalists and early modernists are two separate groups that have tended to ignore the questions of transition from one major period to another. Moreover, the approach to Tokugawa history in English-language works has tended to link it to the Meiji Restoration and the subsequent phase of industrialization and modernization. Tokugawa history, including village history, has often been viewed as important for what it paved the way for, not for what it was.

86. And for the remaining years to the present, only eleven documents are extant in the Imabori collection.

87. Nakada, "Tokugawa jidai ni okeru mura no jinkaku," in his *Hōsei shi ronshū*, pp. 963–77.

88. Doc. no. 733, Kanpō 3 (1743).2.6: Imabori-mura ryō shōya miyada kaihatsu hitofuda.

89. Doc. no. 296, Kan'ei 16 (1639).8.21: Imabori sōbun rensho sadamejō.

90. Doc. no. 247, Genna 3 (1617).12.27: Imabori-mura okibumi; Doc. no. 296, Kan'ei 16 (1639).8.21: Imabori sōbun rensho sadamejō.

91. *YS*, III: 150. A document issued to Mitsuya village proposing the mutual defense of a communal grass-cutting area against possible encroachment by outsiders at the time of a cadastral survey.

92. Doc. no. 8, Tenshō 20 (1592).3.18: Imabori-mura ie kazuchō an. The character for *shō* (of *shōya*) is incorrectly written in the document. This error has been noted in *YS*, III: 151.

93. Sale and purchase of land was an important communal matter in that it restructured the apportionment of villagewide tax obligations. For example, see Doc. no. 961, Meireki 4 (1658).2.11: Shōya Jiuemon tō rensho hatake baiken.

94. To be discussed further under the heading "The Sō in Intervillage Disputes."

95. In this case, the headman was the addressee. Codes were usually written by the heads of the five-household groups (discussed below). See Kanbun 10 (1670).8.11: Nakano-mura okite, for an illustration. *YS*, VI: 49–50.

96. For a fuller discussion of village governance in English, see Befu; and Asakawa, "Notes on Village Government." For examples of the range of a shōya's activities, see Henderson.

97. Genbun 3 (1738).11: Nakano-mura shōya yaku gōriki no oboe and Genbun 3 (1738).12.11: Nakano-mura shōya yaku gōriki ni tsuki tatsusho, in *YS*, VI: 149–50.

98. Villages set salary rates for their own officials. Shibawara, for instance, paid 4 *koku* of rice to the headman and 1.6 *koku* to elders. *YS*, III: 244.

99. *YS*, III: 243–44.

100. As with many other aspects of Tokugawa village life, there was much local variation in the way the shōya came to be chosen. In some villages, it was a position passed down among the members of several locally powerful lineages. For our region, we can find instances of the election of officials in Shibawara and Fuse as well. The election is described in *YS*, III: 245. For documentary evidence, see Genbun 3 (1738).12.9: Nakano-mura shōya yaku kōtai mōshi watashi and Genbun 3 (1738): Nakano-mura shōya atoyaku irefuda ginmi ni tsuki jōshin, both in *Nakano kyōyū monjo*, in *YS*, VI: 153–54.

101. We may recall that Imabori had eight elders and Hebimizo, ten.

102. Enkyō 5 (1748).3: Nakano-mura shōya kimoiri toshiyori tsutome kata sadame, in *Nakano kyōyū monjo*, in *YS*, VI: 151–52.

103. For example, see Doc. no. 733, Kanpō 3 (1743).2.6: Imabori-mura ryō shōya miyada kaihatsu hitofuda. Here the shōya of the "Hikone (Ii) side" and "Sendai (Date) side" as well as their delegates (yokome and kimoiri) gave seals of approval to the sō's plan to "develop a piece of land that had lain waste since ancient times and turn it into shrine land." Also see Doc. no. 298, Genroku 7 (1694).11.30: Imabori-mura men aisadamejō an, for the signatures of both the shōya and the eight otona. For the signature of a hyakushō-dai, see Doc. no. 1011, Kyōhō 10 (1725).10.26: Hirako tame ikken sumijō.

104. One of the major uprisings of the Tokugawa period in which peasants and Christians of Kyushu (Hizen and Higo provinces) rebelled (1637–38) against the oppressive rule of their domainal lord, Matsukura.

105. Cremation and cemeteries for the bone-filled urns, both associated with Buddhist funerary practices, became widespread in Japan only in the Tokugawa period. But even then, rural villages were slow to adopt these customs and continued to practice interment. Toyoda, *Shūkyō seido shi*, p. 115; Takeda, p. 272.

106. Compulsory donations were the primary source of funds for running most small temples. Toyoda, *Shūkyō seido shi*, p. 108.

107. *YS*, III: 521. The survey, conducted in 1871–79, covered the villages in Gamō and Kanzaki counties.

108. Information regarding Renkōji is inconsistent. *Ōmi Gamō-gun shi* provides 1713 as the date of opening, but the Imabori collection contains a priest's statement from 1710 regarding the origins of a Kannon statue housed there. Doc. no. 228, Hōei 7 (1710).4.18: Renkōji kannon sonzō yuraisho an. It is certain, nonetheless, that this temple originated in the mid-Tokugawa period. See *GS*, VII: 21.

109. *YS*, III: 522. Where the majority of Imabori residents registered themselves before 1713 is unknown.

110. Takeda, pp. 268–69.

111. Ibid., p. 272.

112. *YS*, III: 526.

113. *YS*, III: 524.

114. Hieizan, pp. 64–65. The Meiji Restoration brought the total separation

of Hie Shrine from Enryakuji. At that time, images of Buddha, sutras, and other Buddhism-related items in the shrine were all destroyed or removed.

115. *YS*, III: 525.

116. *YS*, III: 514–15, table 59. The number of registered households is an approximation based on oral research conducted in 1925. It is assumed that there is fundamental continuity in affiliation from the Tokugawa period to modern times.

117. Of the others, two were Zen temples and two were Shin.

118. The term *ujigami*, which characterizes the community's collective relationship to local deities from the Tokugawa period on, can be found in Doc. no. 718, Bunka 12 (1815).2: Tani Junpei ujigami jimen shakuyō shōmon.

119. Doc. no. 270, Tenshō 13 (1585).4.10: Imabori sōbun eboshi naoshibun ukejō an; Doc. no. 679, Genroku 11 (1698).11.4 and Genroku 12 (1699).11.23: Eboshi naoshijō; Doc. no. 262, Tenshō 15 (1587).2.6: Otona naoshi nikki; Doc. no. 663, Genroku 4 (1691).11.3: Otona naoshi kechi naoshichō.

120. Of course, the diminution in shrine assets was countrywide. In the mid-seventeenth century, Uwanishi Shrine in Wakasa Province retained only about 16 percent of the land it had held in the 1260s. Takamaki, p. 337.

121. Ono Takeo, pp. 72–76.

122. *YS*, III: 555–56.

123. Doc. no. 470, Tenshō 19 (1591).8.21: Imabori sōbun rensho sadamegaki. These three households were obligated to pay taxes left unpaid by the absconding neighbor. An undated document from the pre-Hideyoshi period has a reference to a "seven-person group" that was accountable to the sō. Doc. no. 291: Imabori-mura sōchū okibumi. This document still uses the term *gō*, suggesting the approximate date of compilation.

124. Ono Takeo, pp. 76–78; Maeda, p. 9.

125. See Doc. no. 291: Imabori-mura sōchū okibumi, for a specific mention of seven-household groups in Imabori. Doc. no. 291 is translated in Appendix B.

126. *YS*, III: 164–65. The increasing authority of the five-household group coincides with the greater systematization of the household registration system. Perhaps greater control of the villagers by the headman through the use of registration requirements helped to consolidate the surveillance system as well.

127. The government (Date) ordered construction of a village assembly hall (*yoriai dō*) in 1664; it served as the place for keeping accounts and making announcements. *YS*, III: 179–80.

128. The four mura were Nakano, Imazaike, Kanaya, and Koima. *GS*, V: 94–100. In the Tokugawa period, the former lower four gō included the following mura: Hebimizo, Imazaike, Kanaya, Nakano, Koima(zaike), Higashi-Kobochizuka, and Imabori. Doc. no. 1021, Genroku 6 (1693).10.27: Honai shimo-gō nanaka-mura Fuse-mura suiron sumijō utsushi.

129. *GS*, V: 94.

130. *GS*, V: 97–99. The document is dated Genna 3 (1617).6.15 and was signed by Nakano, Imazaike, Koima, and Kobochizuka-mura.

131. *GS*, V: 99–100. The relevant documents are dated Genna 3 (1617).9.16 and 9.20 and were addressed to the shōya of Imazaike, Nakano, Koima, and Higashi-Kobochizuka.

132. For Imabori, see *YS*, III: 109, graph 2. The increase in Ōmi was from 775,279 *koku* to 830,594 *koku*. *YS*, III: 110, 290.

133. *YS*, III: 291–92.

134. Entry dated Kan'ei 15 (1638).12.16: Nakano-mura okite, in *YS*, VI: 43–44. No female names were included among the signatories.

135. So designated in 1678. *Ōmi Kanzaki-gun shi kō*, 2: 717.

136. For an informative discussion of villages assisting post stations, see Vaporis. Doc. no. 693: Yōkaichi tenma oboe demonstrates that on this particular occasion, 31 men were summoned. The duty was for one day for all but two men, who were required to serve two days. One of the two commuted the second day of his service to a cash payment of 148 *mon*.

137. *Ōmi Kanzaki-gun shi kō*, 2: 719–21.

138. Meiwa 1 (1764).12.15: Chōsenjin shonyūyō gin kumi gō wari chō, in *YS*, VI: 119–122.

139. Doc. no. 254, Keichō 4 (1599).5.10: Imabori sōbun okibumi.

140. Doc. no. 255, Kan'ei 3 (1626).6.3: Imabori sōchū okibumi an.

141. Doc. no. 1004, Kan'ei 2 (1625).3.1: Hebimizo-mura sōchū okime an.

142. Doc. no. 1005, Kan'ei 10 (1633): Hebimizo-mura jige okitegaki.

143. Contemporary parlance separated the legal codes into two categories: *kōgi*, or *jitō hatto* (regulations issued by a public office), and *mura hatto* (regulations issued by a village). Harada Toshimaru, *Kinsei sonraku no keizai to shakai*, p. 42. The separation of the "public" order and the local (and "private") order was visible in many aspects of society.

144. To ascertain their rights, they first went to a priest of the temple Ishidōji (the former headquarters of the Rokkaku) for arbitration. This became the background of an interesting subplot in the larger dispute. Shibawara, a village in the Upper-ho, intervened in the process at the temple, claiming that the dispute was not between Fuse and the Lower-ho villages but between Fuse and both the Lower- and Upper-ho (thereby claiming rights to access). Shibawara was proven wrong in this claim. Document dated Genroku 7 (1694).3.10, in *Hebimizo kuchō mochimawari monjo*.

145. Document dated Hōei 2 (1705).int.4, in *Hebimizo kuchō mochimawari monjo*.

146. *Hebimizo kuchō mochimawari monjo* contains dispute-related documents dated as follows: Enpō 5 (1677).8.19; 1677?.8; Genroku 7 (1694).3.10; Genroku 8 (1695).11.2; Hōei 2 (1705).1.25, 1.27, 2, int.4, 10.20, 11.4.

147. Doc. no. 367, Tenshō 16 (1588).7.11: Imabori sōbun okijō.

148. Doc. no. 290, Kan'ei 16? (1639?).11.19: Imabori murando rensho oboegaki.

149. Doc. no. 290 (ibid.) is suggestive of the outcome of the tribunal. Numbers are written next to some of the names listed; for example, "30" is written next to Nikkei's name, "10" next to Saburōemon, and "50" next to Matazō. Whether these numbers represent the votes or not is unclear.

150. Doc. no. 296, Kan'ei 16 (1639).8.21: Imabori sōbun rensho sadamejō.

151. For an example of expulsion in the Tokugawa period, see Doc. no. 255, Kan'ei 3 (1626).6.3: Imabori sōchū okibumi an, which stipulates ostracism by the sō for damaging plant leaves, among other things.

152. Enpō 2 (1674).9.27: Hatto ukegaki, in *Nakano kyōyū monjo*, in *YS*, VI: 26–27. See Appendix B for pre-Tokugawa regulations.

153. For example, laws issued by the Date in 1652, 1658, 1679, and 1682.

154. For example, the code of Chōsokabe Motochika states: "Quarreling and bickering are strictly forbidden." Jansen, p. 105.

155. Manji 1 (1658).10.9: Date ke daikan kyūka jō hatto, in *Nakano kyōyū monjo*, in *YS*, VI: 17–18. The village officials acknowledged the receipt of this order on the tenth day of the tenth month, addressing it to the Date officials. The order also requested similar acknowledgments by the ten-household groups. Thus, six days later (11.16), 142 villagers belonging to 12 groups (kumi) acknowledged receipt, addressing their reply to the shōya and the kimoiri.

156. Manji 1 (1658).12.2: Nakano-mura kumi gashirachū ukegaki, in *Nakano kyōyū monjo*, in *YS*, VI: 46–47.

157. Doc. no. 955, Shōwa 45 (1960): Imabori no otehan (inzen) no densetsu, by Murata Sōkichi. Murata Sōkichi is a prominent member of Imabori's miyaza today.

Conclusion

1. Asakawa, "Agriculture," pp. 225–26. The quotation appears on p. 226.

2. Keirstead explains the similar phenomena by focusing on the coded and ritualized tropes of peasant rebellion that created a meaningful dialogue between peasants and proprietors in medieval Japan, in "The Theater of Protest."

3. Skinner has articulated the interaction between local systems, on the one hand, and the benefits of prestige, on the other, in "Chinese Peasants," pp. 276–77.

Appendix A

1. *Sonpi bunmyaku*, Genji 10.

2. Entry dated Bunji 1 (1185).10.11, in *Azuma kagami*, in *Zenyaku Azuma kagami*, 1: 235.

3. Uwayokote, pp. 178–80; *YS*, II: 18–19.

4. *YS*, I: 290. It is said that Sasaki-no-yama-no-kimi received the prestigious title of "kimi" from Emperor Keidai in the late fifth century.

5. *Engi-shiki*, 10, in *Kogaku sōsho*, 3: 207. Sasaki Shrine was counted as one of the eleven shrines in Gamō County.

6. *GS*, II: 5–6. Sasaki-no-yama-no-kimi Kahi was an *uneme* who received the Junior Lower Fifth Rank in 787; Miyako was also granted the same rank in 860. According to the *Man'yōshū*, a *naishi* by the name of Sasaki-no-yama-no-kimi accompanied Emperor Kōken and her mother to Fujiwara Nakamaro's residence. Poem no. 4267, in *Man'yōshū*, p. 379.

7. *YS*, II: 18.

8. *YS*, II: 17–19.

9. The reference to the shugo Sadatsuna in *Azuma kagami* entry dated Bunji 1 (1187).2.9 is anachronistic. In 1187, shugo posts as such did not exist. He should have been called *sōtsuibushi* at that time. But another entry, dated Kōchō 1 (1261).5.13, clearly indicates that the brothers were granted shugo posts in seventeen provinces. See *Zenyaku Azuma kagami* 1: 333 and 5: 443. See also *YS*, II: 24–25, 37.

10. *Kusatsu-shi shi*, 1: 466–70.

11. *GS*, I: 151; *YS*, II: 52–62. The awarded stewardships were in Sasaki Toyoura-no-shō, Wani Katata-no-shō, and Kurimoto Kita County, according to an entry dated Antei 1 (1227).9.22 in *Azuma kagami*, in *Zenyaku Azuma kagami*, 3: 453. In addition, Kutsuki-no-shō (certainly) and Ōhara-no-shō

(most likely) were designated as Nobutsuna's jitō land. Of these, the jitō-shiki in Kurimoto Kita County was annulled later, in order to reduce the animosity of Enryakuji priests who had private holdings in the same area. Toyoura-no-shō was exchanged for Nagaoka-no-shō in Owari at a later date also. In English, Mass describes the development and the outcome of the Jōkyū War in his *The Development*. See p. 22 for the involvement of the Sasaki.

12. Doc. no. 9849, Bun'ei 5 (1268).1: Ōmi Namazue-no-shō yurai ki, in *Kamakura ibun*, 13: 327–28; entry dated Kangen 1 (1243).11.1, in *Azuma kagami*, in *Zenyaku Azuma kagami*, 4: 366; *YS*, II: 69–71.

13. *YS*, II: 72–77; Shimosaka, "Omi shugo Rokkaku-shi," pp. 56–57.

Appendix B

1. Kanamoto, "Mura okite," p. 37; Nakamura Ken, "Muromachi," p. 7.
2. Hashiuragaki.
3. "Paid 38 *mon*" was added to the document at a later date.

Bibliography

The place of publication for Japanese-language books is Tokyo unless otherwise noted.

Unpublished Primary Sources

Gōshū Gamō-gun Imazaike-mura kenchichō oyobi hyakushō nayosechō. Facsimile (*eishabon*). Tokyo Daigaku Shiryō Hensanjo.
Hebimizo-chō kyōyū monjo. Private copy of Nakamura Ken's. Catalogued by Dōshisha Daigaku Jinbun Kagaku Kenkyūjo.
Hebimizo kuchō mochimawari monjo. Private copy of Nakamura Ken's.
Imabori Hiyoshi jinja shaki. Compiled by Murata Sōkichi in 1973.
Imazaki Onjōji monjo. Facsimile. Tokyo Daigaku Shiryō Hensanjo.
Nakano kyōyū monjo. Private copy of Nakamura Ken's.
Sonpi bunmyaku, Genji. Vol. 10. Facsimile. Tokyo Daigaku Shiryō Hensanjo.

Published Primary Sources

Chūsei seiji shakai shisō. Vol. 1. Edited and compiled by Ishii Susumu, Ishimoda Shō, Kasamatsu Hiroshi, Katsumata Shizuo, and Satō Shin'ichi. Nihon shisō taikei, no. 21. Iwanami Shoten, 1976; originally published 1972.
Daijōin jisha zōjiki. Vol. 4. Edited by Tsuji Zennosuke. Kadokawa Shoten, 1964.
Dainihon shiryō. Ser. 4, 5, and 8. Compiled by Tokyo Daigaku Shiryō Hensanjo. Tokyo Daigaku Shiryō Hensanjo, 1905–.
Engi-shiki. In *Kogaku sōsho,* compiled by Mozume Takami. Kobunko Kankōkai, 1927.
Genpei seisuiki. Compiled by Kokumin Tosho. Nihon bungaku taikei, no. 15. Kokumin Tosho, 1926.
Imabori Hiyoshi jinja monjo. Compiled by Hiyoshi Monjo Kankōkai. Shiga-ken: Hiyoshi Monjo Kankōkai, 1975.
Imabori Hiyoshi jinja monjo shūsei. Compiled by Nakamura Ken. Yūzankaku, 1981.
Inryōken nichiroku. Vol. 5. Compiled by Shiseki Kankōkai. Kyoto: Shiseki Kankōkai, 1954.
Kamakura ibun. 31 vols. Compiled by Takeuchi Rizō. Tokyodō, 1971–86.
Kanmon gyoki. Compiled by Hanawa Hokinoichi and Ōta Toshirō. Zoku Gunsho ruijū, bui, no. 2. Zoku Gunsho Ruijū Kanseikai, 1958–59; originally published 1916–30.

Kutsuki monjo. Vol. 1. Compiled by Okuno Takahiro and Katō Akira. Zoku Gunsho Ruijū Kanseikai, 1978.

Kyōō Gokokuji monjo. 3 vols. Compiled by Akamatsu Toshihide. Kyoto: Heirakuji Shoten, 1961.

Mansai Jugō nikki. Compiled by Hanawa Hokinoichi and Ōta Toshirō. Zoku Gunsho ruijū, bui, no. 1. Zoku Gunsho Ruijū Kanseikai, 1974–75; originally published 1928.

Man'yōshū. Edited by Takagi Ichinosuke et al. Nihon koten bungaku taikei, no. 7. Iwanami Shoten, 1962.

Masamoto-kō tabi hikitsuke. Compiled by Kunaichō Shoryōbu. Nara: Yōtokusha, 1961.

Mibuke monjo. Vol. 3. Compiled by Kunaichō Shoryōbu. Meiji Shoin, 1981.

Nagaoki Sukune nikki. Compiled by Kondō Heijō. Kaitei shiseki shūran, no. 24. Kondō Kappansho, 1902.

Oda Nobunaga monjo no kenkyū. 3 vols. Compiled by Okuno Takahiro. Yoshikawa Kōbunkan, 1970, 1973, 1984.

Ōshima jinja, Okutsushima jinja monjo. Compiled by Shiga Daigaku Keizaigakubu Fuzoku Shiryōkan. Shiga-ken: Shiga Daigaku Fuzoku Shiryōkan, 1986.

Ryō no gige. Edited by Kuroita Katsumi and compiled by Kokushi Taikei Henshūkai. Shintei zōho Kokushi taikei, no. 22. Yoshikawa Kōbunkan, 1939.

Sugaura monjo. 2 vols. Compiled by Shiga Daigaku Keizaigakubu Shiryōkan. Yūhikaku, 1967.

Taiheiki. Edited by Gotō Tanji and Kamada Kisaburō. Nihon koten bungaku taikei, no. 34. Iwanami Shoten, 1965.

Tokitsugu-kyō ki. Edited by Hayakawa Junsaburō. Kokusho kankōkai sōsho, ser. 4, vols. 7–10. Kokusho Kankōkai, 1914–15.

Wamyō ruijūshō gun gō ri ekimei kōshō. Edited by Ikebe Wataru. Yoshikawa Kōbunkan, 1981.

Zenyaku Azuma kagami. Edited by Nagahara Keiji and Kishi Shōzō. Vols. 1, 3, 4, and 5. Shinjinbutsu Ōraisha, 1976–77.

Local Histories with Documents and Commentaries

Gifu-ken shi. Vol. 3. Edited by Gifu-ken. Gannandō, 1969.

Izumi Sano-shi shi. Edited by Shibata Minoru. Osaka: Izumi Sano Shiyakusho, 1958.

Kōga-gun shi. 2 vols. Edited by Shiga-ken Kōga-gun Kyōikukai. Kyoto: Seibunsha, 1926.

Kusatsu-shi shi. Vol. 1. Edited by Kusatsu-shi Shi Hensan Iinkai. Kusatsu, Shiga-ken: Kusatsu Shiyakusho, 1981.

Ōmi Echi-gun shi. Vols. 2–5. Edited by Shiga-ken Echi-gun Kyōikukai. Kyoto: Naigai Shuppan, 1929.

Ōmi Gamō-gun shi. 10 vols. Edited by Nakagawa Senzō. Shiga-ken: Shiga-ken Gamō-gun Yakusho, 1911–12.

Ōmi Hino-chō shi. Vol. 2. Edited by Shiga-ken Hino-chō Kyōikukai. Kyoto: Naigai Shuppan, 1930.

Ōmi Kanzaki-gun shi kō. 2 vols. Edited by Ōhashi Kinzō. Shiga-ken: Shiga-ken Kanzaki-gun Kyōikukai, 1928.

Ōmiwa-chō shi. Compiled by Ōmiwa-chō Shi Henshū Iinkai. Ōmiwa, Nara-ken: Ōmiwa-chō Yakuba, 1956.
Shiga-ken Hachiman-chō shi. 2 vols. Edited by Shiga-ken Gamō-gun Hachiman-chō. Kyoto: Naigai Shuppan, 1940.
Shiga-ken shi. 3 vols. Edited by Shiga-ken. Shiga-ken: Shiga-ken, 1928.
Takashima-gun shi. Edited by Shiga-ken Takashima-gun Kyōikukai. Kyoto: Naigai Shuppan, 1927.
Yōkaichi-shi shi. 6 vols. Edited by Yōkaichi-shi Shi Hensan Iinkai. Yōkaichi-shi: Yōkaichi-shi Shiyakusho, 1983–86.

Dictionaries

Kadokawa Nihon chimei daijiten. Vol. 25, *Shiga-ken.* Compiled by Takeuchi Rizō et al. Kadokawa Shoten, 1979.
Nenjū gyōji jiten. Compiled by Nishitsunoi Masayoshi. Tokyodō, 1981.
Nihon chishi. Vol. 13. Compiled by Nihon Chishi Kenkyūsho. Ninomiya Shoten, 1976.
Ōmi no kuni yochi shi ryaku. Vol. 1 of *Dainihon chishi taikei,* no. 22. Edited by Samukawa Tatsukiyo. Yūzankaku, 1929.
Shūkyō saijiki. Compiled by Gorai Shigeru. Kadokawa Shoten, 1982.

Secondary Sources and Translations

Akamatsu Toshihide. "Za ni tsuite." *Shirin* 37.1 (February 1954): 1–25.
Amino Yoshihiko. *Muen, kugai, raku: Nihon chūsei no jiyū to heiwa.* Heibonsha, 1982; originally published 1978.
———. *Nihon chūsei no hi-nōgyōmin to tennō.* Iwanami Shoten, 1984.
———. "Some Problems Concerning the History of Popular Life in Medieval Japan." *Acta Asiatica* 44 (March 1983): 77–97.
Andō Seiichi. "Han shakai to shō miyaza—Kishū Naka-gun Kishi no shō no baai." In *Han shakai no kenkyū,* edited by Miyamoto Mataji, pp. 275–92. Kyoto: Mineruba Shobō, 1970.
———. *Kinsei miyaza no shiteki kenkyū—Kihoku nōson o chūshin to shite.* Yoshikawa Kōbunkan, 1960.
Aoyagi Masaru. "Chūsei makki ni okeru ichi shōnin no katsudō—Kosodeya no baai." *Kokugakuin zasshi* 89.3 (March 1988): 54–69.
Araki Moriaki. *Bakuhan taisei shakai no seiritsu to kōzō.* Ochanomizu Shobō, 1959.
Asakawa Kan'ichi. "Agriculture in Japanese History: A General Survey." *Economic History Review* 2.1 (January 1929): 81–92. In *Land and Society in Medieval Japan,* edited by the Committee for the Publication of Dr. K. Asakawa's Works, pp. 219–30. Tokyo: Japan Society for the Promotion of Science, 1965.
———. "Notes on Village Government in Japan After 1600" (parts 1 and 2). *Journal of the American Oriental Society* 30 (1909–10): 259–300; 31 (1911): 151–216.
Asao Naohiro. "Heinō bunri o megutte—shōryōshusō no dōkō o chūshin ni." *Nihon shi kenkyū* 71 (March 1964): 39–60.
———. "Toyotomi seiken ron." In *Iwanami kōza Nihon rekishi,* vol. 9, pp. 159–210. Iwanami Shoten, 1963.
Ashikaga Kenryō. "Gamō-no no keisei—Yōkaichi shiiki no chikei to kodai

kaihatsu ni tsuite." In Yōkaichi-shi Shi Hensan Iinkai, ed., *Yōkaichi-shi shi hensan dayori* 6 (July 1980): 1–3.

Aston, W. G., trans. *Nihongi: Chronicles of Japan from the Earliest Times to A.D. 697.* London: George Allen and Unwin, 1956; originally published 1896.

Befu, Harumi. "Village Autonomy and Articulation with the State." In *Studies in the Institutional History of Early Modern Japan,* edited by John W. Hall and Marius B. Jansen, pp. 301–14. Princeton: Princeton University Press, 1968.

Berry, Mary Elizabeth. *Hideyoshi.* Cambridge: Harvard University Press, 1982.

Blacker, Carmen. *The Catalpa Bow: A Study of Shamanistic Practices in Japan.* London: George Allen and Unwin, 1986; originally published 1975.

Bloch, Marc. *French Rural History: An Essay on Its Basic Characteristics.* Berkeley and Los Angeles: University of California Press, 1966.

Bourdieu, Pierre. *Outline of a Theory of Practice.* Cambridge Studies in Social Anthropology, no. 16. Cambridge: Cambridge University Press, 1977.

Bray, Francesca. "Patterns of Evolution in Rice-growing Societies." *Journal of Peasant Studies* 11.1 (October 1983): 3–33.

Brown, Delmer. "The Japanese Tokusei of 1297." *Harvard Journal of Asiatic Studies* 12 (1949): 188–206.

Brown, Philip C. "The Mismeasure of Land: Land Surveying in the Tokugawa Period." *Monumenta Nipponica* 42.2 (Summer 1987): 115–55.

Cort, Louise Allison. *Shigaraki: Potter's Valley.* Tokyo: Kodansha International, 1979.

Davis, Winston. "Parish Guilds and Political Culture in Village Japan." *Journal of Asian Studies* 36.1 (November 1976): 25–36.

Egashira Tsuneharu. *Gōshū shōnin.* Shibundō, 1965.

Eisenstadt, S. N., and Louis Roniger. "Patron-Client Relations as a Model of Structuring Social Exchange." *Comparative Studies in Society and History* 22.1 (January 1980): 42–77.

———. *Patrons, Clients and Friends: Interpersonal Relations and the Structure of Trust in Society.* Cambridge: Cambridge University Press, 1984.

Endō Motoo. "Shokunin no soshiki to shite 'za' no ichi kōsatsu." *Shakai keizai shigaku* 3.2 (May 1933): 1–30.

Fujiki Hisashi. *Sengoku shakai shi ron—Nihon chūsei kokka no kaitai.* Tokyo Daigaku Shuppankai, 1982; originally published 1974.

———. "Tōitsu seiken no seiritsu." In *Iwanami kōza Nihon rekishi,* vol. 9, pp. 33–79. Iwanami Shoten, 1975.

Fujiki Hisashi with George Elison. "The Political Posture of Oda Nobunaga." In *Japan Before Tokugawa: Political Consolidation and Economic Growth, 1500–1650,* edited by John W. Hall, Nagahara Keiji, and Kozo Yamamura, pp. 149–93. Princeton: Princeton University Press, 1981.

Fujitani Toshio. "Shimizu Mitsuo no shōgai to sono gyōseki." In Shimizu Mitsuo, *Chūsei shōen no kiso kōzō,* pp. 242–58. Vol. 3 of *Shimizu Mitsuo chosakushū.* Kyoto: Itakura Shobō, 1975.

Fukuo Takeichirō. "Kinsei shoki ni okeru toshi shōgyō to shōnin no seikaku—shu to shite Ōmi Azuchi, Hachiman jōkamachi o megutte." *Shigaku kenkyū* 93 (May 1965): 1–21.

———. "Ōmi shōnin no hassei to sono hatten ni tsuite." *Shirin* 22.1 (January 1937): 135–54; 22.2 (April 1937): 109–30.

———. "Ōmi shōnin zen shi kenkyū no shiten—kodai Ōmi no keizaiteki chii to chūsei Ōmi no bussan." In *Yokota Ken'ichi sensei kanreki kinen Nihon shi ronsō,* edited by Yokota Ken'ichi Sensei Kanreki Kinenkai, pp. 545–62. Osaka: Yokota Ken'ichi Sensei Kanreki Kinenkai, 1976.

Fukutake Tadashi. *The Japanese Social Structure: Its Evolution in the Modern Century.* Translated by Ronald P. Dore. University of Tokyo Press, 1982.

Gay, Suzanne Marie. "The Muromachi Bakufu in Medieval Kyoto." Ann Arbor, Mich.: University Microfilms, 1982.

Geertz, Clifford. *The Interpretation of Culture.* New York: Basic Books, 1973.

Goodwin, Janet R. "Alms for Kasagi Temple." *Journal of Asian Studies* 46.4 (November 1987): 827–41.

Grapard, Allan G. "Linguistic Cubism—A Singularity of Pluralism in the Sannō Cult." *Japanese Journal of Religious Studies* 14.2–3 (June–September 1987): 211–34.

Hagiwara Tatsuo. *Chūsei saishi soshiki no kenkyū.* Yoshikawa Kōbunkan, 1962.

———. *Kamigami to sonraku—rekishigaku to minzokugaku to no setten.* Kōbundō, 1978.

Hall, John W. "Feudalism in Japan—A Reassessment." In *Studies in the Institutional History of Early Modern Japan,* edited by John W. Hall and Marius B. Jansen, pp. 15–51. Princeton: Princeton University Press, 1968.

———. "Kyoto as Historical Background." In *Medieval Japan: Essays in Institutional History,* edited by John W. Hall and Jeffrey P. Mass, pp. 3–38. New Haven: Yale University Press, 1974.

Harada Toshiaki. *Mura no saishi.* Chūō Kōronsha, 1975.

Harada Toshimaru. "Kinsei sonraku no jichi to ryōshu no shihai—Ōmi no kuni Sugaura-mura ni tsuite." *Hikone ronsō* 36 (March 1957): 9–21.

———. *Kinsei sonraku no keizai to shakai.* Yamakawa Shuppansha, 1983.

———. "Sonraku no jichi ni kansuru ichi kōsatsu—Ōmi no kuni Sugaura-mura ni tsuite." In *Han shakai no kenkyū,* edited by Miyamoto Mataji, pp. 242–74. Kyoto: Mineruba Shobō, 1970.

Hatai Hiromu. *Shugo ryōgoku taisei no kenkyū: Rokkaku-shi ryōgoku ni miru Kinai-kingokuteki hatten no tokushitsu.* Yoshikawa Kōbunkan, 1975.

Hattori Hideo. "Kaihatsu, sono shinten to ryōshu shihai—Hizen no kuni Nagashima no shō no Tachibana Satsuma ichizoku." *Chihō shi kenkyū* 152 (April 1978): 11–38.

Hazama Jikō. "The Characteristics of Japanese Tendai." *Japanese Journal of Religious Studies* 14.2–3 (June–September 1987): 101–12.

Henderson, Dan Fenno. *Village Contracts in Tokugawa Japan: Fifty Specimens with English Translations and Comments.* Seattle: University of Washington Press, 1975.

Hieizan Enryakuji, ed. *Hieizan.* Kyoto: Seki Shoin, 1959.

Higo Kazuo. *Miyaza no kenkyū.* Kōbundō, 1942.

———. *Ōmi ni okeru miyaza no kenkyū.* Tokyo Bunrika Daigaku, 1938.

Higuchi Setsuo. "Ashiko shōnin no chiriteki seikaku." In *Rekishi chirigaku no shomondai,* edited by Jinbun Chiri Gakkai, pp. 50–58. *Jinbun chiri* 3.5 and 3.6 combined. Kyoto: Yanagihara Shoten, 1952.

Hōgetsu Keigo. *Chūsei kangai shi no kenkyū.* Yoshikawa Kōbunkan, 1983; originally published 1943.

Hori Ichirō. *Minkan shinkō shi no shomondai.* Miraisha, 1971.

———. "On the Concept of Hijiri (Holy-Man)." *Numen* 5 (1958): 128–60, 199–232.

Horikawa Tatsunosuke. "Yōkaichi-shi no rekishiteki haikei." *Gamō-no* 14 (1977): 29–34.

Hoston, Germaine A. *Marxism and the Crisis of Development in Prewar Japan.* Princeton: Princeton University Press, 1986.

Imai Rintarō. "Nobunaga no shutsugen to chūseiteki ken'i no hitei." In *Iwanami kōza Nihon rekishi,* vol. 9, pp. 47–84. Iwanami Shoten, 1963.

Ishida Yoshihito. "Gōsonsei no keisei." In *Iwanami kōza Nihon rekishi,* vol. 8, pp. 35–78. Iwanami Shoten, 1963.

————. "Sō ni tsuite." *Shirin* 38.6 (November 1955): 67–90.

————. "Sōteki ketsugō no shoruikei." *Rekishi kyōiku* 8.8 (August 1960): 24–38.

Ishii Susumu. "'Masamoto-kō tabi hikitsuke' ni arawareta chūsei sonraku." *Chūsei no mado* 13 (November 1963): 33–40.

Ishimoda Shō. *Chūseiteki sekai no keisei.* Tokyo Daigaku Shuppankai, 1970; originally published 1946.

Itō Hiroko. "Sōson no seiritsu to hatten: Kōyasanryō Kii no kuni Tomobuchi no shō ni oite." *Nihon shi kenkyū* 120 (July 1971): 1–12; 121 (September 1971): 30–50.

Itō Yuishin. "14, 15 seiki no sonraku ni okeru kanjin ni tsuite—Ōmi kotō, konan no jinja kanjin o jirei to shite." In *Nihon shūkyō shakai shi ronsō,* edited by Mizuno Kyōichirō Sensei Shōju Kinenkai, pp. 263–83. Kokusho Kankōkai, 1982.

Jansen, Marius B. "Tosa in the Sixteenth Century: The 100 Article Code of Chōsokabe Motochika." In *Studies in the Institutional History of Early Modern Japan,* edited by John W. Hall and Marius B. Jansen, pp. 89–114. Princeton: Princeton University Press, 1968.

Kageyama Haruki. *Hieizanji—sono kōsei to shomondai.* Kyoto: Dōhōsha, 1979.

Kamiki Tetsuo. *Nihon chūsei shōhin ryūtsū shi ron.* Yūhikaku, 1980.

Kanamoto Masayuki. "Chūsei Imabori-gō ni kansuru Shirin, Kurokawa ronbun o hyōsu." *Chūsei no mado* 7 (December 1960): 49–65.

————. "Chūsei kōki ni okeru Ōmi no nōson—Tokuchin-ho Imabori-gō no rekishi." In *Nihon shakai keizai shi kenkyū,* edited by Hōgetsu Keigo Sensei Kanreki Kinenkai, vol. 2, pp. 243–304. Yoshikawa Kōbunkan, 1967.

————. "Chūsei Ōmi shōnin no seikaku—Tokuchin-ho Imabori shōnin no bunseki." *Shigaku zasshi* 70.8 (August 1961): 58–80.

————. "'Imabori Hiyoshi jinja monjo' ni tsuite no ni san no kōsatsu." In *Tōyō Daigaku bungakubu kiyō,* no. 31: Shigakuka, 3 (December 1977): 1–43.

————. "Mura okite." *Rekishi to chiri* 301 (September 1980): 29–42.

————. "Tokuchin-ho Imabori-gō no sonmin." In *Tōyō Daigaku bungakubu kiyō,* nos. 32 and 33: Shigakuka, 4 (December 1978): 1–33; 5 (December 1979): 1–23.

Kanda, Christine G. *Shinzō: Hachiman Imagery and Its Development.* Cambridge: Harvard University Press, 1985.

Kanno Watarō. *Ōmi shōnin no kenkyū.* Yūhikaku, 1941.

Katō Mieko. "'Musume' no za kara nyōbō-za e—chūsei sonraku to bosei." In *Bosei o tou: Rekishiteki hensen,* edited by Wakita Haruko, vol. 2, pp. 204–27. Kyoto: Jinbun Shoin, 1985.

Katsumata Shizuo. "Baibai, shichi ire to shoyū kannen." In *Futan to zōyo,* pp. 181–209. Vol. 4 of *Nihon no shakai shi,* edited by Asao Naohiro et al. Iwanami Shoten, 1986.

————. *Ikki.* Iwanami Shoten, 1983; originally published 1982.

————. *Sengokuhō seiritsu shi ron.* Tokyo Daigaku Shuppankai, 1979.

————, ed. "Rokkaku-shi shikimoku." In *Chūsei seiji shakai shisō*, vol. 1, edited and compiled by Ishii Susumu, Ishimoda Shō, Kasamatsu Hiroshi, Katsumata Shizuo, and Satō Shin'ichi, pp. 279–307. Nihon shisō taikei, no. 21. Iwanami Shoten, 1976; originally published 1972.

Katsumata Shizuo with Martin Collcutt. "The Development of Sengoku Law." In *Japan Before Tokugawa: Political Consolidation and Economic Growth, 1500–1650,* edited by John W. Hall, Nagahara Keiji, and Kozo Yamamura, pp. 101–24. Princeton: Princeton University Press, 1981.

Kawai Yūnosuke. "Kinsei shoki no shōgyōteki nōgyō keiei—Nonogō chagyō no hatten to zasetsu." *Shigaku kenkyū* 5.43 (March 1951): 63–78.

Kawane Yoshiyasu. "Chūsei zenki sonraku ni okeru josei no chii." In *Nihon josei shi,* edited by Josei Shi Sōgō Kenkyūkai, vol. 2, pp. 1–28. Tokyo Daigaku Shuppankai, 1982.

Keirstead, Thomas E. "Fragmented Estates: The Breakup of the Myō and the Decline of the Shōen System." *Monumenta Nipponica* 40.3 (Autumn 1985): 311–30.

————. *The Geography of Power in Medieval Japan.* Princeton: Princeton University Press, forthcoming.

————. "The Theater of Protest: Petitions, Oaths, and Rebellion in the Shōen." *Journal of Japanese Studies* 16.2 (Summer 1990): 357–88.

Kelly, William W. *Irrigation Management in Japan: A Critical Review of Japanese Social Science Research.* Cornell University East Asia Papers, no. 30. Ithaca, N.Y.: China-Japan Program, Cornell University, 1982.

Kikuchi Takeo. "Sengoku daimyō no kenryoku kōzō." *Rekishigaku kenkyū* 166 (November 1953): 1–17.

Kiley, Cornelius J. "Estate and Property in the Late Heian Period." In *Medieval Japan: Essays in Institutional History,* edited by John W. Hall and Jeffrey P. Mass, pp. 109–24. New Haven: Yale University Press, 1974.

Kimura Motoi. *Nihon sonraku shi.* Kōbundō, 1980; originally published 1978.

Kitamura Toshio. "Chihō shijō no hatten, zanson to sono yōin ni kansuru rekishi chiriteki kenkyū—Ōmi Yōkaichi o chūshin to shite." *Jinbun chiri* 2.4 (October 1950): 1–13.

Kiyama Hideki. "Social Organization of the Eighth-Century Japanese Villages: A Statistical Reconstruction Based on the Contemporary Registration." Ann Arbor, Mich.: University Microfilms, 1978.

Kobayashi Kentarō. "Chūsei jōkan no rekishi chirigakuteki kōsatsu—sengoku daimyō ryōgoku no chiiki kōzō kenkyū e no kokoromi." *Jinbun chiri* 15.4 (August 1963): 40–64.

————. "Kannonjijō no jōkamachi—sono puran sōtei e no tegakari." In *Chūbu daimyō no kenkyū,* edited by Katsumata Shizuo, pp. 230–33. Sengoku daimyō ronshū, no. 4. Yoshikawa Kōbunkan, 1983.

Koizumi Yoshiaki. "Nairanki no shakai hendō." In *Iwanami kōza Nihon rekishi,* vol. 6, pp. 123–65. Iwanami Shoten, 1975.

Kumada Tōru. "Jiyū shijō no seiritsu ni tsuite—chūsei makki Higashi Ōmi no nōson kōzō." *Shigaku zasshi* 59.4 (April 1950): 42–57.

Kuroda Hideo. *Kyōkai no chūsei, shōchō no chūsei.* Tokyo Daigaku Shuppankai, 1986.

————. "Sengoku Shokuhōki no gijutsu to keizai hatten." In *Kōza Nihon rekishi*, vol. 4, edited by Rekishigaku Kenkyūkai and Nihonshi Kenkyūkai, pp. 275–316. Tokyo Daigaku Shuppankai, 1985.

Kuroda Hiroko. *Chūsei sōson shi no kōzō*. Yoshikawa Kōbunkan, 1985.

Kuroda Toshio. "Chūsei jisha seiryoku ron." In *Iwanami kōza Nihon rekishi*, vol. 6, pp. 245–95. Iwanami Shoten, 1975.

———. "Chūsei no kokka to tennō." In *Iwanami kōza Nihon rekishi*, vol. 6, pp. 261–301. Iwanami Shoten, 1963.

———. *Jisha seiryoku—mō hitotsu no chūsei shakai*. Iwanami Shoten, 1980.

———. *Nihon chūsei hōkensei ron*. Tokyo Daigaku Shuppankai, 1974.

———. *Nihon chūsei no kokka to shūkyō*. Iwanami Shoten, 1975.

———. "Shintō in the History of Japanese Religion." *Journal of Japanese Studies* 7.1 (Winter 1981): 1–21.

Kurokawa Masahiro. "Chūsei Imabori-gō no nōmin kōzō to Enryakuji." *Shirin* 43.5 (September 1960): 95–119.

———. "Chūsei Imabori shōnin ni kansuru hitotsu no shiryō ni tsuite." *Nihon rekishi* 273 (February 1971): 102–7.

———. *Chūsei sōson no shomondai*. Kokusho Kankōkai, 1982.

———. "Sugaura shō to sō." *Rekishi kyōiku* 8.8 (August 1960): 46–51.

Kurokawa Naonori. "15, 16 seiki no nōmin mondai." *Nihon shi kenkyū* 71 (March 1964): 28–38.

Levy, Ian Hideo, trans. *The Ten Thousand Leaves: A Translation of the Man'yoshu, Japan's Premier Anthology of Classical Poetry*. Princeton: Princeton University Press, 1981.

Maeda Masaharu. *Nihon kinsei sonpō no kenkyū*. Yūhikaku, 1950.

Maki Kenji. "Chūsei makki ni okeru sōson kannen no seiritsu." *Keizai shi kenkyū* 16.1 (July 1936): 1–20.

Makino Shinnosuke. *Buke jidai shakai no kenkyū*. Tōe Shoin, 1928.

———. "Chūsei makki ni okeru sonraku no ketsugō o ronzu." *Keizai ronsō* 16.5 (May 1923): 862–77; 17.1 (June 1923): 106–19.

———. *Tochi oyobi shūraku shi jō no shomondai*. Kawade Shobō, 1938.

Maruyama Kōtarō. "Eiroku 3 nen Rokkaku Shōtei jōgaki ni tsuite." *Gifu shigaku* 72 (October 1970): 17–23.

Maruyama Yoshihiko. "Chūsei kōki shōen sonraku no kōzō—Imabori-gō ni okeru sonraku kyōyūden no keisei o chūshin ni." *Nihon shi kenkyū* 116 (January 1971): 1–33.

———. "Ōmi no kuni Tokuchin-ho Nogata shogō ni okeru nōgyō seisan no arikata." In *Akamatsu Toshihide kyōju taikan kinen kokushi ronshū*, edited by Akamatsu Toshihide Kyōju Taikan Kinen Jigyōkai, pp. 683–96. Akamatsu Toshihide Kyōju Taikan Kinen Jigyōkai, 1972.

———. "Shōen sonraku ni okeru sōyūden ni tsuite—Ōmi no kuni Tokuchin-ho o chūshin ni." In *Chūsei no kenryoku to minshū*, edited by Nihonshi Kenkyūkai Shiryō Kenkyūbukai, pp. 297–323. Osaka: Sōgensha, 1970.

Mass, Jeffrey P. *The Development of Kamakura Rule, 1180–1250: A History with Documents*. Stanford: Stanford University Press, 1979.

———. *The Kamakura Bakufu: A Study in Documents*. Stanford: Stanford University Press, 1976.

Matsumoto Shinpachirō. *Chūsei shakai no kenkyū*. Tokyo Daigaku Shuppankai, 1981; originally published 1956.

Matsunaga, Alicia. *The Buddhist Philosophy of Assimilation: The Historical Development of the Honji-Suijaku Theory*. Monumenta Nipponica Monograph, no. 31. Tokyo: Sophia University in cooperation with Charles E. Tuttle, 1969.

McClain, James L. *Kanazawa: A Seventeenth-Century Japanese Castle Town.* New Haven: Yale University Press, 1982.

McMullin, Neil. *Buddhism and the State in Sixteenth-Century Japan.* Princeton: Princeton University Press, 1984.

———. "The Enryakuji and the Gion—Shrine-Temple Complex in the Mid-Heian Period." *Japanese Journal of Religious Studies* 14.2–3 (June–September 1987): 161–84.

———. "The Sanmon-Jimon Schism in the Tendai School of Buddhism: A Preliminary Analysis." *Journal of the International Association of Buddhist Studies* 7.1 (1984): 83–105.

Miura Kaneyuki. *Hōsei shi no kenkyū.* Iwanami Shoten, 1919.

———. "Rekishi jō yori mitaru Ōmi." In *Rekishi chiri: Ōmi gō,* edited by Nihon Rekishi Chiri Gakkai, pp. 1–36. Sanseidō, 1912.

Miura Keiichi. "Chūsei no tanomoshi ni tsuite." *Shirin* 42.6 (November 1959): 1–22.

———. "Sōson no kigen to sono yakuwari." *Shirin* 50.2 (March 1967): 1–31; 50.3 (May 1967): 33–63.

Miyagawa Mitsuru. "Chūsei sonraku ni okeru nōmin to jizamurai." In *Shigaku kenkyū kinen ronsō,* edited by Hiroshima Bunrika Daigaku Shigakuka Kyōshitsu, pp. 2–23. Kyoto: Yanagihara Shoten, 1950.

———. "Gōson seido to kenchi." *Nihon shi kenkyū* 19 (February 1953): 2–28. Published in his *Taikō kenchi ron,* vol. 2, pp. 1–44.

———. *Taikō kenchi ron.* 3 vols. Ochanomizu Shobō, 1964, 1965, and 1963; vols. 1 and 2 originally published 1957, 1959.

Miyake Hitoshi. "Kyōdōtai no denshō to kosumorojii." In *Minzoku to girei: Sonraku kyōdōtai no seikatsu to shinkō,* edited by Miyake Hitoshi, pp. 18–30. Bukkyō to Nihonjin, no. 9. Shunjūsha, 1986.

Miyata Noboru. *Kami no minzoku shi.* Iwanami Shoten, 1984; originally published 1979.

Miyajima Keiichi. "Sengokuki ni okeru Rokkaku-shi kenryoku no seikaku—hakkyū monjo no seikaku o chūshin ni shite." *Shichō,* n.s., 5 (1979): 136–63.

Mizumoto Kunihiko. "Mura shakai to bakuhan taisei." In *Higashi Ajia sekai no saihen to minshū ishiki,* edited by Rekishigaku Kenkyūkai, pp. 97–107. Special supplementary issue of *Rekishigaku kenkyū.* Aoki Shoten, 1983.

Morisue Yoshiaki. *Chūsei geinō shi ronkō.* Tokyodō, 1971.

Morris, Dana Robert. "Peasant Economy in Early Japan, 650–950." Ann Arbor, Mich.: University Microfilms, 1980.

Murai Yasuhiko. "Shōen to yorisakunin—kondenchikei shōen no tokushitsu ni tsuite." In *Chūsei shakai no kihon kōzō,* edited by Nihonshi Kenkyūkai Shiryō Kenkyūbukai, pp. 43–80. Osaka: Sōgensha, 1978; originally published 1958.

Murata Chōzō. "Chūsei za shōnin no ichi shōkō." *Gamō-no* 8 (May 1973): 13–20; 9 (January 1974): 10–14.

Nagahara Keiji. "Chūsei kōki no sonraku kyōdōtai." In *Nihon kodai chūsei shi no chihōteki tenkai,* edited by Toyoda Takeshi Kyōju Kanreki Kinenkai, pp. 321–48. Yoshikawa Kōbunkan, 1973.

———. "Chūsei no shakai kōsei to hōkensei." In *Kōza Nihon rekishi,* edited by

Rekishigaku Kenkyūkai and Nihonshi Kenkyūkai, vol. 4, pp. 317–57. Tokyo Daigaku Shuppankai, 1985.

————. *Gekokujō no jidai.* Chūō Kōronsha, 1965.

————. *Nihon chūsei shakai kōzō no kenkyū.* Iwanami Shoten, 1973.

————. *Nihon hōken shakai ron.* Tokyo Daigaku Shuppankai, 1966.

————. *Nihon no chūsei shakai.* Iwanami Shoten, 1972.

————. "Shōensei shihai to chūsei sonraku." *Hitotsubashi ronsō* 47.3 (March 1962): 51–72. Later published in *Nihon hōkensei no shakai to kokka,* vol. 1, edited by Toda Yoshimi, pp. 215–38. Rekishi kagaku taikei, no. 4. Itakura Shobō, 1973.

Nagahara Keiji and Kozo Yamamura. "Shaping the Process of Unification: Technological Progress in Sixteenth- and Seventeenth-Century Japan." *Journal of Japanese Studies* 14.1 (Winter 1988): 77–109.

Nagahara Keiji and Yamaguchi Keiji, eds. *Kōza Nihon gijutsu no shakai shi.* 8 vols. Hyōronsha, 1983–85.

Nagashima Fukutarō. "Chūsei Nara no san ichi." *Hisutoria* 3 (March 1952): 23–30.

Nakada Kaoru. *Hōsei shi ronshū.* Vol. 2. Iwanami Shoten, 1938.

Nakagawa Seiji. "Kinki ni okeru miyaza no kenkyū to kodai sonraku no shakai jōtai." *Kokugakuin zasshi* 33.8 (August 1927): 60–80; 33.9 (September 1927): 107–129.

Nakamura Ken. "Baiken, kishinjō kara mita sonraku seikatsu—Imabori Hiyoshi jinja monjo no baai." In *Nihon shūkyō shakai shi ronsō,* edited by Mizuno Kyōichirō Sensei Shōju Kinenkai, pp. 285–310. Kokusho Kankōkai, 1982.

————. "Chūsei kōki ni okeru Ōmi no kuni Tokuchin-ho Imabori-gō no nōgyō." *Nōgyō keizai kenkyū* 48.4 (April 1977): 149–57.

————. "Chūsei kōki no sonraku." *Nihon shi kenkyū* 90 (April 1967): 22–41.

————. "Chūsei ni okeru gimonjo no kōyō." *Nihon rekishi* 303 (August 1973): 13–37.

————. *Chūsei sōson shi no kenkyū: Ōmi no kuni Tokuchin-ho Imabori-gō.* Hōsei Daigaku Shuppankyoku, 1984.

————. "Honai, Edamura kami sōron no tenmatsu." *Gamō-no* 14 (1977): 2–20.

————. "Honai shōgyō no tenkai katei: Obata, Ishidō to no sōron o chūshin ni." *Shakai kagaku* 23 (December 1977): 210–53.

————. "Imabori Hiyoshi jinja monjo zakkō." *Gamō-no* 5 (May 1971): 1–10.

————. "Muromachi, sengoku jidai no sonraku seikatsu—Imabori Hiyoshi jinja monjo no mura okite o chūshin ni." *Gamō-no* 11 (November 1974): 1–10.

————. "Ōmi no kuni Tokuchin-ho Imabori-gō kenkyū no seika to kadai." *Shakai kagaku* 20 (March 1976): 88–211.

————. "Ōmi no kuni Tokuchin-ho Imabori-gō no mura okite." In *Nihon shūkyō no rekishi to minzoku,* edited by Takeda Chōshū Hakushi Kanreki Kinenkai, pp. 229–50. Ryūbunkan, 1976.

————. "Ōmi no kuni Tokuchin-ho Imabori-gō no 'sō' oboegaki—Kanamoto Masayuki-shi no shoron o megutte." *Shakai kagaku* 11 (January 1970): 110–60.

————. "Ōmi Tokuchin-ho no sarugaku noh oboegaki." *Gamō-no* 13 (November 1976): 1–7.

————. "Shin hakken no Hebimizo kyōyū monjo ni tsuite." *Nihon rekishi* 318 (November 1974): 13–23.

————. "Sōson monjo no seikaku—Imabori Hiyoshi jinja monjo no bunrui o megutte." *Shakai kagaku* 26 (November 1979): 156–211.
Nakamura Naokatsu. "Gimonjo monogatari." *Komonjo kenkyū* 1 (June 1968): 29–47.
————. *Shōen no kenkyū.* Kyoto: Hoshino Shoten, 1939.
————. "Tochi baiken no ichi baai." *Komonjo kenkyū* 7–8 (February 1975): 29–42.
————. "'Za' no yūsuru gimonjo no igi." *Keizai shi kenkyū* 11.5 (May 1934): 1–17.
Nakamura Tadashi. *Doreisei, nōdosei no riron.* Tokyo Daigaku Shuppankai, 1977.
Neale, Walter S. "Reciprocity and Redistribution in the Indian Village: Sequel to Some Notable Discussions." In *Trade and Market in the Early Empires: Economies in History and Theory,* edited by Karl Polanyi, Conrad M. Arensberg, and Harry W. Pearson, pp. 218–36. Glencoe: Free Press, 1957.
Nishiyama Katsu. "Sengokuki daimyō kenryoku no kōzō ni kansuru ichi shiron." *Nihon shi kenkyū* 236 (April 1982): 21–37.
Nose Asaji. *Nohgaku genryū kō.* Iwanami Shoten, 1956; originally published 1938.
Oda Yūzō. "Kodai, chūsei no suiko." In *Futan to zōyo,* pp. 91–116. Vol. 4 of *Nihon no shakai shi,* edited by Asao Naohiro et al. Iwanami Shoten, 1986.
Oguri Hiroshi. "Common no kaitai to Nihon no iriai rinya no baai." In *Sanchi kōgen no rekishi chiri,* edited by Rekishi Chiri Gakkai, pp. 107–25. Kanagawa: Rekishi chiri gakkai, 1981.
Ohnuki-Tierney, Emiko. *The Monkey as Mirror: Symbolic Transformations in Japanese History and Ritual.* Princeton: Princeton University Press, 1987.
Ono Kōji. *Nihon sangyō hattatsu shi no kenkyū.* Hōsei Daigaku Shuppankai, 1981; originally published 1931.
Ono Takeo. *Nihon sonraku shi gaisetsu.* Iwanami Shoten, 1981; originally published 1936.
Ooms, Herman. *Tokugawa Ideology: Early Constructs, 1570–1680.* Princeton: Princeton University Press, 1985.
Ōyama Kyōhei. "Kugonin, jinin, yoriudo." *Shakaiteki shoshūdan,* pp. 249–84. Vol. 6 of *Nihon no shakai shi,* edited by Asao Naohiro et al. Iwanami Shoten, 1988.
Polanyi, Karl, Conrad M. Arensberg, and Harry W. Pearson. "The Place of Economics in Societies." In *Trade and Market in the Early Empires: Economies in History and Theory,* edited by Karl Polanyi, Conrad M. Arensberg, and Harry W. Pearson, pp. 239–42. Glencoe: Free Press, 1957.
Popkin, Samuel L. *The Rational Peasant: The Political Economy of Rural Society in Vietnam.* Berkeley and Los Angeles: University of California Press, 1979.
Ruch, Barbara. "Medieval Jongleurs and the Making of a National Literature." In *Japan in the Muromachi Age,* edited by John W. Hall and Toyoda Takeshi, pp. 279–309. Berkeley and Los Angeles: University of California Press, 1977.
Sakurai Eiji. "Nihon chūsei shōgyō ni okeru kanshū to chitsujo." *Jinmin no rekishigaku* 94 (December 1987): 1–15.
Sasaki Gin'ya. "Chūsei makki shōhin ryūtsū keitai no henka ni tsuite." *Risshō Daigaku keizaigaku kihō* 4 (June 1953): 19–43.
————. *Chūsei shōhin ryūtsū shi no kenkyū.* Hōsei Daigaku Shuppankai, 1981; originally published 1972.

————. "Rakuichi rakuzarei to za no hoshō ando." In *Sengokuki no kenryoku to shakai,* edited by Nagahara Keiji, pp. 157–230. Tokyo Daigaku Shuppankai, 1983; originally published 1976.

————. *Shōen no shōgyō.* Yoshikawa Kōbunkan, 1964.

————. "Shōensei makki no tochi chōbo no henka to nōson kōzō." *Risshō Daigaku keizaigaku kihō* 9 (October 1954): 51–78.

Sasaki Junnosuke. *Daimyō to hyakushō.* Nihon no rekishi, no. 15. Chuō Kōron-sha, 1971.

Satō Kazuhiko. *Nanbokuchō nairan.* Nihon no rekishi, no. 11. Shōgakkan, 1974.

Scott, James C. *The Moral Economy of the Peasant: Rebellion and Subsistence in Southeast Asia.* New Haven: Yale University Press, 1976.

————. *Weapons of the Weak: Everyday Forms of Peasant Resistance.* New Haven: Yale University Press, 1985.

Sekiguchi Tsuneo. "Sō ketsugō no rekishiteki ichi ni tsuite." *Rekishigaku ken-kyū* 291 (August 1964): 45–51.

Shibata Minoru. "Chūsei shōmin no seikatsu—Izumi no kuni Hine no shō ni tsuite." In *Kokushigaku ronsō,* edited by Uozumi Sensei Koki Kinenkai, pp. 337–47. Uozumi Sensei Koki Kinenkai, 1959.

————. *Shōen sonraku no kōzō.* Osaka: Sōgensha, 1955.

Shiga Setsuko. "Chūsei kōki ni okeru honjo kendan ni tsuite no ichi kōsatsu." *Nihon shi kenkyū* 274 (June 1985): 1–26.

————. "Chūsei kōki shōen sonraku to kendan—sonraku 'jichi' no saikentō." *Rekishigaku kenkyū* 569 (July 1987): 17–34.

Shimada Jirō, ed. *Nihon chūsei sonraku shi no kenkyū—Settsu no kuni Toshima-gun Esaka-gō chiiki ni okeru.* Yoshikawa Kōbunkan, 1966.

Shimizu Mitsuo. *Chūsei shōen no kiso kōzō.* Vol. 3 of *Shimizu Mitsuo chosaku shū.* Kyoto: Itakura Shobō, 1975; originally published 1956.

————. *Jōdai no tochi kankei.* Itō Shoten, 1946; originally published 1943.

————. *Nihon chūsei no sonraku.* Nihon Hyōronsha, 1943; originally published 1942.

Shimosaka Mamoru. "Ōmi shugo Rokkaku-shi no kenkyū." *Komonjo kenkyū* 12 (October 1978): 55–95.

————. "Sanmon shisetsu seido no seiritsu to tenkai—Muromachi bakufu no Sanmon seisaku o megutte." *Shirin* 58.1 (January 1975): 67–114.

Shōtoku Chūgakkō Kyōdo Kenkyūkai, ed. *Shiga-ken Yōkaichi-chō shi no ken-kyū.* Shiga-ken: Shōtoku Chūgakkō, 1951.

Skinner, G. William. "Chinese Peasants and the Closed Community: An Open and Shut Case." *Comparative Studies in Society and History* 13 (1971): 270–81.

————. "Cities and the Hierarchy of Local Systems." In *Studies in Chinese Society,* edited by Arthur P. Wolfe, pp. 1–79. Stanford: Stanford University Press, 1978.

————. "Marketing and Social Structure in Rural China." *Journal of Asian Studies* 24.1 (November 1964): 3–44; 24.2 (February 1965): 195–228; 24.3 (May 1965): 363–99.

Smith, Carol A., ed. *Regional Analysis.* 2 vols. New York: Academic Press, 1976.

Smith, Robert J. "The Japanese Rural Community: Norms, Sanctions, and Ostracism." *American Anthropologist* 63.3 (June 1961): 522–33.

Smith, Thomas C. *The Agrarian Origins of Modern Japan.* Stanford: Stanford University Press, 1959.

Sugimura Yutaka. "Honai shōnin no shijō katsudō keitai: Ōei-Kanshōki o chūshin to shite." *Kokushigaku* 112 (October 1980): 42–59.

———. "Tokuchin-ho shōgyō no kisoteki kōsatsu—sono honza tokken no sōshitsu." *Kokugakuin Daigaku daigakuin kiyō* 7 (1975): 225–35.

Sugiyama Hiroshi. *Shōen kaitai katei no kenkyū.* Tokyo Daigaku Shuppankai, 1959.

Suma Chikai. "Yamashiro no kuni Kii-gun ni okeru sanzai shoryō to sonraku no chiriteki kōsatsu." *Chūsei no mado* 4 (February 1960): 2–12.

———. "Yamashiro no kuni Kii-gun ni okeru shōensei to nōmin." In *Chūsei no shakai to keizai,* edited by Inagaki Yasuhiko and Nagahara Keiji, pp. 81–149. Tokyo Daigaku Shuppankai, 1962.

Suzuki Atsuko. "Chūsei kōki ni okeru chiiki keizaiken no kōzō." In *Sekai shi ni okeru chiiki to minshū,* pp. 61–70. Special supplementary issue of *Rekishigaku kenkyū.* Aoki Shoten, 1980.

———. "Honai shōnin kenkyū no saikentō—toku ni enkakuchi ryūtsū o megutte." *Zenkindai shi kenkyū* 3 (November 1976): 80–90.

Tabata Yasuko. "Chūsei kōki ni okeru ryōshu shihai to sonraku kōzō: sōshō, sōgō no kinō to yakuwari." *Nihon shi kenkyū* 187 (March 1978): 68–86. Later published in her *Chūsei sonraku no kōzō to ryōshusei,* pp. 286–306.

———. *Chūsei sonraku no kōzō to ryōshusei.* Hōsei Daigaku Shuppankyoku, 1986.

———. "Daimyō ryōgoku kihan to sonraku nyōbō za." In *Nihon josei shi,* edited by Josei Shi Sōgō Kenkyūkai, vol. 2, pp. 209–50. Tokyo Daigaku Shuppankai, 1982.

Takamaki Minoru. *Miyaza to sonraku no shiteki kenkyū.* Yoshikawa Kōbunkan, 1986.

Takashige Susumu. "Chūsei ni okeru sonraku no keisei to shijō—Niimi no shō o rei to shite." *Shigaku kenkyū* 95 (August 1966): 1–14.

———. *Kodai, chūsei no kōchi to sonraku.* Daimeidō, 1975.

Takeda Chōshū. "Kinsei shakai to bukkyō." In *Iwanami kōza Nihon rekishi,* vol. 9, pp. 263–302. Iwanami Shoten, 1975.

Tonomura, Hitomi. "Forging the Past: Medieval Counterfeit Documents." *Monumenta Nipponica* 40.1 (Spring 1985): 69–96.

———. "Women and Inheritance in Japan's Early Warrior Society." *Comparative Studies in Society and History* 32.3 (July 1990): 592–623.

Totman, Conrad. "Tokugawa Peasants: Win, Lose, or Draw?" *Monumenta Nipponica* 41.4 (Winter 1986): 457–76.

Toyoda Takeshi. *Chūsei Nihon no shōgyō.* Toyoda Takeshi chosakushū, no. 2. Yoshikawa Kōbunkan, 1982.

———. *Chūsei Nihon shōgyō shi no kenkyū.* Iwanami Shoten, 1944.

———. "Chūsei ni okeru jinja no saishi soshiki ni tsuite." *Shigaku zasshi* 53.10 (October 1942): 67–118; 53.11 (November 1942): 84–128.

———. *Chūsei no shōnin to kōtsū.* Toyoda Takeshi chosakushū, no. 3. Yoshikawa Kōbunkan, 1983.

———. "Japanese Guilds." *Annals of the Hitotsubashi Academy* 5.1 (1954): 72–85.

———. *Nihon shūkyō seido shi no kenkyū.* Daiichi Shobō, 1973; originally published 1938.

———. "Ōyamazaki abura jinin no katsudō—Uozumi, Sawai ryōshi no kyōcho o yomite." *Rekishi chiri* 62.5 (November 1933): 57–64.

———. "Sengoku shokō tōseika no za ni tsuite." *Keizai shi kenkyū* 28.2 (August 1942): 1–29.

———. *Shūkyō seido shi.* Toyoda Takeshi chosakushū, no. 5. Yoshikawa Kōbunkan, 1982.

———. *Za no kenkyū.* Toyoda Takeshi chosakushū, no. 1. Yoshikawa Kōbunkan, 1982.

Toyoda Takeshi and Sugiyama Hiroshi. "The Growth of Commerce and the Trades." In *Japan in the Muromachi Age,* edited by John W. Hall and Toyoda Takeshi, pp. 129–44. Berkeley and Los Angeles: University of California Press, 1977.

Toyoda Takeshi and Kodama Yukio, eds. *Ryūtsū shi.* Vol. 1. Yamakawa Shoten, 1969.

Tsuboi Hirofumi. "Matsuri no chiikiteki shokeitai—Miyaza kenkyū no shiten." In *Matsuri no shokeitai,* edited by Misumi Haruo and Tsuboi Hirofumi, vol. 2, pp. 257–90. Nihon saishi kenkyū shūsei, no. 4. Meicho Shuppan, 1977.

Tsuji Hiroyuki. "Chūsei ni okeru Ōmi Sakamoto no hatten to toshi keikan." *Hisutoria* 88 (September 1980): 1–30.

Uejima Tamotsu. *Kyōkō shōen sonraku no kenkyū.* Haniwa Shobō, 1970.

Uwayokote Masataka. "Inseiki no Genji." In *Gokeninsei no kenkyū,* edited by Gokeninsei Kenkyūkai, pp. 153–92. Yoshikawa Kōbunkan, 1981.

Vaporis, Constantine N. "Post Station and Assisting Villages: Corvee Labor and Peasant Contention." *Monumenta Nipponica* 41.4 (Winter 1986): 377–414.

Wakita Haruko. "Cities in Medieval Japan." *Acta Asiatica* 44 (1983): 28–52.

———. "Muromachiki no keizai hatten." In *Iwanami kōza Nihon rekishi,* vol. 7, pp. 51–98. Iwanami Shoten, 1976.

———. *Nihon chūsei shōgyō hattatsu shi no kenkyū.* Ochanomizu Shobō, 1981; originally published 1969.

———. "Nihon chūsei toshi no kōzō." *Nihon shi kenkyū* 139–40 (March 1974): 15–35.

———. *Nihon chūsei toshi ron.* Tokyo Daigaku Shuppankai, 1981.

———. "Towards a Wider Perspective on Medieval Commerce." *Journal of Japanese Studies* 1.2 (Spring 1975): 321–45.

Wakita Osamu. *Kinsei hōkensei seiritsu shi ron: Shokuhō seiken no bunseki.* Vol. 2. Tokyo Daigaku Shuppankai, 1977.

———. "Nobunaga seiken no za seisaku." *Ryūkoku shidan* 56–57 (December 1966): 471–81.

———. *Oda seiken no kiso kōzō: Shokuhō seiken no bunseki.* Vol. 1. Tokyo Daigaku Shuppankai, 1975.

Yamamoto Keishirō. "Chūsei shōnin no gimonjo sakusei." *Rekishi to Seikatsu* 6.3–4 (July 1943): 23–28.

Yamamoto Masakazu. "Sengo Ōmi no sonraku ni okeru miyaza kenkyū no hōkō." *Shakai kagaku* 26 (November 1979): 71–98.

Yamamoto Takashi. "Kamakuraki no mura to hyakushō—Bingo no kuni Ōta no shō o chūshin ni." *Rekishi hyōron* 374 (June 1981): 29–44.

Yamamura, Kozo. "The Development of Za in Medieval Japan." *Business History Review* 47.4 (Winter 1973): 438–65.

Yōkaichi-shi Shi Hensan Iinkai, ed. *Yōkaichi-shi shi hensan dayori.* 20 issues. Yōkaichi-shi, Shiga-ken: Yōkaichi-shi Shi Hensan Shitsu, 1978–85.

Yokoyama Haruo. "Chūsei makki ni okeru Rokkaku-shi no dōkō." *Koku-shigaku* 68 (March 1957): 74–87.
Yoshida Toshihiro. "'Sōson' no tenkai to tochi riyō—Tokuchin-ho Imabori-gō no rekishi chirigakuteki monogurafu to shite." *Shirin* 61.1 (January 1978): 122–49.
Yoshie Akio. "Ho no keisei to sono tokushitsu." *Hokkaidō Daigaku bungakubu kiyō* 34 (March 1974): 121–50.
Yoshimura Tōru. "Rokkaku seibatsu to Konoe-ke ryō." *Ōmi chihō shi kenkyū* 5 (May 1977): 8–19.

Index

In this index an "f" after a number indicates a separate reference on the next page, and an "ff" indicates separate references on the next two pages. A continuous discussion over two or more pages is indicated by a span of page numbers, e.g., "57–59." *Passim* is used for a cluster of references in close but not consecutive sequence.

Library of Congress Cataloging-in-Publication Data

Tonomura, Hitomi.
   Community and commerce in late medieval Japan : the corporate
villages of Tokuchin-ho / Hitomi Tonomura.
      p.   cm.
   Includes bibliographical references and index.
   ISBN 0-8047-1941-1 (cloth) :
      1. Manors—Japan—Yōkaichi-shi—History.   2. Village communities—
Japan—Yōkaichi-shi—History.   3. Yōkaichi-shi (Japan)—Commerce—
History.   I. Title.
HD920.Y59T66 1992
307.72'0952'185—dc20
91-14323
   CIP

♾ This book is printed on acid-free paper

22021000